designing with
progressive
enhancement

building the web that
works for everyone

Todd Parker

Patty Toland

Scott Jehl

Maggie Costello Wachs

New
Riders

VOICES THAT MATTER™

**DESIGNING WITH PROGRESSIVE ENHANCEMENT:
BUILDING THE WEB THAT WORKS FOR EVERYONE**
Todd Parker, Patty Toland, Scott Jehl, Maggie Costello Wachs

NEW RIDERS
1249 Eighth Street
Berkeley, CA 94710
510/524-2178
510/524-2221 (fax)

Find us on the Web at www.newriders.com
To report errors, please send a note to errata@peachpit.com
New Riders is an imprint of Peachpit, a division of Pearson Education

Acquisitions Editor: Wendy Sharp
Project Editor: Wendy G. Katz
Technical Editor: James Craig
Production Editor: Myrna Vladic
Composition: David Van Ness
Indexer: Jack Lewis
Interior Design: Mimi Heft
Cover Design: Aren Howell

ISBN-13:   978-0-321-65888-3
ISBN-10:   0-321-65888-4

9 8 7 6 5 4 3 2 1

Printed and bound in the United States of America

Contents

SECTION I THE TEST-DRIVEN PROGRESSIVE ENHANCEMENT APPROACH

chapter 3   writing meaningful markup   49

SECTION II PROGRESSIVE ENHANCEMENT IN ACTION

chapter 7 building widgets with progressive enhancement 143

chapter 8 collapsible content 147

chapter 9 tabs 161

acknowledgments

First, we want to thank Peachpit/New Riders for giving us the opportunity and the incentive to write this book. We've been considering accessibility and using test-driven progressive enhancement in our projects and on our site for years, but Peachpit's encouragement prompted us to take the plunge and articulate the principles and techniques we've pieced together into a cohesive whole for this important topic. If only for our own benefit, the exercise has been incredible. We deeply appreciate the invaluable input we've received along the way.

Specifically, a huge thanks to our two Wendys at Peachpit/New Riders: Wendy Sharp, who found our online lab and reached out to invite us to write this book, and provided invaluable insights and expertise about shaping our ideas for this medium; and Wendy Katz, whose careful and thoughtful editing, and infinite humor, wit, and patience, were essential to getting us through to the end. Thanks also to Glenn Bisignani for his marketing insights and support; and Aren Howell, Mimi Heft, and David Van Ness for their beautiful designs.

We owe our technical editor, James Craig, an enormous debt. His thoughtful advice and invaluable expertise in accessibility and ARIA have measurably improved the quality of our recommendations. Where we get accessibility recommendations right, it is very frequently thanks to his contributions. (And, importantly, if we get it wrong, that responsibility is our own.)

Thanks to John Resig and everyone on the jQuery and jQuery UI teams for their support and the incredible JavaScript library that we so enjoy working with—throughout this book and in our everyday work. And very special thanks to Brandon Aaron, for contributing to, and significantly improving, the performance of our EnhanceJS framework.

We want to acknowledge our valued clients and colleagues, who have encouraged us think about these important ideas in our work for them and provided real-world challenges that inspired many of the solutions in these pages. We thank Steve Krug for his advice and encouragement, and Derek Jones for his help with book production.

And we would also like to recognize many organizations that have been incredibly generous in offering a public forum for us to share, discuss, and refine many of ideas and techniques that went into this book: *A List Apart Magazine,* Delve UI Conferences, MIT WebPub, the Markup & Style Society, jQuery, Ajaxian, and *Smashing Magazine.*

Our work is built upon a foundation of ideas, techniques, and code that countless generous and brilliant people have shared publicly, and taught us personally, including: Tony Aslett, Doug Bowman, Andy Budd, Corey Byrnes, Dan Cederholm, Tantek Çelik, Steve Champeon, Andy Clarke, Jeff Croft, Derek Featherstone, Seth Ferreira, Nick Finck,

Becky Gibson, Brandon Goldsworthy, Scott González, Marc Grabanski, Aaron Gustafson, Chris Heilmann, Dorothy Hesson, Molly Holzschlag, Shaun Inman, Paul Irish, Yehuda Katz, Jeremy Keith, Peter-Paul Koch, Bruce Lawson, Ethan Marcotte, Michael McGrady, Eric Meyer, Cameron Moll, Jon Reil, Richard Rutter, Travis Schmeisser, Dave Shea, Chris Smith, Jonathan Snook, Krista Stevens, Nicole Sullivan, Karl Swedberg, Randy Taylor, Dan Webb, Richard Worth, Jörn Zaefferer, Jeffrey Zeldman, and countless others.

Many of the techniques in this book were forged and refined with the help of the many talented and thoughtful individuals who read and comment on our lab blog; we greatly appreciate your encouragement, technical expertise, and criticism. And more importantly, we hope you will continue to embrace these ideas and contribute to both the commentary and the code that comprises our demos and downloadable plugins. (Please feel free to go to www.filamentgroup.com/dwpe to join the discussion.)

* * *

PERSONAL ACKNOWLEDGEMENTS

We all thank Christine Fichera for generous use of her photos throughout the book; and Todd thanks Christine and Nathan especially for letting this book intrude on bath and story time.

Patty thanks Judy Kohn and Jeff Cruikshank for being such great mentors and role models, and all the Tolands for their infinite patience and support even when they still don't understand exactly what she does for a living.

Scott thanks his wife Stephanie and all his family and friends for their patience and encouragement while writing this book, and his parents for their uncompromised support and encouragement from day one.

Maggie thanks her husband Michael, family, and friends for their endless support, encouragement, and good humor; special thanks to her mom, Barbara Thompson, for a lifetime of inspiration, and to those who acted as sounding boards for many of the ideas expressed in this book.

introduction

the case for designing with progressive enhancement

In many ways, right now is the best possible time to be a web designer.

New sites and applications emerge at an astounding rate and transform the way we work, communicate, and live. We manage our businesses, build our relationships, voice our opinions, educate ourselves about world affairs, and find a whole range of entertainment online. Advances in web standards are making the web easier, faster, and more dynamic and powerful all the time. And "online" has been liberated from the "line" itself—an explosion of web-enabled mobile phones and compact netbooks keeps us connected virtually everywhere.

But this bounty of Internet riches has a downside: while advanced interactions tend to work beautifully on the newest browsers that support advanced CSS and JavaScript, there's a whole universe of web-enabled devices—from the newest Kindle or Wii gaming system to a wide range of older computers and mobile phones—that have limited or no support for these features, and can be left with a broken and unusable experience. And even with a modern browser, sites can exclude blind or vision-impaired users if web developers don't take care to support keyboard interaction and layer in specific accessibility features required by screen-reader software and other assistive devices.

As web designers and developers, we are always balancing three somewhat conflicting objectives. We want to embrace all the exciting new technologies available to deliver compelling, interactive experiences. But at the same time, we're deeply committed to ensuring that our sites are universally accessible, intuitive, and usable for everyone. And from a development perspective, it's equally important to write the cleanest and most maintainable code possible. It's been our quest to find a development approach that will satisfy all three objectives in an elegant way that will work on real-world projects.

Happily, we think we have found a way. *Designing with Progressive Enhancement* is a practical guide to web design and development that focuses specifically on how to create sites that deliver the highly interactive experiences that JavaScript, advanced CSS, and Ajax afford, and at the same time ensure that the very same codebase will work everywhere. Our approach is built on the basis of a coding methodology called *progressive enhancement*, which, simply put, recommends that all web content and functionality be based on semantic HTML that's usable on any web-enabled device, and advanced CSS- or JavaScript-based enhancements be layered unobtrusively on top of it.

Building sites with progressive enhancement doesn't necessarily take much more effort, but it definitely requires a shift in your development approach and perspective. Some might argue it's not worth the effort—that current development methods capture enough of the audience to cover "the majority" of users, and that improving support for web standards among web browsers will close the gap.

However, if recent trends in Internet usage and device development are any indicator, the *opposite* is true: some of the most cutting-edge, web-enabled devices have browsers with poor web standards support, and the number of older computers or mobile phones that are running outdated and less capable browsers is growing rather than shrinking.

Regardless, the bottom line is that people use a wide range of browsers, platforms, and devices in their daily lives, and they expect their favorite websites and applications to work seamlessly across the lot. Building sites that work only in a handful of specific browsers isn't a realistic approach when facing this increasingly complex universe of devices, especially when progressive enhancement provides a way to build sites that will work anywhere, for everyone.

But we know just saying these things won't convince the skeptics. So let's take a look at some of the facts about the global web audience and current technology, and also examine how common coding approaches can misfire—with results from mild inconvenience to full failure of functionality.

The ever-widening world of the web

It's easy to forget how quickly and dramatically the Internet has grown and changed our lives. Even a decade ago, web access was limited to a fairly narrow demographic of users, all generally using fairly consistent hardware. Today, the web is truly a global phenomenon, and the diversity of its audience is constantly expanding; and users are accessing the web on a vast array of web-enabled devices.

By understanding the trajectory of who is using the web today, how they get online, and where the growth is most likely to happen tomorrow, we can better plan for this new world where the web is everywhere and used by everyone.

Everyone is getting on the web (or will be soon)

At the start of the Internet boom in the mid-1990s, the majority of Internet users lived in wealthier Western countries, were educated (because the web required technical skill), and tended to be professionals or more affluent individuals, as systems ran on prohibitively expensive PCs that required expensive monthly access plans and a strong infrastructure.

Over the past decade, computers have become much easier to use, and the plummeting cost of hardware, software, and online access has made them far more accessible. With that, the mix of people on the web has shifted to a much more global population with a full gamut of ages, education levels, and socioeconomic classes represented, leading to a democratization of the web's information and tools.

The brisk pace of Internet adoption continues to drive the growing diversity of people online—the global population of Internet users grew more than 450%—from 361 million in December 2000 to more than 1.78 *billion* (or more than 25% of the world's population) in September 2009 (www.internetworldstats.com/stats.htm, as of June 30, 2009). This growth was dramatic across the global stage: Internet users in Africa surged fourteenfold from 4.5 million to 66.9 million, and in Asia grew 6x from 114 million to 738 million, compared with the 4x increase in Europe from 105 million to 402 million (www.internetworldstats.com/stats.htm, as of June 30, 2009).

In the United States, Internet users spread to a broader demographic in the decade, with more than 92% of 18–29-year-olds and nearly half of all seniors online, and a far wider range of education and economic levels. The web is quickly becoming ubiquitous: more than 73% of the U.S. adult population reported using the Internet and email, access in rural areas surpassed 50% (Pew Research Center's Internet & American Life Project (www.pewinternet.org), and fully 93% of all public elementary school classrooms have Internet access (U.S. Department of Education, National Center for Education Statistics. 2006. *Internet Access in U.S. Public Schools and Classrooms: 1994-2005.* NCES 2007-020).

But it's perhaps most interesting to consider these facts: at 798 million users, Asia's Internet penetration is less than 20% of its population, and Africa's 66.9 million represent less than 7%, while the U.S. and most western European countries are generally in the 70–80% range. As Internet access continues to grow, the largest areas of potential growth are much more likely to happen across the globe, where users have not only different languages and cultures, but also very different equipment, connections, infrastructure, and access expectations than people in the Western world.

Evolving user expectations

Along with huge growth of the global user base and web-enabled devices, there is an equally dramatic change in *what* the Internet delivers today. A confluence of new web content and interaction innovations has fundamentally changed user expectations about website behaviors and capabilities. Consider, for example, just this short list of changes since 2000:

▶ Established online-only businesses like Amazon, eBay, and Netflix introduced much more richly-layered content, embedded media, dynamic interactions, and immersive experiences, which set a new bar for user experience.

▶ The emergence of user-generated content—from blogs to YouTube, Facebook, Digg, Twitter, and beyond—has democratized website content and structure, and raised users' expectations of being able to create, reference, and creatively repurpose web content to suit their needs.

▶ The real-time web has caused people to expect up-to-the-second updates of their social network on Facebook, followers on Twitter, and collaborators on Google Docs or Wave, which has prompted a big move away from the static page-by-page underpinnings of the web and towards an Ajax-powered environment that may never require an old-fashioned page refresh.

▶ The rise of web-based applications that attempt to offer desktop-quality user experiences in web browsers, like rich data visualizations, drag-and-drop gestures, and rich interactivity, support the overall trend of software being offered as a web service instead of installed on a computer.

▶ As users now access the web through multiple desktop browsers at work and home and on the move with their mobile phones and other devices, they expect their data to be accessible on any device at any time.

These innovations have transformed the Internet into to a powerful global platform that delivers application-like features and functionality in the browser, and puts the power of instant communication in the reach of all users.

Expanding user accessibility needs

With a significantly broader demographic online, including a larger proportion of older users, and the vast array of new interaction models emerging in advanced websites, there is also a new set of considerations that impact how we design websites.

As people age, they typically suffer from decreased or impaired vision, hearing, and motor skills, all of which are critically important for successfully navigating the Internet. Conditions such as cataracts, blindness, hearing impairments, reduced joint mobility, loss of fine motor control, or hand tremors can make using a traditional website difficult at best.

These older users may require larger type and more contrast, especially for extended reading; it's critical that websites be structured to allow the adjustment of text settings to suit their needs. Many blind users, and those with more extremely impaired vision, leverage assistive technologies such as screen-reader software programs on their desktops to read application content and web pages aloud; properly structured semantic content and full keyboard support to promote navigation without vision or a mouse are essential to successfully using screen readers on the web. And users with compromised mobility frequently feel more control using the keyboard for navigation rather than a mouse.

In 1998, the U.S. Federal Government passed Section 508, an amendment to the Rehabilitation Act that requires federal agencies to make their electronic and information technology accessible to people with disabilities, and established national standards for accessibility of digital media for people with physical and mental disabilities. Although these rules apply only to government agencies and companies that supply goods and services to the federal government, Section 508 presents a clear set of enforceable standards for providing access to all users, and has become a de facto legal standard that many private organizations have also embraced.

The World Wide Web Consortium (W3C) has been very active in creating specifications for accessibility on the web through its Web Accessibility Initiative (WAI) and related projects. The W3C's Web Content Accessibility Guidelines (WCAG 2.0) provides both high level principles and a checklist of specific guidelines and criteria for ensuring that websites are accessible. The Accessible Rich Internet Applications (WAI-ARIA) specification provides a set of attributes that can be added to markup (like HTML) to describe advanced UI widgets such as sliders and tree controls in a way that is meaningful to screen readers.

Together, these advances provide both a clear mandate and a set of tools that can be used today to provide full access to the web, regardless of users' physical abilities. Both building accessibility features into sites and testing on screen readers should be priorities to all developers, because lack of accessibility equates to discrimination in the eyes of users, and possibly of the law.

Consider, for example, Target Corporation's experience: in early 2005, the National Federation for the Blind (NFB) approached Target, alerting them to the fact that a number of features on their website rendered it unusable for many disabled users. The company claimed that their brick-and-mortar stores were adequately accessible for those users. Unsatisfied with Target's response, in February 2006, NFB brought a lawsuit against Target, citing a violation of the Americans with Disabilities Act of 1990. After several years in the court, the case settled in August 2009, with Target establishing a $6 million settlement fund, paying nearly $3.8 million for NFB's legal fees, and agreeing to substantially redesign their website to introduce accessibility features, with usability testing by NFB on a scheduled basis.

While such lawsuits are rare, design and development best practice precedent is being set in this and similar cases that promote accessible coding standards. The guidelines and specifications for creating universally accessible sites are advancing. With the democratization of the web, our designs and code need to be developed for universal access—a web that works for everyone, regardless of their language, culture, age, physical abilities, or technology platform.

Rise of the non-desktop web

As the web's audience, user expectations, and online content norms have evolved, there has been a parallel shift in where and how users connect online—in particular with the emergence of web-enabled mobile phones, video game systems, and dedicated web appliances.

By 2008, of the 1.4 billion Internet users worldwide, fully 75% had accessed the Internet on a mobile device, and 29% of world Internet access was *exclusively* on a non-desktop browser (Tomi Ahonen, *Thought Piece: Mobile Telecoms Industry Size,* 2009, www.tomiahonen.com). The adoption of the mobile phone has been faster than any other technology in the history of invention, and its impact on how we design for the web is just now being felt.

Back in the earliest days of the mobile web, mobile handsets had tiny screens, slow processors, and understood only a simplified version of XML called WML (Wireless Markup Language). Few developers, or users, expected websites to work seamlessly on these devices.

A first wave of web-enabled "smartphones" appeared on the scene around 2000–2002—including the Nokia 9210 Communicator, the Palm Treo, and the first RIM Blackberry and Microsoft Windows CE devices—and ushered in a new level of expectation about real-time access to data and functionality. These devices could access standard HTML sites and even had rudimentary support for JavaScript and CSS. In a very short time, literally hundreds of different models of mobile phones capable of accessing the "real" web emerged and sparked off the mobile web revolution.

By 2009, the number of active mobile phone subscriptions has reached 4.6 billion ("Explaining 4.6 billion mobile phone subscriptions on the planet," Communities Dominate Brands blog, 11/6/09, http://communities-dominate.blogs.com/brands/2009/11/explaining-46-billion-mobile-phone-subscriptions-on-the-planet.html)—a number that dwarfs the current total population of Internet users. Even though all these mobile devices may not have smartphone-like web browsers, it's fair to say that mobile is a massive and growing channel that can no longer be ignored when building a website.

Even the definition of "mobile device" is constantly evolving and mutating, to include web-enabled touchscreen tablets, micro-laptops, and other gadgets. Each device has its own unique set of browser capabilities, plugin support, installed fonts, screen dimensions, and interaction norms—from a RIM's Blackberry thumbwheel and keyboard interaction, to Amazon's Kindle's mini-joystick controller, to Apple's iPhone multi-touch interaction model, and beyond.

A large number of video game systems like the Nintendo Wii, Sony Playstation 3, and Microsoft Xbox all have web browsers available—these systems take liberties with website design to "adapt" it in a way that is usable on a television screen ten feet away with a gaming controller. And other consumer electronics —e-book readers, television sets, home telephones, even clock radios and refrigerators—are gaining web browsers. The diversity of devices on which our designs will appear has exploded.

Expanding "shelf life" of devices and browsers

For each new computer, mobile phone, or gadget purchased, there is a good chance it replaces an older device that is recycled down the tech "food chain." Millions of mobile phones and computers stay active, either handed down within families, shared with schools and community centers, or donated to all kinds of social programs; many end up in faraway countries via donations to military families or global development NGOs. In the developing world, where materials reuse and recycling is far more common, the vast majority of devices are carefully maintained far beyond their typical "useful" life in the West. With each passing year, an ever-growing number of machines in homes, libraries, schools, and Internet cafes are running "antiquated" versions of browsers that aren't updated, for various reasons.

Along with this large universe of older devices in current rotation, there is an equivalent group of "fringe" browsers that run on alternative operating systems. Unix-based operating systems are frequently used in low-cost computers like netbook mini-laptops and the One Laptop Per Child (OLPC) project's XO computer. Technical power users frequently use Unix-based computers that run a wide array of "alternative" browsers like Konqueror, and purely text-based browsers like Lynx, that can render pages very differently than mainstream browsers. Each may have marginal market share individually, but together they constitute millions of web visitors worldwide.

* * *

The massive scale and range of people now on the web, coupled with the shifting expectations of user experience and the explosion of web enabled devices we need to support, translates into an exponentially more complicated design and development challenge than the one designers faced even a few years ago.

The common approach of developing only for a target group of the newest and most popular desktop browsers and ignoring the rest almost surely leaves millions of potential readers, customers, job seekers, dates, or political supporters with a broken, unusable experience. At the same time, we appreciate that it's daunting for any developer to accept responsibility for testing and debugging sites on even a tiny representative set of the vast array of desktop browsers, mobile phones, gaming systems, and other specialized devices because time and effort are always a constraint in a real-world project.

Still, if you're not convinced that the standard approach to developing advanced websites is a problem, consider the following real-world cases where current sites fall down.

The landmines of Web 2.0

Many of the more interesting and engaging features in the explosion of Web 2.0 sites and applications developed in the past decade are supported by JavaScript for rich interactivity, Ajax for dynamic data, and advanced CSS.

These advances paralleled the launch of scores of different desktop browser versions over the past decade—and this doesn't take into account the vast array of web-enabled devices and mobile phones in recent years. While many contemporary browsers embrace web standards, they don't render the web uniformly, and collectively require a complex system of coding, testing, and occasional hackery to get sites to appear and function in a consistent manner.

There are a number of common web design and development trends that are undermining the promise of universal access that the web is built on.

Browser tunnel vision

To make development and testing manageable in the real world, all companies and individual developers (ourselves included) focus their coding and testing on a specific set of browsers. This is reasonable from a contractual perspective: clients ask us to commit (in writing) that our code will look and function exactly as designed, and we know that not every browser can handle the styles and scripting that a modern site design requires. So part of our agreement involves testing the code in some agree-upon list of browsers or environments, depending on the project.

But what about all the users who aren't using a supported browser? Is it acceptable to exclude them from accessing the site and display a message asking them to upgrade their browser? Many people don't upgrade their browsers—either because they're not technically savvy enough to upgrade, aren't allowed to install software on their machines for security reasons (especially true in corporate environments), or are tied to a legacy browser because a crucial-to-them web application works only in that specific browser.

It's easy to dismiss users in non-supported browsers as unimportant because they represent a marginal percentage of the audience, or because it's assumed they are generally less savvy or technically adept and, therefore, not a target user. But poor browser capabilities are not limited to outdated devices or to Luddites: Amazon's Kindle, a device commonly considered to be "cutting edge" and used by very demanding early adopters, has a monochrome display and a text-based browser that offers only limited CSS and JavaScript support as "experimental" features.

Enforcing access to a specific set of target browsers through user agent detection is fundamentally unreliable. For example, many versions of the popular Blackberry smartphone provide a preference that lets users identify their browser as either Blackberry, Firefox, or Internet Explorer, precisely to get past these developer roadblocks.

This leads to situations where developers may take risks with their use of JavaScript and CSS, assuming that they've locked out all the "bad" browsers, and will deliver a very broken experience to anyone who switched a preference setting to gain access.

The notion of a list of supported browsers oversimplifies a host of other assumptions: developers commonly assume that supported browsers will have all features enabled—like images, CSS, cookies, JavaScript, and plugins like Flash, Java, or Silverlight—and that all of these enabled features will behave as they expect. What if a user has a supported browser but decides to disable cookies or JavaScript for security or privacy reasons? What if a user has disabled CSS or images in their mobile device to make pages load faster? When developers estimate that a chosen list of supported browsers will cover 95% of the general web population, they overlook situations where users technically have a supported browser but have disabled a feature that is critical for the design to work.

In the real world, code probably fails far more often than developers know (or care to admit) because the majority of testing happens in a relatively safe and controlled environment—a limited set of modern browsers in their default configuration, on a "typical" screen resolution, at default font size. The real world is much more unpredictable and varied. The notion that we need only consider a small set of "target" browsers creates a false sense of security. This "tunnel vision" prevents us from really seeing all the browsers and devices that we need to support and working on ways to make our code more compatible and bulletproof.

"JavaScript required" may leave many users out

Many sites now rely on JavaScript for essential functionality, like populating page content with Ajax or submitting and validating forms—which means that when scripting isn't available, entire pages or features can break completely.

A search for statistics on the percentage of users who have JavaScript enabled yields numbers from 85–98%; the most quoted source, W3schools' browser statistics site, estimates that about 5% of Internet users have JavaScript disabled. (At current internet usage rates, this translates to roughly 83 million people!) We work with several clients who use custom enterprise browser configurations with selected JavaScript features modified or disabled for security reasons; these browsers will properly "register" as JavaScript enabled, but not all sites or pages will function.

Many popular JavaScript- and AJAX-powered sites—including Adobe's e-commerce store, the travel-booking site Kayak, and the project-management tool Basecamp—simply require JavaScript for core functionality, and present an error message when scripting isn't enabled.

These error messages usually tell the user to turn on scripting and use a supported browser. But what if a person is at the airport and needs to check alternative flights, or see the status of a project, on an older Blackberry or Palm Treo that doesn't support JavaScript? Downloading a new browser isn't an option.

A surprising number of large e-commerce sites build essential features that drive revenue in a way that works only when scripting is available. On the Sears.com website, newly relaunched in the fall of 2009, when a customer either searches for a product or navigates to any product listing page (for example, Home > Appliances > Microwaves > Countertop) without JavaScript, the results area that should display products remains blank except for an Ajax "loading" animation.

The page is served with only a placeholder spinner animation, which is clearly intended to be replaced with a list of products by an Ajax request after the page loads; there is no meaningful markup on the page when it loads. The search filters and featured product blocks are also JavaScript-dependent. For users without scripting, the Sears site completely fails in its primary purposes: helping shoppers do research and buy products.

Although it would be nice to assume this is an isolated situation, it's a widespread problem. On the current Walmart.com site, every Add To Cart button is added to the page with Ajax; without JavaScript, there are no purchase-related buttons. Both the Toys R Us and The North Face sites have an Add To Cart button on their product detail pages, but clicking that button calls a JavaScript function that does nothing at all in a browser with scripting disabled.

All of these are lost revenue opportunities that could have been easily avoided by simply including a functioning Add To Cart button in the page that submits a simple form.

Assuming CSS is another potential a point of failure

Assumptions about CSS support, either alone or combined with JavaScript, introduce another whole range of potential failures.

Many older desktop browsers don't render CSS according to web standards. On popular smartphones like the Palm Treo and older Blackberry devices, users often disable CSS completely because of the browser's poor CSS support. We sometimes see complex and advanced CSS applied to the page and served to every device. When rendered incorrectly by browsers with spotty or no CSS support, the page may not look as intended, and it could even cause sections or the entire page to become unusable if elements end up positioned incorrectly or styled illegibly.

Compounding this issue, developers sometimes rely on JavaScript to add or manipulate CSS styles in order to make a page functional. This is a common point of failure: if either CSS or JavaScript isn't properly supported, the page may be rendered unusable, regardless of how nicely structured the markup may be under the covers.

On the Ford cars home page (www.fordvehicles.com), both the global navigation bar and footer links rely on JavaScript to position them correctly on the page. Without scripting, the global navigation is invisible, and the footer navigation links are positioned over the main product image, making much of the page illegible and unusable.

The international landing page for Nike.com has a JavaScript- and Flash-enabled list of countries to route shoppers to a country-specific site. With scripting disabled, a customer sees only a blank, black page that completely prevents them from shopping. Ironically, in the HTML source for the page, there are perfectly usable links for each country, but they're hidden with hard-coded CSS to make room for the JavaScript enabled experience they assume everyone will see. This simple choice denies untold numbers of potential shoppers every day for Nike.

The black box of plugins

Plugins like Adobe Flash, Microsoft Silverlight, and Sun Java are popular with developers and many users—they can provide powerful capabilities like visualizing interactive charts, maps, and other information; playing media; connecting with a computer's file system; and more. But because they can require manual installation and updating by users, and are not supported on every platform and browser, they frequently offer the frustrating "update your system" roadblock to users without the most current version installed.

On mobile devices, plugin support is currently piecemeal, as carriers, handset manufacturers, and plugin developers work to balance performance with the less powerful processors found in mobile devices. For example, Apple has steadfastly refused to allow Adobe Flash support in the iPhone's browser, meaning that the tens of millions of iPhone users cannot currently access any form of Flash content.

In addition to concerns about mobile access, any content delivered with a plugin is stored within the proprietary plugin code structure, so despite the efforts of plugin makers to improve accessibility, the content is not as accessible to screen readers or search engines as it would be if coded with simple, semantic HTML.

Finally, there is small but alarming trend that Adobe Flash and PDF are being targeted as the most popular vectors for malicious tampering, as they have generally broad support on the most popular browsers and platforms. This emerging security risk may have implications for both user adoption and corporate security standards that will influence users' willingness to access plugin-based content. (Sources: "Adobe Flash's security woes: How to protect yourself," *Computerworld*, 12/14/09, www.computerworld.com/s/article/ 9142223/Adobe_Flash_s_security_woes_How_to_protect_yourself?taxonomyId=63, and "Adobe to patch zero-day Reader, Acrobat hole," *CNET news*, 12/16/09, http://news.cnet. com/8301-1009_3-10416816-83.html.)

New devices introduce unanticipated interaction norms

Many popular mobile phones have excellent browsers that rival the latest desktop versions in terms of CSS and JavaScript capabilities, but have introduced radically different ways for users to interact with the page than on standard desktops—which can have significant usability implications.

For example, touchscreens that support multi-touch gestures have emerged as the new standard for interactions in many mobile devices. The combinations of tap and drag gestures on a touchscreen introduce a new set of interaction norms that allows users to zoom, click, and scroll pages. However, there are a few important interactions that an iPhone or Android user cannot duplicate easily in a multi-touch environment:

▶ On a multi-touch mobile device, the gesture of dragging a finger across the screen is used to pan or scroll the visible area of the web page. Since the drag gesture is already used for panning around the screen, there isn't any gesture to let users drag and drop items on the screen. If you build an interactive experience where users can add items to their cart only by dragging, this feature won't work on these advanced mobile devices.

▶ Some web applications mimic the desktop multi-select capability by clicking items with the mouse while pressing the Control or Shift key on a keyboard. On a touchscreen, any interaction that requires simultaneous keyboard and mouse clicks is not supported without some custom workaround.

▶ Sites that break pages up into small scrolling panels by setting the CSS overflow or using frames—like an Outlook-style email reader with a list view and reading pane, for example—won't work on an iPhone, as there are no persistent scrollbars within the web browser. In fact, the iPhone could render the whole interface perfectly, but the internal scrollbars for the message list or detail pane won't be displayed—the user would need to intuit that they aren't seeing the full list or message and know to use a two-finger drag gesture to scroll within the sub-pane.

* * *

Many site developers assume that everyone who can render the enhanced experience has all the features and tools to fully support it, and has a desktop browser with a keyboard and mouse for input. But we hope we've convinced you that, increasingly, these are dangerous assumptions to make.

As companies and individuals launch new sites, or build new capabilities into their existing systems, they face important decisions about how to design and implement the front-end code. Since the web is inherently an unpredictable environment, assumptions about browsers and plugins deliver a false sense of security. In reality, any technology used in a web page that isn't simple HTML markup will break somewhere, and could ruin the user experience.

To avoid these pitfalls, any content or transaction that is essential to the core purpose or business of a site should be developed to work on any browser that understands basic HTML—this is the cornerstone of the underlying design of the web, and the key goal of universal access. CSS, JavaScript, cookies, and images can all enhance some browser experiences, but inhibit or break in others; a design approach that makes them secondary and optional is the one that will deliver an optimal experience for the broadest possible spectrum of users.

Progressive enhancement to the rescue

When faced with the incredible range of different users and devices we needed to support on our day-to-day projects, we began to wonder how to provide a site or application that would work for everyone, feature the most advanced interface elements for those who were capable, and still be manageable to develop and test for real-world client projects. We needed a pragmatic approach that provides a solid, usable baseline experience for any device, and reserves the richly designed features that require the tight coordination of JavaScript, CSS, and plugins for a subset of popular, modern desktop and mobile visitors.

What we really wanted was a "magic bullet:" a single, manageable codebase that would work everywhere, created with the cleanest, most efficient and future-compatible development approach.

We believe we've found a near-perfect solution with progressive enhancement. First coined by Steven Champeon and Nick Finck at the March 2003 South by Southwest conference ("Inclusive Web Design for the Future" by Steven Champeon and Nick Finck, delivered 3/11/03 at SXSW, http://hesketh.com/publications/inclusive_web_design_for_the_future), progressive enhancement is as much a mindset as a methodology. It focuses first and foremost on content and functionality. The goal is to build a perfectly functional and usable page that uses only the expressive potential of HTML semantics, creating a page that is accessible from the start and guaranteed to work on any web-enabled device—mobile phones, gaming systems, web-browsing refrigerators, and anything else you can think of.

Only after the HTML markup is as descriptive and clear as possible do we develop CSS and JavaScript—both written to external files and then unobtrusively applied to the HTML markup to transform it into a rich, interactive experience. We avoid inline styles or event handlers whenever possible. The key to progressive enhancement starts with the careful separation of content (HTML), presentation and styles (CSS), and behavior (JavaScript), which allows us to deliver a workable and appropriate experience for each browser.

Progressive enhancement and graceful degradation: same difference?

Progressive enhancement is frequently compared to, and sometimes confused with, the coding practice of graceful degradation. While the two move toward the same goal—making sure users receive a functional experience—their methods are radically different.

Graceful degradation, also known as "fault tolerance," begins with the principle that some parts of complex systems will fail, and then seeks to build in alternate paths that "degrade" to a lesser but still functional experience. The principles of graceful degradation and fault tolerance long precede web design—in fact, many examples of the ideas behind graceful degradation reference networks like managing load balancing in a failure of the electrical grid or other similarly complex infrastructures. A common web example of graceful degradation is the **noscript** tag, an HTML element intended as a way to deliver content only to users without JavaScript support—it's a fallback alternative to the intended experience.

Progressive enhancement's core development principles take an fundamentally different approach. It assumes that all web-based systems can be reduced to a simple, functional experience captured in a single codebase that will "work" anywhere—that is, it will deliver a usable, legible, and fully functional and satisfying experience to the widest range of devices, browsers, and platforms. Once the needs of the many have been met in the simplest way, the robust enhancements that modern browsers can handle are layered on progressively (hence the "progressive" in the name) to build up to the complete, complex experience.

We've been using progressive enhancement as a cornerstone of our development process for years, and have realized that it is a currently practical and future-compatible methodology for site development:

▶ It allows for "universal access," not only by providing wide accessibility for screen readers and other assistive technologies, but also for users with JavaScript or CSS disabled or for outdated and less capable browsers.

▶ It promotes coding clarity: thinking from the bottom up encourages cleaner and more modular code, where each functional component has a single purpose and can be reused throughout the interface in multiple contexts.

▶ It keeps things centralized and simple, allowing organizations to maintain a single, unified codebase that is compatible across all desktop, mobile, and video game devices.

▶ It positions sites for future compatibility: the simplest version that works today will continue to work tomorrow, and features included based on capabilities can be easily adapted without requiring major retrofit or removal of fussy hacks.

▶ It allows for a simpler interface with the back-end. We always use native, fully functional elements to serve as the single data connection to the server, and use scripting to create proxy connections to keep enhanced custom elements in sync with the basic elements.

▶ It allows for a single, common codebase across experiences. Each site we develop can use the same HTML page for both the basic and enhanced experiences because the only difference is how CSS and JavaScript are layered on top of this foundation markup.

Over the past few years, progressive enhancement has been quietly adopted by some of the biggest and best sites on the web, precisely because it allows them to reach the widest possible audience. Browse Google, Facebook, Amazon, or Digg with JavaScript and/or CSS turned off, and you'll see that the sites will work surprisingly well. Each site may approach progressive enhancement a bit differently, but each achieves the same goal of delivering a usable experience to anyone who visits.

In most cases, implementing progressive enhancement and delivering on the promise of universal access doesn't take more work; it's mostly a matter of unlearning some bad habits, looking at design and development from a different perspective, and ensuring that a lot of small things that need to be done right *are* done right.

The goal of this book is to help anyone develop a universally accessible site by applying simple, workable progressive enhancement techniques that have been tested in the real world.

In the first section, we'll review our approach to implementing progressive enhancement, including a different way of thinking about planning designs, and our unique methodology for testing the capabilities of each browser before applying enhancements. Then we'll review the HTML, CSS, and JavaScript best practices that will arm you with all the tools you'll need to build sites a new and better way.

After that, we'll look at a dozen specific interface components or widgets and take you step by step through a process to show the specific markup, style, scripting, and enhanced accessibility features you'll use when working with progressive enhancement. These examples individually provide specific how-tos, and collectively represent a set of principles and methods that can be extended to other coding situations to broadly apply progressive enhancement in any situation.

We've used these techniques on our own site and in a number of client engagements, and have found that our approach helps to make progressive enhancement practical and actionable. We hope that by the time you've finished this book, you'll agree.

section one

the test-driven progressive enhancement approach

chapter one

our approach

The latest innovations in web technologies—largely enabled by advanced CSS, client-side JavaScript and Ajax, and browser plug-ins like Flash—bring visual appeal and rich inter-action capabilities to modern websites. But they come with a big limitation: browsers and devices have varying levels of support for these technologies. Though modern brows-ers and the latest mobile devices are capable of rendering very complex interfaces, they account for only a portion of the device universe. And as we discussed in the introduc-tion, creating a site or application that works only on a limited set of high-end browsers and devices can seriously limit your ability to reach to the widest possible audience.

We want to ensure that our clients' content, message, and functionality reach everyone—not just those with modern browsers that support the latest web technologies, but any user with a web-enabled device. This is why we decided a few years ago to start incorpo-rating the philosophy of progressive enhancement into our client work.

Progressive enhancement is simple in theory: serve standards-compliant, HTML-only pages to increase the likelihood that any device will render the content in a usable way. Then, only for browsers that understand CSS and JavaScript, unobtrusively layer style and script enhancements onto the page.

However, when we started building sites this way and testing the results, we made an important discovery: this method doesn't take into account that many older browsers and newer mobile browsers offer only *partial* support for JavaScript and CSS, or that users can intentionally disable these technologies for speed, security, or usability reasons. In the real world, CSS and JavaScript must work hand in hand to power complex application interfaces and widgets. (Imagine trying to use a calendar widget or slider in a browser that has JavaScript enabled but doesn't properly support CSS positioning; the result would be unusable.)

In testing our progressive-enhancement-based sites, we found a number of browsers that would "enhance" a perfectly usable HTML page into a non-functioning mess by running scripts or applying styles that weren't entirely supported. But how can we know which browsers will be able to render enhancements correctly?

We realized that to be sure progressive enhancement delivers on its promise of providing a usable experience to everyone, we need to do three things:

▶ Examine our designs with a critical eye and make sure that every component—even the whizziest Web 2.0 or Ajax widget—is based on well structured, semantic HTML that delivers a fully functioning basic experience in any browser with no CSS or JavaScript at all.

▶ Test a browser's CSS and JavaScript capabilities *before* enhancements are applied, to make better decisions about whether it should stick with the basic experience or get enhancements.

▶ For browsers that are upgraded to the enhanced experience, ensure that great care is given to maintaining accessibility by supporting keyboard navigation and layering in features to support screen readers.

In this chapter, we'll discuss the browser capabilities test we developed to determine which browsers should receive the enhanced experience and what types of features it can test. Then we'll dive into the progressive enhancement approach that we use on our day-to-day client projects. It starts with an activity we call "the x-ray perspective," in which we analyze a complex interface design, map out the semantic HTML that will support a basic functioning experience, and plan for developing advanced CSS and JavaScript that will create the enhanced experience for capable browsers that maintains full accessibility for screen readers.

Testing browser capabilities

Our initial research on progressive enhancement revealed that most developers decide to enhance a page in one of two ways: by delivering enhancements to all browsers with JavaScript enabled, or by only delivering enhancements to a specific set of browsers by using *browser sniffing* (detecting specific user agents like Internet Explorer or rendering engines like WebKit).

We immediately shied away from browser sniffing for several reasons:

▶ Effective sniffing requires meticulous knowledge of each browser's behaviors (and all its versions' variations), making maintenance of this script a large, complicated, and ongoing challenge.

▶ By definition, it's not future-compatible. You can only sniff for browsers that exist today; if a new browser is released tomorrow that is capable of the enhanced experience, it will be locked out until it's added to the list.

▶ Even the most comprehensive white list of user agents can be foiled, because browsers can be configured to report the wrong user agent to get around these techniques (also known as *browser spoofing*).

So the first approach—delivering enhancements to all browsers with JavaScript enabled—seemed the better option, because the majority of browsers with JavaScript support could render the enhanced experience. However, as we mentioned earlier, we saw a surprising number of cases where the enhancements were only partially supported in certain browsers, causing scrambled layouts and JavaScript errors.

When we looked at these situations, we noticed that these broken experiences were rooted in two broad patterns: some browsers failed to render the CSS correctly because they didn't properly support the box model, positioning, floats, or other common CSS properties according to web standards; others didn't properly execute common JavaScript functions like DOM manipulation, event handling, window resizing, and performing Ajax requests.

Applying our progressive enhancement approach would be much easier and more reliable if we had a solid way to check for a reasonable cross-section of browser *capabilities*, and then deliver enhancements only when we were confident that both CSS and JavaScript could be counted on to work together correctly.

With this goal in mind, we developed our browser capabilities testing framework through a process of trial and error. The basic checklist for JavaScript was fairly straightforward: we tested using a method called object detection, in which we could effectively ask the browser whether it recognized native objects such as the **document.getElementById** function, for example, and get back a clear "true" or "false" statement. Each test was written in a fault-tolerant and unobtrusive way such that if a browser didn't understand a JavaScript method, it wouldn't throw errors.

The more challenging question was how to determine whether a browser could correctly render advanced CSS techniques. There is no inherent way to use object detection to ask whether a browser properly renders specific CSS capabilities, such as floats, positioning, vertically layered elements, or transparency.

So we devised a set of CSS capabilities tests to do just that. Each CSS test uses JavaScript to inject invisible HTML elements into the page, applies a specific set of advanced CSS rules, and then runs a JavaScript function that measures the result. For example, to see whether the browser correctly supports positioning, the test places a div at a specific position using CSS, and then runs a script that compares the measured coordinates to see if they match the reference.

When a browser passes the complete suite of capabilities tests, we can feel fairly confident that it handles both CSS and JavaScript in a consistent, standards-compliant way and should be able to properly render the enhanced experience. At this point, the test dynamically loads in the advanced style sheets and scripts that transform the basic HTML markup into the enhanced experience, and adds a link to the page that allows users to opt out of the enhanced experience if they prefer the simpler basic version. Lastly, the test sets a cookie so it can avoid running the capabilities test again, to speed up page performance.

As we put the test framework through its paces, we saw real benefits emerge in our progressive enhancement implementations. First, it gave us a very reliable way to delineate between browsers that could correctly display the enhanced experience and those that couldn't, so the danger of breaking a usable basic page with enhancements was dramatically reduced. And because the test loaded the enhanced CSS and JavaScript files only for browsers that passed, it allowed us to deliver a much smaller, more streamlined basic experience—no heavy markup, styles, or scripts are loaded up front—resulting in much faster download times and fewer unnecessary server calls.

The test framework is designed to be highly flexible and modular, and can be customized to test the specific CSS and JavaScript capabilities required for particular client project. For example, if there are no complex CSS floats or Ajax scripting, we can remove these features from our testing criteria.

On our projects, we typically apply a capabilities test suite to simply divide browsers into binary groups of "basic" or "enhanced" to keep coding and maintenance manageable. We view this basic and enhanced split as a way to provide access to the broadest possible range of devices in the world with minimal effort. From this baseline level of support, it's fairly easy to further customize the test script to more finely slice browsers into multiple levels of capabilities or provide optimized experiences for specific devices, such as an iPhone or Kindle.

We'll review the structure and mechanics of the capabilities test in detail, and discuss some of the scenarios where a modular approach may make sense, in Chapter 6.

Planning for progressive enhancement: the x-ray perspective

As we went through iterative rounds of capabilities test refinement, we started to develop a methodology for taking a complex web interface design and breaking it down for development with progressive enhancement and the capabilities test.

Sometimes the process of finding the right native HTML element to support an advanced design component was quite easy—a custom-styled dropdown menu looks and behaves so much like a native **select** element that it only made sense to start with one. Similarly, custom-styled checkboxes might pose a styling challenge, but we knew from the start that they were checkboxes.

But other cases were not so clear: what should be the basic markup for a Netflix-style, Ajax-powered star-rating widget? Or a tabbed "most popular/emailed/commented" content widget like the ones we see on so many news sites? Or the custom date- or price-range sliders used for filtering results seen on Kayak and other ecommerce sites? And what about still more complex but ever-more-popular Ajax-powered applications that use drag-and-drop and other rich interactions like Gmail? Nothing in the commonly supported HTML element toolbox is an exact match for these scenarios.

Still, while these examples are highly customized and richly interactive, the user actions they support—choosing an option on a scale, switching from one content block to another, setting the low and high points in a range, sorting, searching and retrieving—are clearly possible with standard HTML. We just need to do a little creative thinking to deconstruct these widgets and interactions to identify the native HTML elements that can accomplish the same task.

The main challenge is how to look beyond the customized styles, animations, and other behaviors and see the basic moving parts beneath. We likened this process to putting the widget under an x-ray—for example, the neat CSS and scripting features that made a custom slider interactive and were really skin and clothing, but the "bones" of a slider could be presented as a text input to set low and high numeric values, or radio buttons for a small set of options, or even a select menu for a large list of options, in the basic experience.

The x-ray perspective gets more complex, and more interesting, when considering complex designs, including sites that assemble multiple content types and interactive widgets, web-based applications with dynamic content and complex layouts, or workflows that provide content conditionally within a page based on user interaction, to name just a few examples.

At a macro level, there's an x-ray process to identify how the larger pieces of the page (or patterns across multiple site pages) fit together, to look for patterns of behavior that might inform the combination of key pieces of content and functionality, and to assess how the sequencing of these resources can be optimized to make sure they function well in both the basic and enhanced environments.

Once this higher-order analysis happens, the basic principles at a component or element level remain the same: in each case, it's a simple process of identifying all essential content and functionality required to enable the user, considering the possible HTML elements that could be used for a particular situation (based on content formats, data requirements or business rules, overall flow), and deciding on standard HTML markup that will provide the best user experience.

We'll talk much more about the x-ray perspective, and consider some complex design scenarios that explore the deconstruction process in detail, in Chapter 2. And we'll put individual interface widgets under the x-ray in Chapters 8–19, to see how progressive enhancement techniques achieve the goal of making both the basic and enhanced experiences as fully accessible, functional, and usable as possible.

But before we get into the details of how to apply the x-ray perspective on actual sites and components, let's review the process we've developed for successful progressive enhancement development on our projects.

From x-ray to action: the building blocks of progressive enhancement development

As we refined the capabilities test framework and applied the x-ray perspective over time, a vocabulary and methodology began to emerge that defined our progressive enhancement development process. We have two experiences to support: a "basic" one that works universally on all web-enabled devices (inasmuch as we can make that happen), and an "enhanced" experience that's delivered to more feature-capable browsers. The markup for the former provides a foundation on which everything else is built, so we named it exactly that: "the foundation markup." And as our more feature-rich experience relies on advanced presentation and behaviors, we designated any markup, style sheets, or scripts developed to enable it to be our "advanced" or "enhanced" resources.

To successfully deliver these experiences, it's essential that we honor three key principles of progressive enhancement:

▶ Start with clear content and well-structured markup.

▶ Maintain strict separation of layout and presentation.

▶ Unobtrusively layer in advanced behavior and styling, with careful consideration of accessibility implications.

As our goal for the basic experience is universal access, our development approach must be to *start with clear content and well-structured semantic HTML markup*. Semantic and well-ordered markup serves as a meaningful, functional foundation upon which enhancements can be made; is more likely to be usable on a wider range of devices; and provides a clear road map for users navigating a site with assistive technology.

How you construct the markup around the page's content has a huge impact on how enhancements like CSS and JavaScript may be layered, and also greatly impacts how accessible your page's content will be to non-visual users. A site built with clean, organized, well-formed, and precise markup is much easier to style and make interactive, and allows for code reuse.

Understanding the features, capabilities, and constraints of semantic HTML and the range of elements, tags, and attributes that are available in the current approved HTML specification (not to mention looking forward to new features in the emerging specifications that may be used to position code for future compatibility) is essential to achieving the strongest foundation markup for both basic and enhanced experiences. We review those available options, and discuss the best practice approaches that we recommend in detail, in Chapter 3.

A second key principle we adopt strictly with our progressive enhancement development is to *separate layout from content*. We build out the wireframe of the page before we fill it with content because it greatly simplifies the work of creating consistent template system across an entire project, and we strictly maintain all CSS affecting presentation and style separately from content.

When the structure and style of a page are built independently of its content, it's easy to create variations on the same layout and deliver experiences that work optimally for a wide variety of browsers and devices without any of the structural CSS affecting the content styles. This, in turn, gives us a flexibility to consider extended media types—standard desktop screens, mobile, print, and assistive devices—and selectively apply the basic and advanced CSS features to accommodate them. In Chapter 4, we'll explore understanding which types of styles can be safely applied in most environments, how more complex CSS rules behave and influence one another, and how styles can be centralized and optimized for the cleanest basic and most robust enhanced experiences.

Advanced behaviors and presentations enabled by JavaScript can dramatically enhance an experience—and, if done improperly or carelessly, render a component, page, or whole site completely unusable for large segments of an audience. There are good guidelines and clear best practices for structuring and referencing scripts to *unobtrusively layer in enhanced behaviors* so that they safely improve the experience for browsers that are capable, and also ensure that the basic experience is not compromised. We will look at these principles and techniques, and relevant accessibility considerations, in detail in Chapter 5.

Armed with a better understanding of how HTML markup, well defined CSS, and unobtrusive JavaScript work together, we'll then take an in-depth look at the capabilities test in Chapter 6, and see how it uses the above principles and approaches to enable a more reliable progressive enhancement experience.

Putting theory into action

The next several chapters attempt to condense and highlight the best practices you need to know to successfully implement progressive enhancement on real-world client projects. We'll start in the next chapter by diving into using the x-ray approach; then, in subsequent chapters, we'll cover writing meaningful HTML markup, applying CSS effectively, using JavaScript to build enhancements and add behavior. We'll wrap up with a detailed walkthrough of our browser capabilities test suite.

chapter two

progressive enhancement in action: the x-ray perspective

Our primary goal when building a website is to ensure that everyone gets the best possible experience within the capabilities and constraints of their browser. We believe progressive enhancement makes it possible to achieve this goal by delivering all the benefits that advanced coding affords to those with modern browsers, while still serving the needs of users on older browsers, screen readers, and web-enabled mobile phones—all with a unified code base.

Over the course of many client projects, we've devised a custom progressive enhancement-based methodology which has two important keystones: a capabilities test to conclusively determine each browser's specific capabilities, and a design and development planning process we call "the x-ray perspective."

The x-ray perspective is based on the principle that even within the most complex modern web designs—including dynamic, Ajax-driven applications with desktop-like behaviors—essential content and functionality can and should be expressed with simple, semantic HTML to provide a usable, accessible experience for all visitors. Taking an x-ray perspective means looking "through" the complex widgets and visual styles of a design, identifying the core content and functional pieces that make up the page, and finding a simple HTML equivalent for each that will work universally. It also means identifying the complex styles and behaviors of each component, and creating a strategy for conditionally applying these enhancements when the browser is capable, and in a way that maintains accessibility.

The x-ray process is a powerful tool for thinking strategically about how to layer on page enhancements in the best possible way; it can make the difference between a fully accessible experience and a series of frustrating dead-ends. It's simply a matter of "unlearning" some common bad coding habits, and getting into the habit of thinking strategically about first building the most complete basic experience possible on the page, and then layering the cool stuff on top of it.

In this chapter, we'll summarize the mechanics of our x-ray method, and then review four real-world design cases that include a range of advanced interface elements and interactions. The case studies will show how we evaluate a complex design with the x-ray perspective, review the development and coding decisions we make when building foundation and enhanced markup, CSS, and scripts, and also discuss some of the additional enhancements we add to ensure broad accessibility. Finally, we'll finish up with a summary checklist of criteria to consider when testing code to verify that all the effort put into progressive enhancement will actually deliver a satisfying experience to all users.

An overview of the x-ray perspective

The x-ray perspective is a methodology we've developed to evaluate a complex site design, break it down into its most basic modular parts, and build it back up in such a way that a single coded page will work for modern browsers with full functional capabilities as well as all other browsers and devices that may understand only basic HTML and nothing else.

The x-ray process starts with a target design that shows how the final page should look and behave on a modern browser, with all the advanced bells and whistles. With that target design in hand, we follow a planning and development process comprised of three key parts:

1   Define overall content hierarchy and priority, and map components to a basic HTML equivalent.

2   Build "foundation" markup that provides all essential content and functionality with minimal "safe" styles and no JavaScript.

3   Write advanced markup, CSS, and JavaScript to layer visual and functional enhancements in browsers that can support them.

Constructing the basic and the enhanced experiences in code is often an iterative process; as we write a first draft of the foundation markup and begin working through where to add enhancements, we often find cases where slight tweaks to the foundation markup will be necessary to make those enhancements possible.

Defining content hierarchy and mapping components to HTML

The first step is an exercise in prioritization that simultaneously looks top-down to identify the overall content grouping and hierarchy, and bottom-up to define basic HTML equivalents for all content and functionality.

With content grouping and hierarchy, there are a few questions to consider:

▶ What are the most important pieces of content on the page, and what do users need to read/focus on to understand the intended purpose or message? Is there a literal or implied order of that content?

▶ Looking across the full site design, are there common content, functionality, or behavior patterns that can and should be reused in the template system?

▶ Are there any tasks that must be completed? If so, what are the steps in the process, and the tools the user will need? Are steps required or optional? Are the content and/or the choices for any step contingent on a prior user decision?

These higher-order questions tease out opportunities to establish interface rules and norms, and become a foundation for the centralized style and functional behavior rules for the coding process.

Concurrent with the high-level analysis, we look with a critical eye at the detailed page content and functionality, and how it would work in the basic vs. enhanced experience:

▶ Does the design call for content that's inserted dynamically via Ajax? (In the foundation markup, this content must either be served with the page or be contained in a separate, linked HTML page.)

▶ Are there parts of the interface that constitute a workflow where choices in one step determine options in another, or require detailed connections back to a server to validate a selection? We need to make sure any contingencies are properly segregated in the basic experience to help users be most efficient, and to minimize errors or complications.

▶ Are there parts of the interface that may be prohibitively bandwidth-intensive or difficult to use in the basic experience, constructed only with standard HTML? If so, we can either provide simpler components in the foundation markup, or encourage basic users to accomplish a goal through an alternate, offline method.

Finally, we do a detailed analysis of each individual component on the page to identify its purpose and determine the basic HTML elements that would best support it. At the same time, we consider how we could apply CSS and JavaScript enhancements to this markup, and assess whether enhancements introduce any specific accessibility concerns.

In our own work, we often find ourselves in interesting debates as we figure out how to express a very complex user interface with the limited vocabulary of HTML. Some basic HTML decisions are quite straightforward—simple page headers and body content, for instance, clearly lend themselves to being formatted as headings and paragraph elements. But others—particularly more complex interactive components that don't clearly map to standard HTML elements—occasionally require more careful thought.

Consider, for example, a custom slider control that filters for flight times and prices:

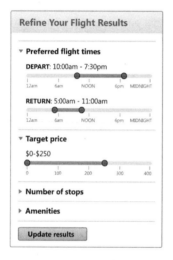

Figure 2-1 Sliders used as filters on a travel search website.

What's the proper HTML equivalent for a slider that sets a start and end timeframe? Or a low and high dollar amount? Are they the same?

This is where the x-ray perspective kicks in. Instead of looking at the appearance or user-interaction of an element in the final design, we focus on what information the element is supposed to convey or what data needs to be collected from the user. What's really going on inside Kayak's sliders, beneath the surface?

Consider that each timeframe slider is designed to collect two values—a start time and an end time—within a 24-hour period. A few standard HTML elements for collecting user input could very effectively capture those values, including a text input or a select element, but which element provides the best user experience? The time chooser also has a fixed set of options on a continuum, so a pair of select elements—say, with standard time increments at 15-minute intervals—would be a good choice for the foundation markup, because it provides clear user constraints analogous to markers on the slider's scale (it allows only valid times to be selected). For an enhanced experience, we'd leverage the select elements' markup—their options, values, and any other relevant attributes—to create a full-featured slider widget with CSS and JavaScript that "communicates" its values back to the original select elements so they're submitted with the form. (We'll discuss detailed recommendations for implementing accessible sliders with progressive enhancement in Chapter 16.)

Considering higher-level content hierarchy, priorities, and groupings, and then mapping detailed content and component functionality to basic HTML equivalents yields an initial roadmap for building the simple markup and minimal styles in a basic experience, followed by the more complex markup, styles, and scripts that will be delivered as enhancements.

Building foundation markup and minimal, safe styles

When the overall hierarchy of the page and the purpose of each component is planned out, it's much easier to efficiently write semantic HTML code that will serve as the basis for both the basic and enhanced experiences. We refer to this HTML as the "foundation" markup because it literally forms the foundation on which we'll build CSS and JavaScript enhancements to bring the finished design to life.

When coding the foundation markup, we tackle the major layout sections first—including all main container elements like the masthead, footer, and column configurations—to solidify the basic page structure before we move on to more detailed components. Then we fill out the content and functionality for all the individual elements on the page with a particular focus on using semantic HTML to create a basic experience that is easy to use. (In Chapter 3, we review how to write semantic markup that supports both the basic and enhanced experiences.)

There are some situations where HTML elements are needed to make the basic experience functional but won't be necessary in the enhanced experience, or alternately, cases where markup is only relevant and usable in the enhanced experience. For example, a **select** used as a filter on a results page requires a button to submit a form in the basic experience; that button isn't necessary in the enhanced code, where JavaScript can automatically submit on "blur" (when the user has completed their selection, and focused elsewhere on the page). Conversely, a Print button requires JavaScript to function; it should be excluded from the foundation markup so it doesn't confuse users in the basic experience, and added with JavaScript when the page is enhanced.

◆ Tip

When writing the foundation markup and noting where enhancements should be made, keep track with HTML comments written directly to the markup, for example:

`<!-- This radio button set will be enhanced into a slider -->`

or

`<!-- Print button goes here -->`

This annotation keeps important enhancement-related information clearly in place during development, and also provides useful signposts when returning to a design to update it, or for communicating among larger collaborative design teams.

When writing foundation markup, we periodically preview the page in a wide range of browsers and screen readers to check that the content hierarchy is intact and that the page reads well, makes sense, and is functional on its own. Well-structured markup that is written with proper semantics is inherently accessible—links and form controls are all keyboard accessible; **alt** text on images adds meaning for screen readers and search engines; well-organized source order makes the page easy to read.

This is also a good time to validate the markup, which can be extremely helpful in unearthing markup errors and avoiding bugs down the road.

◆ Tip

A validation tool we frequently use is provided by the W3C: http://validator.w3.org.

Once the foundation markup is in good shape, there are a small number of "safe" style rules that can be applied to improve the visual appearance and usability of the basic experience. Safe styles are very simple CSS rules that render reliably on a wide range of browsers and degrade gracefully if they aren't supported.

Safe styles are applied to the foundation markup through an external style sheet and can include a font family and a very minimal set of background colors, borders, padding, and margins—just enough to convey basic branding and create comfortable spacing between content objects, to underscore the hierarchy and make the page easier to read or scan.

Some CSS properties can render in unexpected ways across older and mobile devices, so it's crucially important to avoid using them in the safe style sheet for the basic experience. These include floats; reversing text on darker background colors or images; and setting fixed width or height dimensions, overflow properties, or negative margin or position values. (We'll discuss how to write safe styles in greater detail in Chapter 4.)

When foundation markup and safe styles are completed, the page should be fully functional and usable to everyone. Next, we'll plan the enhanced experience.

Applying markup, style, and script enhancements

When coding enhanced components, like a custom slider control, we often need to tweak the foundation markup so it will better enable the enhanced experience. For example, we will often add IDs and classes to HTML elements in the foundation markup to establish the "hooks" needed to apply styling and behavior enhancements. If extra markup is needed to apply multiple background images or other visual effects in the enhanced experience, **span** and **div** tags may also be selectively added. Since these attributes and tags are invisible to a user in the basic experience, they are harmless to add to the foundation markup and will make the enhancement process much easier to style and make interactive with JavaScript. Still, we recommend using extra markup selectively and in moderation—additional tags add weight to the page, and too much additional complexity and page weight could negatively impact the basic experience (read: increase download time).

Once the markup is complete, enhanced styles will do most of the heavy lifting to move content into floated or positioned columns, layer in background images, and apply styles necessary to make interactive widgets function properly. As such, they may not work for all browsers the same way, and may need to be divided among multiple style sheets that are applied conditionally when the capabilities test passes.

This is also the time to add any JavaScript functions that transform the foundation markup, manipulate styles and add behavior to transform the page into the enhanced experience, and to remove markup that is useful only in the basic version of the site.

It's also critical to ensure that any content that will be added or updated by Ajax in the enhanced experience be delivered to the page in an accessible way for users in the basic experience. For example, a data grid, search results page, or product description should be populated with data in the foundation markup, not structured as an empty **div** that is populated by Ajax after the page loads. Any filtering, paging, or navigation to update page data should be built with standard HTML forms and links to make sure the navigation works without scripting enabled. This seemingly simple rule is frequently overlooked—presumably in the name of speed or responsiveness—but as we saw in the examples in this book's introduction, neglecting to serve necessary content with the page can result in unacceptably poor experiences for users on devices without complete JavaScript or CSS capabilities.

* * *

Designing and developing web pages with the x-ray perspective requires a little more planning time up front, but it pays off in huge dividends in the form of cleaner separation of markup, presentation, and behavior, and most importantly, it makes the goal of progressive enhancement attainable.

Next, we'll look at four real-world design scenarios—a news website, a retail check-out form, a dynamic budget-planning tool, and a photo-manager application—featuring advanced interface designs that present rendering or accessibility challenges. Each case study will illustrate how to deconstruct a design into foundation markup and style and script enhancements, with emphasis on how to maintain accessibility in both the basic and enhanced experiences.

Case 1: Planning structure and organization in a news website

News sites have transformed in recent years to incorporate a broad range of enhanced styles and JavaScript-enabled features like animated slideshows, compact filtering and sorting controls, dynamic charts, maps, and other rich data-display tools. While these enhanced features dramatically improve the experience, they require a more complex code structure and present potential challenges to accessibility, which make this site an ideal case for building with progressive enhancement.

Let's take a look at the target news site design:

Figure 2-2 News website target design with interactive features

The target design incorporates a number of interactive components, including a prominent rotating feature block, a list of story links with several filtering options, and a custom stock-quote search tool.

Evaluating content organization and naming

First, we'll evaluate the final design to understand how content is grouped, and to identify any components with advanced features that will need to be mapped to simple standard HTML.

The first step is to organize and name the high-level regions of the page. This layout is pretty straightforward: starting at the top, there is a masthead with the search box and logo, followed by a two-level global navigation bar, a large content section in the main part of the page with three columns of content, and a footer with copyright and support links. We'll assign a descriptive ID to each region that is brief and clearly describes its purpose and priority on the page, rather than its position or style (which may evolve if the site is expanded or redesigned).

To organize these regions, we'll name the top bar's ID "masthead," the global navigation "navigation," and the footer bar "footer." Naming IDs for the three columns within the main page is a bit trickier. The fairly neutral ID scheme of "featured-content" for the feature slideshow column, "main-content" for the wider center column, and "sidebar" for the right-hand column with search and advertising is a workable naming convention that sufficiently describes the priority and relationships among the columns.

We should also assign WAI-ARIA landmark roles to each content region. ARIA is a specification created by the W3C for assigning additional semantic meaning to markup for screen readers, like the role or dynamic state of specific components. Landmark roles can be assigned to static content blocks to identify their primary purpose, and also provide a quick way for screen reader users to navigate around the page, as many newer screen readers enable this functionality. Landmarks are assigned with the **role** attribute and an accepted value, like **navigation** or **main**; the complete list of accepted roles and their descriptions are listed in the latest WAI-ARIA specification at www.w3.org/WAI/PF/aria/roles#landmark_roles.

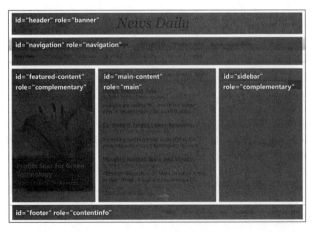

Figure 2-3 The news website's primary layout blocks are assigned logically named IDs and given landmark roles.

Leveraging native HTML hierarchy features for content organization

In the basic experience, advanced CSS and JavaScript aren't available to create multi-column layouts, or use slideshows or tabs to streamline the content presentation. Instead, the basic experience must rely completely on source order and semantic markup structure to express the content organization and priority. One of the most important tools for visually organizing content on the page is the heading element, which has built-in hierarchy in its structure, and provides additional semantic meaning for search engines and people using screen readers. We'll leverage the native capabilities of headings to provide the majority of the structure here.

When coding the foundation markup, it's important to analyze all the page content and sketch out a heading structure that is parallel, comprehensive, and consistent. Here is how we'll set up the heading structure for the news page to provide a clear overview of the document organization:

▶ The masthead, including the name of the publication, "News Daily," is marked up with an **h1** element, because it's the most prominent and important heading on the page.

▶ The main section of content is divided into three columns for Features, Stories, and a sidebar with a stock quote search tool and advertising. The top heading for each column is marked up with an **h2** element.

▶ Content objects within each column, like slideshow titles, linked article titles, and market data tabs, are marked up with **h3** elements.

Headings used in this way help both visual and screen-reader users discern the content hierarchy. By default, browsers render heading elements in graduated font sizes, from very large (**h1**) to small (**h6**); in the basic experience, we rely on the browser's default sizes to style headings so that they appear larger than normal text.

Headings introduce hierarchy and order on the news page, and build in an added benefit for users of screen readers who rely on markup structure alone to navigate; most modern screen readers now provide a control to browse the content by page headings (as well as paragraphs and lists).

Structuring navigation

Top navigation in the enhanced experience is a compact horizontal bar; a background color shift indicates on-state feedback for the selected primary navigation option, and groups it with secondary navigation options:

Figure 2-4 News site top navigation in the target design

In the basic experience, this navigation is best represented as an unordered list, because it will support the hierarchical relationship between the selected primary navigation option and its list of sub-navigation options. Each list item contains a link that will refresh the page in both the basic and enhanced experiences when clicked. The unordered list of navigation links renders in the basic version of the page as a long, nested list of links:

When it's placed at the top of the source order (just below the mast-head), users navigating the page with keyboard commands on mobile devices and screen readers may have to scroll or read through this long list of options before reaching the more important, featured content, so it's good practice to provide an optional link that lets users skip any navigation elements that are repeated on every page. Simply include an anchor link that reads "Skip to content," and point its **href** value to the main content area's **id**, in this case, **content**:

```
<a href="#content">Skip to content</a>
```

We're choosing to show only the sub-navigation for the selected option in our design, but keep in mind that the submenus associated with all ten top-level news categories could number 50–80 items or more. For complex or deeply nested navigation systems with hundreds of options, we sometimes place navigation markup below the page content in the source order so that users don't encounter—and have to skip—the complete navigation every time they load a new page. This allows the main content to display closer to the top of the screen, and makes it easier for users with mobile phones or screen readers to access it quickly.

◆ Tip

When employing this alternate approach, it helps to provide keyboard users a "Jump to navigation" link at the top for quick access to the navigation block at the bottom.

Accommodating layered and animated content

The first column of content in the main page content area contains a featured slideshow with animated transitions and Pause/Play controls. The slideshow is slick, but at a fundamental level it's really just a compact way to display links to multiple feature stories, each with an image, a story title that links to a detail page, and a caption. Looking at this widget from an x-ray perspective, this slideshow could simply be built from a series of content blocks, written to the page as part of the foundation markup so they're accessible without JavaScript, and then enhanced into a slideshow for capable browsers.

Skip to content

- Top Stories
- World
- U.S.
- Politics
- Business
  - Overview
  - Global Business
  - Markets
  - Economy
  - Small Business
  - Personal Finance
- Technology
- Sports
- Arts
- Travel
- Classifieds

Figure 2-5
Top navigation unordered list seen in the basic experience, with the "Skip to content" link above.

In the basic experience, all slideshow content can be formatted like a static film-strip, with the photos and their captions all displayed at once. This way, all the content is visible and accessible, and we can easily transform the set of content blocks into the enhanced slideshow experience.

The slideshow controls—the Pause/Play, Previous, and Next controls for navigating through the slides—are necessary only in the script- and CSS-enhanced experience; they can be omitted entirely from the foundation markup and created and inserted by JavaScript when the capabilities test passes.

In some situations, serving all feature stories may be too bandwidth-intensive for the foundation markup. If this is the case, it's equally valid to include a single feature story in the foundation markup to reduce page weight, and then load the remaining stories' markup into the page with Ajax for users in the enhanced experience.

Enhanced experience

Basic experience

Figure 2-6 The animated slideshow in the enhanced experience is based on a fully accessible series of content blocks in basic experience.

Supporting dynamic filtering and sorting

Next to the Features block, the page displays a Stories list that users can filter by the latest, most popular, most emailed, or most blogged:

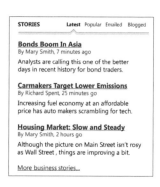

Figure 2-7 In the enhanced experience, the filter links dynamically load new stories with Ajax.

From an x-ray perspective, we see that this feature will be accessible to all users in the basic experience if the page loads an initial set of stories based on a default filter option

("Latest"), and the filter controls are coded as standard links that reload the page with an alternate set of stories:

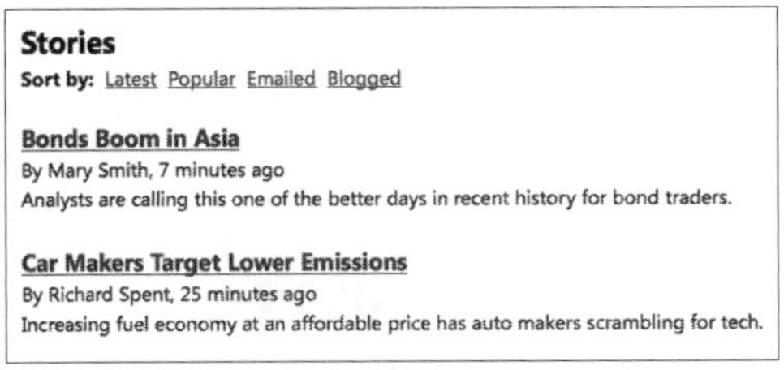

Stories
Sort by: <u>Latest</u> <u>Popular</u> <u>Emailed</u> <u>Blogged</u>

Bonds Boom in Asia
By Mary Smith, 7 minutes ago
Analysts are calling this one of the better days in recent history for bond traders.

Car Makers Target Lower Emissions
By Richard Spent, 25 minutes ago
Increasing fuel economy at an affordable price has auto makers scrambling for tech.

Figure 2-8 Filtered story views are accessed with simple links in the basic experience.

In the foundation markup, each filter link's **href** attribute will contain parameters to reload the page with a filtered story list. In the enhanced version, we can use JavaScript to intercept the click on a link, parse the link's **href** value, and repopulate the list of stories dynamically with Ajax, instead of requiring a page refresh.

This feature could also be implemented as a small form with radio buttons, or a **select** control with sort options, and a Go button to submit the form. The choice of how the basic markup is built for a particular interaction like this depends on the server configuration, and what feels most usable and appropriate for the design.

Case 2: Workflows, validation, and data submission in a checkout form

Consider an online scenario that commonly employs enhanced dynamic features: an ecommerce checkout form.

Many contemporary checkout pages use JavaScript-, Ajax-, and advanced CSS-controlled features to deliver highly efficient and engaging transactions that minimize opportunities for error and result in far higher user confidence. For example, checkout pages commonly include features such as form elements that progressively reveal required fields based on user input: in-place data validation and highlights and error feedback on form elements; tooltips with helper text and instructions next to or even within form fields; and highly efficient data-entry widgets like sliders and calendars. These features visually organize a form, place focus and information where users need it most, and make it more attractive and easier to use.

The downside is that these features function poorly or not at all without JavaScript and CSS, possibly leaving some percentage of users on older browsers, slower systems, and mobile phones out in the cold. Since most companies that sell on the web spend a great deal of time and effort convincing shoppers to purchase on their site, it really isn't acceptable to lose even a single customer on the final checkout page because the developer decided to take a shortcut.

So let's take a look at a checkout page design with some advanced features to see how we could devise a plan that provides all required content and functionality in the foundation markup, and pave the way for the addition of enhanced features for capable modern browsers.

Breaking down the checkout form design

Our target design is a compact checkout workflow that groups several distinct steps into a single page:

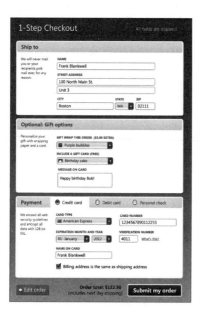

Figure 2-9 Target design for an advanced checkout transaction page

The first step in building an accessible checkout form is to take a high-level pass through the target design to identify any features or components that don't map exactly to standard HTML. A host of advanced features immediately jump out:

▶ Richly designed form sections with multi-column layout

▶ Custom-styled dropdowns with branded visual styles and, in the case of the gift options and credit card chooser, a thumbnail image to deliver feedback

▶ A radio button-driven set of payment options that function as tabs, each displaying a unique set of form controls for collecting that type of payment

▶ A custom-styled Submit button

We need to understand how the features and interactivity should work in the basic experience, since we won't be able to rely on JavaScript for constraints, validation, feedback, or interactivity.

With data-entry-intensive form interfaces in particular, we should focus our x-ray view specifically on identifying and isolating any cases in the enhanced interface that employ sophisticated error-condition feedback, dynamically populate data from one area to another, or reveal options contingent on user decisions. These features need to be handled through server interactions in the basic experience, so it's critical to identify any key workflow points with functionality that requires server input or validation, and structure the experience to properly support the user in a logical and error-free way.

Starting at the top of the form, we have a shipping address block that is pretty straightforward; it contains a combination of text inputs and dropdowns and requires no JavaScript for interactivity in the enhanced experience. While the Gift Options block's design calls for custom features, like icons displayed with each option, the data input mechanism has similarly straightforward functionality, just like a standard **select** element, and doesn't require extensive validation or introduce any complex business rules.

When we apply the x-ray perspective to the payment section, we arrive at an important decision point: The enhanced version is organized into a radio button-driven tab strip that reveals specific form controls unique to each payment method, based on user interaction; the server retrieves the appropriate set of form controls dynamically, based on the chosen radio-button option. But in the basic experience, we don't have the luxury of dynamically activating and disabling multiple form fields.

We could present a very long form in a single page, with the three payment methods listed out under their respective radio buttons, but this format is not very usable. It places unreasonable burden on the shopper to understand the technical constraints, fill out only the fields related to their selected payment method, and skip the form elements related to the other payment types. This can lead to errors, confusion, frustration, and ultimately, of course, abandoned checkouts.

A better option is to break the form into multiple screens, splitting the process into logical steps to provide server-side validation and properly branch the experience based on user input. This separation of steps affords an added benefit: it allows for content captured in earlier steps to be directed into successive steps—shipping address information entered into the first block can populate the payment section in the third, for example.

With this plan in mind, the next step in our x-ray process is to look at each part of the enhanced target design to identify the contingencies in detail, and map our enhanced components to basic HTML equivalents.

The first two sections—Ship To and Gift Options—include no dependencies, and they logically fit together, so we'll combine these two sections into the first step in our basic experience:

Figure 2-10 The first two sections of the enhanced form (left) are grouped into the first step of a multi-screen checkout wizard for the basic experience (right).

The enhanced design for the Gift Options section calls for custom select menus for the gift-wrap and gift-card fields, in order to provide thumbnail images for each option. By starting with a standard **select** element in the foundation markup, we can provide a perfectly functional version in the basic experience that lacks only thumbnails, and then enhance it to a custom select when the browser is capable. (We'll discuss how to create custom selects in detail in Chapter 17).

The gift-card message is applicable only if the shopper chooses to include a card, so this field will be hidden in the enhanced experience until a gift card is chosen. However, the card message field should be included in the foundation markup so it's accessible in the basic experience; these shoppers will simply skip the card message field if they choose not to include a card. While it's not ideal to show an unnecessary form field, it's only a single, clearly labeled field, so its presence isn't likely to cause confusion or place too much burden on the user.

Now let's address the Payment section. In the enhanced experience, the interface presents the payment-type option in a single, compact row of radio buttons, and pre-fills the default page with the form fields and content for the most common option, Credit Card:

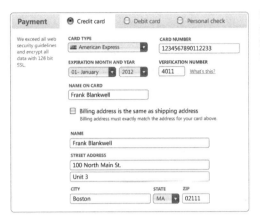

Figure 2-11 The Payment section of the enhanced experience defaults to the most popular option—in this case, the Credit Card form.

In the basic experience, we could include the payment options at the bottom of the first step, below the shipping address and gift options, since there are technically no contingencies that must be met before this step. But from a user perspective, payment options may seem out of place here—a logical disconnection—and that could be confusing. Also, we want shoppers to be able to jump back to specific steps from the final confirmation page to edit their choices, which will be easier to implement if we maintain a crisp divide between the shipping and payment steps (this requirement won't be necessary in the enhanced experience, as all content is visible on the single-page form).

So the second step in the basic checkout experience will be a fairly simple page with three radio buttons for the various payment options; when submitted, the form will send a request to the server and retrieve the correct payment fields based on the user's choice:

Figure 2-12 In the basic experience, a simple payment chooser retrieves the correct form fields.

The next screen will be conditionally written by the server to display one of three different payment forms depending on whether credit card, debit card, or personal check was selected.

For credit card and debit card payments, a billing address block is used to validate the card information. Since the shipping address has already been sent to the server, we can provide a checkbox to let shoppers skip the billing address entry if it's the same as the shipping address. In the enhanced experience, checking this field will hide the billing address fields with JavaScript. In the basic experience, the billing address form presented on the subsequent screen can be skipped completely if the checkbox is checked:

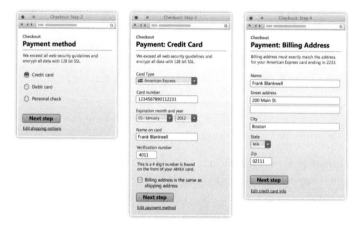

Figure 2-13 Payment workflow in the basic experience. Users who check the "same billing address" checkbox on the Credit Card screen (middle) will skip the Billing Address screen (right).

The basic checkout experience includes a final review page that provides feedback on all the data entered throughout the workflow, with an Edit button next to each section that navigates the user back to that step. Since the basic checkout experience involves a series of forms across multiple pages, users' data entries and selections should be presented for review before the form is submitted, to give them the opportunity to catch and edit errors:

Figure 2-14 Order review and confirmation page in the basic experience

This page is unique to the basic experience—in the enhanced experience, the whole checkout takes place on a single page, so the ability to review and edit the information is always available.

To recap: the basic checkout experience consists of five discrete steps that branch the user workflow based on business rules, and provide validation along the way:

1 Shipping address and gift options

2 Payment method (credit card, debit card, check)

3 Payment details (with custom form fields based on the user choice in step 2)

4 Payment billing address (for credit and debit options only)

5 Review order

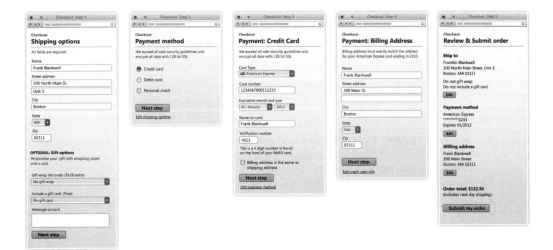

Figure 2-15 The five sequential steps of the basic checkout experience

Marking up the form to ensure accessibility

To build our checkout form in the most accessible way, it's essential that we make good choices about HTML markup structure, taking special care to consider underlying semantics. Are the form elements organized and coded to be as descriptive and usable as possible? For instance, every form element should have a properly associated label, and provide the best possible user experience in terms of ease of use and proper constraints to avoid errors.

In the foundation markup, each checkout page must start with a **form** tag with an **action** attribute directed to the server resource—for example, a PHP file—that will process the form. For each step in the checkout sequence, form controls are logically grouped within a **fieldset** element, and labels are stacked above each **input** with only minimal styles applied—no float or width/height properties should be set on form elements. At the bottom of each page, a Next Step button is provided to submit the form and move the user to the next step in the process, and a Back link navigates the shopper back to the previous page.

Our enhanced checkout form design includes several custom-styled select menus with embedded thumbnail images: gift-wrap options, gift-card options, and a custom credit-card chooser. It's essential to use a basic HTML **select** in the foundation markup to ensure that any user can make all relevant functional choices, and then enhance that **select** with custom styles once a browser has passed the capabilities test.

Figure 2-16 The basic experience uses a standard HTML **select** (left), which is transformed into a custom-styled **select** with thumbnail images in the enhanced experience (right).

■ Note

For a detailed explanation of how to style custom selects, see Chapter 17.

The custom-styled Submit My Order button is another case where proper markup choice is crucial. The latest HTML specification (4.01) provides two elements: an **input** with the **type** attribute set to **submit**, or a **button** element. Both natively submit form data, but the **button** element was omitted from a subset of XHTML called XHTML-MP (mobile profile), and as a result is not supported in browsers that render according to the XHTML-MP specification. The **input element**, on the other hand, is supported by every browser that implemented HTML 2 or later and will work on the widest range of browsers, including obscure or older mobile devices. We want to make sure that any transaction process works reliably everywhere and for everyone, so we recommend using the **input** here.

Figure 2-17 A universally compatible submit **input** is used in the foundation markup (left), and custom-styled in the enhanced experience (right).

With some custom styles applied to make the submit **input** look and behave like a button, users get a satisfying, predictable, and reliable experience everywhere. (We describe the recommended process for developing custom-styled buttons in Chapter 14.)

Applying constraints and validation

Ensuring that shoppers enter valid information during the checkout is essential to completing the transaction. As designers, we have three techniques to ensure that valid data is entered: provide instruction and helper text to demonstrate proper formatting, impose constraints to prevent invalid entry, and provide validation logic in the form of user feedback (tell the user on-screen that they entered invalid input and need to correct it).

Providing instruction and example data is the friendliest of our validation options; hints about proper formatting from the start can go a long way toward reducing invalid data. We recommend either displaying helpful content directly on the page or providing in-context assistance in tooltips next to specific fields, to keep the overall experience clean and help the user focus on the question at hand.

Figure 2-18 Instructions can help reduce data errors. They should be placed on the page in the basic experience (left), and can be selectively shown in the enhanced (right).

We can also constrain user entry to valid data values by providing controls and enhanced widgets that accept only valid entries (like checkbox, radio button, select, auto-complete text input, slider, or calendar date picker), and showing only the necessary form elements for the task at hand using progressive disclosure.

When the design calls for a free-text entry control such as a text **input**, for example, for a credit card number, we can provide text instruction in the basic experience and configure server-side validation to check the value to makes sure it's the right type (e.g., numeric), within the acceptable value range (e.g., 15 digits), and, if needed, add more sophisticated algorithms to recognize number patterns that map to specific card types.

Figure 2-19 Credit card number validation requires form submission in the basic experience (left). The input can be validated in real time with JavaScript in the enhanced experience, and the error message displayed as a tooltip (right).

The basic experience requires server interaction to provide validation feedback and hide/show form fields based on relevant context. When a user clicks the Submit My Order button, the server can validate form data to check for required fields that are not filled out or fields that don't have valid data values, and return the user to the relevant page with clear messaging about what needs to be corrected. The server can also coordinate which form fields should be seen next, like which payment form to show based on the user's payment choice.

In the enhanced experience, much of this user-constraint and validation behavior can happen in real time by using Ajax, and feedback is provided as the user types or completes their selection. This technique allows us to reuse the same server-side validation rules in both the basic and enhanced experiences.

Assembling the basic and enhanced experiences

The single-page enhanced experience is broken down into so many steps for the basic experience that it may seem like the foundation markup for both experiences is too different to use the same code. However, we can serve up the first step of the basic experience to everyone, run the capabilities test, and use the power of JavaScript (specifically, Ajax) and CSS to assemble the foundation markup from our five basic steps into the single enhanced page. Or, to speed up page load, the server could check for the cookie set by the capabilities test to see if the browser has already passed, and then assemble the entire page for users of the enhanced experience.

It's also possible to leverage the same back-end logic created to serve the proper forms and implement validation rules for both the basic and enhanced experiences. In this case, the server logic would be configured to simply retrieve requested data; the enhanced experience would employ Ajax to make the request, while the basic experience would use a standard page request.

Case 3: Interactive data visualization in a budget calculator

Our next case study is perhaps our most visually rich example: a dynamic budget calculator tool for planning a financial budget. It works with an interactive set of sliders, calculates data on the fly, and delivers real-time feedback in the form of an interactive pie chart with hover tooltips and monthly and yearly totals.

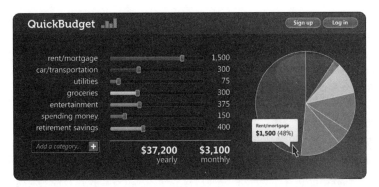

Figure 2-20 Target enhanced design for the budget calculator

At first glance, this tool may not immediately seem like a good candidate for progressive enhancement. But with an x-ray perspective, this tool's core functionality is very straight-forward and lends itself to a universal design approach: the advanced slider elements simply allow users to enter a numeric value for several categories, and the summary table and pie chart display the calculated sum of those values and show their relative weight by category and sum total.

Choosing basic markup for the budget line components

The budget calculator uses a slider widget to set and adjust the numeric value of each budget line item. There's a range of "best" foundation markup options for an enhanced slider widget, with the right element depending on the number and length of options available. For example:

▶ In cases with 2–5 simple choices (Rate: Great, Good, Fair, Poor, Not Applicable) or up to 10 numeric levels, a **radio button** set is a great choice, because it displays all options for easy scanning and has built-in constraints to avoid user input errors.

▶ For larger or more custom continuum situations where the slider is populated with 5–20+ fixed options (like financial ratings levels, for example: AAA, AA+, AA, AA–, A+, A, A–, BBB+, BBB, etc.) a **select** is optimal, because it provides good constraints, and larger lists of options can be visually divided into groups using the **optgroup** element. On the downside, select menu options are not easy to scan because they're hidden from view by default (contained in a dropdown menu) and may require scrolling.

▶ Where users can enter a wide range of numeric values (Maximum price: $0–1,000), a **text input** would be appropriate—with the caveat that there is no native way to constrain input to numeric values, so this approach would require server-side validation.

For each budget slider, we'll use a simple text **input**, because we want to allow users to enter any numeric dollar value, including decimal points for added precision.

The budget calculator foundation markup starts with a **form** tag that has an **action** attribute directed to a resource for processing the form. Each budget category line item is presented in a **div** that includes a **label**, an associated text **input** for entering a budget dollar value, and a **span** to display the calculated percentage for the category. Our markup for each category looks like this:

```
<div>
  <label for="category-1">rent/mortgage</label>
  <input type="number" min="0" max="5,000" value="1,500" id="category-1" />
  <span class="budget-percentage" title="Percent of total budget">48%</span>
</div>
```

The input has an attribute of **number**, and additional **min** and **max** attributes to set its acceptable high and low range; its actual number value and calculated percentage would both be blank to start, and then populated with the necessary values with each page refresh.

■ Note

The input number type is a new attribute in the HTML5 specification, but can be used safely now as it defaults to an attribute type of text in browsers that don't support it. We will talk more about input attributes in Chapter 3, "Writing meaningful markup."

At the bottom of the list of categories, the form needs a Calculate Budget button in the basic experience to submit the form data and calculate totals and category percentages on the server.

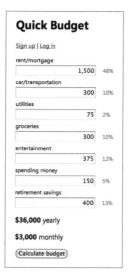

Figure 2-21 The basic calculator offers simple text inputs, calculated percentages and totals, and a button to update changes server-side.

We'll have to accommodate one error case: text inputs for entering the budget amount don't natively provide good constraints to prevent people from entering letters or special characters. For this reason, the inputs will need to be validated by the server each time the form is submitted.

We can also support the ability to add new budget categories in the basic experience by providing a set of "blank" text inputs. Just like the Submit button to recalculate the budget, the Add button will submit the whole form and reload the page with the new category and calculated values.

Figure 2-22 A small form adds a new category to the basic experience and reloads the page.

With these two simple forms for collecting budget information and adding a new category, we're supporting all the essential functionality to provide a satisfying and informative basic experience.

Creating accessible sliders from the foundation markup

While simple form fields in the basic experience do the job, for users with capable browsers, the tactile nature of slider controls in the enhanced experience encourages more exploration—and is a lot of fun.

Figure 2-23 Interactive, color-coded sliders update the dollar-number feedback and pie chart visualization as they are dragged.

There are a few key principles about how the basic and enhanced experience can work together in the context of progressive enhancement and the x-ray perspective.

First, whenever we build an enhanced widget that collects user input or data entry, we build it using a "proxy" pattern. For example, at page load, the enhancement script that creates the slider looks for any pre-existing value in the corresponding foundation **input,** and uses that value to set the initial position of the slider handle. Whenever the slider is moved, the script resets the **input** value to match, and the script continuously keeps the two in sync. In many cases, we'll keep both the slider and the editable **input** on the page at the same time and let the user choose which one to use. The benefit of this approach is that the server can process the data the same way in both basic and enhanced experiences, because it interacts only with the **input**.

Second, since there aren't any HTML elements that natively map to the semantics of a slider, we'll use non-semantic markup for this enhanced widget—which means we need to factor in accessibility features to mirror the native behaviors that users expect. In this case, we'll code it with a series of **div**s for the slider container, track, and gripper handle. But users on assistive devices won't know that this pile of **div**s is an interactive widget unless we add accessibility features to "translate" it. Specifically, we'll add an ARIA **role** attribute with the value of **slider** to identify this as a slider widget, and attributes to set the minimum, maximum, and current value for the slider so newer versions of screen readers can interpret this widget. For users on older screen readers that don't support ARIA features, the ability to interact with the original inputs is an essential accessibility feature.

Lastly, since sliders rely on a drag behavior to move the handle, it's also important to consider that many newer mobile devices like the iPhone, Palm Pre, and Google Android use drag events for general scrolling around the screen. To ensure that sliders are still usable on those devices, the slider script must allow users to click on a handle to give it focus, and then click elsewhere on the track to set the new value. Similar behaviors also support keyboard access—the Tab key focuses on a slider handle, and arrow keys move the slider to a specific value.

Building the pie chart

Seeing the pie chart update on the fly as the budget sliders move is a prominent feature of the enhanced experience, and really adds to the interaction. But relying on a plugin like Adobe Flash or a server-side tool to generate a static pie chart image doesn't embrace the inclusive progressive-enhancement principles we're striving for. Luckily, we can embrace a more universal—and future-forward—approach by using the HTML5 **canvas** tag to generate charts natively in HTML across a broad range of modern browsers. (Even Internet Explorer will render the chart without plugins, with a Google script called ExplorerCanvas, http://excanvas.sourceforge.net.)

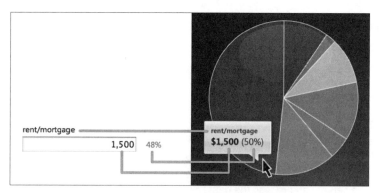

Figure 2-24 Pie chart tooltips in the enhanced experience are populated with the same values as the basic experience: category label, value, and percentage.

The pie chart's values are pulled from the same JavaScript code that generates the percentage feedback next to each input, and passed into a script that generates the canvas chart. (We'll cover accessible charting with **canvas** in detail in Chapter 12.)

The pie chart's tooltips display the label, budget dollar amount, and percentage when the user places their mouse over a portion of the pie. These data are just a different presentation of the label, input, and percentage values in the "enhanced" table (and the foundation markup).

Note

We'll talk about creating accessible custom tooltips in detail in Chapter 10.

From an accessibility standpoint, a pie chart image, regardless of how it's rendered, doesn't provide useful information for a non-sighted user. Therefore, in the enhanced experience we'll add a bit of context for screen-reader users, so they understand that the **canvas** tag and any associated markup for the chart are strictly presentational. We'll put the **canvas** in a containing **div** and add a **role** of **img** to communicate that the canvas is performing the role of an image, and also provide instructional message text in an **aria-label** attribute that explains the chart's purpose and its data values. For users on older screen readers that don't have ARIA support, we'll provide a second message in a **span** tag (which we'll hide from sighted users and ARIA-aware screen readers) that explains that the chart markup is purely presentational, along with a "skip" link so they can easily move past that markup.

In the basic experience, the percentage feedback expresses the same information as the pie chart in text form, so you may not need to include the pie chart at all. However, if a chart is desired, it's possible to generate a static image of the pie chart with each recalculation of the budget and add it to the page as an **image** tag.

We now have a fully usable and accessible budget-planner tool that will work on any device—and some interesting x-ray techniques in the toolbox to reuse in other contexts.

Case 4: Supporting full-featured application capabilities in the browser—the Photo Manager

Our final example, a photo-manager interface, is a product of the more recent Web 2.0 era, with complex application functionality previously found only on the desktop, replicated within a web browser:

Figure 2-25
Web-based
photo-manager
application

Today, many sites and online tools include complex Ajax-powered application features similar to the ones in this example, including scalable and resizable panes for navigation and content display, simple single-object drag-and-drop gestures, complex multiple selection abilities enabled by mouse-drag selections or Control/Shift-clicking, and Ajax-powered edit-in-place actions.

There is so much interactivity expressed in this design that it's almost difficult to see how all the capabilities might be supported in a basic experience! In fact, a big part of the x-ray exercise for such complex interfaces is to take a critical eye to functionality and decide how it will be handled: there may be a simple equivalent for select features; more complex interactions or gestures may be structured as multi-step or staged workflows; or, in some cases, we may determine that certain types of advanced functionality are so complex that their basic HTML equivalent may not be warranted for all users and devices.

As with our other target designs, we'll start by looking at the photo manager at a high level to understand the content and functionality groupings, look for any complex data-submission contingencies, determine which content and components are essential to the function of the site for all users, and map back to basic HTML equivalents to support them.

Marking up global navigation elements

We'll start with the overall page layout, for which the x-ray analysis is easy enough: the top bar with the product name and primary navigation sections (Organize, Upload, Shop, Account) can be coded as a standard set of links. Each link will reload the entire application window in both the basic and enhanced experiences, because the corresponding sections of the application will have different functionality. We'll use a heading element (**h1**) in the foundation markup for the product name ("Filament Photo Manager"), and style it to make it look more refined in the enhanced experience:

Figure 2-26 The heading and global navigation as seen in the basic experience

For section-specific secondary navigation, the left-hand navigation pane should also be coded as a set of standard links in the foundation markup, with headings to identify and group the two types of content (photos and albums):

Figure 2-27 The left navigation pane is coded as a series of headings and list of links.

In the enhanced experience, when the user clicks a link in the left navigation pane we'd like a seamless, application-like interaction to populate the right pane with the corresponding photos. We'll use JavaScript to intercept the link's **href** value to formulate an Ajax request that grabs photos from the selected album and populates the right-hand pane.

Figure 2-28 In the enhanced experience, clicking on an album name in the left pane loads the grid of album photos in the right pane via Ajax.

At the bottom of the left navigation pane there's also a New Album button. In the enhanced experience, clicking this button dynamically creates a new album link in the left navigation list with a default name, ready to be edited; in the basic experience, it navigates the user to a separate page with a simple form to name the album:

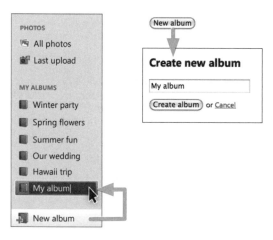

Figure 2-29 The enhanced New Album button creates an editable node in the left navigation pane; in the basic experience, the button navigates to a separate form page to name the album.

Supporting complex album and multi-photo interactions

In the enhanced experience, each album is displayed in a clean, simple interface with the album name at the top and secondary actions tucked into a menu in the upper right corner. The bottom toolbar has a set of action buttons for selected photos, and a slider to change the thumbnail photo size:

Figure 2-30 The enhanced experience album detail offers Album Actions at the top of the screen, and an actions toolbar (Delete, Email, Print) for selected photos at the bottom.

One feature that makes the enhanced photo manager really feel like a desktop application is the ability to select multiple photos in the album grid view by dragging a lasso around a group of photos, or holding down the Control or Shift key and clicking on a set of photos. When a selection is made, the interface allows users to click on the actions toolbar at the bottom to edit, delete, email, or print the selected photos, or drag and drop them over an album name in the left-hand pane to add them to an album.

Figure 2-31 Multiple photos can be selected and added to an album by dragging and dropping, just like a desktop application.

These rich interactions may not seem to be compatible with a progressive enhancement approach at first glance, but it's actually easy to provide the same functionality by using standard HTML form elements.

The basic experience of the album view looks quite a bit less styled, but provides all the same functionality. The album page starts with a heading followed by a series of album action buttons that route the user to separate pages to complete or confirm the actions:

Figure 2-32 In the basic experience, the album detail shows the album name and Album Actions headings first in the source order after the navigation.

When considering the complex mouse-drag and Control-click interactions from an x-ray perspective, they simply allow users to select multiple photos—and we can easily replicate this in the basic experience with native form elements. In the foundation markup, each photo can be coded with a **label** containing the image name, and a **checkbox** for selecting the photo. The album markup is wrapped in a **form** tag with several **submit** buttons to perform delete, email, and print actions, as well as a select menu grouped with an Add button to assign the selected photos to an album.

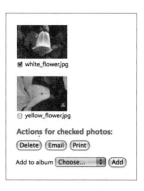

Figure 2-33 In the basic experience, checkboxes make it easy to select multiple photos and perform actions on the set with a series of buttons.

This form-style interaction is perfectly usable in the basic experience, and may even be preferable for users who are less comfortable with using drag-and-drop gestures, not to mention screen-reader users or mobile-phone users with multi-touch interfaces who can't perform drag gestures at all. (We always like to provide a fallback link with our capabilities test to let users access the basic experience from the enhanced experience—this is a classic example where even users with capable browsers may want to simplify the experience, and providing a link lets them choose which version best suits their needs.)

In the enhanced experience of the album view, the user double-clicks on a thumbnail image to replace the album thumbnails view with a full-size photo detail:

Figure 2-34 In the enhanced experience, double-clicking on a photo thumbnail image loads a full-size photo into the right pane via Ajax.

This fluid transition between the album grid and photo detail view is possible only with JavaScript. To allow users in the basic experience access to the photo detail and relevant editing tools, we'll place a link on each thumbnail photo, which will open a separate HTML photo-detail page. As with the albums above, we'd use Ajax to pull this exact foundation HTML markup for the photo-detail content into the pane in the enhanced version and style it appropriately, so there is no difference in the markup between these two experiences.

Figure 2-35 Photo-detail view in the enhanced experience

The photo-detail page in the enhanced experience has the photo name, a Back To Album button, and along the bottom, an actions toolbar that makes it easy to rotate, crop, delete, email, and print the photo. We'll create standard form submit buttons in the foundation markup that allow users to perform these actions on the photo; these same buttons are simply styled and positioned differently in the enhanced experience. Implementing keyboard shortcuts (such as mapping the Delete key to deleting the photo) and mouse gestures (such as supporting drag-and-drop to add the photo to an album in the left navigation list) will add interactive richness that mirrors behavior found in a native desktop application.

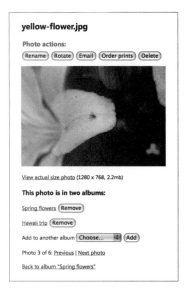

Figure 2-36 In the basic experience, clicking a linked photo navigates the user to a separate photo-detail page with optimized tools and navigation.

In the basic experience, we'll add a few unique features beneath the photo to enhance usability. First, we'll provide clear feedback about albums in which the photo is stored, with a Remove button next to each. The same "add to album" functionality from the album grid is presented here, to make it easy to add this photo to additional albums. Each of these actions would submit a form and reload the page to provide accurate feedback.

At the very bottom of the screen, navigation links enable browsing to next and previous photos in the album, and navigating back to the album grid view. When breaking up the basic experience into multiple pages (as we have here), it's always a good idea to provide additional navigation options to improve the overall flow for users.

What happened to the Crop button?

You may notice that we've omitted the Crop button from the basic experience. This is intentional. There are some cases in the x-ray process where you encounter functionality that is too complex when expressed in standard HTML elements to be comfortably usable in the basic experience. For us, the cropping tool was one such case: how could we replicate the drag-and-resize functionality of the crop box in a basic experience? If we were to deem this functionality absolutely essential, we could explore accessible solutions—for example, calculating the total pixel size of the image from the server or providing a set of text inputs for the users to enter pixel coordinates for top-left and bottom-right corners of the image. But either of these options seemed far worse user experiences than simply suggesting to the user in the basic experience that images be properly cropped before uploading.

We believe it's best to try to achieve as much parity as possible between basic and enhanced versions of any site or application, but concede that sometimes features need to be cut from the basic experience when the usability or development effort doesn't make sense.

Creating custom forms and overlays

In addition to the navigation among albums and between the album grid and detail views, there are a number of situations where the addition of small overlays and dialog boxes would make an enhanced experience feel truly responsive and application-like. For example, clicking the Email button in the actions toolbar could slide a semi-transparent overlay over the photo that prompts the user to specify recipients and a message before sending via Ajax.

Figure 2-37 In the enhanced experience, the Email Photo form opens in an overlay that is appended to the page via Ajax.

To make this work in the basic experience, the Email button would navigate users to a separate page containing the email form. (This same form foundation markup can be used in both the basic and enhanced experiences; in the latter, it's pulled in via Ajax and styled to look like the overlay design.) After the email is successfully sent, the page should refresh with a confirmation message and have a button or link to return to the photo detail page.

Figure 2-38 In the basic experience, the Email Photo form is a separate HTML page.

This plan for supporting the navigation and functional actions in the core screen types and functional actions follows a common set of patterns: providing discrete screens for workflow in the basic experience, and repurposing the foundation markup with overlays and in-place features in the enhanced experience.

Building in Back-button support

One last crucial point we feel is worth considering carefully when building complex websites or web-based applications, especially those that use Ajax: how the browser's Back button will work.

While web users are becoming more comfortable with complex application-like interactions within the browser, they still expect some native browser conventions to behave consistently, including the idea of using the browser's Back button to navigate to the previous page. When an application uses Ajax, by default the Back button doesn't recognize the interim Ajax-enabled steps, and instead navigates users back to the last real "page" it loaded (frequently, this can be the login page!), which may seriously confuse and frustrate users. Even in sites or applications coded without Ajax, there may be cases where the user can toggle large panes of content that are on the page that they would consider a new "page," and to which they would expect to "return" when they click the Back button.

In the case of our photo application, we anticipate that people would probably expect the Back button to move them back through their previous navigation views (Album 1 > Photo detail A > Photo detail B > Album 5), but not undo any of the actions they've performed (add to album, email, and so on) in between. In simple terms, by adding a unique URL hash—a string preceded with a # in the URL—and using JavaScript to check every time users navigate to a unique album or photo view, the Back button will work as expected, and all the normal browser actions, like bookmarking and emailing a link, will also work as expected.

Each website is different, so the specifics of how to make the Back button behave in a predictable and useful way will depend on the particular system model, but it plays an important role in making an application work well, and as such requires attention. We discuss specific techniques for tracking state this way when we discuss building a tabs widget in Chapter 9.

Checklist for implementing the x-ray in action

Once we've mapped the functionality to standard HTML, created foundation markup, layered on enhancements, and iteratively tested and refined a couple of times, the final step to the x-ray approach is to run through a checklist of questions to test progress:

▶ Is the basic experience fully functional and usable with HTML only?

▶ Does the foundation markup encode all the information, including layout and structure, that the enhanced experience needs?

▶ For both basic and enhanced experiences, does the page read and work in a sensible order, and promote the most important content and function?

▶ Are the pages navigable and form elements usable (selections can be made and submitted) using only keyboard commands?

▶ Do the pages make sense when navigated with a screen reader? Can the user navigate the header structure alone?

▶ Is there a clear way for all users—including those on mobile devices or using screen readers—to switch between the basic and enhanced experiences (for example, with a "View low/high bandwidth version" link) as a matter of preference, or if for some unforeseen reason the enhanced version fails?

While these questions may not reveal *every* exception case for accessibility and rendering support for every browser experience, they highlight many of the key factors that will help achieve the goal of universal access.

* * *

We've only scratched the surface of all the elements one could encounter in the broad range of sites and web-based applications that could possibly be designed. But we hope this overview gives a good sense of how many enhanced interactions can be translated into simple HTML for the basic experience, and more importantly, serve as inspiration when thinking about how to tackle complex applications with progressive enhancement.

Progressive enhancement in general, and our x-ray approach and capabilities test in particular, work effectively only when your coding approach strictly applies best-practice coding approaches for HTML markup, CSS, and JavaScript. In the next three chapters, we'll review the key points and features we believe are essential to understand in order to properly implement progressive enhancement design.

Once we've laid that foundation, we'll then walk through the specifics of how our capabilities testing framework works, and how you can refine and even extend it to work in even more creative ways for your own unique needs.

And then we'll get into some detailed widget components to demonstrate the real in-the-trenches techniques you can employ to make progressive enhancement work in today's browsers, and tomorrow's.

chapter three

writing meaningful markup

These days it's tempting to overlook proper markup and structure: there's an arsenal of web technologies that can completely transform HTML, and experienced designers and developers can apply CSS and JavaScript to a pile of **divs** and **spans** to impose hierarchy, make it look pretty, or script it to behave as they want. But what happens when you take CSS and JavaScript away? Is the content hierarchy still in place? Does the most important information appear at the beginning of the page? Where is the navigation? Is it easy to find? Does everything still work?

In this book, we recommend integrating progressive enhancement and capabilities testing into your development process to ensure that all content and functionality reaches everyone with any web-enabled device. But this approach works only when the site is built on a proper foundation of clean, well-organized, and properly structured semantic markup.

What is semantic markup? In the 2001 *Scientific American* article, "The Semantic Web," Tim Berners-Lee defined it as a way to "bring structure to the meaningful content of Web pages" (Tim Berners-Lee, James Hendler and Ora Lassila, "The Semantic Web," *Scientific American Magazine,* May 2001, www.scientificamerican.com/article.cfm?id=the-semantic-web). In other words, semantic markup is the vocabulary, grammar, pronunciation, and composition that helps the browser—and, by extension, the user—make sense of the web. We've found that we can express surprisingly powerful and complex ideas by combining semantic HTML tags together in smart ways—ways that make even the basic experience without CSS or JavaScript clear and usable.

Coding foundation markup so that it works on all possible browsers and properly supports enhancements requires careful consideration of which elements to use, and where they'll be most effective. Markup is like any language—without a strong knowledge of its structure and rules, it's just an assembly of sounds or symbols.

In this chapter, we'll examine commonly used HTML elements, and describe how good semantic choices can improve browser interpretation and optimize the user experience on any web-enabled device. We'll consider semantic markup options in four basic sections:

▶ *Marking up text and images*: The basic building blocks of any site work best when marked up as accurately and precisely as possible. This section explores the range of semantic tags to intelligently identify web content and impart hierarchical meaning.

▶ *Marking up interactive elements*: Forms and other interactive elements incorporate very specific capabilities, and choosing proper markup is crucial to support expected behaviors and promote optimal user interaction.

▶ *Creating context in the page*: How you group individual content items and related form objects offers opportunities to help the browser—and the audience—understand your message and purpose.

▶ *Setting up an HTML document*: Finally, using markup that defines the HTML document and identifies the page offers its own methods to encode meaning and inform the browser or other user agent how to interpret it.

As we go, we'll review how to interpret contemporary design challenges and break them down into their individual parts so that you can best structure and mark up the content as a foundation layer for CSS and JavaScript enhancements.

Marking up text and images

As designers, we know that every good experience starts with clear, well-defined content. Once the site's narrative, or the application's workflow, is complete, translating the content into markup is just a matter of knowing which elements to use.

Some elements, like headings, serve a dual purpose: browsers render them in a fairly consistent way that's visually distinct from the rest of the content, and under the hood they provide instructions to assistive technologies (like screen readers) and machines (like search engines) that interpret the content without any visual cues from the design.

The following sections explore the range of semantic elements we recommend to imbue foundation text, images, and rich media with useful meaning.

Elements for meaningfully marking up text

Conventions for presenting the printed word have been in place for centuries—including paragraphs, headers, quotations, and many more—that help readers parse and understand the hierarchy and meaning of a text. These rules are as valid on the web as they were when Gutenberg invented the printing press, and semantic markup provides a rich array of precise tags to help impart meaning to text web content. Thoroughly and accurately employing the range of these elements can dramatically improve how a browser or search engine interprets and presents text content.

HEADINGS

Heading elements are used to mark up titles and subtitles, divide content into sections and create hierarchy on the page.

Standard semantic heading elements number from **h1**, which represents the highest hierarchical level on the page; each successive heading is encoded with relative importance, down to the **h6** heading—the smallest available.

```
<h1>The most important header</h1>

<h2>Next most important heading</h2>

<h3>Sub-level heading</h3>

<h4>Sub-level heading</h4>

<h5>Sub-level heading</h5>

<h6>Smallest sub-level heading</h6>
```

Headings also serve an important role in page meaning and accessibility for both search engines and screen readers.

Though search engines don't publish their algorithms, it is believed by many that some engines interpret relative importance of content based on the headings in the content hierarchy—placing more relative rank weight on the words found in heading elements than standard running text. A paragraph, **div**, or **span** styled to look like a heading, by comparison, would not be assigned the same level of importance.

Screen readers like JAWS, NVDA, Apple's VoiceOver and WindowEyes are used by the visually impaired to access web content and functionality; for example, many take advantage of heading elements for quick content scanning and navigation. They allow users to easily traverse a page's heading elements with simple keystrokes, and some provide a dedicated panel for listing those headings as a quick table-of-contents navigation (www.w3.org/TR/WCAG-TECHS/H69.html).

Because headings are helpful in page navigation and in parsing content visually, it's also good form to use them in logically consistent ways and not skip levels—for example, use an **h1** followed by an **h2**, not by an **h3**. Though markup will validate with an omitted heading level, it may be confusing for users trying to understand how the content is organized.

To confirm that you've used headings effectively in your markup, consider viewing the page with CSS disabled. Like an outline, the content hierarchy (including any interactive functionality) should be clear. Without an explicit and predictable heading structure, users may have a difficult time scanning the page for high-level messages and content organization.

In the enhanced experience, headings can be transformed with CSS and JavaScript to become clickable labels for interactive widgets like an accordion or group of tabs. These enhanced capabilities also rely on proper and consistent structure—for example, headings that sit parallel to one another in a tab strip should be marked up with **h** elements of the same level. (In later chapters we'll discuss in detail how to transform headings in these ways—for disclosure accordions see Chapter 8; for tree widgets, Chapter 11; and for tabs, Chapter 9.)

PARAGRAPH TEXT

Paragraphs are block-level elements used to organize narrative content into discrete thoughts or ideas within a web page.

```
<p>This is a paragraph of text wrapped in a paragraph tag.</p>
<p>I'm a second paragraph. My two sentences complete an idea.</p>
```

We advise against using paragraph elements to mark up anything other than straight paragraph text. Layout structure like columns and higher-level content groupings should be marked up with a **div**, or, when grouping sections in a form, a **fieldset**.

QUOTES

Quotations can be marked up in a couple of ways; however, only one—the **blockquote**, an element meant for longer quotations, like those in paragraph form—should be used for foundation markup because it will render consistently across browsers without any CSS or JavaScript workarounds.

A quote's content is placed within the **blockquote** element, and its source URI may be noted in a **cite** attribute on the opening tag:

```
<blockquote cite="http://www.filamentgroup.com">We design engaging user
interfaces for web applications, mobile devices, and touchscreen kiosks
that are simple and accessible to everyone.</blockquote>
```

Controlling line breaks and spacing, the right way

Since the invention of HTML, developers have been tempted to use line breaks and non-breaking spaces to control content layout and spacing in place of proper paragraph or other semantic notation and CSS, because sometimes it's just easier to append one or more line break tags. However, misuse of these tags may greatly reduce content readability.

A **line break**—using the **
** tag—denotes a hard carriage return at a specific location in the text. While there are legitimate uses for this element, such as the breaks between lines in an address, it should not be used for adding vertical spacing to a page layout. It's important to keep in mind that a line break that looks good on a 1024x768 resolution screen may look skewed or leave orphaned words hanging on a much smaller screen, like those on handheld devices, or on a standard or screen with the text size magnified. Whenever possible, it's best to let text wrap naturally and fill the available space. If precise line breaks are necessary to read a block of content properly, like when displaying source code or lines from a poem, one might also consider using the **pre** element for pre-formatted text.

Similarly, the **non-breaking space**—specified in character notation as ** ** or as a character entity with ** **—is intended to connect two words that have a space between them but should stay together on the same line and not wrap independently. There are legitimate uses for this, like ensuring that proper names, product names, or trademarked phrases always appear together. However, non-breaking spaces are often misused as a quick way to add horizontal spacing between elements. Doing this, like overusing line breaks, introduces the risk that some of your audience may see odd spacing, orphaned words, or awkward line breaks. It's safer to conditionally use margin or padding with CSS to create space between elements.

When a source should be displayed with the quote, use the **cite** element nested within **blockquote**:

```
<blockquote cite="http://www.filamentgroup.com">We design engaging user
interfaces for web applications, mobile devices, and touchscreen kiosks
that are simple and accessible to everyone.

<cite>Todd Parker, Principal, Filament Group, Inc.</cite>

</blockquote>
```

The HTML 4 specification also lists an inline element—the **q** element—which is meant for shorter quotations, like dialogue within a sentence:

```
<p>The Donald exclaimed, <q>You're fired !</q></p>
```

In theory, the browser should render the proper quotation marks in context based on the page's language settings or whether the quote is nested. According to the HTML 4 specification, "Visual user agents must ensure that the content of the **q** element is rendered with delimiting quotation marks" (www.w3.org/TR/REC-html40/struct/text.html#edef-Q). But browsers implement the **q** element inconsistently; most notably, Internet Explorer fails to render quotation marks in the **q** element at all.

Fixing the unpredictable q element

Since the rendering of **q** is very unpredictable, we recommend using it cautiously, and using CSS resets to try to style it in a consistent way across browsers.

We recommend reading the following articles for information on styling the **q** element consistently across browsers:

"CSS reset and quirky quotes:" www.paulchaplin.com/blog/css-reset-and-quirky-quotes

"Fixing Quotes in Internet Explorer:" http://juicystudio.com/article/fixing-ie-quotes.php

PREFORMATTED TEXT AND CODE

For text that has been preformatted and must be displayed exactly as written, use the **pre** element. The **pre** element instructs the browser to display every line break or character space and usually styles the text in a fixed-width font. It can be useful for displaying poetry, text art, equations—any content that requires special formatting.

```
<pre title="Excerpt from a poem by Emily Dickenson">
The daisy follows soft the sun,
And when his golden walk is done,
  Sits shyly at his feet.
He, waking, finds the flower near.
"Wherefore, marauder, art thou here?"
  "Because, sir, love is sweet!"
</pre>
```

When specifically formatting code, such as lines of HTML or JavaScript, you can use the **code** element together with the **pre** element. Used together, **code** and **pre** will preserve line breaks at specific points in the content. Keep in mind that characters used in markup—like ampersands, or less-than and greater-than symbols (<, >) for open and close tags—must be encoded as character entities to be interpreted as text by the browser.

```
<pre>
<code>
// Include the following script block:
&lt;script&gt;
  var el = document.getElementById(&quot;foo&quot;);
  alert(el);
&lt;/script&gt;
</code>
</pre>
```

ABBREVIATIONS

Use the **abbr** element to provide immediate explanation of abbreviated terms or acronyms for people who may not be familiar with them, as well as for screen readers, search engine spiders, or translation systems. To add the full or expanded text to an **abbr** element, include a **title** attribute, which displays as a tooltip in most desktop browsers when the mouse hovers over the word.

```
<p>The United States is a member of <abbr title="North Atlantic Treaty
Organization">NATO</abbr>.</p>
```

■ Note

A similar element, acronym, identifies acronyms in text, but it is slated to be dropped from the HTML5 specification. We recommend using abbreviation instead. (http://dev.w3.org/html5/html4-differences)

EMPHASIZED CONTENT

To emphasize a word or phrase, use the **em** or **strong** element (**strong** implies greater emphasis). These elements can be applied separately or nested:

```
<p>This sentence uses <em>multiple <strong>emphasis</strong></em> tags.</p>
```

While most browsers by default display text within **em** tags as italic, and text within **strong** tags as bold, these elements should not be used to simply apply visual formatting when added emphasis is not necessary.

When text should be given lower priority in the content hierarchy, such as in footnotes and captions, use the **small** element:

```
<p>Man first landed on the moon in 1964. <small>Wikipedia, 2009</small></p>
```

◼ Note

You might expect screen readers to pronounce text within these elements with varying emphasis, but as of this writing the latest versions of the popular screen readers JAWS and Window-Eyes do not read text marked up in these elements any differently than plain text (www.paciellogroup. com/blog/?p=41). Even so, it remains good practice to use them for giving semantic emphasis to words or phrases in your content, and to lay a foundation in the event that newer screen readers add this functionality later.

SUPERSCRIPT AND SUBSCRIPT

Superscript and subscript characters—necessary in certain languages and scientific contexts—can be added inline with the **sup** (superscript) and **sub** (subscript) elements.

```
H<sub>2</sub>O
```

```
E = mc<sup>2</sup>
```

◼ Note

When extensive use of mathematical expressions or scientific notation is necessary, consider using a markup language with more accurate semantic tags, like MathML to mark them up instead.

Lists

Lists group listed items within a container, and come in three basic types:

Unordered lists present a set of items in no implied order, like a shopping list, and are rendered in most browsers with a bullet preceding each item.

```
<ul title="My shopping list">
  <li>Milk</li>
  <li>Eggs</li>
  <li>Butter</li>
</ul>
```

◼ Note

It's good practice to mark up navigation links with an unordered list because modern screen readers can identify these lists in the markup structure and provide a way for users to jump to/from this content from other areas of the page.

Ordered lists incorporate priority or sequence and are rendered in most browsers with a sequential numeric value next to each item. They're useful for presenting tables of contents or a movie queue.

```
<ol title="Table of Contents: A Brief History of HTML">
  <li>The early days</li>
  <li>The current state of the art</li>
  <li>The future!</li>
</ol>
```

Unordered and ordered lists can be nested—you can place **ul** elements within **li** elements to create new levels of hierarchy.

Definition lists are similar to unordered lists, except that instead of a single **li** element for each list item, they contain *sets* of elements: **dt** (term) and **dd** (definition). Just like a dictionary entry, a term in a definition list can have more than one definition, so multiple **dd** elements are allowed per **dt**. Definition lists are ideal for marking up a list of features and descriptions, names and bios, or questions and answers.

```
<dl title="Famous people born in the 1800s">
  <dt>Abe Lincoln</dt>
  <dd>US president, born 1862</dd>
  <dt>Albert Einstein</dt>
  <dd>Genius physicist, born 1879</dd>
  <dt>Babe Ruth</dt>
  <dd>Baseball hero, born 1895</dd>
</dl>
```

Tabular data

Tables are intended to display tabular data. Every table must have at least the **table**, **tr** (table row), and **td** (table data cell) elements to validate, and in most cases they should also have the **th** (table header) tag to identify rows or columns of data values. Several optional tags are also useful for adding semantic meaning to tabular data, like the **caption**, **thead**, **tfoot**, and **tbody** tags for identifying and grouping sections of the table.

The structural elements you choose depend on the data's complexity and how it's meant to be used or visually displayed. For example, compare the two tables below, both constructed with valid, accessible markup. The first is a table in its simplest form, marked up with only rows, headers, and cells:

```
<table>
  <tr>
      <th>State</th>
      <th>Capital city</th>
  </tr>
  <tr>
      <td>Massachusetts</td>
      <td>Boston</td>
  </tr>
  <tr>
      <td>Minnesota</td>
      <td>St. Paul</td>
  </tr>
</table>
```

The second table has a complex structure and includes a **caption** that will act as the table title, and content is further divided with sections for the header (**thead**), footer (**tfoot**), and body (**tbody**):

```
<table cellspacing="0">
  <caption>Annual Sales:</caption>
  <thead>
      <tr>
          <th rowspan="2" id="department">Department</th>
          <th colspan="4" id="year-2008">2008</th>
      </tr>
      <tr>
          <th id="Q1">Q1</th>
          <th id="Q2">Q2</th>
          <th id="Q3">Q3</th>
          <th id="Q4">Q4</th>
      </tr>
  </thead>
```

```
<tfoot>

    <tr>

        <td colspan="5">Data valid as of December 2009</td>

    </tr>

</tfoot>

<tbody>

    <tr>

        <td headers="department">Toys &#38; Games</td>

        <td headers="Q1 year-2008">1.4M</td>

        <td headers="Q2 year-2008">2.2M</td>

        <td headers="Q3 year-2008">2.8M</td>

        <td headers="Q4 year-2008">2.1M</td>

    </tr>

    <tr>

        <td headers="department">Appliances</td>

        <td headers="Q1 year-2008">1.4M</td>

        <td headers="Q2 year-2008">2.2M</td>

        <td headers="Q3 year-2008">2.8M</td>

        <td headers="Q4 year-2008">2.1M</td>

    </tr>

  </tbody>

</table>
```

According to the HTML specification, the **tfoot** should immediately follow the **thead** (and precede the **tbody**) so that the header and footer load to the page before rows of data. Grouping sections of a table into **thead**, **tfoot**, and **tbody** elements like this is especially useful when structuring very large data sets that could take a few seconds or more to load—the header and footer elements will load much faster and provide feedback to users.

Segregating the header and body cells into sections lets you scope CSS rules to the **thead**, **tfoot**, and **tbody** elements separately to make them visually distinct, or use a combination of CSS and JavaScript to set an **overflow** property on the table body so the header bar remains static (CSS alone can be used to create this effect in WebKit- and Mozilla-based browsers; JavaScript is necessary to make it work in Internet Explorer).

In more complex tables like the second example above, where a single header spans multiple columns or rows, the relationship between the header and its data cells may be made clear by it presentation when displayed in a browser, but that same connection may not be obvious when the markup is interpreted by non-visual user agents like screen readers. To ensure that users of assistive technology don't miss out on valuable data associations, assign a unique ID to each **th**, add the **headers** attribute to each table cell, and then map each table cell to its header by writing the relevant header's ID into the **headers** attribute. Each **headers** attribute can point to more than one ID, separated by a space.

You can also use the **caption** element to identify the table or provide additional information that users may need to interpret the data. The **caption** element should be written into the table structure immediately after the opening **table** tag and before the table's main content. By default, a caption is displayed directly above its table, like a title.

◼ Note

The summary attribute assigned to the `table` tag is largely redundant with the caption, and consequently has been dropped from the specification for HTML5. For that reason, we recommend using `caption` rather than summary when additional helpful explanation is warranted.

In the enhanced experience, tabular data can be transformed into charts, graphs, and other visualizations. See Chapter 12 for a review of how this can be done.

No more tables for layout—finally!

Before CSS became a web standard supported by most browsers, developers frequently relied on tables to lay out page content. They often constructed intricately nested tables to format every content block on the page, and even incorporated "spacer" images to approximate padding and margin.

Now that CSS is widely used, we no longer need to rely on tables this way, and we can return them to their intended purpose: displaying tabular data. We never recommend using tables to achieve layout.

Images

The **img** tag embeds an image in a web page. Because images don't contain semantic meaning except for the source filename, it's important to provide descriptive text using the **alt** attribute for screen readers, search engines, and readers with images disabled to understand the content conveyed by the image.

```
<img src="acme-logo.png" alt="Acme Corporation" />
```

Here are a few guidelines to keep in mind when filling in **alt** values:

▶ The **alt** attribute's value will appear or be read in place of a missing or unseen image, so think of **alt** text as a replacement for the image rather than simply a description. Consider what purpose the image serves on the page, and whether its content is crucial or optional to understanding the greater narrative.

▶ Any image that is in the page markup for purely cosmetic reasons, like a design flourish, should include an empty **alt** attribute, like **alt=""**, so screen readers will read the filename aloud and move on. Make every attempt to limit the number of presentation-only images embedded in the markup, and, whenever possible, use them as background images specified with CSS instead.

▶ Charts and graphs should have **alt** text that concisely describes any relevant conclusion, trend, or relationship in the data. An **alt** description of "Line chart of total sales in 2009" is nowhere near as useful as "Total annual sales graph showing an 18% increase in 2009 from 10.2 million to 12.1 million (USD)."

▶ Photos and illustrations should be described in detail only if they are true content and critical to the narrative. Don't treat **alt** as a caption for the visual image, like "portrait of John Doe." But do describe useful information that adds context to the narrative, like "Portrait of 20-year-old John Doe, a scruffy wild-haired cowboy in rumpled white shirt and jeans surveying the rugged terrain of his Montana ranch."

▶ There's no need to include the word "image" as part of the description, as screen readers will generally speak the **role** along with the text. For example, use **alt="a horse and rider"** rather than **alt="image of a horse and rider"**, as it may be spoken as "image of a horse and rider *image*."

Embedded rich media

Best practices for embedding rich media in websites have long been disputed; they change frequently to keep up with the competitive landscape of proprietary content-delivery platforms. Rich media is most commonly delivered on the web using technologies that require browser plugins such as Adobe Flash, Apple QuickTime, Sun Java, or Microsoft Silverlight, and is embedded into a page in various ways, like using **object** elements, or non-standard elements such as **embed**, or frequently a combination of the two.

While plugins are prevalent, there are many downsides:

▶ For users, it can be a hassle to continually download and update plugins in order to browse the web; for developers, rich media content requires continual maintenance as plugins are released, updated, or discontinued.

▶ Plugin formats encapsulate content, which can make that content difficult to access for search engines, screen readers, and mobile devices. Users with disabilities are often left out of rich media content altogether when providers deem it too costly or complex—or sometimes, technically impossible—to deliver accessible content with a given plugin.

▶ Content delivery depends upon the plugin companies' continuing support for their products, which is worrisome to those interested in ensuring content viability.

For all these reasons, the need for a standardized delivery system for rich media has never been more pressing. Fortunately, the HTML5 specification has introduced several elements for embedding rich media—**video**, **audio**, and **canvas** for image and animation—that are simple, accessible, and forward-looking.

The HTML5 **video** element allows you to embed video content in a web page in much the same way you would an image. Simply insert the **video** tag in the markup and direct its **src** attribute to a video file URL, and supporting browsers—currently, the latest versions of Safari, Firefox, and Opera—will provide a native interface for the user to view and control that video's playback.

```
<video src="myvideo_320x240.ogg" />
```

The HTML5 **audio** element is similar to the **video** element, except that, of course, it embeds an audio file in the page. Simply insert an **audio** tag into the markup and set its **src** attribute to an audio file URL:

```
<audio src="myfavoritesong.wav"></audio>
```

Both the **audio** and **video** elements also include native JavaScript APIs for controlling playback, with many events to leverage for creating interactivity that rivals any plugin-based offering. These APIs are documented in the HTML5 spec at w3.org.

For graphical rich media, such as an interactive chart or an animated feature graphic, HTML5 offers the **canvas** element, which you can think of as an image element that offers a JavaScript API for drawing graphics. (We'll provide an example of how to transform tabular HMTL data into **canvas**-based charts that work across all major browsers in Chapter 12, "Charts with HTML canvas.")

All three elements support the placement of markup within the opening and closing tags, which may be used to reference an image or text-based equivalent of the embedded media or to provide instruction and/or links to access the source for browsers that don't support the HTML5 standard.

```
<video src="myvideo_320x240.ogg">
Oops, you're seeing this message because your browser does not support the
<code>video</code> element. To view this video, <a href=" myvideo_320x240.
ogg">download myvideo_320x240.ogg</a> to play it in another application.
</video>
```

Though the HTML5 specification is still under consideration, we strongly recommend using these elements now to embed rich media in place of proprietary plugins because they are more semantically rich (each opening tag identifies the type of content and its source), and more importantly, they support the addition of alternative markup for browsers that don't support them. If it's necessary to provide a rich media alternative for other browsers, you could, for example, write a script that checks whether the browser supports the **video** element, and if not, injects a different element, like an **object**, that directs the browser to the video file in a format it does understand.

Embedding external page content

Before Ajax introduced the ability to dynamically update regions of a page without a full refresh, developers used **frames** and **iframes** for similar—albeit less sophisticated—purposes.

The **frame** and **iframe** elements are both designed to bring external content into a page, loading entire HTML pages as well as all of their dependencies. The **frame** element fits into a larger framework of grouped elements known as a **frameset**, which replaces the body tag and divides the page into regions that may be related or interdependent. The **iframe** element is meant to be inserted inline, alongside other markup.

The flexibility afforded by **frame** and **iframe** elements—to build extremely complicated sites with deeply nested sets of frames that mimic the complex dependency structures commonly found on the server-side—introduced severe problems in accessibility, navigation, and page performance. Consequently, the **frame**, **frameset**, and **noframes** elements were dropped from the HTML5 specification because "their usage affected usability and accessibility for the end user in a negative way" (www.w3.org/TR/html5-diff/#absent -elements).

Thankfully, the days of constructing pages with nested **frameset**s are long gone. But even today there are occasions when content that must be on the page can't be included in the page markup—possibly because it may be hosted on an external website, or because the formatting of the content causes visual conflicts when injected directly into the page. In these cases, it may make sense to use an **iframe** to present that content (though we recommend this be done very sparingly, due to performance and accessibility drawbacks).

In situations where it makes sense to use an **iframe**, we recommend writing the basic version of the page using an anchor element that references the resource and contains a text description, and then using JavaScript to generate and insert an **iframe** element and then populate its **src** with the value of the anchor element's **href** attribute.

For example, we'd write a standard anchor tag into the foundation HTML that's served to all browsers:

```
<a href="http://filamentgroup.com" class="inline-content">My favorite
design firm</a>
```

If capabilities tests pass, we use the anchor link's **src** attribute to create an **iframe** that displays the full site inline within the page:

```
<iframe src="http://filamentgroup.com"></iframe>
```

Once the **iframe** is in the page, you can either hide the anchor or keep it in the enhanced experience, to offer the user a way to visit the page on its own:

```
<iframe src="http://filamentgroup.com"></iframe>
<a href="http://filamentgroup.com">Filament Group's website</a>
```

Marking up interactive content

Interaction is a fundamental aspect of the web, and semantic markup provides a host of options to support a range of specific interaction types, from simple links to complex forms for data entry.

Native HTML elements for interaction are rich with inherent functionality: they facilitate movement; capture and submit data, showing feedback in the process; and support keyboard and mouse interactions appropriate for the browser and device context. HTML form elements provide the primary way to capture user input and submit it back to a server for storage or processing.

Understanding the semantic meaning and unique capabilities of native interactive elements takes on greater importance when considering how to construct the foundation markup for a page with fancy CSS- and JavaScript-enhanced interactive widgets. Unlike code for the enhanced experience, the foundation markup must function—make it possible for the user to complete all required tasks—without any assistance from CSS or JavaScript.

In the previous chapter, we described the x-ray perspective, a way to break down a complex design into its basic, functioning parts—for example, seeing that a custom dropdown menu is really just a souped-up **select** element, or that a slider is another incarnation of two text input boxes that capture a range of values. In Section 3, we'll consider a number of enhanced interactive widgets in detail and the optimal semantic choices for their foundation markup.

Now, we'll review the overall structure of interactive and form elements, their primary purpose, and any important issues to explore when considering each element for inclusion in the foundation markup. When applicable, we note any important changes to an element from the HTML 4 to the HTML5 specification; we also list ways it may be upgraded for an enhanced experience.

Anchor links

Anchor links are the basic navigation element of the web, used for linking between pages and to content within the same page.

To link to another page on the same site or an external site, specify a destination URI in the link's **href** attribute:

```
<a href="http://www.acmecorp.com" title="Official site of Acme corp">
Acme</a>
```

To link to a location within the same page, specify the location's unique **id** preceded by a pound sign (#):

```
<a href="#content">Learn what we've done</a>

...

<div id="content">

  <h1>What we've done</h1>

  <p> We've worked on a wide variety of website, application interface,
  branding and print projects in a broad range of industries.</p>

</div>
```

In the enhanced experience, there are a host of powerful things we can do to transform anchor links. For example, the title attribute or a local anchor can be used to populate a tooltip that appears on hover. External link URLs can be "hijacked" with JavaScript to steal the mouse click event on a link to kick off an Ajax request based on the **href** value.

Form structure

Any transaction or data-entry scenario on the web is accomplished with form elements. Well-structured forms consist of several basic semantic elements to lay out the workspace, along with one or more form controls to collect user input and submit values for processing.

FORM

The first element that every form needs is, not surprisingly, the **form** element, with an **action** attribute that points to a resource that will process the form when submitted:

```
<form action="edit-account.php">

    ...form elements go here...

</form>
```

■ Note

The HTML5 specification states that "The new form attribute for input, output, select, textarea, button, and fieldset elements allows for controls to be associated with a form. I.e., these elements can now be placed anywhere on a page, not just as descendants of the form element" (www.w3.org/TR/html5-diff/#new-attributes). As more browsers support this specification, we can make use of this new attribute; however, for the time being we recommend wrapping all form controls that should be submitted together within a single form element to remain compatible with all browsers.

FIELDSET AND LEGEND

The **fieldset** element is an optional element that can be used to organize form elements into logical sections—for example, contact information, billing information, a username and password pair, or a set of radio button or checkbox inputs grouped together under a common title. The **legend** element sits within the **fieldset** element and serves as a title for the set.

```
<form action="edit-account.php" method="post">

  <fieldset>

      <legend>Contact information</legend>

      ...

  </fieldset>

</form>
```

■ Note

The HTML5 spec allows the disabled attribute for the fieldset element, thereby "disabling all its contents when specified" (www.w3.org/TR/html5-diff/#new-attributes).

LABEL

Each form control should have a **label** element to identify it and provide an additional way for the control to receive focus. When properly associated with its control, clicking a label will automatically transfer focus to its control, meaning that you could check a checkbox by clicking its label; this is an ideal way to create a larger click target and make the form more accessible to users with visual or motor control impairments.

The **label** is associated with its element by assigning a **for** attribute and providing the control's ID as the value:

```
<label for="filling-1">Peanut butter</label>
<input type="checkbox" value="pb" name="sandwich" id="filling-1" />
```

This relationship between labels and their elements also comes in handy with checkboxes and radio buttons. We can leverage the shared click event to customize labels—for example, to create a polling widget, like the star rating on Netflix. (See Chapter 15 for an example of how this works.)

When a design calls for form controls without visible labels—for example, an address field may have two stacked text inputs, but with a single label for both—we advocate creating a label for each input and simply hiding the label that shouldn't be displayed:

```
<label for="address-1">Address</label>
<input type="text" id="address-1" />

<label for="address-2" class="hidden-label">Address, line 2</label>
<input type="text" id="address-2" />
```

The first label, "Address," is visible on the page and receives focus when users tab to that field; the second label, "Address, line 2," is present in the markup but hidden in an accessible way so it's still available to screen readers. To accessibly hide the second label, absolutely position it off the page with a large left value:

```
.hidden-label { position: absolute; left: -9999em; }
```

Form controls

Semantic markup includes a range of form elements, or controls, each governed by business rules that define their capabilities—including specific structure and format of their data options, whether they support single or multiple selection, whether choices are limited by the system or can be defined by the user—as well as a wealth of native interaction behaviors. These elements provide a solid foundation for reliable interaction, and also offer many possibilities for transformation in enhanced contexts.

TEXT INPUT

The simplest and probably most common form element is the text input, which accepts a single line of alphanumeric text:

```
<input type="text" name="address" />
```

The text input is an ideal form control to use when considering foundation markup for many widgets because it is so open-ended and can capture any combination of alphanumeric characters.

HTML5 provides a number of input types for stricter validation of text inputs, such as **number**, **telephone**, **range**, and more. We recommend using these input types in your foundation markup whenever they make sense, since browsers will simply default to a type of **text** when the specified type is not recognized.

For example, the following markup demonstrates an input with a **type** of **range**, including **min** and **max** attributes to describe the acceptable values:

```
<input type="range" min="0" max="50" value="25" />
```

The input type **range** appears differently depending on the browser—Safari 4 and Opera 10 render the input as a slider, while other browsers like Firefox 3.5 simply render it as a text input.

Figure 3.1 Input type range in several browsers (top: Safari 4 Mac, middle, Opera 10 Mac, bottom, Firefox 3.5 Mac).

The most current Opera browser, Opera 10, includes the most extensive level of support for these input types. By setting the type to **number**, Opera 10 will render the input with "spinner" arrows, making it simple for the user to increase or decrease the value with their mouse or arrow keys. Similarly, a type of **date** will render the input as a select menu with a custom calendar control.

Figure 3.2 The year formatted with input type **date** in the Opera 10 browser.

(We'll use the input type **number** to manipulate a custom slider's value in Chapter 16.)

Also new in HTML5, the **placeholder** attribute can be applied to text **input** elements (as well as **textarea**s) to provide hint text inside the field to inform the user of a particular expected format:

```
<label for="groceries">Groceries:</label>

<input type="text" name="groceries" id="groceries" placeholder="Add grocery
items separated by commas" />
```

Groceries: Add grocery items separated by commas

Figure 3.3 Text input with **placeholder** attribute in the Safari 4 browser.

Developers have often achieved this effect by prepopulating the value attribute with hint text, which causes accessibility issues and requires validation to prevent the hinted value from submitting with the form. In browsers that don't support the placeholder attribute, JavaScript can be used to manipulate its text to mimic native implementation.

TEXTAREA

The **textarea** element is designed to capture a multiple-line text entry and is frequently used for entering gift messages or comments. A **textarea** element has an open and close tag; all content contained between the tags is displayed inside an editable text field. Although you can control the width and height with CSS, you should also consider specifying the **cols** (width) and **rows** (height) attributes to set the general dimensions of the **textarea** in the basic experience:.

```
<textarea cols="30" rows="10">

Four score and seven years ago, our fathers brought forth upon this
continent a new nation...

</textarea>
```

In capable browsers, a **textarea** can be transformed into a rich text editor; or a **textarea** that contains a comma-delimited list of items can be enhanced into a recipient list builder like Facebook's message recipient field. (We'll demonstrate how to convert a **textarea** into a list builder in Chapter 18.)

CHECKBOXES

The **checkbox** element provides a way for users to choose one or more options from a set. All options are displayed on the page inline by default and can be toggled on or off with a mouse click or by focusing on the checkbox and hitting the spacebar. And checkboxes can be checked by default by appending the **checked** attribute, which accepts a single value: **checked**. (Easy to remember, eh?)

In order for checkboxes to submit properly, the **name** attribute on all checkboxes within a set must match:

```
<label for="filling-1">Peanut butter</label>
<input type="checkbox" value="pb" name="sandwich" id="filling-1" />

<label for="filling-2">Jelly</label>
<input type="checkbox" value="j" name="sandwich" id="filling-2" />

<label for="filling-3">Marshmallow Creme/label>
<input type="checkbox" value="m" name="sandwich" id="filling-3" />
```

Checkboxes can be enhanced into helpful widgets, like a custom toggle button. Because checkboxes are notoriously difficult to style with CSS in a consistent way across browsers, we developed a method for customizing checkbox and label pairs to match a custom design in the enhanced experience, which we'll outline in Chapter 15.

■ Note

Most browsers interpret an empty checked attribute (`checked=""`) to mean that the checkbox is in fact checked; they ignore the empty quotation marks, and just look for the presence of the checked attribute itself. The checked attribute was originally introduced as a Boolean option that could be appended to a form element: `<input type="text" checked>`. When XHTML came along, the syntax changed accordingly (to `checked="checked"`) to comply with XHTML's syntax rules. HTML5 allows you to use either syntax.

It's important to keep this in mind when toggling a checked state using JavaScript. Manipulating the checked state via the DOM (`this.checked = true`) is more reliable than toggling the checked value of the checked attribute.

RADIO BUTTONS

Radio buttons work very similarly to checkboxes, except they allow only a single selection from a set of mutually exclusive items, where checkboxes allow multiple selections.

For that reason, radio buttons are ideal for marking up interfaces that require a single selection from a smaller group of options (say up to 10) and in cases where it's helpful to see all options simultaneously on the screen—like multiple choice tests or survey questions, ratings or polls, or shipping options in a retail checkout process. Radio buttons, like checkboxes, can be pre-checked with the checked attribute, but only one at a time can be checked within a set.

Again like checkboxes, radio buttons are difficult to style with CSS, but can easily be updated for an enhanced experience with a combination of CSS and JavaScript. We'll discuss scenarios where radio buttons can be enhanced into a single slider widget, like a volume control, or a star rating widget, in Chapter 15.

SELECT

The **select** element allows users to choose a single option from a predefined list, much like a radio button. Because the native **select** element is rendered with only the currently selected option shown instead of the whole list, it's ideal for use with a large list of options that must fit into a compact space. When activated, the **select** opens to reveal a menu with each **option** element listed:

```
<select name="north-american-countries">

  <option value="canada">Canada</option>

  <option value="mexico">Mexico</option>

  <option value="united-states">United States</option>

</select>
```

◆ Tip

Although theoretically a select can hold a large number of options, for the sake of usability it's best to limit this number to roughly 50 or fewer to avoid a lengthy scrolling list. When exceeding this number, it may help to group items using optgroup elements if the content lends itself to sub-groupings. In all cases—even with option lists of as few as 8–10 values—it's thoughtful to present the options in a logical sort order that users will understand to facilitate easy scanning and scrolling.

Each **option** element contains a word or phrase that displays in the **select**'s dropdown menu, as well as a number of attributes that may be leveraged when the form is submitted and/or when transforming a basic select element into a widget for the enhanced experience:

▶ **value** — The value to be submitted with the form (required)

▶ **selected** — May be set to **selected** to display the **option** as selected when the page loads. If multiple selections are permitted, more than one **option** may have this attribute.

▶ **disabled** — Makes the option visible, but not selectable, in the select menu

▶ **label** — An abbreviation of the option's enclosed text value. (This attribute is valid, but not well supported in all browsers. For that reason, we don't recommend using it for essential information required in the basic experience, but it does prove very useful for encoding additional meaning for use in enhanced controls.)

Select **option**s can also be grouped into subsections with **optgroup** elements. While this is valid markup, the **optgroup** is displayed in different ways across browsers, and as a result can't be styled consistently. Though CSS support is somewhat limited, we recommend using **optgroup** in foundation markup to provide additional semantic meaning to the list.

Multiple options may be selected at once by setting the **multiple** attribute on a select element to **multiple** (similar to setting the **checked** attribute on an input), but we don't recommend using this feature because there is no visual indicator that multiple items can be selected. A user has to know to press the Control or Shift key while clicking to make a multiple selection (or instructional text must be provided to that end). In this situation, we find a set of checkboxes to be significantly more intuitive and usable.

When the design calls for a **select** element or its menu to have a customized appearance—for example, to display icons next to each option, or use custom typography to highlight part of the text—consider starting with a **select** element as the foundation markup. See Chapter 17 to see how to build a custom select in this way.

INPUTS AND BUTTONS FOR FORM SUBMISSION

HTML provides two elements that submit form data: an **input** element, with the type set to **submit**, or a **button** element (also with a type of **submit**). The **input**'s **value** attribute is displayed on the button as text, while **button** displays the text contained in its tags. Both lines below render as similar-looking buttons:

```
<input type="submit" value="Save changes" />
```

```
<button type="submit">Save changes</button>
```

Submit **inputs** and **buttons** share a single purpose—when they're properly enclosed in **form** tags, they send form data to the server when clicked.

They're also easy to style using CSS; however, the **button** element allows nested child elements, meaning it can support more advanced CSS styling than **input**, including text hierarchy and "sliding door" background images.

Button element value submission in Internet Explorer

Most browsers handle form submission the same way whether the user clicks an **input** or **button** element. However, older but still popular versions of Internet Explorer—including IE 6 and 7—present an exception when the **input** or **button value** attribute must be sent along with the data. When the button is clicked in IE 6 or 7, the **innerHTML** of the button element, i.e., "Save changes," rather than the specified **value**, is sent to the server. This is corrected in IE 8, but until earlier versions are phased out, a JavaScript workaround is necessary to properly submit the **button**'s **value** across all browsers.

For more information, check out Coping With Internet Explorer's Mishandling of Buttons (http://allinthehead.com/retro/330/coping-with-internet-explorers-mishandling-of-buttons).

In the foundation markup, we recommend using the submit **input**, as it's one of the core founding elements of HTML, dating back to one of the first complete versions of the HTML specification, 2.0, released in 1995. As an older element, the **input** is more likely to work in older or obscure browsers, or in browsers that only partially support the current HTML specification. By comparison, the **button** element is relatively new—introduced in the latest complete specification for HTML, version 4.01—and experiences occasional dodgy support on older mobile devices. While **buttons** are likely to work in most browsers, the safer bet is to use the **input** element in foundation markup.

If your design requires a custom-styled button containing more than one HTML element, then use JavaScript to transform the **input** into a **button**. We review this technique in Chapter 14.

Creating context in the page

The semantic tags described above in this chapter provide the tools you need to properly structure the most common content types displayed on the web, but those individual pieces often need an additional level of organizational structure, in the form of layout containers or groupings, to make sense of them in the context of a web page. It's necessary to make a few simple but important choices to ensure that content is grouped logically to deliver the most appropriate semantic meaning for the range of people and agents consuming your content, and to present it in a way that delivers the most efficient and satisfying user experience.

Know when to use block-level vs. inline elements

Block-level and inline elements serve different purposes within the page structure, and have different default display properties that could affect how foundation markup is rendered in the basic experience. It's important to understand this distinction to make the right choices for your site.

Block elements—including headings, paragraphs, block quotes, lists, tables, and **divs**—are intended to form the high-level structure and content hierarchy of a page. By default, block-level elements stack vertically in the page and may also contain both block and inline child elements. Inline elements—like anchors (**a**), elements for adding emphasis (**em**, **strong**, **small**), and **spans**—are exactly that: they're meant to flow and wrap inline with text within block-level containers.

◆ Tip

When coding foundation markup for a page, consider how the default display properties of block and inline elements affect how the page renders without CSS or JavaScript to aid in formatting.

Grouping content with HTML5 elements

Several HTML5 elements are slated to replace **div** for specific layout components, including **section**, **aside**, **nav**, **article**, **header**, and **footer**. While they're more semantically correct than their generic counterparts, these future-compatible HTML5 elements and may not be supported in older or very basic browsers, meaning they may not obey CSS rules directed at them. Until browser support improves, these elements should be used only as an enhancement to, not a fundamental part of, the foundation markup. Or, consider wrapping them around your existing structural elements to reap their semantic benefits without risking problems in browsers that don't support them. For example, a **div** element acting as a header could be enclosed in a header element, or vice-versa:

```
<header><div id="header"></div></header>
```

Also, some of these elements convey more semantic meaning than their names imply. For instance, **section**, like **div**, is a block element that groups any type of content on the page, but it serves another important function—each **section** represents a node in the page "outline." If you were to take all of the headings and content in a document and convert them to outline form, each **section** would constitute a new line item in that hierarchical structure.

For more information on these elements, we recommend the A List Apart article, "A Preview of HTML5" (www.alistapart.com/articles/previewofhtml5).

Most semantic elements are intended to describe specific pieces of content, like headings and paragraphs; however, the **div** and **span** elements are less well defined. Both are primarily used for grouping content when a more specific semantic element isn't available to do the job.

A **div** is a block element, commonly used for structuring layout components like headers, columns, and footers; it can also be used to construct page components that don't have semantic equivalents in HTML, like the structure for a calendar widget. For example, you might use **divs** to create a columnar layout, and use heading and paragraph elements to structure the content of a news article:

```
<div>
  <p>I'm a block-level paragraph inside a div.</p>
</div>

<div>
  <h3>Article Title</h3>
  <p>I'm a block-level paragraph inside a div.</p>
</div>
```

A **span** is used inline and is ideal for grouping phrases within lines of text. Inline elements may only validly contain other inline elements.

```
<p>Product strategy, <span>user-centered workflow design</span>, concept
demos and UI prototypes...</p>
```

Identify elements with IDs and classes

Id and **class** attributes can be applied to most HTML elements. Classes and IDs make elements easier to address with CSS and JavaScript, and serve a number of other useful purposes as well.

An ID must be unique within a page, meaning that it can be used only once on a single element, like a header, footer, or particular form control. ID attributes have a number of additional uses:

▶ As a local target for an anchor link. Users can click a link directed to a specific ID (preceded by a pound sign) — **<a href="#table-of-contents">Table of Contents</a>** — to scroll to the page to that element or create a bookmark for later reference.

▶ To draw a meaningful relationship between elements, like connecting a **label** element to the form field it describes, so users can click the label to focus its field.

▶ To allow users with assistive technology to understand relationships that may otherwise be apparent only to sighted users, such as the currently active node in an enhanced tree widget, or the relationship between a menu button and its drop menu body.

Classes, by contrast, are designed to label elements that occur repeatedly in a page or site, making them handy for applying CSS or JavaScript to several elements at once. In addition to their use in applying enhancements, classes are used in *microformats* to describe standard content types commonly found on the web, such as a person's contact information or an event's date and location. While not an official W3C web standard, microformats have gained traction, and a number of websites and browsers leverage their semantics to connect content across the web in interesting ways. (To find out more, visit microformats.org.)

Regardless of the reason for adding classes or IDs to your markup, we recommend choosing names that meaningfully describe the element's content and purpose, so that the markup is understandable to developers, rather than tying it to a specific visual design or behavior characteristic; design-based class and ID names can quickly become irrelevant and confusing if the design changes even in subtle ways. To that end, also use a consistent naming convention throughout a website (for example, use hyphenation to join words together) to keep code tidy and predictable, and consequently simplify code maintenance and extension should the site be expanded. And because neither **divs** nor **spans** convey any semantic meaning about the content they hold, it's especially useful to assign descriptive classes and IDs to clearly identify their purpose within the code.

Identify main page sections with WAI-ARIA landmark roles

WAI-ARIA, the Accessible Rich Internet Applications suite, is a W3C specification that includes recommendations for applying meaning to markup used in dynamic and advanced user interface controls. The ARIA suite also provides attributes, called *landmark roles*, which can be assigned to HTML elements in foundation markup.

Landmarks identify the major sections of a page—header, footer, main content, and more. Newer screen reader versions allow the user to navigate between landmarks on a page using keystrokes (the semicolon key in JAWS, for instance). Landmark roles that identify static sections of content include:

▶ **banner** — for a global header that appears throughout the site

▶ **complementary** — for supporting content, like sidebars

▶ **contentinfo** — information about the content on this page, like a footnote or copyright statement

▶ **main** — for the primary content on the page, like the body of a news article

▶ **navigation** — for lists of navigation links

▶ **search** — for a search form

You can assign a landmark to a segment of the page with the **role** attribute:

```
<ul role="navigation">
  <li><a href="home.html">Home</a></li>
  <li><a href="about.html">About the Company</a></li>
  <li><a href="contact.html">Contact Us</a></li>
</ul>
```

Though ARIA is a fairly new specification—its support is limited to recent versions of browsers and screen readers—ARIA attributes are safe to use in browsers that don't understand them (they'll simply be ignored), and require minimal work that pays big dividends to users of screen readers, so we recommend implementing them in your projects now. (In several chapters in Section 2 we'll discuss how to assign ARIA attributes to markup generated dynamically with JavaScript.)

Maintain legible source order

Source order is simply the order in which you write markup into an HTML document. Some elements must appear before others in order for the page to validate—for example, the **head** element must appear before the **body**. But within the **body** tag, it's up to the developer to determine where code blocks for particular page components appear in the markup. Should the main content column come before the sidebar, or vice versa? Does it matter, since both are floated into columns using CSS anyway? Actually, it *does* matter to users who don't rely on visual cues to read a page; and how the markup is ordered can have a big impact for them.

Structuring markup in a meaningful order from top to bottom, and applying that logic consistently across the entire site, is essential to making your site legible to users of browsers that don't fully support modern CSS techniques—including those on older or some mobile devices—and those with assistive technologies like screen readers. Organized markup conveys content hierarchy and provides a clear path for navigation; inconsistent, poorly grouped markup is a barrier to understanding and navigating the content.

It may be tempting to rely on CSS to do the hard work of organizing content, because it provides myriad ways to position and highlight prioritized content with images, color, and font size (to name just a few style characteristics). But writing the markup without CSS applied ensures that it's legible to all users, and lowers the likelihood that you'll make the page *appear* well organized when really it's a confusing maze of tags under the hood. To stay on the safe side and ensure that your markup's source order is clear, stick to the rule that CSS should be applied only after the source order of your markup is firmly in place.

As a fun test, pick a favorite website, and then turn off CSS entirely using a developer toolbar option (in Firebug, a plugin for Firefox, disabling all CSS is an option in the CSS menu), or comment out the style sheet references from a page of your own, and view the result. What do you see? Compare your results to the following statements:

▶ The most important or timely content is at the top of the page, and less important content is located farther down, below the fold.

▶ Content groupings are clear, with headings that identify and are followed by relevant paragraphs.

▶ Headings properly convey the content hierarchy; those with more priority appear in larger font (**h1** or **h2** elements, for instance) followed by those with lower priority.

▶ Links appear in the correct context (for example, a "More..." link follows an abbreviated list of links).

▶ Embedded images appear before captions.

▶ Global navigation elements are in a consistent location on each page and don't push the main content too far down the page.

If your results conform to the statements above, then the source order is correctly organized and accessible; if not, users of older, mobile, or screen reader browsers may not be able to make sense of your site. Users should see the highest priority message as soon as the site loads onto their BlackBerry®—if they have to scroll to find it, the message, and the opportunity, may be lost.

GLOBAL NAVIGATION PLACEMENT AND THE "SKIP" LINK

Global navigation elements are especially tricky to place in the source order. The number of links in the global navigation is an important factor to consider, so we follow a general rule when choosing where to place the global navigation markup:

▶ If the total number of navigation links is relatively small (10–25 or fewer options total, including primary- and sub-level links), we keep it at the top of the page, where most users (even those on screen readers) expect to find it.

▶ If the navigation is more extensive (especially multi-level navigation menus), place the navigation markup *after* the content in the source order.

A very short list at the top of the page is easy to scroll past, or skip when a link is provided; a longer list may push more valuable, unique content down the page so that users must scroll to find it. If you anticipate that users may be viewing the page on very small mobile screens, it's worth considering that scrolling a long list of options to find the good stuff may feel tedious, or worse, be a deterrent to reading further.

Whether the navigation markup is located before or after the main content area is less important than whether it has a consistent home. When the navigation moves within the source order from one page to the next, screen reader users have to relearn where it's located, and may possibly endure listening to repeated navigation options.

In either case, we maintain that it's good practice to include a "skip navigation" anchor link (or, when the navigation is at the bottom of the page, a "skip *to* navigation" link for easy location) to allow keyboard or mobile users to jump ahead to the main content and avoid repeating the options on every page they visit.

The skip link should be written into the foundation markup's source order immediately before the content it governs, like a top navigation list that's repeated on every page:

```
<a href="#content" id="skip-navigation">Skip navigation</a>
<ul id="nav" role="navigation">
  <li><a href="home.html">Home</a></li>
  <li><a href="products.html">Products</a></li>
  <li><a href="contact.html">Contact Us</a></li>
</ul>
```

```
<div id="content">
  <!-- page content is here -->
</div>
```

The link may be hidden from the enhanced experience using CSS, but be sure to hide it in an accessible way by positioning it off the page; using display or visibility properties to hide the link may render it useless to screen reader users.

```
a#skip-navigation { position: absolute; left: -9999em; }
```

And for visual keyboard users, it's good practice to style the link so it appears on focus and active states to show that it's available when they encounter it while tabbing through the link structure:

```
a#skip-navigation:focus,
a#skip-navigation:active { left: 0; top: 0; }
```

Some may argue that the skip link is no longer necessary because the latest screen reader browsers are making better use of semantic markup: they provide mechanisms for users to navigate via headings, lists, and paragraphs, and are adopting the WAI-ARIA specification, which instructs developers to identify the main sections of a page with landmark roles so that users can easily move from one section to the next. However, the skip link is still useful for "power" users who prefer to use the keyboard for website navigation, or for users who are limited to keyboard navigation, like those on older, pre-smartphone mobile devices. Without a built-in way to skip repeated navigation content, users in these scenarios must scroll to get to the right place, which could be prohibitive when the screen size is small and narrow.

Use the title attribute

Applying the optional **title** attribute to elements is a simple way to build meaning and helpful instruction into your markup, and it comes with an added bonus: by default, most browsers render the **title** value as a tooltip, or block of helper text that appears when users hover over its element. Some screen readers also read title values aloud.

In the foundation markup it's useful to identify linked images, for example, with **title** attributes:

```
<label for="email" title="To keep spammers out, we'll send a confirmation
email to make sure this is a valid email address">Email Address</label>
<input type="text" name="user" id="email" class="text" />
```

Figure 3-4 Native browser tooltip displayed below label on cursor hover

The **title** attribute can be applied to most elements, and it accepts a text phrase of any length, but it's best to keep **title** values concise and to the point as longer phrases or sentences may be truncated when they appear as tooltips, or may distract from the main content when read by screen readers.

We also frequently use this feature to help users understand how to use icon-only buttons within an enhanced application interface—for example, in a data table with editable rows that may be deleted by the user, the **title** attribute allows us to provide a text instruction in the form of a tooltip when the user hovers the mouse over the button.

In the enhanced markup, **title** values may be converted with CSS and JavaScript into custom tooltips that include more interactive functionality, or even follow the mouse as it moves over an area of the page. (We'll review a method for enhancing **title** values into custom-styled tooltips in Chapter 10.)

■ Note

The title *attribute is valid on* link *elements, including links that reference external style sheets. When a style sheet is specified on the page as* preferred *or* alternate, *the* title *attribute is required to assign the style sheet reference a unique name:*

```
<link rel="alternate stylesheet" href="styles.css" type="text/css" media="screen"
title="enhanced">
```

Setting up an HTML document

Now that we've established a solid system for marking up and organizing our HTML using the guidelines described above, it's time to place our content into a proper HTML document.

The most basic structure of an HTML document is pretty simple—every well-formed web page starts with an **html** element that holds the following additional elements:

▶ A **head** element—which will contain the **title** element and any **meta** tags, external style sheets, and script references (more on these elements and their related attributes in a moment)

▶ A **body** element that contains the page content

Structurally, it looks like this:

```
<html>
  <head></head>
  <body></body>
</html>
```

A document comprised of this very pared-down structure will work in a browser—technically. But in order for it to appear and work in a consistent way across a wide range of browsers, it needs a few more elements that identify markup syntax and describe what the page is about.

The DOCTYPE

A valid **DOCTYPE** declaration is a tag that should appear on every page in the site; it identifies the markup syntax used on the page and references a particular markup specification for validation purposes. In short:

▶ It instructs the browser to operate in standards-compliant mode; without it, the browser operates in *quirks mode*, meaning that it makes a best guess about how to render the markup and styles.

▶ It provides the necessary information to validate the page according to a particular markup specification (i.e., XHTML 1.1).

To work properly, the **DOCTYPE** must be the first tag listed in the page (no other tags or even white space before it), and must also conform to a particular syntax. Most **DOCTYPE**s must include a reference to the *document type definition* or DTD (which defines the markup language type and version used in the document), and a link to the relevant DTD posted on the W3C's server for verification purposes.

Each markup language specifies a particular **DOCTYPE** tag. For example, the HTML 4.0 and XHTML 1.1 **DOCTYPE** tags are unique; the first value in quotations is the DTD, and the second value is the DTD link:

```
<!DOCTYPE HTML PUBLIC "-//W3C//DTD HTML 4.01//EN" "http://www.w3.org/TR/
html4/strict.dtd">
```

```
<!DOCTYPE html PUBLIC "-//W3C//DTD XHTML 1.1//EN" "http://www.w3.org/TR/
xhtml11/DTD/xhtml11.dtd">
```

The following HTML5 **DOCTYPE** is also valid, though it's missing the DTD and link:

```
<!DOCTYPE html>
```

Why is this **DOCTYPE** different? The W3C wants to eliminate the need to denote specific versions of HTML and encourage developers to simply code with web standards.

Documents with the HTML5 **DOCTYPE** applied will validate against the HTML5 specification, which allows the use of XHTML syntax (like closing all tags), and instructs browsers to render in standards-compliant mode.

Why validate your code?

"Invalid" markup is simply markup that doesn't exactly conform to the specification it's written against. For example, closing an image tag with a space and forward slash is valid XHTML 1.1, but is invalid HTML 4.0:

```
<img src="tree.gif" alt="The American elm tree" />
```

Valid HTML 4.0 images are not closed:

```
<img src="tree.gif" alt="The American elm tree">
```

In most cases, invalid markup will still render correctly. In fact, many websites, including those built by industry standouts, are not made up of valid markup (see "The XHTML 100" at www.goer. org/Journal/2003/04/the_xhtml_100.html).

So what's the point in validating code if invalid code works just the same? Here are two reasons why it remains a core part of our development practice:

▶ Code validation often reveals hidden problems in the markup that may not be revealed until much later, when they're more difficult to fix.

▶ A validated page conforms to web standards and is therefore forward-compatible (validator. w3.org/docs/why.html).

The document header

The **head** of an HTML page is reserved for links to external style sheets and JavaScript files, and for descriptive information about the content that may help your page perform better with search engines. Configuring these elements correctly will help your page perform better and be more legible to user agents, including standard browsers and screen readers. We'll cover the most important elements you'll need to address to properly structure the page **head**.

CONTENT TYPE AND CHARACTER ENCODING

The content type, or MIME type, tells the browser what kind of markup to expect, and can be set by adding a **meta** tag to the page **head**:

```
<!doctype html>

<html>

  <head>

     <meta http-equiv="content-type" content="text/html" />

  </head>

  <body></body>

</html>
```

You can also set the content type globally for your site by defining it at the server level as the **http-equiv** header. For example, on an Apache server you could specify an **.htaccess** file with a content type for the entire site:

```
<Files abc.html>

  ForceType text/html; charset=UTF-8

</Files>
```

Like the content type, you can also specify the type of character encoding, or how the browser should interpret the characters written into the markup. For example, if your content is primarily in Russian, you should specify a character encoding that includes the Cyrillic alphabet. The most common encodings specified in web pages include:

▶ UTF-8, which is based on the Unicode encoding model, is backwards compatible with ASCII, and covers a wider range of characters than ISO-8859-1 in languages spanning from Western European to East Asian.

▶ ISO-8859-1, which is based on ASCII and includes mainly Western European characters (http://en.wikipedia.org/wiki/ISO/IEC_8859-1). ISO-8859-1 is the default encoding when none is specified in documents with the content type **text/html** (www.w3.org/Protocols/rfc2616/rfc2616-sec3.html, section 3.7.1).

We recommend using UTF-8 because it supports a wider range of languages than ISO-8859-1.

You can specify the character encoding in the same **http-equiv** header set by the server, or at the document level with the same **meta** tag:

```
<!doctype html>

<html>

  <head>

     <meta http-equiv="content-type" content="text/html; charset=utf-8" />

  </head>
```

```
<body></body>

</html>
```

■ Note

Characters not included in the specified encoding can be written to the page markup, either as named entities, like   for a non-breaking space, or numeric character references (NCR), which specify   for a non-breaking space.

See the following sites for complete encoding references:

www.webstandards.org/learn/articles/askw3c/dec2002

http://en.wikipedia.org/wiki/Character_encoding

PAGE TITLE

Clients frequently ask us how to improve their website's placement in search result listings. One simple way to do that is make sure all pages have a unique, descriptive page title:

```
<html>

  <head>

    <title>What we've done: UI design & development client examples |
    Filament Group, Inc., Boston, MA</title>

  </head>

  <body></body>

</html>
```

Every page should have a unique **title** element that describes the content and purpose of the page. Giving every page in your site the same boilerplate title (e.g., Acme Corporation Inc.) will not only hurt your search engine optimization (SEO) ranking, but it's also not very useful to visitors. When writing a title, keep these facts in mind:

▶ The title will display as the default bookmark name and in the tab bar of a browser, so make the first word or two as specific as possible.

▶ Search engines like Google or Bing use the title as the link for each result and truncate it to a single line of roughly 60–70 characters (though it's commonly assumed that they will still take the full title into account). Using concise language and leading with words that most specifically describe the page will help it stand out in a result list.

▶ Users may think about different words for an appropriate page title than you (for example, the manufacturer) would. Be sure to use customer-centric language that maps to what your target users will expect, rather than company jargon or technical terms. For example, on a product page, "Product detail: Acme Solarfox 100B lantern" isn't as useful as "Solar powered camping lantern with LED light – Solarfox 100B."

▶ If you add your name (or company name) to every page title, make sure to list it at the end to give more emphasis to the words that describe that page's content.

▶ Lastly, consider geographic keywords that help search engines know where you're located, like "Boston, MA USA," but again, put this closer to the end of your title.

And be concise: don't load up your titles with unnecessary keywords just to boost your traffic. Some search engines may detect when page titles are loaded with numerous repeated or superfluous keywords, and actually assign a lower ranking, or, worse, ban a site from search result pages. Ultimately, an accurate, thoughtful page title like "Solar powered camping lantern with LED light – Solarfox 100B – Acme Corp Boston MA USA" will be more informative to people and search engines alike.

DESCRIPTION AND KEYWORD META TAGS

The keyword and description **meta** tags were originally designed to give search engines a summary of the page's content. Over the years, SEO marketers have abused these tags to the extent that some speculate that they no longer hold much weight in search engine ranking or relevance, but it still makes sense to add a thoughtful set of **meta** tags to the page because they add valuable meaning to the document.

The content of the description **meta** tag is sometimes displayed in search-engine results and other contexts; for that reason, it should be structured as a concise, readable statement of the page's purpose. It should summarize the page content or functionality in a sentence or two, and use words that expand on the page title but are more descriptive and conversational. It can also be a bit longer than the title because it's not as limited to a specific character count:

```
<meta name="description" content="Solarfox 100 solar powered camping
lantern with LED light, wide range of colors and completely waterproof,
made in the USA by Acme Corp." />
```

The keywords **meta** tag, by contrast, is primarily used to inform search engine spiders and other automated systems how to interpret and evaluate the key information on the page:

```
<meta name="keywords" content="solarfox, solar, rechargeable, lantern,
green tech, camp, camping, acme, made in the usa, boston, massachusetts,
new england" />
```

Present the most important terms that a user may search for as a comma delimited list, including logical variants on the same theme (i.e., solar, rechargeable). Like in the title, going overboard with a list that's lengthy or contains repeated words can bloat the page and, in theory, hurt its ranking, so it's best to keep the list to no more than 40 words.

LANGUAGE

The language **meta** tag is used to identify the language in which the HTML page is authored and to help aid user agents in interpreting the content:

```
<meta name="language" content="en-us" />
```

Each language has a code, and sometimes a suffix that clarifies the particular dialect (such as en-us for American English). Syntax for language codes and their usage is outlined in the HTML specification (www.w3.org/TR/html401/struct/dirlang.html#langcodes).

ROBOTS

The robots **meta** tag is used to tell search engine spiders how to index the contents of the page and whether to follow links listed in the page markup.

By default, a spider will index all page contents and follow any links, which is the same as explicitly instructing search engines to do so with this tag:

```
<meta name="robots" content="all" />
```

To tell a robot *not* to index the content, set the **content** attribute to **noindex**; to prevent links from being spidered, add the **nofollow** attribute, like this:

```
<meta name="robots" content="noindex, nofollow">
```

Keep in mind that not all spiders will respect your robots tag, so you should take precautions to protect sensitive content from spammers and other malevolent software that scans for email addresses and sensitive information by obscuring or encrypting it.

STYLE SHEET AND SCRIPT REFERENCES

Placing style rules and JavaScript in external files that are referenced in the **head** is the most standards-compliant and progressive enhancement-friendly way to organize and manage these assets.

Each style sheet should be referenced in a **link** element, with either an absolute or relative path, after any **meta** tags:

```
<link rel="stylesheet" type="text/css" href="/styles/basic.css" />
```

By default, a style sheet will apply to a page on all devices and in all formats the same way (as much as the device or format allows). It can be targeted to affect the page only when it's displayed on a PC (**screen**) or mobile device (**handheld**), or when printed (**print**) by specifying the appropriate **media** attribute:

```
<link rel="stylesheet" type="text/css" media="print"
href="/styles/print.css" />
```

As a rule, JavaScript file references (denoted with **script** tags) should follow any style sheets; this ensures that styles are applied to the page before interactions:

```
<script type="text/javascript" src="/scripts/ajax.js"></script>
```

FAVORITE ICONS

A nice finishing touch to setting up an HTML document is to reference a favorite icon, or *favicon*, image. When specified, an icon will appear in the browser's address bar or tab and also in a bookmark menu, to make it easier to identify your page. The image should be sized to at least 16x16 pixels. Though modern browsers will accept a favicon in any image format—including JPG, GIF, or PNG—in order for it to appear on the widest range of browsers we recommend using the legacy icon (ICO) format, which uses the file extension **.ico**. Simply reference it like this:

```
<link rel="shortcut icon" href="/favicon.ico" />
```

There are a number of web tools available that convert a JPG, GIF, or PNG icon into the ICO format. We've used the following with great results:

▶ www.favicon.cc

▶ www.degraeve.com/favicon

◆ Tip

For a site with many Apple iPhone and iPod touch users, you can also create a special icon that will appear on the device's home screen. The image must be sized at 57x57 pixels and in PNG format, with the filename apple-touch-icon.png:

```
<link rel="apple-touch-icon" href="/apple-touch-icon.png" />
```

Building in accessibility

Creating accessible markup is as simple as writing clean, well-structured, and clearly identified markup, and abiding by a few simple design rules to ensure that text is legible and links maintain good affordance. Markup written in compliance with these criteria is more usable by screen readers or other assistive technologies, search engines, and users of conventional browsers alike, because it encodes additional meaning and helpful feedback that contribute to the overall usability of the site. It's a win for all.

There are two sets of guidelines that outline specific criteria that you should strive to meet in your code: Section 508 and the Web Content Accessibility Guidelines (WCAG). Each should be considered when thinking about how to achieve a fully accessible site, so we'll cover these at a high level here, and then work though specific accessibility examples in later chapters.

■ Note

Following the guidelines outlined here does not guarantee that your project will be accessible; the only way to be sure of that is to incorporate thorough accessibility testing into your quality assurance process.

Accessibility guidelines and legal standards

There are a number of domestic and international standards that describe legally acceptable levels of accessibility consideration for different judicial bodies, including Section 508 of the Americans with Disabilities Act (ADA) in the U.S., and EU guidelines for Interactive Media, for example.

These rules and standards apply to a range of information technologies, from software applications to telecommunications products. For example, US ADA Section 508 includes a host of standards that specifically apply to web development:

a   A text equivalent for every non-text element shall be provided (e.g., via an **alt** attribute, or within element content).

b   Equivalent alternatives for any multimedia presentation shall be synchronized with the presentation.

c   Web pages shall be designed so that all information conveyed with color is also available without color, for example from context or markup.

d   Documents shall be organized so they are readable without requiring an associated style sheet.

e   Redundant text links shall be provided for each active region of a server-side image map.

f   Client-side image maps shall be provided instead of server-side image maps except where the regions cannot be defined with an available geometric shape.

g   Row and column headers shall be identified for data tables.

h   Markup shall be used to associate data cells and header cells for data tables that have two or more logical levels of row or column headers.

i   Frames shall be titled with text that facilitates frame identification and navigation.

j   Pages shall be designed to avoid causing the screen to flicker with a frequency greater than 2 Hz and lower than 55 Hz.

k A text-only page, with equivalent information or functionality, shall be provided to make a web site comply with the provisions of this part, when compliance cannot be accomplished in any other way. The content of the text-only page shall be updated whenever the primary page changes.

l When pages utilize scripting languages to display content, or to create interface elements, the information provided by the script shall be identified with functional text that can be read by assistive technology.

m When a web page requires that an applet, plug-in or other application be present on the client system to interpret page content, the page must provide a link to a plug-in or applet that complies with §1194.21(a) through (l).

n When electronic forms are designed to be completed on-line, the form shall allow people using assistive technology to access the information, field elements, and functionality required for completion and submission of the form, including all directions and cues.

o A method shall be provided that permits users to skip repetitive navigation links.

p When a timed response is required, the user shall be alerted and given sufficient time to indicate more time is required.

We encourage our clients, specifically those who supply services to government agencies or populations that receive government funding, like schools, to understand their obligations according to these standards. And in general, we recommend applying them as much as possible as good coding practice.

More information about the Section 508 standards and how to apply them are at the Section 508 website, www.section508.gov.

Web Content Accessibility Guidelines (WCAG)

Currently in version 2.0, Web Content Accessibility Guidelines (WCAG, pronounced *wh-kag*) were created by the WCAG working group and are reviewed and approved by the World Wide Web Consortium (W3C), the standards body that produces and maintains the cornerstone markup and CSS specifications.

At the high level, WCAG promotes coding that follows four high-level guidelines:

▶ Make things perceivable

▶ Make things operable

▶ Make things understandable

▶ Make things robust

And in practice, WCAG stipulates the following common-sense rules to achieve these high-level goals:

▶ Provide text alternatives for any non-text content so that it can be changed into other forms people need, such as large print, Braille, speech, symbols, or simpler language.

▶ Provide alternatives for time-based media. (Time-based media include pre-recorded or live video and audio.)

▶ Create content that can be presented in different ways (for example, simpler layout) without losing information or structure.

▶ Make it easier for users to see and hear content, including separating foreground from background.

▶ Make all functionality available from a keyboard.

▶ Provide users enough time to read and use content.

▶ Do not design content in a way that is known to cause seizures.

▶ Provide ways to help users navigate, find content, and determine where they are.

▶ Make text content readable and understandable.

▶ Make Web pages appear and operate in predictable ways.

▶ Help users avoid and correct mistakes.

▶ Maximize compatibility with current and future user agents, including assistive technologies.

See the full list, with detailed explanation and usage guidelines, at the WCAG site, www.w3.org/TR/WCAG.

* * *

We've (hopefully!) covered how to build a well-structured, semantic HTML page that will power our basic experience and set the foundation for the enhanced experience. Next we'll discuss to how to use CSS in the most effective way for progressive enhancement.

chapter four

applying styles effectively

Cascading Style Sheets (CSS) define the visual styling of a page and allow for a clean separation of presentation from content. A range of advanced typography, visual effects, and sophisticated layouts are all possible with CSS. Applied correctly, these styles can have a huge impact on both the aesthetic appeal and usability of a site.

One of the basic principles of progressive enhancement, and of modern coding practices in general, is to separate presentation from the markup by grouping all style rules into one or more external style sheets. While writing all styles into an external style sheet is an essential best practice for progressive enhancement, on its own this practice does not guarantee a satisfying experience for all users. Every browser will attempt to render any style sheet referenced on the page, regardless of whether or not it properly supports the CSS properties specified. When rendered in capable devices, a style sheet can make a page easier to read or a workflow simpler to follow, but when rendered in browsers that only partially support CSS, it can make the experience confusing or unusable.

When we develop with progressive enhancement, we take the basic principle of separating presentation a step further: we separate styles into "safe" styles that can be served with the foundation markup to all browsers (including those that only partially support CSS), and layer on more complex style enhancements and CSS techniques only after we've tested the browser with our EnhanceJS testing suite and determined that a browser is capable of rendering them properly.

In this chapter, we'll review the best practices we commonly employ when applying CSS with progressive enhancement, including a review of how to divide styles into basic and enhanced style sheets, and highlight techniques to improve the accessibility, usability, and performance of styles.

Applying CSS to the page

There are a number of CSS best practices that apply globally to both basic and enhanced experiences. It's essential to structure styles in external style sheets so they may be logically applied based on browser capabilities, to reference them properly, to target intelligently when appropriate, and to use meaningful naming conventions that characterize styles by their purpose or function rather than their visual characteristics.

Maintaining styles in external style sheets

The first step in maintaining clean separation between markup and styles is to reference all style rules in an external style sheet. This best practice of separating styles from markup has been widely adopted by developers, and is important because:

▶ It allows a page to be styled in many ways and easily changed because it doesn't "bake in" a particular appearance

▶ It simplifies maintenance by keeping all style rules in one place

▶ It minimizes code weight by centralizing shared styles with common classes and IDs rather than repeating them multiple times in the markup

This approach is fundamentally different from the commonly used (but frequently problematic) practice of writing styles inline—for instance, assigning styles to specific elements in the markup with the **style** attribute (e.g., **style="padding: 5px"**), or in a style block in the page. Inline styles introduce a number of challenges:

▶ They can't be reused across multiple elements on a page or website, meaning inline styles must be duplicated in every place they're needed.

▶ They are difficult to maintain and update, because they're embedded within the content of HTML, rather than being stored in a single external location. Long term, this becomes a maintenance headache, especially if a design changes in any significant way.

▶ They won't be controlled by style rules referenced in external CSS. Even if global styles are maintained externally, each instance of an inline style rule in the markup will override any global external styles.

▶ Styles served with markup will be rendered by the browser, even if they are not fully supported. Not all browsers handle CSS the same way, or even fully support all CSS2 properties, so in some situations an inline style may render content unusable.

Even in situations where a style is used only once or twice throughout a site, we still recommend listing it in an external style sheet along with all other style rules for the site.

WHEN IT'S OK TO USE INLINE STYLES: A FEW EXCEPTIONS

There are a few very specific cases in advanced UI design where we've found inline styles to be necessary: dynamically positioning elements on the screen, animating elements' style properties, and creating CSS-based charts.

For instance, if you need to center a modal dialog in the screen or iterate the opacity of an element to create a fade transition, it's not practical to create a class for every possible set of position coordinates or for every increment of animated movement. In these cases, it makes sense to use JavaScript to apply a **style** attribute and modify CSS properties on the fly. We also use inline dimensions to create pure CSS-based charts by styling an element with a percentage width or height for each bar in a chart.

That said, we recommend keeping these inline style rules to an absolute minimum, and using externally referenced CSS for visual presentation whenever possible.

Linking to external style sheets

When we start coding a project, one of the first things we do is create an external style sheet that will house all style rules for the foundation markup, and reference it in the page **head**:

```
<link type="text/css" rel="stylesheet" href="basic.css" />
```

A valid style-sheet link contains the following attributes:

▶ **type** specifies the content type for the server to interpret (for style sheets, it should always be **text/css**)

▶ **rel** states the relationship of the linked resource to the HTML document (**stylesheet**)

▶ **href** contains a relative or absolute path to the CSS file

According to the HTML 4 spec, the **link** element is valid only when listed in the document **head**, but there's a more important reason to always list it there: any resources listed in the **head** are loaded before elements in the **body**. In other words, placing the **link** element in the **head** puts styles in place before the page content shows up, so that when it does, it is styled appropriately. Referencing style sheets elsewhere in the page increases the likelihood that the page will load as unstyled HTML, and users will see one or multiple steps of design transformation as styles load—often a suboptimal user experience.

You can also reference multiple style sheets within a single page. When doing so, keep in mind that each style sheet referenced on a page will require a separate HTTP request to the server, and the browser will load every style sheet referenced within the **head** section of the HTML page before displaying the page content. For these reasons, we recommend combining CSS into the smallest number of files possible.

Referencing with @import—more risk than reward

Some developers prefer the **@import** notation to reference external style sheets within style tags or another style sheet alongside other CSS selectors. It's often used to organize multiple style sheets and manage dependencies. For example, a few **@import** rules could organize all of the styles for screen presentation within a master style sheet that's referenced on the page:

```
@import url(screen-global.css);

@import url(screen-article-formatting.css);

@import url(screen-admin-tools.css);
```

While this may seem like an efficient way to organize CSS files, **@import** may actually slow down the page loading process. Each **@import** reference requires a separate, full HTTP request from the browser to the server. In addition, **@import** requests are made asynchronously, meaning the browser will not wait for these requests to load before rendering page content. This approach increases the likelihood that as the page starts to load, users will see plain, unstyled HTML before the styles fully load into place.

For these reasons, we recommend bypassing this method for referencing style sheets, and instead using **link** tags and the smallest number of files possible.

TARGETING PARTICULAR MEDIA TYPES

By default, style sheets referenced with the **link** element are applied to all media formats, including standard computer screens, mobile devices, and printers.

To flag a style sheet so that it applies only to a particular format, use the **media** attribute of the **link** element to apply one or more media types (separating multiple values with commas). For example, this style sheet will apply formatting to print output only:

```
<link type="text/css" rel="stylesheet" href="basic.css" media="print" />
```

Media types can also be specified for individual blocks of CSS within a style sheet, to target a few style exceptions to a particular type within a style sheet that applies to a broader range of formats:

```
@media print {

  h1 { font-size: 16pt; }

  h2 { font-size: 14pt; }

  h3 { font-size: 12pt; }

  #navigation, #advertisement { display: none; }

}
```

The HTML specification lists a number of media types to choose from, three of which apply to websites and applications:

▶ **screen** renders all associated styles in browsers on standard computer screens

▶ **print** applies formatting for printer output, where layouts are typically set in points and inches, and dimensions are often based on paper sizes

▶ **handheld** applies styles to handheld devices with presumably low bandwidth connections, smaller screens, and limited graphics capabilities

Of these, the **handheld** media type is, unfortunately, the least reliable. As of this writing, few mobile browsers actually obey this media type and parse styles accordingly. The best way to ensure that appropriate styles are served to mobile devices is to develop with test-driven progressive enhancement to ensure that low-bandwidth, low-capability devices are served a usable experience.

Using meaningful naming conventions

When naming classes and IDs, we recommend using names that describe the content's purpose or role in the content hierarchy, not how it's presented on the screen. Think of classes and IDs as an extension of semantic markup—does the name accurately categorize and identify the content within?

Choosing meaningful naming conventions is a best practice when developing with progressive enhancement for a couple reasons:

▶ An element labeled with a class or ID may be styled differently in the basic and enhanced experiences. For example, a column of text in the basic site may be pulled into a modal dialog in the enhanced version. Naming that content according to its purpose provides a logically described hook for applying both safe and enhanced styles, as well as for applying interactivity with JavaScript.

▶ Visual design can change, even within a single development cycle. For example, a left navigation bar may be moved to the top or the right side of the page, in which case an ID of **left-nav** no longer makes sense. It's better instead to use a name that describes the purpose of the navigation, such as **primary-nav** or **secondary-nav**.

This point is particularly relevant when CSS may be maintained or extended by multiple developers. As a professional services firm, 90% of the code we write is handed off to clients or provided as open source code to the public. As such, the naming conventions we use should make sense to developers who were not part of the initial build process. Keeping names simple and purposeful, and avoiding cryptic acronyms or jargon that's known only among members of a development team, strengthens the code throughout the life cycle of a project.

Styling the basic and enhanced experiences

When referencing external CSS with our test-driven PE approach, there are additional considerations to be made. Since our capabilities testing framework allows us to provide both a basic and an enhanced presentation of the same page, we need to decide which portions of the CSS should be sent to everyone, and which portions should be reserved for users with more capable browsers.

The testing framework allows us to make a very clean division between the CSS that's delivered to all browsers (including those that fail any part of the capabilities test suite) and browsers that pass all test criteria. For the sake of clarity in the examples that follow, we'll assume that the styles for each experience are going to be stored in separate style sheets named **basic.css** and **enhanced.css**. Any styles included in **basic.css** will be referenced in the page source when it's first served, and if the browser passes our capabilities tests, we will then load **enhanced.css** into the page as well. (We'll detail the mechanisms for referencing these CSS files using the framework in Chapter 6, "Testing browser capabilities.")

Safe styles for the basic experience

Most browsers have a default style sheet that does a good job of communicating content hierarchy with these defaults, so we generally let the browser's style sheet take precedence and override it as little as possible. In our experience with test-driven PE, we've discovered that a number of "safe" CSS properties are OK to use in the basic experience, so we typically set these in our **basic.css** style sheet. These properties will render fairly consistently across browsers that support any level of CSS, new and old—and while some browsers won't respect these properties, they won't break the site if they aren't recognized:

▶ *Text formatting*: The default fonts for a site can be set on the **body** tag with a font "stack" that lists the most preferred fonts first (**font-family: "Segoe UI", Helvetica, Arial, san-serif**); we recommend that the stack should include fonts that are commonly installed on many systems. Other text formatting, such as bold (**font-weight: bold**), italic (**font-style: italic**), strikethrough (**text-decoration: line-through**), capitalization (**text-transform: uppercase**), alignment (**text-align: center**), leading (**line-height:1.2**), and tracking (**letter-spacing: 0.3em**) are all fairly well supported by most browsers. (We recommend *not* setting font sizes, or changing the **text-decoration** property to modify the default underline on links, in the basic experience.)

▶ *Text color and backgrounds*: In general, text color (**color: red**), background colors (**background-color:#224466**), and background images (**background-image: url(images/texture.png)**) are safe to use in the basic experience, as long as the text is legible when background image or color is not applied. Keep in mind that some mobile browsers support text color but not background color, so that reversed-out text (light text on dark background color, for example) may not be visible. Also, it's important to note that many mobile browsers will always render linked text in blue, so you could end up with blue text even if you specify a legible link color. (If the background were dark blue, links could be completely invisible.) As a rule of thumb, we recommend reserving reversed-out text for the enhanced experience.

▶ *Padding and margin*: When used very sparingly, padding (**padding:1em**) and margin (**margin-top:1.5em**) can space elements apart and enhance the readability of a page in the basic experience . Floating, positioning, stacking, or setting negative margins, dimensions, or overflow properties should never be set in the basic style sheet.

▶ *Border*: Used in moderation, borders (**border:1px solid black**) can draw attention to groups of content, and greatly improve the basic experience.

Combined, these style properties are often sufficient to add light branding to a site to make it unique and recognizable, and to enhance user-friendliness.

There is one additional advantage in keeping **basic.css** very simple and clean: it may be able to function as both the basic screen experience and a print style sheet. To do this, be sure to add a print-specific **@media** block to **basic.css** that hides any elements in the enhanced experience that would be irrelevant when printed (navigation, advertisements, etc.):

```
@media print {
  h1 { font-size: 16pt; }
  h2 { font-size: 14pt; }
  h3 { font-size: 12pt; }
  #navigation, #advertisement { display: none; }
}
```

Styling the enhanced experience

By using capabilities testing to send our enhancements only to browsers that will understand them, we can apply advanced CSS layout techniques—like floats, positioning, and more—with confidence that they won't cause usability problems. This practice also allows us to write enhanced CSS that assumes JavaScript is available and well supported.

There are a number of best practices we follow when writing enhanced CSS that we recommend considering:

▶ *Let CSS do the work.* When a page component has multiple, dynamic visual states that react to the user's input or manipulation (such as default, highlight, or disabled states), write a class for each state and toggle it on/off using JavaScript. This lets CSS do the heavy lifting, and prevents situations where unnecessary inline styles are added with JavaScript.

▶ *Embrace the cascade.* If a basic CSS is written with a light hand, the enhanced CSS can cleanly extend it without having to negate any styles that were already declared. This is why we advocate using very little CSS in the basic experience.

▶ *Keep resets minimal.* If your enhanced CSS rules depend on reset styles that normalize or negate the browser's default styles, we recommend including them at the top of **enhanced.css** (and avoid using them altogether in **basic.css**). We highly recommend resetting as few styles as possible, and building on top of the styles provided by the browser. This is especially important with form elements, which have certain default styles that users will recognize, and it's best to leave them intact whenever possible.

▶ *Adopt forward-looking CSS when possible.* A number of newer CSS3 features that allow for rich visual styling—like rounded corners, drop shadows, variable opacity, and animated transformations—are gaining support in the latest browsers, can reduce code bloat, and provide more powerful selectors for associating style rules with markup structure. For example, using CSS3 **border-radius** to round the corners of an element eliminates the need to use several HTML elements to hold background images for each corner of a box. While many of these features will not work in older browsers like IE6, they are safe to use in enhanced experiences, because they'll be ignored in browsers that don't understand them.

▶ *Be mindful of setting type with images.* A design may call for a custom font that isn't commonly installed on computers and devices. We never recommend setting type in images (even when applied with accessible techniques, like **alt** attributes). There are many custom font techniques that ensure that page content is available to all users (including those on screen readers) and make it possible to provide the site content in various languages. Custom type can be rendered in Canvas or Flash to visually replace portions of a page's text, and many browsers also support CSS **@font-face** to reference custom fonts by URL.

Accessibility considerations

When applying style to a page, there are a multitude of usability and accessibility issues to consider for all users, including those with disabilities.

The W3C offers an extensive recommendation called "Web Content Accessibility Guidelines 2.0" (WCAG), which covers a range of accessibility best practices, including meaningful markup choices, visual design considerations, and use of JavaScript to improve accessibility. There are several we feel are very important that are worth highlighting:

▶ *Text size and scaling*: Design pages with text sizes that are large enough for the average user to read easily. CSS written using flexible units such as **em** and **%**, or keywords like **small**, **medium**, and **large,** allows users to easily resize the text to their preference. While most modern browsers can resize page content regardless of its CSS units, Internet Explorer versions 6 and earlier require the use of flexible units for text scaling to work.

▶ *Contrast ratios*: To ensure that text content is comfortably readable for a broad audience, WCAG recommends a text color-to-background contrast ratio of no less than 3:1 for large text and 5:1 for smaller text. (For reference, black text on a white background is 21:1, and the mid-gray for hex#666 on white is 5.74:1.) There are many tools to test specific contrasts and ensure acceptable contrast levels.

▶ *Color accommodations*: Interfaces frequently build in color-based visual cues—from colored text for links, to red/green indicators for performance, to highlights for alerts. Six to nine percent of the population suffers from some level of color-blindness, with the most common type manifesting itself in a difficulty distinguishing red and green values. For this reason, any visual indicator should have both a shift in color value and a secondary visual indication like a distinctly different shape or pattern to make it usable for people with color-blindness.

▶ *Clear link affordances*: Users expect that text located in certain locations on the page—at the top, along the left column, and at the bottom—will be links regardless of style; for text links in the body of the page, it's important to style them with adequate difference from surrounding text, and consider underlining them at all times, or at least on hover, for optimal clarity.

▶ *Background color fallback*: When using a background image behind text, be sure to set a complementary background color behind the image as a fallback in case the image fails to load or the user has images disabled. (Contrast-ratio considerations, described above, should be applied in this case as well.)

There are also a number of our own accessibility best practice guidelines we always keep in mind when considering overall page layout and structure:

▶ *Consider screen resolutions*: When designing pages with fixed widths, we recommend designing within the common screen resolution of 960 pixels wide, to ensure most users will not need to scroll horizontally.

▶ *Present comfortable column and line widths*: Columns of text that are roughly 80 characters wide (about 9–10 words) are most comfortable to read. For very text-heavy sites, we consider even narrower columns to facilitate comfortable scanning and reading.

▶ *Work with native browser focus styling when possible*: Most browsers handle focus with a dotted or glowing outline that allows users to easily navigate a page with their keyboard. While this outline treatment sometimes clashes with the intended user interface design, we recommend that you don't disable it; if you do, be sure to create another style, like a border or background color shift, that appears on focus to provide clear feedback to users navigating the page without a mouse.

▶ *Follow established conventions*: Across the web, users are trained to find common features in specific locations—primary navigation at the top or left of the page; account tools, shopping-cart feedback, and logout links at the top right; and user help links at the bottom of the page, for example. Positioning elements in a predictable and consistent location helps users find what they need efficiently.

▶ *Hide and show content safely*: Whenever you use CSS to hide text from visual users, be sure to do so in an accessible manner. Using **display: none** or **visibility: hidden** will likely hide the text from screen readers as well, meaning they won't be able to access that content. One accessible hiding solution is absolutely positioning an element off the page, out of view to visual users, by setting a large negative **left** value (don't set a **top** value, as this could inhibit accessibility). Another solution is to set a large negative text indent on the element, and a hidden **overflow**, to move the text out of view.

▶ *Try to avoid scrolling areas within a page*: The **overflow** property is used to specify how content should appear when it overflows the boundaries of its container (visible, cropped, or scrollable). Some mobile browsers, like the iPhone, support scrolling overflow, but don't display scrollbars, and require two fingers to scroll these areas, making scrolling areas are difficult to use—others don't support scrolling at all.

Dealing with bugs and browser inconsistencies

Writing CSS that works consistently across browsers is often more difficult than it looks. Hacks—the "creative" syntax developers use to target or exclude a specific browser—should be used as a last resort, and applied selectively, because they're difficult to maintain and may cause rendering issues as newer, standards-compliant browser versions are released. Fortunately, hacks are usually avoidable if you approach CSS the right way. For the limited cases where it's unavoidable, we have some recommended techniques.

Conditional comments

Internet Explorer is infamous among web designers for its quirky handling of CSS, but given its share of the browser market, even minor rendering differences are hard to ignore. For situations where you simply can't make your layout render properly in versions of Internet Explorer, there are conditional comments—a proprietary feature of Internet Explorer that let you specify HTML markup that only IE will see. (Since they use standard HTML comment syntax, other browsers will disregard them.)

When CSS workarounds for IE are necessary, you can list those style rules in a separate style sheet and reference it on the page within conditional comments:

```
<!--[if IE]>
    <link rel="stylesheet" type="text/css" href="ie_fixes.css" />
<![endif]-->
```

Conditional comments can be targeted to a particular version of IE. We always recommend specifying a version, or all versions prior to a particular one, by using **lt** so later, more standards-compliant versions of IE won't see them. For example, the following conditional comment is read only by versions of IE released before version 7 (that is, earlier than IE 7):

```
<!--[if lt 7]>
    <link rel="stylesheet" type="text/css" href="ie_fixes.css" />
<![endif]-->
```

When writing CSS within IE-specific style sheets, we recommend the following:

▶ *Target exceptions only*: An IE-specific style sheet should contain a minimal number of workarounds that cascade off styles that are served to all browsers.

▶ *Use filters sparingly*: Many versions of Internet Explorer include proprietary CSS properties known as filters, which enable advanced effects such as shadows and blurs, and allow fixes for IE's rendering of semi-transparent PNGs (see sidebar). Unfortunately, IE filters are invalid CSS, and can also slow down page performance. Use with caution, if at all.

PNG transparency in IE 5 and 6

Versions of Internet Explorer prior to 7 do not natively support alpha transparency in PNG 24 images. Because of this, the semi-transparent areas in PNG images will appear gray or blue when viewed in IE 5 and 6. Fortunately, it's possible to achieve a more graceful fallback in these browsers if you save your images as PNG 8 instead, which can be done using Adobe Fireworks, or with several command-line-based scripts available free online. When a PNG 8 image is viewed in these browsers, its semi-transparent channels will fall back to fully transparent, which is much less obtrusive in the user interface.

Common issues and workarounds

Through our experience in creating CSS layouts that work across a wide array of browsers, we've noticed a number of issues that seem to occur in almost every project. Here are some workarounds we commonly use to fix them.

CLEARING AND CONTAINING FLOATS

When a CSS float is applied to an element, its height is no longer recognized by its parent element. This layout behavior sometimes conflicts with how the layout should render, so there's a need for a workaround to make the parent element wrap around its floated children. The simplest fix for the problem is to float the parent element, or to set its **overflow** property to **auto,** but this doesn't work in every situation.

◼ Note

For more details, read Eric Meyer's "Containing Floats," http://complexspiral.com/publications/ containing-floats.

As an alternate approach, we can apply a workaround known as "clearfix." The clearfix technique works by injecting an element just after the last floated child element, and using CSS to give it **block** and **clear** properties. Since this new element is not floated itself, it will cause the parent to recognize its location and wrap around it.

The CSS for clearfix is pretty clever. It uses the **:after** pseudo-element selector to create and style an element—in this case, a single character—without the need for

JavaScript. Simply add the following style rule to your enhanced style sheet, and apply **class="clearfix"** to an element to force it to wrap around all floated child elements:

```
.clearfix:after {
  content: " ";
  display: block;
  height: 0;
  clear: both;
  visibility: hidden;
}
```

The **:after** selector is not supported in Internet Explorer versions 7 and earlier, so it's necessary to include a second selector to ensure the clearfix technique works. The proprietary **zoom: 1** property triggers **hasLayout** (described later in this chapter) in Internet Explorer, which will cause it to wrap its floated child elements. Keep in mind that it's good practice to store IE-specific styles in a separate style sheet and reference that style sheet using a conditional comment:

```
/* for Internet Explorer */
.clearfix {
  zoom: 1;
}
```

There is an alternate, and less obtrusive, approach to assigning the **clearfix** class throughout the markup. The clearfix style rules can be scoped to all elements that need them by listing their selectors in the style sheet:

```
#header:after,
div#primary-navigation:after,
#primary-content:after,
#footer:after {
  content: " ";
  display: block;
  height: 0;
  clear: both;
  visibility: hidden;
}
```

```
/* for Internet Explorer */
#header,
div#primary-navigation,
#primary-content,
#footer {
   zoom: 1;
}
```

This change keeps the markup free of classes for visual workarounds, and can reduce page weight.

A tip of the hat

The clearfix approach to float clearing was originally described in the article "How To Clear Floats Without Structural Markup" at *Position is Everything* (www.positioniseverything.net/easyclearing.html).

ADDRESSING Z-INDEX ISSUES

In modern websites, it's common for user interface components to not only be positioned next to each other, but also stacked in front of or behind other elements. In CSS, this stacking is handled through a property called **z-index**.

The **z-index** property can be applied to any element with **relative**, **absolute**, or **fixed** position (assigned with the **position** property), and accepts a number that represents its vertical stack position among other elements on the page; an element with a higher **z-index** value appears in front of elements with lower (or no) **z-index** values. The entire document has a stacking context—elements are stacked relative to sibling elements on the page—and every container element with a **z-index** applied creates a new stacking context for child elements, meaning that child **z-index** values are relative to one another, and not to the rest of the page.

Internet Explorer versions 7 and earlier interpret this stacking model incorrectly: they create a new stacking context for all positioned elements, even those without a specified **z-index**. This can make it difficult to layer stacked elements in a predictable way. For example, an absolutely positioned tooltip that sits inside a relatively positioned **fieldset** element may appear behind other positioned elements on the page, because IE treats them like stacked elements when they should just appear in the document flow.

To combat this issue for absolutely positioned elements, we use JavaScript to append the markup (in this case, the tooltip) just before the end of the **body** element. Doing this ensures that the tooltip will sit in the document's stack order (not a particular element's), and if we assign a high enough **z-index** value, it will appear in front of all other page elements. In general, we recommend taking this approach when dynamically appending any overlaid content, because it removes any guesswork about where an element should be inserted to layer correctly above all other page content.

Another Internet Explorer **z-index** issue is that "windowed" elements such as **select**, **iframe**, **object** (used for plugins like Adobe Flash), and anything with scrollbars, all tend to stack in front of everything else, regardless of source order or **z-index** value. Unfortunately, the workaround for this issue is not pretty: we use JavaScript and CSS to inject an empty, hidden **iframe** element directly behind any content that is intended to appear in front of the rest of the page, with dimensions large enough to act as a shield, blocking windowed content from leaking through.

◆ Tip

For an automated approach to this fix, we recommend using the bgiframe jQuery plugin
(http://docs.jquery.com/Plugins/bgiframe).

FIXING HASLAYOUT BUGS IN INTERNET EXPLORER

When you test CSS layouts in Internet Explorer, you're bound to run into seemingly random rendering bugs—elements that appear partially visible, act oblivious to style rules, blink while scrolling, or reveal fragments of text in unexpected places on the page.

These types of bugs are often the result of issues with IE's rendering engine, and are typically caused by an element lacking a quality Microsoft refers to as **hasLayout**. The details of what exactly **hasLayout** means are somewhat mysterious. In general, block-level elements are considered to have **hasLayout** in IE's rendering engine, but sometimes the engine forgets to apply **hasLayout** where it should.

There are a few CSS properties that can be applied to an element to trigger **hasLayout**:

▶ **position: relative;**   This property is often the safest **hasLayout** workaround; we generally try it first.

▶ **zoom: 1;**   An invalid and proprietary, yet somewhat harmless, CSS property that assigns a page-zoom level of 100% to an element, rendering it as it would by default.

▶ **height: 1%;**   or any **height** setting, for that matter, will usually trigger **hasLayout**.

To ensure that future browser versions with better standards support won't see these styles, consider placing **hasLayout** style fixes in an IE-specific style sheet that is targeted only to the specific versions of Internet Explorer that need them.

* * *

We've covered how to effectively write and organize your styles so they can be cleanly targeted to the basic and enhanced experiences. Next, we'll discuss how to transform the foundation markup by unobtrusively layering on JavaScript to enhance the page and add interactivity.

chapter five

scripting enhancements and interactivity

From its humble beginnings—when it was often misunderstood as a quirky "toy" language—to its current status as one of the most widely used programming languages in the world, JavaScript has come a long way in a short time. Today's browsers are built on powerful processing engines that enable us to create rich experiences with JavaScript that rival those found on the desktop, with speed and capabilities advancing at a rapid pace.

Using a test-driven progressive enhancement approach, we can apply JavaScript in a more targeted manner, enhancing foundation markup in powerful ways to create the highly interactive web applications users want, while making sure we protect accessibility for browsers that lack JavaScript support.

In this chapter, we'll discuss how to apply JavaScript unobtrusively to extend a page's functionality, while preserving and even enhancing its accessibility. We'll consider JavaScript development in the context of four basic areas:

▶ Applying JavaScript to HTML

▶ Understanding JavaScript's place in the basic experience

▶ Scripting the enhanced experience

▶ Preserving and enhancing usability and accessibility

As we go, we'll detail the ways to structure JavaScript unobtrusively and write it as generically as possible so that it may be reused in different contexts.

How to properly reference JavaScript

Separating JavaScript-driven behavior from HTML markup is an essential best practice in making progressive enhancement possible; clean separation allows scripting enhancements to be targeted to capable browsers. When coding with a PE approach, JavaScript should be applied unobtrusively by placing it in an external file and referencing it in the page **head.**

Avoiding inline JavaScript

It's very common to see inline JavaScript code blocks or event handlers—like markup such as **onclick** or **onmouseover** attributes—added to HTML markup. Inline JavaScript may seem like a convenient way to quickly add interactivity, but there are several important reasons why this approach is a bad idea:

▶ It increases code weight. When events are applied inline, they must be repeated on each individual element in the markup, bloating the page file size and slowing load times.

▶ It increases maintenance complexity. Maintaining inline scripts requires meticulously noting where instances of events are written into the markup, and then painstakingly finding and updating each instance where JavaScript is embedded directly in the content of HTML documents. If individual instances are missed, they could cause errors.

▶ It applies behavior in all browsers that support JavaScript, including those with poor support. Some users may experience errors and accessibility problems when certain scripting techniques fail.

Fortunately, in the vast majority of cases, inline scripts are entirely avoidable; JavaScript provides native methods for traversing the markup structure of a document to apply events without having to add attributes or edit the markup.

Referencing external JavaScript

Well-formatted script-file references are easy to construct and apply in HTML. For each file, add a script element to the **head** of the HTML document, and set its **src** attribute to the path of an external JavaScript file:

```
<script src="js/enhancements.js" type="text/javascript"></script>
```

The **type** attribute is also necessary to communicate the file's content type—in this case, **text/javascript**—for the server to interpret it properly.

There is an ongoing debate in the development community around where script files are best served: Does it belong in the **head** element along with CSS references, as noted in the HTML 4 specification? Or at the end of the document so that content loads first?

From our perspective, these are not the critical questions. When coding for progressive enhancement, the most important aspect of referencing external scripts is not *where* they go, but *when* they're introduced. Script files should be loaded to the page only after it's certain that the browser can render them properly. To determine which script files will work on a device, it's necessary to test the scripts before the browser loads them, and then serve only the script enhancements that pass the test. (We'll describe in detail how to load scripts in this way in the next chapter, "Testing browser capabilities.")

Understanding JavaScript's place in the basic experience

In the previous chapter, we listed several "safe" CSS properties that we recommend for making small visual improvements to a page's basic experience that don't run the risk of introducing usability problems.

In the case of JavaScript, however, there is no such list. When JavaScript encounters a problem—whether due to poor browser support or faulty developer logic—it has a tendency to go out with a bang and expose errors to the user regardless of their severity. Worse, JavaScript errors can stop a process from running, and leave a page partially enhanced or entirely unusable.

For this reason, we recommend including one JavaScript reference in the foundation markup: the very limited JavaScript to run the capabilities test suite. We always build the basic experience—foundation markup and safe styles—with standard HTML static elements and form controls, to build a functioning interface that works universally across devices without any JavaScript events attached. If—and only if—the browser passes all capabilities tests required for the enhanced experience, do we use EnhanceJS to load in additional JavaScript for layering on enhancements.

Best practices for scripting enhancements

JavaScript can be used to enhance a page in a number of ways, from minor content show/hide toggles to complex transformations that alter the user experience entirely. In this section, we'll demonstrate some best practice approaches for applying JavaScript to a page using progressive enhancement, to add enhanced behaviors to content already on the page, generate or request new markup, apply enhanced styles, and manage content visibility.

Running scripts when content is ready

Unlike CSS, JavaScript requires that the HTML elements it manipulates be present the moment it executes; if a required element is not available for the script, the browser will throw errors. To avoid this situation, JavaScript must be delayed from executing until the markup has finished loading.

JavaScript's native **onload** event handler triggers when all contents contained within the element it's bound to—including all dependencies like images and iframes—have finished loading. Enclosing a script in an **onload** event handler ensures that the elements acted on by the script are loaded and ready before it runs:

```
document.body.onload = function(){

  // Do something to the body content

};
```

In many cases, scripts can safely execute once the HTML markup is available, and before the complete page assets (images, iframes, etc.) have finished loading. There is no single native JavaScript method that works across all current browsers, but popular JavaScript libraries provide custom event handlers—such as jQuery's **ready** method—that execute a script as soon as the basic markup structure is in place:

```
$(document).ready(function(){

  //DOM-related code goes here!

});
```

Applying behavior to markup

In the enhanced experience, one of the main activities JavaScript controls is unobtrusively applying behavior to respond to user interaction. There are two ways to attach or bind JavaScript event handlers to enhanced markup:

▶ *Event binding* applies event handlers like mouse clicks or keypresses to specific elements on the page.

▶ *Event delegation* takes advantage of JavaScript's event bubbling feature to apply event listeners to a parent container, instead of binding handlers directly to individual elements.

USING EVENT BINDING

JavaScript is an event-driven language, meaning that it can either execute the moment it loads, or it can "listen" for an event to trigger it at a later time. JavaScript events correspond to environmental actions such as **load** and **error**, and to user actions like **mousedown**, **mouseup**, **click**, **mouseover**, **mouseout**, **keypress**, and more.

JavaScript event handlers are built-in methods for applying behavior to page elements. When behavior is bound to elements using an event handler, its execution will delay until the event occurs. JavaScript's event-listening capability is a major factor in building web applications that feel smart and responsive.

For example, the following code shows how to bind a **click** event handler to an anchor element after finding it by its **id**:

```
var myAnchor = document.getElementById('myAnchor');

myAnchor.onclick = function(){

  //JavaScript placed here will execute when myAnchor is clicked

};
```

This method of binding event listeners, however, will overwrite any listener previously applied to the same event on that element. To add event listeners without overwriting others, the W3C's DOM Level 2 event model specifies the **addEventListener** method. Internet Explorer implemented its own event binding method, **attachEvent**, meaning a cross-browser solution for adding event listeners requires a check to utilize the supported method.

To simplify binding multiple event listeners, JavaScript libraries provide custom methods, such as jQuery's custom **bind** method. Libraries also provide selector engines that allow elements to be found with CSS style syntax, making it simple to bind events by ID, class name, or any CSS selector. The following code demonstrates a **bind** method that accepts two arguments: an event name (in this case **click**, but it could also accept others like **mouseover**, **mouseout**, etc., or even multiple events) and a callback function to execute when that event is triggered:

```
$('#myAnchor').bind('click', function(){

  //JavaScript placed here will execute when myAnchor is clicked

});
```

The jQuery **bind** method's callback function executes within the scope of the DOM element to which the event is bound, which allows you to refer to the element with the JavaScript keyword, **this**. For example, an element's **class** attribute can be modified using the **this** keyword when the element is clicked:

```
$('#myAnchor').bind('click', function(){
  this.className = "clicked";
};
```

USING EVENT DELEGATION

Binding events directly to elements is useful, but when you're building complex applications with lots of elements that should behave in a similar way, it's more efficient and manageable to use event delegation to assign events.

One advantage of event delegation is that events bound to a parent element automatically apply behavior to child elements, even if they are not yet on the page. This makes it a particularly useful technique for scripting enhancements on pages where markup is added after the widget is created. Event delegation also applies events quickly, and is very efficient with memory consumption: instead of looping through every node in a tree to bind individual events, all the logic can be assigned once at the parent level.

Events have native properties—such as **pageX** and **pageY** (referring to the mouse coordinates) and **target** (referencing the element that triggered the event)—and jQuery normalizes these properties' names across browsers. The **target** property is particularly useful for applying event delegation because it can be used to find out which element triggered an event.

Event delegation refers to the practice of binding an event to a parent element, like a widget container or the **body** element; when an event is triggered on an element nested inside the parent, the event "bubbles" up to the parent node and triggers the execution of a script that checks which element was the **target** of the event, and if that **target** matches the element we're looking for, the appropriate script will run.

The first argument passed to an event handler's callback function references its **event** object, which contains all of that event's properties. The following code shows an event bound to the **body** element, with conditional logic enclosed to check if the target of the click was an anchor:

```
$('body').bind('click', function(event){
  if ($(event.target).is('a')){
    // an anchor was clicked!
  }
});
```

jQuery simplifies event delegation even further through its **live** method, which automates event delegation by applying the event to the document itself, and checking the **target** of the event to see if it matches element to which the live method was applied:

```
$('#myAnchor').live('click', function(){
  this.className = "clicked";
});
```

Building enhanced markup with JavaScript

It's often necessary to use JavaScript to create and insert additional HTML for an enhanced experience. For example, a select menu in the basic experience may be transformed into a slider in the enhanced experience. Since this slider markup isn't usable without JavaScript behavior, and would just add extra bandwidth and clutter to the foundation markup, it should not be included in the foundation markup. Instead, the new slider markup must be inserted during the enhancement process.

Enhancement-specific markup can come from one of two places: it's either generated with JavaScript based on information derived from the foundation markup, or retrieved from the server with an Ajax request.

USING THE FOUNDATION MARKUP AS A GUIDE FOR GENERATING ENHANCED MARKUP

When possible, it's good practice to use the basic foundation markup as the reference when generating the enhanced markup.

For example, imagine you want to create a slider from a native HTML **select** element in the foundation markup. We can use JavaScript to parse text from each **option** element and find out which is currently selected in the native **select**. With this data, we populate a generic slider markup "template" in the script, and then inject the resulting enhanced markup into the page. Dynamically generating content is much faster than requesting additional content with Ajax, because everything is already in the page. And by writing the script generically to grab the foundation markup as a data source to populate the template—rather than embedding content into the script—we can reuse the same script logic for many different sliders in a site. (We'll present two examples of this technique in detail in Chapters 12 and 17.)

There are situations where we choose to encode data in the foundation markup so that it's available to be used by the enhancement script. For example, the location of external content that will populate a tooltip can be encoded in a **data** attribute that the enhancement script will use to generate an Ajax request. The HTML5 **data** prefix can be added to any string of text to create a custom attribute that complies with web standards.

In rare cases, storing a small fragment of content or markup in a script *is* the best course of action. Consider, for example, the text for a Close button in a dialog's title bar. While the dialog's main content could come from either the foundation markup or a separate file via server request, its title bar controls and Close button are necessary only for using the dialog itself. The content has no place in the foundation markup, and from a performance standpoint, it's very inefficient to make a server request for this small bit of text. In specific cases like this, we believe it makes sense to put content into JavaScript; when we do, we're careful to store the text in a configurable JavaScript variable, and to define variables in a convenient location such as at the top of the JavaScript file.

REQUESTING ADDITIONAL CONTENT WITH AJAX

In some cases, adding additional markup to the page using Ajax makes more sense than keeping it in the foundation markup—for page size or speed optimization, to avoid confusing the basic experience with extra markup, or for other business reasons.

Ajax—a technology that began as a proprietary feature of Internet Explorer 5, and was later adapted as a web standard and integrated into most modern browsers—lets JavaScript request data from the server to update portions of a page without having to reload the entire page.

Requesting content from the server using Ajax is a straightforward process: a script sends a request to the server for a particular piece of HTML; the server returns a text response that can be in plain text, XML, JavaScript (JSON), or HTML format; and the script inserts the text into the page.

jQuery offers several methods for Ajax functionality, such as:

▶ The **ajax** method, which is the most robust, offering a normalized interface to the browser's XMLHttpRequest API, as well as various events and properties unique to jQuery

▶ The **get** and **post** methods, which offer shortcuts to the **ajax** method, to make requests with more concise configuration

▶ The **load** method, which is similar to **get**, except that you call it on a DOM element within which you'd like the response to be inserted

The **load** method comes with the additional benefit of letting you specify a request filtered to a subset of the response content. For example, the following code requests only a portion of a page (**news.php**) by specifying a CSS selector (**#latest**):

```
$('div#news-ticker').load('news.php #latest');
```

Loading HTML fragments in this way is particularly helpful for retrieving a small subset of content from a larger page.

One potential downfall of requesting content with Ajax is the time required for a server response, which can cause noticeable delays in the user interface on slower connections or with larger requests. When retrieving data from the server, it's good practice to display a "loading" indicator while the request is in progress.

DECIDING WHEN CONTENT SHOULD BE INCLUDED IN THE FOUNDATION MARKUP

In most situations, all content or functionality should be presented in the foundation markup. But there may be situations where a particular feature may be too complicated to use comfortably without JavaScript behavior. For example, in Chapter 2, we noted that recreating the enhanced photo-cropping tool in the photo manager—in which the user needs to specify the exact pixel coordinates for crop points—would be too difficult to use in the basic experience. Given the complexity, cases like this might best be reserved for the enhanced experience.

There also may be cases where content doesn't make sense when JavaScript is disabled. For example, a "Print this page" link relies entirely on JavaScript to work, so it will appear broken to users when JavaScript is unavailable or disabled. Similarly, markup for a custom form control that requires JavaScript to function will only confuse users in a non-JavaScript environment. Markup for these types of features should be excluded from the foundation markup, and added with JavaScript only in the enhanced experience.

Managing content visibility

When adding additional content and markup to an enhanced page with JavaScript, there is a decision to be made about whether the original foundation markup should remain visible.

Sometimes the enhanced content acts as a supplement to the foundation markup, allowing both to meaningfully coexist on the page. Consider a **canvas**-based chart generated from an HTML data table in the foundation markup: the visual chart presentation and the detailed data table could work together and provide additional richness and meaning for users, so we would definitely consider displaying both in the page together. Similarly, if we enhance an **input** or a custom **select** element to a slider, we frequently keep both the native element and the enhanced slider on the page to give users a wider range of interaction opportunities.

There are cases, though, where the enhanced content completely replaces the foundation markup version, like when we replace a native **select** element with a custom-styled version of that control. Having them both visible at once is not only redundant, but also potentially confusing to the user. In these cases, it's important to hide the native control from users.

HIDING CONTENT VISUALLY, BUT NOT AUDIBLY

When we think about showing and hiding, we're always considering the broadest range of users, including those using screen readers. As we discussed above, when we use HTML **table** data to create a chart using the HTML5 **canvas** element (described in detail in Chapter 12), the chart and the table are somewhat redundant content; since they're repetitive, some designers might choose to hide the data table and display the chart. But the chart is useful to sighted users only—removing the table of data values from the page entirely would render the content inaccessible to people using screen readers.

When hiding content from display that is still necessary for screen readers, it's crucial avoid using CSS properties like **display: none** or **visibility: hidden**; they'll not only hide content from sight, but potentially from screen readers as well. To hide content safely, it should be absolutely positioned with a large negative left value (**position: absolute; left: -99999px;**) that moves it reliably off screen.

HIDING CONTENT FROM ALL USERS

A few custom form controls generate content in the enhanced experience that performs the same essential function as the foundation markup; keeping both the native and enhanced version of the control on the page is a nuisance to all users. Take the case of a custom-styled select menu (described in detail in Chapter 17), which uses elements such as **a**, **ul**, **li**, and **div** to create a CSS-friendly, functional replacement for a native **select** element. Once the enhanced control is generated and inserted into the page, the foundation **select** element is wholly redundant, and seeing both may be very confusing.

Many designers/developers would remove the native control entirely from the page with JavaScript, and leave only the enhanced control. Unfortunately, this can cause big problems: the new markup, while perfectly functional for making a selection, has no way of submitting its data along with the rest of the form—it's just **div**s and a list.

In this case, it's necessary to create a *proxy*, which means we hide the native form control visually from the screen using **display: none**, but still keep it in the page markup to hold the value for form submission. Then, we use JavaScript to connect the replacement enhanced control to its native counterpart, so it manipulates the hidden **select** element programmatically as the user changes its values. When coded properly, a proxy allows the form to be submitted with the value from the native control—as far as the server is concerned, it's as if the enhanced control is not even there.

Applying style enhancements

Loading and manipulating CSS to style the HTML markup is fundamental to creating an enhanced experience. JavaScript can facilitate enhancement in a number of ways:

▶ *Dynamically loading additional CSS files.* JavaScript can be used to load style sheets into a page. This is a key factor of our approach: we keep complex styles that we know are inconsistently supported in some browsers in external style sheets, use EnhanceJS to first test whether a browser can successfully render style enhancements, and then inject one or more enhanced style sheets when those certain conditions are met. This technique is useful for making large-scale enhancements that require application of complex styles, like transforming a linear page into a multi-column grid layout.

▶ *Toggling HTML classes.* We advocate using JavaScript to add, remove, and toggle CSS classes, instead of writing inline CSS rules with JavaScript. Because style rules are contained in external CSS files and not sprinkled throughout the script logic, we can maintain a crisp separation between style and behavior, and simplify debugging and maintenance. JavaScript also provides a way to extend CSS support to browsers that don't natively support pseudo-classes such as **:hover** or **:focus**—for example, JavaScript makes it possible to dynamically assign a "hover" class when the user places the mouse over an element.

▶ *Applying style inline with the* **style** *attribute.* There are very limited situations where it's *not* practical to manipulate CSS classes. For example, when JavaScript needs to dynamically set or animate style rules—where the position and dimension properties of a dialog window may need to be manipulated hundreds of times as it's animated, resized, and repositioned on the screen—creating a fixed set of static classes would be impractical. In this case, limited use of setting inline styles dynamically provides the most efficient option. When an animation requires dynamic style scripting, like a cross-fade effect, it's also good practice to remove any inline styles when the animation is complete and replace them with class attributes to maintain their visual appearance and avoid leaving inline styles in the page. Finally, in cases where markup is used to present data visually—such as a **div** element styled to appear as a bar in a bar chart—it's practical to use JavaScript to generate an inline style and apply it to that **div** so its appearance matches the data dimension.

Preserving and enhancing usability and accessibility

Basic pages built with semantic HTML tend to be naturally accessible. Screen readers and other assistive technologies are designed to understand HTML and convey its content to the user; foundation markup will rarely need to be tested in these environments—quite frequently, it just works.

Unfortunately, with enhanced experiences, this rule doesn't usually apply. Even enhancements built with the most descriptive markup possible are likely to run into situations where HTML simply doesn't have elements to describe every feature. A sighted user can easily recognize a custom-styled select menu as the equivalent to a native **select**. By contrast, a screen reader will recognize it only by the elements used to make the control—a standard HTML link, a **div** or two, and an unordered list—which are hardly descriptive of its role in the user interface. Fortunately, ARIA attributes help alleviate this problem—at least for users with modern screen-reader software—which we'll discuss later in this section.

When users recognize a familiar control, they often expect they'll be able to use familiar keyboard conventions—like opening a select menu with the spacebar, navigating through its options with arrow keys, and making a selection by pressing the spacebar again. When creating custom controls, the developer is often responsible for manually implementing behaviors that are native to HTML controls. Building custom controls that are both keyboard accessible and meaningful to screen readers requires additional effort and coding time, and unfortunately is often left to the last minute and implemented sloppily—or left out of the finished product entirely.

This is a major problem, not only for users with disabilities, but also for those who choose to browse the web with, or are limited to, keyboard navigation. Custom controls that lack keyboard shortcut functionality are a step behind their native equivalents, and can frustrate users to the extent that it negates the benefits of the enhancements.

For these reasons, it's important that custom controls replace the native control's functionality, and not only support the spacebar, Enter, and arrow keys, but also Page Up, Page Down, Home, End, and more. These features require additional time and careful attention to develop well and accurately (which is why, when in doubt, we recommend always considering native controls first). But there are definitely cases where custom enhanced controls are worth the effort, and that's why we feel it's crucial to factor in all the accessibility and usability features of the native control into a custom component.

Implementing keyboard access

When developing custom components, it's important to replicate native functionality before extending it with additional features. This is especially critical with keyboard events, because users have preconceived expectations about how they can interact with a familiar control. In this section, we'll discuss the two main areas to consider with keyboard access: tab focus and scripting events.

MANAGING TAB FOCUS

Of all the HTML elements, only a few—including **a**, **input**, **button**, **select**, and **textarea**—can receive native keyboard focus. Focus is handled via the Tab key, and tabbing repeatedly will move focus between eligible elements on the page.

In basic pages, the order in which elements are tabbed through is called the *tab order*, and that order can be controlled with the **tabindex** attribute, which accepts two values: zero to make an element focusable and assign it to the tab order in default source code order; or negative one (**-1**) to remove an element from the tab order entirely. (Though it's technically valid to assign a positive integer to override the default tab order, doing so is not recommended because, when done incorrectly, it can introduce usability issues.)

Managing focus within an enhanced web page requires the use of JavaScript to make a custom control behave like its native counterpart: specifically, it's important to write logic that assigns focus to the control with the Tab key, and once focused, enables the spacebar, Enter, arrow keys, and others to navigate within the control, depending on its intended use. Similarly, pressing the Tab key should move focus away from one control and onto the next.

Some elements within a custom control will sometimes have native focus capabilities that we don't want to replicate. For example, in our custom-styled select menu, we use an unordered list with a set of anchor links (which would natively receive Tab focus) for our options. In that case, we want our anchors to behave like standard select **option** values, which are natively accessed using arrow keys—we can set the **tabindex** of each link (**a**) to **-1** to prevent it from receiving Tab key focus. It's crucial to note that once an element's **tabindex** is set to **-1**, its focus can be managed only programmatically, using JavaScript. (We'll demonstrate in detail how to manage focus with a custom select menu control in Chapter 17, "Select menu.")

SCRIPTING KEYBOARD EVENTS

A number of keyboard events in JavaScript—such as **keydown**, **keyup**, and **keypress**—can be bound to elements. Once a keyboard event is bound, you can use conditional logic to determine which key was pressed, and which actions should occur as a result.

The keyboard events provide a property called **keyCode**, which stores a number corresponding to the key that was pressed to trigger an event. (Keycode number references are freely available online.) The following code demonstrates binding a **keypress** event to an anchor, using jQuery:

```
$('#myAnchor').keypress(function(event){
  if(event.keyCode == 39){
    //the right arrow key was pressed!
  }
}
```

Building on this logic, you can map functionality in a custom component to keyboard equivalents. For example, the previous code example binds a **keypress** event to a link, and executes a script when the Right Arrow key is pressed. This particular code could be useful when adding keyboard support to a tree control, for example, to focus on a tree node and toggle its child elements' visibility with the arrow keys.

Assigning WAI-ARIA attributes

When keyboard support is integrated into a custom control, it's much more accessible to all users. But screen readers must still be properly notified when markup is playing the role of a custom component, and isn't simply there to organize content. To handle this, we use attributes outlined in the W3C WAI-ARIA specification (commonly referred to simply as "ARIA").

In Chapter 3, "Writing meaningful markup," we introduced ARIA and discussed how applying roles to elements in the foundation markup enables a logical set of navigation options for screen-reader users. ARIA attributes can also play an important role in identifying and describing dynamic content in the enhanced experience. For example, a clickable Print button may be built with a standard HTML anchor link; it can be appropriately described as a button by applying an ARIA **role** attribute with the value **button**.

The majority of ARIA attributes and their associated values are intended for use in enhanced experiences, and as such are commonly applied using JavaScript. Like any HTML attribute, ARIA attributes can be set or modified using JavaScript's native **setAttribute** method. The following code demonstrates assigning a role of **button** to an anchor link:

```
document.getElementById('myAnchor').setAttribute('role','button');
```

And jQuery makes the same code significantly shorter:

```
$('#myAnchor').attr('role','button');
```

Testing accessibility

Enhanced experiences often depart from and change native behaviors, so it's critical to test them using assistive technology such as screen readers. Developers need to not only make sure their code is technically compatible with these devices, but also that the page makes sense from the user's perspective.

Some of the most popular screen readers are quite expensive, to the point of being cost-prohibitive for many developers. Luckily, there are many free readers available that are comparable and quite useful for accessibility testing:

▶ The Mac operating system comes with a very robust built-in screen reader called VoiceOver, which can be enabled by launching System Preferences and navigating to the Universal Access section. (There are also a number of other useful features for testing accessibility under Universal Access, like the ability to toggle the screen into grayscale to check for appropriate levels of contrast.)

▶ For Windows users and developers testing on a PC, we recommend downloading and installing the free NVDA screen reader, available at http://nvda-project.org.

◆ Tip

For a great intro on installing and using NVDA, visit www.marcozehe.de/articles/how-to-use-nvda-and-firefox-to-test-your-web-pages-for-accessibility.

▶ JAWS, one of the most popular screen readers on the web, is available as a free 40-minute demo version. This version is slightly inconvenient to use (it requires restarting Windows after 40 minutes of usage), but we still think it's worth it, given the popularity of this commonly used screen reader. (At Filament Group, we install VMWare Fusion on our Macs to run Windows alongside our other applications, so we can test all three screen readers mentioned above.)

In addition to internal testing with screen readers, one other very valuable way to know if a website is accessible is to perform live usability testing with disabled users. The authors of *Just Ask: Integrating Accessibility Throughout Design* maintain a very helpful resource site with helpful tips, guidance, and resources at www.uiaccess.com/accessucd/ut_plan.html.

Maintaining state and preserving the Back button

Ajax applications in particular introduce a unique accessibility problem: as users interact with the page, a disconnect may develop between the content represented on the screen and the page state as shown in the browser's address bar. Ajax calls are not natively tracked in browser history, so changes may not reflect the user's perception of his or her actions.

A good rule of thumb when deciding whether to track page changes in the browser's history is whether a user would likely think that their action moved them to a new "page." For example, if a JavaScript-based tab strip controls enough of the page that it feels like a primary navigation element, each tab click may be worthy of tracking via history, so the user has the option of going back through the history of tab views or bookmarking that page. Tracking may also be appropriate on a search-results page for navigating among sets of results, or for keeping one's place in a set of tabs.

Tracking state in Ajax applications requires JavaScript to update and watch for changes to the URL hash (a segment of the page URL intended for linking to a section of a document by its ID attribute). For example, the following URL would scroll the page to the element with an ID of **content**:

```
http://example.com/#content
```

In the "Taking it further" section of Chapter 9, we review how to build a plugin that manages history within an Ajax application using the URL hash.

* * *

Now that we've reviewed how to apply JavaScript unobtrusively, as well as how to write semantic HTML, and cleanly separate and write effective styles, you have all the core elements of progressive enhancement in hand. Next, we'll show you how to tie it all together using capabilities testing to ensure that you're delivering enhancements to only capable browsers.

chapter six

testing browser capabilities

When a design includes advanced CSS or JavaScript, developing with progressive enhancement—building content and functionality in semantic HTML, and then layering on more complex styles and behavior—is a strong first step to ensure you can provide a usable experience. But simply separating the markup from presentation and behavior doesn't ensure that enhancements are served only to browsers capable of rendering them.

Fortunately, there is a way to eliminate the guesswork: testing browser capabilities. Testing what an individual browser can *actually do* determines with much greater certainty whether it will render page enhancements correctly.

At Filament Group, we consider this to be the most important aspect of developing with progressive enhancement. Our capabilities test checks for both JavaScript and CSS support, and confirms that a range of key features render properly, which allows us to assume that specific required style or behavior dependencies will work as designed. It's been our experience that most complex interfaces and interactive widgets depend on JavaScript and CSS to work together. To that end, we built EnhanceJS, a testing framework that checks capabilities and conditionally applies enhancements, and also adds a fallback option in case the capabilities tests are inaccurate.

In this chapter, we'll review how EnhanceJS is structured and works, explain how to use EnhanceJS in your own projects, and look at how to extend the many customizable levers in EnhanceJS to take more control over the way enhancements are delivered. Finally, we'll discuss how you can take the principles of capabilities testing further by creating your own tests.

EnhanceJS: a capabilities testing framework

EnhanceJS is a lightweight JavaScript framework that runs through a suite of script and style-capabilities tests the first time a person visits a site. If all tests "pass"—that is, if the test confirms that the browser demonstrably supports all features—it appends CSS or script enhancements to the document. If any single test fails, no enhancements are made, and the page is left as is: a fully functioning basic experience.

When the test passes, the script applies enhancements to the page in two ways:

1   It assigns a class named **enhanced** to the **html** element. Any style rules scoped to this class in an attached style sheet will take effect when the class is assigned.

2   If specified, any number of script or style sheet files will be appended to the document **head**.

EnhanceJS then saves the browser's pass or fail result in a cookie to prevent the framework from running through the capabilities tests at every page load. When EnhanceJS runs on subsequent pages, it first checks the cookie and then proceeds by adding enhancements (or not); if no cookie is found, it runs through the suite of tests again.

As a fallback option, the framework script appends a toggle link to the document body for users to manually switch between the basic and enhanced versions of the site. This level of user control is valuable for those occasions when a browser passes the tests and enhancements are applied, but something doesn't work correctly. While we test browser capabilities to prevent this scenario from occurring, there is always a possibility that a user may encounter issues with an enhanced experience (especially given the variety of internet-capable devices today). The ability to toggle the page back to its simpler, fully functional basic experience is a critical feature in our progressive enhancement methodology. It's also a handy feature for any user who prefers to view a simpler, potentially faster version of the site.

The EnhanceJS framework consists of three main parts:

▶   A short script block written to each page that calls the **enhance** function. This function accepts several options, including which JavaScript or CSS files should be appended if capabilities are supported by the browser. When JavaScript is not enabled, this function is simply ignored, and the browser renders the basic version of the page.

▶   The framework script, housed in a separate file (**enhance.js**). This is the brains behind the entire operation: it runs through the suite of capabilities tests and notes which ones pass or fail. When all tests pass, it assigns the **enhanced** class to the **html** element, and, optionally, injects any files that are specified on the page.

► A suite of one or more capabilities tests that is plugged into the framework script. Each test in the suite addresses a single JavaScript method or CSS property; if the feature is supported by the browser, the test returns a **true** value. By default, we've included several tests that cover a representative cross-section of JavaScript and CSS features that can be edited or extended to meet the needs of a particular project.

Capabilities testing provides a mechanism for targeting enhancements only to browsers that can handle them.

Capabilities testing frameworks

Testing browser capabilities is an emerging technique, and we're happy to say that we already know of at least one other library that complements and extends EnhanceJS: Modernizr (http://modernizr.com) provides detailed test cases for many of the features found in HTML5. As the discussion of progressive enhancement and capabilities testing evolves, we plan to keep an eye on new libraries and techniques. Check the book's website (www.filamentgroup.com/dwpe) for links to other useful capabilities testing frameworks as well, as we'll try to update it with more useful resources as we find them.

The mechanics of EnhanceJS: how the tests work

The EnhanceJS framework uses two testing mechanisms to determine browser support: object detection for JavaScript features, and a custom script-based method to test CSS rendering accuracy.

For JavaScript feature support, the well-established method of object detection provides a way to determine whether a browser supports a particular JavaScript object, method, or property, by simply wrapping it in a conditional statement and running it.

For example, **getElementById** is a commonly used method that finds an element in the DOM using its **id** value:

```
var myEl = document.getElementById('myElement');
```

We can test the browser to see if it supports a method like **getElementById** as follows:

```
if (document.getElementById) {
  // this object is supported by the browser
}
```

We use this simple object-detection model to test for JavaScript support in EnhanceJS, testing the following capabilities when **enhance()** is called on a page:

▶ **document.getElementById**—finds elements by their ID

▶ **document.getElementsByTagName**—finds elements by their tag name

▶ **document.createElement**—creates new elements

▶ **xmlHttpRequest**—tests Ajax support (we test for several popular implementations of this object)

▶ **window.resize**—detects adjustments when the window is resized.

▶ **window.print**—triggers the browser's print dialog

We include tests for these objects in the default EnhanceJS test suite because we have found that they represent a good cross-section of the most common actions that need to be supported to successfully access and manipulate elements in the document. (Later in this chapter we'll discuss how to edit this list when configuring EnhanceJS to work in your own projects.)

Testing for CSS support is slightly more complex, for two reasons:

▶ When CSS fails, it fails silently. If a browser understands a CSS property, it will try to render that style, even partially; if it doesn't, it will ignore the property and its attributes without causing an error. While this graceful failure is a benefit of using CSS (it allows us to safely experiment with new CSS properties that may not work everywhere), it also makes CSS support particularly difficult to test.

▶ Even if testing support of CSS properties like we do for JavaScript objects were possible, doing so wouldn't give us an accurate view of how it actually renders, since browser support for CSS spans a wide continuum—from visually accurate and predictable, to slightly off, to extremely buggy. For example, a browser could report that it supports **margin**, but may render margins on actual elements larger or smaller than the values specified in the style sheet.

While there is no simple or reliable way to ask a browser *if* it supports a CSS property and get an answer that will ensure a good experience, we discovered that there is a way to test *how* CSS renders in the page. We developed a number of test scripts that create an HTML element, style and insert it into the document body, and then manually check the various properties to determine whether the browser renders them correctly.

For example, one such test checks a browser's rendering of the CSS box model. The box model states that the actual width of a box (or block-level element) includes the sum of its width, border, and padding CSS properties. In cases where it's not properly supported, it can have a cascading effect that effectively breaks a page layout. EnhanceJS creates a **div**, applies 1 pixel width and 1 pixel left and right padding (2 pixels padding total). It then compares the actual width value against the sum, which should equal 3 pixels if the box model is implemented properly:

```
// function for checking box model support
function boxModelSupported(){
  var newDiv = document.createElement('div');
  newDiv.style.width = '1px';
  newDiv.style.padding = '1px';
  document.body.appendChild(newDiv);
  var divWidth = newDiv.offsetWidth;
  document.body.removeChild(newDiv);
  // compare measured width to expected value (3)
  // the === compares both the type and value
  return divWidth === 3;
}


// check result of function
if (boxModelSupported()){
  //box model is supported
}
else {
  //box model is not supported
}
```

In addition to the box model test, EnhanceJS employs similar functions to test several CSS properties that are known to have spotty support across a wide range of old and new browsers:

▶ **position**—positions elements in the page

▶ **float**—floats elements next to one another

▶ **clear**—clears an element from its floated sibling

▶ **overflow**—controls how overflowed content is rendered

Each method for testing capabilities—JavaScript object detection and testing for CSS rendering accuracy—works well on its own. However, it's our experience that many complex interfaces combine advanced JavaScript and CSS features together rather than applying them individually. For that reason, we package the tests and apply them simultaneously when the page loads, and then used the aggregated results to determine if enhancements may be safely added.

Applying enhancements with EnhanceJS

To run EnhanceJS, the following script references must be present on the page, preferably enclosed within the **head** element to ensure that testing starts immediately (which decreases the likelihood that the page will display before enhancements are appended):

▶ A reference to the enhance.js script file. Download the latest version from http://enhancejs.googlecode.com, copy **enhance.js** into your project's script folder, and append the script reference to the page head, for example:

```
<script type="text/javascript" src="js/enhance.js"></script>
```

▶ A script block listed in the **head** after the file reference that encloses a call to the **enhance** function:

```
<script type="text/javascript">
  enhance();
</script>
```

When a browser passes the test suite, EnhanceJS appends the **enhanced** class to the **html** element, which we can use to scope style rules to layer on style enhancements.

For example, when EnhanceJS passes and confirms that the CSS **float** property is supported, content arranged in a single column in the basic experience could be shifted into a multi-column layout in the enhanced experience.

To do this, prefix any enhanced CSS selectors with **html.enhanced** followed by a trailing space; rules written with this prefix will apply only to elements that are children of an **html** element with a class of **enhanced**.

Styles written without the prefix will apply to both the basic and enhanced experiences:

```
div.contentA,
div.contentB {
  border 1px solid #000;
}
```

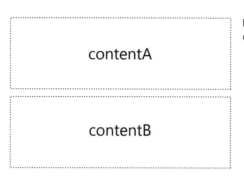

Figure 6-1 With basic styles applied, `divs` are stacked horizontally.

While those with the prefix will apply to the page only after EnhanceJS passes:

```
html.enhanced div.contentA,
html.enhanced div.contentB {
  width: 50%;
  float: left;
}
```

Figure 6-2 When the enhanced class is applied, **divs** float side by side.

For relatively simple sites with a handful of style enhancements, we might put these styles in a basic style sheet, which makes them immediately available without additional server requests. But adding these individual selectors to every enhanced element does additional code weight to the basic experience—there is a breakpoint where the benefit of immediacy can be offset by the drawback of added file size.

For more complex enhancements or large-scale page transformations, we recommend configuring EnhanceJS to append external CSS or JavaScript files to the page. Appending files in this way ensures a faster-loading basic experience for users on less-capable devices, and also may potentially yield bandwidth savings for site hosts since enhancement files are sent only to browsers that can render them.

Preventing a flash of unstyled content (FOUC)

Pages built with progressive enhancement may experience what's known as a flash of un-styled content, or FOUC, where the page loads without its CSS applied before quickly transitioning to its intended styled layout. This effect occurs when CSS is dynamically loaded and applied after a page starts rendering, or when JavaScript manipulates a portion of the page while it's loading, causing the content to redraw or reflow.

Fortunately, EnhanceJS provides a way to hide unstyled content from users until CSS is loaded. EnhanceJS appends a class, **enhanced**, to the **html** element when the test passes, and we can use this class to hide content while it's loading in the enhanced experience. Here's how:

1. In the basic style sheet that's served with the page, hide all body content with a rule scoped to the **enhanced** class:

    ```
    html.enhanced body { visibility: hidden; }
    ```

2. Add a rule to the end of the final style sheet on the page:

    ```
    html.enhanced body { visibility: visible; }
    ```

Because the **enhanced** class is applied to the **html** element immediately upon passing the test, the page remains blank until all styles are loaded.

An alternate, speedier approach to tackling the FOUC is to optimize EnhanceJS by integrating it with server-side scripts, which we discuss later in this chapter.

Configuring EnhanceJS

When we created EnhanceJS, an important goal was to make it flexible so that developers could configure it to work as needed for their site or application. We set up the **enhance** function to accept a set of predefined options in the form of a passed argument in object format, which provides a clean system for specifying a number of key/value pairs (note the curly brackets inside the parenthesis, and the commas after all but the last pair):

```
enhance({
  key1: value1,
  key2: value2,
  key3: value3
});
```

EnhanceJS provides configurable options for:

▶ Loading additional style and script files

▶ Changing the appearance of or disabling the experience toggle link

▶ Throwing an **alert** when a browser fails a test (for testing purposes)

▶ Specifying additional tests of your own

In the next sections, we'll describe in detail how and when to specify these options.

Loading additional style sheets

We frequently design and develop application-style interfaces that require a large number of style enhancements to transform the basic lightly structured HTML into more complex gridded layouts and interactive widgets. We recommend keeping the enhanced styles that will extend style rules written for the basic experience in external style sheets, and using EnhanceJS to append them.

To load an additional style sheet, specify a file path in quotes after the **loadStyles** option:

```
enhance({
  loadStyles: [
      '/css/enhancements.css'
  ]
});
```

The **loadStyles** option accepts an array of values (as noted by the square brackets around the file path), which means you may specify more than one style sheet. Each style sheet must be listed in its own set of quotes, with a comma separating multiples:

```
enhance({
  loadStyles: [
      'css/enhancements.css',
      'css/enhancements2.css',
      'css/enhancements3.css'
  ]
});
```

◆ Tip

Be careful to not *place a comma after the last style sheet in an array; doing so will cause a JavaScript error.*

When EnhanceJS passes, it creates a link element with the specified file path for each specified style sheet, and then appends it to the document head in the order listed:

```
<head>
<meta http-equiv="content-type" content="text/html;charset=UTF-8">
  <title>Custom input</title>
  <link href="css/basic.css" type="text/css" rel="stylesheet">
  <script type="text/javascript" src="js/enhance.js"></script>
  <script type="text/javascript">
  // Run capabilities test
  enhance({
      loadStyles: [
          'css/enhancements.css',
          'css/enhancements2.css',
          'css/enhancements3.css'
      ]
  });
  </script>
  <link href="css/enhancements.css" rel="stylesheet" type="text/css">
  <link href="css/enhancements2.css" rel="stylesheet" type="text/css">
  <link href="css/enhancements3.css" rel="stylesheet" type="text/css">
</head>
```

SPECIFYING STYLE SHEET ATTRIBUTES

Style sheet references may be qualified with a number of attributes that assign additional meaning to the style sheet. Commonly used attributes include:

▶ **title**, which provides a short description of the style sheet and is also a required attribute when specifying alternate or preferred status

▶ **media**, which targets the styles for a particular media format, like print, screen (as in computer screen), or handheld

▶ **rel**, which identifies the relationship of the file specified to the page; the default value is **stylesheet**, but it's also possible to assign alternate status to a style sheet by specifying **alternate stylesheet**.

■ Note

For a more detailed discussion of best practices for assigning style sheet attributes, review Chapter 4 on CSS.

To accommodate specific attributes, the **loadStyles** option also accepts style sheet references in JavaScript object notation, which means that the file path and any additional attributes are specified as comma-separated key/value pairs within curly brackets.

For example, to append a print style sheet to the enhanced version of the page, reference the print style sheet by providing the **href** property with the file path, followed by a **media** property with a value of **print**):

```
enhance({
  loadStyles: [
      'css/enhancements.css',
      { href:'css/enhanced-print.css', media: 'print' }
  ]
});
```

APPLYING CONDITIONAL STYLE SHEETS FOR INTERNET EXPLORER

There are CSS rendering bugs unique to Internet Explorer. To accommodate them, Microsoft introduced conditional comment tags that allow developers to create styles and target them to specific (or all) versions of Internet Explorer only.

We preserved this ability to target style sheets to Internet Explorer in EnhanceJS by providing a property called **iecondition**, which may be passed into the **enhance** function along with a specific version number, or the value **all**, to direct the associated style sheet to all versions of the browser. Notation in the script reference is very similar to how you'd specify a style sheet attribute, except that individual version numbers aren't listed in quotes:

```
enhance({
  loadStyles: [
      'css/enhancements.css',
      { href:'css/ie-fixes.css', iecondition: 'all' },
      { href:'css/ie-6-fixes.css', iecondition: 6 }
  ]
});
```

Loading additional scripts

JavaScript files may be specified and appended to the page when EnhanceJS passes, in much the same way CSS files are appended. Just use the **loadScripts** option, and write an array of one or more comma-separated file paths in quotes:

```
enhance({
  loadScripts: [
      'js/jquery.js',
      'js/enhancements.js'
  ]
});
```

EnhanceJS will load script files in the order specified, so it's important to list any script dependencies first. For example, when referencing a script library, like jQuery or YUI, be sure to list it first, so that EnhanceJS loads it ahead of any custom scripts that rely on the library to work.

When no dependencies between script files exist, you can speed up the loading process by setting an option called **queueLoading** to **false**, which disables the default queuing, or sequential loading, of JavaScript files and allows multiple scripts to load simultaneously (as allowed by the browser).

Customizing the experience toggle link

By default, EnhanceJS appends a link to the bottom of the page that allows users to manually switch between the basic and enhanced experience. It assigns a class to the link—by default, named **enhanced_toggleResult**—that makes it possible to style with CSS, or to manipulate with additional JavaScript. Since this class name is consistent in both the basic and enhanced experiences, its appearance can be styled in both by adding the following style rule to your style sheets:

```
.enhanced_toggleResult { /* CSS to style the toggle link goes here */ }
```

EnhanceJS injects the toggle link at the end of the **body** element, but it's possible to move the link to another location on the page by writing and including a short script. For example, the following script uses the jQuery syntax to find the toggle link and re-append it to another element on the page (in this case, to a **div** element with an **id** of **myFooter**:

```
$('.enhanced_toggleResult').appendTo('div#myFooter');
```

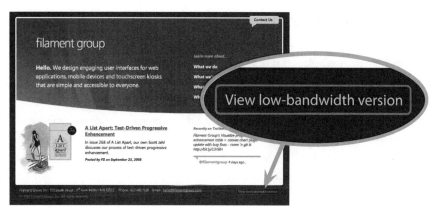

The toggle link text—the text that users see and click on the page—can also be adjusted. By default, links in the basic and enhanced versions of the page read "View high-bandwidth version" and "View low-bandwidth version," respectively. To override this wording, pass in custom text with the **forceFailText** and **forceFailText** options:

```
enhance({
  // shown in the enhanced experience:
  forceFailText: "View mobile site",
  // shown in the basic:
  forcePassText: "View enhanced site"
});
```

DISABLING THE TOGGLE LINK

The toggle link serves an important purpose in providing a way for users to opt out of an experience when it's not working for them, and can also be useful for users who may prefer to override EnhanceJS's result. In the interest of helping users, we would never recommend deleting it outright. However, if you'd rather use another method for toggling between the basic and enhanced experiences, it's possible to hide EnhanceJS's default toggle link to avoid redundant elements on the page.

To prevent EnhanceJS from inserting the link, set the **appendToggleLink** option to **false** when configuring the **enhance** function:

```
enhance({
  appendToggleLink: false
});
```

Forcing EnhanceJS to pass or fail

EnhanceJS stores the pass/fail result of the capabilities tests in a cookie for future page loads. It's possible to manipulate this result and force the page to load either the basic or enhanced experiences when, for example, it's a requirement to serve a separate, "low-bandwidth" version of the site to all mobile devices.

EnhanceJS provides helper methods to simplify switching the page rendering from one experience to the other. Use these methods with caution—and only when necessary—as they bypass the capabilities tests:

▶ The **reTest** method simply deletes the cookie and refreshes the page, causing the test suite to re-run as if it had never been run before.

▶ The **forceFail** method sets the cookie value to **fail** and refreshes the page without any enhancements (the basic experience).

▶ The **forcePass** method sets the cookie value to **pass** and refreshes the page with enhancements displayed, whether the browser can render them correctly or not.

To use the helper methods in your own scripts, first store the pass/fail result in a variable. This variable stores a reference to the result of the **enhance** function which can be used to call the EnhanceJS helper methods:

```
//run default test suite
var myTest = enhance();
```

```
//force fail previous test and refresh page
myTest.forceFail();
```

We use this method exactly in the **forceFail** and **forcePass** methods used by the toggle link: EnhanceJS binds a click event to each toggle link that calls the appropriate method, depending on the experience level currently in view.

Extending the EnhanceJS test suite

The default test suite in EnhanceJS checks for a representative cross-section of JavaScript object support and CSS rendering accuracy. However, it's possible that the project you're working on requires technologies that we don't test by default, like Flash or new HTML5 elements like **canvas** or **video**.

We built the EnhanceJS capabilities test suite to be easily customizable and extensible. You can modify the test suite to your needs in a number of ways: utilizing the built-in configuration options in EnhanceJS to replace or append tests in the suite; creating multiple instances of the test to address specific features or capabilities; and enabling the **alertonFailure** option to perform large-scale browser test scenarios.

Modifying the test suite with EnhanceJS options

EnhanceJS provides two options for adding tests: **addTests** and **tests**. New tests passed in with the **addTests** are added to the existing test suite; tests passed in to the **tests** option replace the default test suite entirely.

Both options accept a single value in object notation—i.e., a group of tests or methods contained in a set of curly brackets. Each method represents a single test and should have a meaningful name—e.g., **canvasSupport**—followed by a colon and a normal JavaScript function that must return a **true/false** value in order for EnhanceJS to process the result correctly. Multiple tests may be listed in the set, and if so, should be separated by commas:

```
enhance({
    addTests: {
        canvasSupport: function(){
            return document.createElement('canvas').getContext;
        },
        videoSupport: function(){
            return !!document.createElement('video').play;
        }
    }
});
```

EnhanceJS executes each test in the order listed; if it encounters a value of **false** at any point, it assigns a cookie indicating a fail result and appends the proper toggle link for the basic experience; if all tests deliver a **true** value, the assigns the passing cookie and enhances the page.

Creating new or multiple instances of EnhanceJS

EnhanceJS takes an all-or-nothing approach to capabilities testing: when a single test in the suite fails, testing stops, and EnhanceJS records a fail grade. However, you may want to enhance the page with a feature that could run in a browser successfully even when other tests in the suite fail.

You can create and run multiple instances of EnhanceJS on each page where capabilities must be tested, which makes it possible to:

▶ Test for a single feature (or group of features) separately from the main capabilities test suite.

▶ Modify an existing instance of EnhanceJS that has already been running on a site for some time. EnhanceJS drops a cookie with the pass/fail result that never expires; to ensure that EnhanceJS is "reset" to ignore the cookie and run again when a feature is added to an existing installation, a new copy of the test must be created.

Each instance of EnhanceJS must be associated with a unique name; by default, the name assigned is **enhanced**. To create a new instance of EnhanceJS, call the **enhance** function, but include a new **testName** option with the name value in quotes:

```
enhance({

    testName: 'enhancedCanvas',

    loadScripts: [

        'js/canvas-enhancements.js'

    ]

});
```

When writing the new instance name, keep in mind that EnhanceJS reuses this name a few times throughout the framework for:

▶ The cookie that captures the pass/fail result

▶ A prefix attached to the toggle link (i.e., **enhanced_toggleResult**)

▶ The class name assigned to the **html** element when the tests pass

Also, for each instance of EnhanceJS, a new experience toggle link is appended to the page, which allows users to switch between the basic and enhanced versions of that particular feature; as such, it should be styled or relocated to appear with that feature so that it's not confused with the toggle link for the rest of the page. For example, you might run a separate instance of EnhanceJS to replace a table with a **canvas**-based chart generated from its data; the toggle link for that unique enhancement could be positioned beneath the chart with the text "View tabular data."

Enabling the capabilities test alert for debugging

When developing and adding your own capabilities tests, it's helpful to know which test is causing a particular browser to fail. EnhanceJS provides the **alertOnFailure** option for just this purpose. Set this option to **true**, and the script will fire a JavaScript alert in the event that a test fails:

```
enhance({

  alertOnFailure: true

});
```

Keep in mind that the **alertOnFailure** option should be used only in a testing environment (never on a live website), as it may cause alerts to fire in any browser that fails the tests and interfere with the user experience.

Why EnhanceJS uses `alert()` vs. console logging

For many developers, console logging tools (like Firefox's Firebug plugin) are preferred when debugging scripts for that browser because they're more fully featured and robust. However, not all browsers support console debugging.

We've found that JavaScript's native **alert** method best reveals when and where tests fail across a broad range of browsers, old and new. It fires in almost any JavaScript-enabled browser, and makes it possible to use helpful tools like BrowserShots (http://browsershots.org), which test a page across a wide range of browsers and shows specifically where failed tests occur.

Optimizing EnhanceJS on the server

The EnhanceJS framework script conditionally loads style and script enhancements when the capabilities tests pass; this process can be greatly optimized by using server-side languages like PHP, Ruby, or Python to serve optimized pages based on the browser's stored pass/fail result.

The process works like this: In the page markup, instead of writing a reference to **enhance.js** and the script block that calls the **enhance** function, place a server-side include reference in the page **head** that checks for the EnhanceJS cookie. When a user loads the page in their browser, one of the following things happen:

▶ If no cookie is present—either because the browser has never loaded the page before, or doesn't support cookies—the page is served with all necessary EnhanceJS scripts that perform the capabilities tests and make enhancements, on the client-side.

▶ If a cookie is present with a passing grade, the page is served with enhancements, including the **enhanced** class on the **html** element, references to additional CSS or JavaScript files, and the experience toggle link. The page arrives in the browser ready to go, so no client-side file loading is necessary. In this case, the server-side scripts also provide an optimized way to add enhanced markup to the page that would otherwise be injected with client-side JavaScript when the test passes.

▶ If a cookie is present with a failed grade, the page is served in its basic form, with foundation markup and a basic style sheet, and without any JavaScript. The experience toggle link is also appended in this case, but instead of using JavaScript to toggle the experiences, it points to a server-side script that performs the same function.

■ Note
_____

For more information and example code for server-side configuration of EnhanceJS, visit the EnhanceJS project site at http://enhancejs.googlecode.com.

★ ★ ★

We've outlined all the basic tools and methodology you'll need to apply progressive enhancement to any project, and effectively test capabilities to ensure universal access. In the next section of this book, we'll walk through a dozen step-by-step examples that show how we apply these techniques to build accessible widgets seen in real-world projects.

section two

progressive enhancement in action

chapter seven

building widgets with progressive enhancement

When building web sites and applications with progressive enhancement, it's important to use the x-ray perspective to decide how the basic and enhanced experiences work together, and then follow the best practices for coding the markup, CSS, and JavaScript in an accessible way to provide the best possible experience to the widest range of browsers and devices.

Synthesizing these best practices can be a bit daunting the first time through. So, in this section, we'll walk step-by-step through detailed examples of a dozen commonly used interactive widgets—like a tabs control, slider, data chart, and dialog—and show how to build them according to our progressive enhancement process.

Before we dive into code examples, we'll take a moment to summarize the general coding approach we'll follow for these widgets, provide an overview of which components we cover, and describe the structure you can expect to see in the chapters in this section.

How the widgets are coded

There are several valid ways to markup a page with HTML, CSS, and JavaScript. In the following chapters, we use standard approaches and syntax that are well documented and easy to follow.

For the foundation markup, we use XHTML syntax, finding its disciplined and precise rules—that all element tags are closed and all attributes quoted, for example—make it easier to read and replicate.

We use elements primarily from the latest official HTML specification, HTML 4.01. We consider this "safe" HTML because, as the approved spec since April 1998, it's universally supported across the widest range of mobile and desktop browsers, including the more "creative" browsers that run on gaming systems and household consoles. Equally important, all the elements we use in our examples will continue to be supported by the next HTML specification, HTML5, so this markup is both backward and forward compatible.

At the time of this writing, the HTML5 specification is in draft form. Though not fully approved, we use a number of HTML5 elements and attributes throughout the widget examples that fall into two broad groups:

▶ A few attributes—like the input **type= number** and the **data** prefix—add information that we can use to build a smarter enhanced experience, add greater semantic value to markup overall, and are either safely ignored by browsers that don't understand them or have a built-in fallback HTML4 element. These are safe to use in foundation markup.

▶ A small group of HTML5 features—like the **canvas** and **video** elements, for example—offer robust standards-based functionality, are likely to be included in the official HTML candidate recommendation, and are already being adopted by several contemporary browsers. In the following widget examples, we recommend using many of these features in your projects today, and we'll demonstrate how best to do that.

■ Note

For more information, review the HTML 4.01 specification (www.w3.org/TR/html4), the list of elements specified in HTML 4.01 (www.w3.org/TR/REC-html40/index/elements.html), and the differences between HTML 4.01 and 5 (http://dev.w3.org/html5/html4-differences).

The WAI-ARIA 1.0 specification is also in draft form at the time of this writing, but is well supported in several of the more popular screen-reader software packages. We apply WAI-ARIA accessibility attributes extensively to markup for both the basic and enhanced experiences to help ensure that our code is well understood by assistive technologies and well positioned for future accessibility advances.

All widget examples use style properties specified in the latest CSS specification, CSS 2.1 (www.w3.org/TR/CSS2). When possible, we include newer properties proposed for the next revision, often referred to as CSS3, like **border-radius** for rounded corners or **text-shadow** for a drop shadow effect (www.w3.org/Style/CSS/current-work#CSS3). Currently, many of these properties will render correctly only in a subset of modern browsers, including the latest versions of Firefox, Safari, and Opera. In browsers that don't support them, they are simply ignored, so we can confidently use them for style enhancements, knowing they will cause no harm.

Finally, our script examples are based on the jQuery JavaScript library, an open-source library of helpful JavaScript properties and methods for writing very concise yet power-ful functions. We use jQuery because its selector and method syntax (its conventions for locating and acting upon specific DOM elements) are particularly easy to read, and can quickly convey the logic behind particular scripting actions. Documentation for the jQuery library, including a full reference of accepted selectors and available methods, is maintained at jquery.com. (Full disclosure: Filament Group actively contributes to the jQuery UI widget library and, collectively, belongs to the jQuery leadership team.)

Navigating the widget chapters

Each chapter in this section of the book covers a specific widget example and, when pos-sible, reviews common variations of that component. The widget chapters are organized into two groups by their primary purpose:

▶ The first six chapters present *content organization widgets*, which arrange informa-tion on the page so that it can be selectively shown/hidden (collapsible content, tabs, tooltip, dialog, tree), or displayed as a data visualization (charts).

▶ The second six chapters feature *data input and submission widgets* that provide con-venient, and often more efficient, ways to collect user input (buttons, custom check boxes and radio buttons, slider, list builder, select menu, custom file input).

Within each chapter, we follow a general format: review the widget's target design with an x-ray perspective and map functional pieces to standard HTML elements, and then write foundation markup, apply safe styles, and layer on style and script enhancements.

When constructing each widget, we follow a few key principles to ensure that both the basic and enhanced experiences deliver the appropriate functionality and are universally accessible to those on screen readers, mobile devices, and desktop browsers alike:

▶ We always start with semantic HTML for the foundation markup and logically define valid attributes. When the target design allows, we'll use this markup for both the basic experience and as the starting point for any style or script enhancements, and when possible, we'll also use it as a content source to help configure an enhanced widget.

▶ To ensure that every enhanced experience is as fully accessible as the native markup on which it's based, we build in ARIA attributes, keyboard access, and any other expected behaviors based on existing precedents (similar form controls, desktop conventions, or WCAG guidelines), and we recommend thorough testing with screen readers like VoiceOver, NVDA, WindowEyes, and JAWS.

For data input and submission widgets, specifically, we're careful to always start with a functional HTML form control to ensure that, in the absence of any CSS or JavaScript enhancements, the component will function as needed and be accessible to all users on any device. We add the fewest enhancements necessary to make the element look and act like a richly styled control, without altering how the user interacts with it—for example, in Chapter 15, we show how to customize checkbox and radio button elements using standard **input** and **label** elements along with CSS and minimal JavaScript.

When it's not possible to enhance a standard form control, we make sure that the enhanced component (whether it works in tandem with the original form element, or replaces it entirely in the user experience) always maintains a continuous connection to the native input for data submission. We do this by scripting a "proxy" connection—any time that either the basic native form control or the enhanced custom widget changes a data value, this script captures user input and updates the other component to keep them continuously in sync. To ensure the simplest and cleanest integration with back-end server logic, we always keep the original native form element in the markup to submit form data.

When running script enhancements that manipulate elements on the page, we do so as soon as the markup is ready, so the enhanced experience appears in a seamless way, and to prevent errors associated with running scripts before the elements are present. To do this, we use jQuery's **ready** method. When not otherwise specified, assume that any DOM-related code presented in our widget chapters is called within this **ready** method. (We reviewed the **ready** method in detail in Chapter 5, "Scripting enhancements and interactivity.")

Example code for download

For every widget in the following twelve chapters, we've developed markup, styles, and plugin scripts—for experimentation and to include in your projects. At the end of each chapter, we provide specific instructions or tips for how to download and use a full-featured version of the code described in the widget example. All code that accompanies the book is available at www.filamentgroup.com/dwpe.

All code and plugins are provided as open source and released under the MIT open source license for both commercial and non-commercial use (www.opensource.org/licenses/mit-license.php).

chapter eight

collapsible content

With the ever-growing complexity of websites and web applications, designers often choose to selectively hide and show content on the screen, either by progressively revealing content based on user actions, or by providing content in collapsible blocks that users can selectively toggle on and off.

Content blocks that let users selectively toggle their display have a myriad of common design forms and even more names—*collapsibles*, *spin-downs*, *toggle panels*, *twisties*, and *content disclosures*, to name just a few. There's a wide range of scenarios where collapsible content is useful:

▶ For detailed information that isn't essential to see at all times or for all users, but may be helpful in select cases, such as documentation describing a technical issue

▶ For optional fields in a form, like user preference settings for a registration form, or the gift-wrap options in an ecommerce checkout workflow

▶ For tool panes or grouped palette panels in desktop-style web applications, where the user can choose which elements should be collapsed or expanded to optimize screen real estate

When content is presented inside a collapsible widget, it's a common best practice to display a visual indicator such as an arrow or plus/minus icon along with a clickable label or other element to let users know there's additional content available.

It's also important to ensure that selectively hidden content remains accessible to screen readers by adding appropriate ARIA attributes, supporting keyboard access, and using the optimal CSS properties to properly manage visibility. In this chapter, we'll discuss how to build collapsible content in an accessible way.

X-ray perspective

Let's consider a common case where collapsible content is used: a feedback message for a technical error. In our photo manager site, when a user has completed uploading a batch of photos, a feedback panel may appear to summarize the total number of issues, and provide details about specific upload issues, and in a simple and compact format:

Figure 8-1 Target design with details panel collapsed

For users interested in knowing which photos have issues and what specific problem occurred, we'll provide a Details heading that, when clicked, will expand a panel to show the full list of photo issues. To indicate that the Details heading will reveal more content, a small arrow is placed to the left; when the panel expands, the arrow orientation points downward.

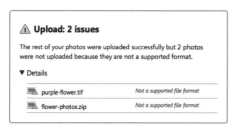

Figure 8-2 Target design with details panel expanded

Looking at the collapsible details panel with our x-ray perspective, we note that the detail content provided in the panel may be necessary to help the user in the basic experience understand what to do next. For that reason, we need to ensure that it is included in its entirety in the foundation markup. In the enhanced experience, we'll use JavaScript and CSS to hide the contents by default, and add the arrow icons and click behavior to expand or collapse the content when users click on the Details heading.

There's one crucial point to consider for the foundation markup: the Details heading acts as a title for the collapsible component, so it should be marked up as a heading element (**h2**) to take advantage of the semantics that headings afford.

Beyond that, the content that sits within the collapsible pane can be formatted with any semantic HTML. In this case, each line contains only two items of data—the filename (we'll use a background image for the icon) and the issue description—and the formatting is quite simple, so we can use an unordered list to keep the markup very lightweight. By wrapping the issue description in an emphasis tag (**em**), we can use CSS to float it right to look like our design. (If our details data included any additional data fields, or would benefit from explanatory headers, we would most likely mark it up as a table.)

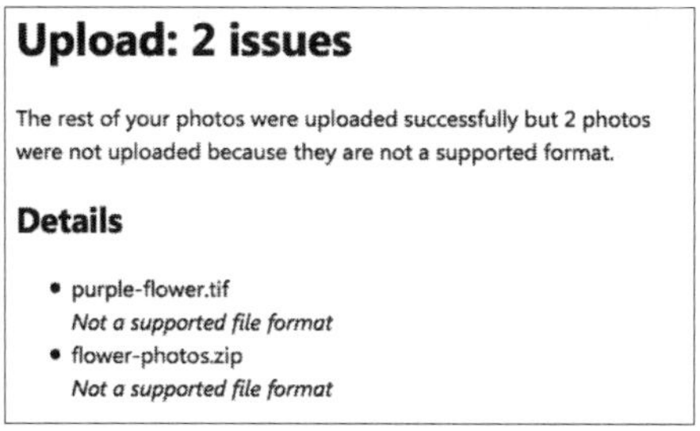

Figure 8-3 The basic experience displays all collapsible content so it's accessible.

A couple of important accessibility features must be factored into the enhanced markup and script to ensure that it follows best practice norms for screen-reader users.

People using screen readers will expect that expanded content will be read, and collapsed content to be skipped, when the page is read aloud. To prevent collapsed content from being read, we hide it using **display: none** in the enhanced CSS, and mark it with **aria-hidden="true"** in the DOM.

Hiding the collapsed content this way is fine, *as long as* screen-reader users are informed that it's there, and are provided with a way to access it. The enhancement script will make the few necessary markup modifications to the Details heading:

▶ The heading needs a cue to let users know it contains more content. To provide clear instructions, the script will insert a **span** before the heading's text, detect the current state of the collapsible pane, and append the text "Show " when content is collapsed or "Hide " when it's expanded (note the trailing space in the text, which makes sure the screen reader pauses before reading the heading text). The screen reader will read the more descriptive "Show Details" or "Hide Details" to explain what will happen when the user clicks. These **span** elements will be accessibly hidden off-screen so they're not visible on the page.

▶ The heading must be able to receive keyboard focus. The script will wrap an anchor element (**a**) around the text inside the heading tag, which makes it navigable when the user presses the Tab key.

Now that we have a good sense of how the basic and enhanced experiences will be created, we can move on to writing the foundation markup and styles.

Creating accessible collapsible content

It's a fairly simple process to create collapsible content widgets that are fully accessible in both the basic experience and with screen readers in the enhanced experience.

In the following code walkthrough, we'll focus specifically on the clickable heading and the collapsible portion of our target design:

Figure 8-4 The collapsible portion of the target design

Foundation markup and style

The foundation markup for the collapsible panel is simply a heading followed by an unordered list. Within each list item, the issue description is wrapped in an emphasis tag to differentiate it from the filename:

```
<h2>Details</h2>
<ul>
  <li>purple-flower.tif <em>Not a supported file format</em></li>
  <li>flower-photos.zip <em>Not a supported file format</em></li>
</ul>
```

For the basic style sheet, we'll set the font on the body tag, and style each **em** element to **display: block** to make the issue description sit on a new line:

```
body { font-family: "Segoe UI", Arial, sans-serif; }
ul li em { display: block; }
```

In the basic experience, all content is visible at all times, with no collapsible behavior. With the safe styles applied, it's easy to read and is organized into a clear visual hierarchy:

Details

- purple-flower.tif
  Not a supported file format
- flower-photos.zip
  Not a supported file format

Figure 8-5 Basic experience with safe styles applied

Enhanced markup and style

To style the expanded and collapsed states in the enhanced experience, we'll need to identify the classes that the script will apply to the markup to add style and enable showing and hiding behavior.

The Details heading is assigned a class of **collapsible-heading**, and the content **ul** is assigned a class of **collapsible-content**. These classes will be used to define the appearance of the expanded state—orienting the heading's arrow icon to point down, and making the details content visible on the screen:

```
<h2 class="collapsible-heading">Details</h2>
<ul class="collapsible-content">
  <li>purple-flower.tif <em>Not a supported file format</em></li>
  <li>flower-photos.zip <em>Not a supported file format</em></li>
</ul>
```

When a user clicks the heading to hide detail content, the script adds a class of **collapsible-heading-collapsed** to the heading that swaps the arrow icon to point to the right, and adds a class of **collapsible-content-collapsed** to the list to hide it both onscreen and from most screen readers. The script will also update the **aria-hidden** attribute to match:

```
<h2 class="collapsible-heading collapsible-heading-collapsed">Details</h2>
<ul class="collapsible-content collapsible-content-collapsed" aria-hidden=
"true">
  <li>purple-flower.tif <em>Not a supported file format</em></li>
  <li>flower-photos.zip <em>Not a supported file format</em></li>
</ul>
```

As we discussed in the x-ray section, the heading needs additional markup to make it accessible with keyboard navigation and provide contextual instruction for screen readers.

First, a link with a class of **collapsible-heading-toggle** is wrapped around the heading text so it's accessible to keyboard users. Adding an ARIA role of **button** identifies the element's function in browsers that are aware of the newer, ARIA markup:

```
<h2 class="collapsible-heading">
  <a class="collapsible-heading-toggle" href="#" role="button">Details</a>
</h2>
```

The script will also inject a **span** before the text, with the class of **collapsible-heading-status**, which we will use to provide instructions for screen readers. The script will include logic to deliver the proper span text depending on the collapsible panel's state.

When the content is expanded and the link has focus, the screen reader will read the link text as "Hide Details":

```
<h2 class="collapsible-heading">
  <a class="collapsible-heading-toggle" href="#" role="button">
  <span class="collapsible-heading-status">Hide </span>
  Details</a>
</h2>
```

When collapsed, the link will be read as "Show Details":

```
<h2 class="collapsible-heading collapsible-heading-collapsed">
  <a class="collapsible-heading-toggle" href="#" role="button">
  <span class="collapsible-heading-status">Show </span>
  Details</a>
</h2>
```

With the markup and class names established, we can write enhanced style rules against it that will apply the necessary styles for the widget.

First, we'll set a global font size in the enhanced style sheet that will simplify how we set font sizes for elements within our widget. We'll assign a **font-size** property to the **body** element that "resets" the standard browser default size.

We prefer to use the relative **em** unit to set font sizes so that users can more easily adjust text size to their liking with browser preferences and key commands. The base font size for most browsers is 16 pixels; by setting the body font size to 62.5% of 16 pixels, we effectively "reset" a single **em** unit (**1em**) to 10 pixels:

```
body { font-size: 62.5% }
```

With the base font size set as a percentage, **em** designations will translate to simple multiples—1.5 **em** equals 15px, 2.2 **em** is 22px, and so on—which greatly reduces our need to calculate each element's text size, and preserves scalability for users who change their default size or use keyboard commands like Ctrl-plus or Ctrl-minus to resize on the fly.

A tip of the hat

This percentage-based font-size solution was inspired by the work of Richard Rutter, whose May 2004 blog post, "How to size text using ems" (www.clagnut.com/blog/348), laid out the principles, code examples, and a very helpful explanation of how to accommodate multiplier effects when em units are nested in the page.

Next, we'll write style rules for the classes, without specifically referencing the elements to which they are applied. This generic approach allows our collapsible behavior to work properly on different combinations of HTML elements, such as an **h3** followed by a **p**.

The **collapsible-heading** needs 15 pixels of left padding to make space for the arrow background image:

```css
.collapsible-heading {
    padding-left: 15px;
    background: url(../images/icon-triangle.png) 0 6px no-repeat;
}
```

The arrow background image is a sprite containing both the expanded (down-facing) and collapsed (right-facing) states. When the collapsed class is present, the background position shifts to display the right-facing arrow:

```css
.collapsible-heading-collapsed {
    background-position: 0 -84px;
}
```

We want our header to match our target design, which means we don't want the **h2** to inherit the toggle link's default underline, so we'll remove it:

```css
.collapsible-heading-toggle {
    text-decoration: none;
}
```

(This is optional; if you *do* want the header of a collapsible container to retain the native underline to look like a link, simply skip this step.)

When the unordered list content has the collapsed state class, we set the **display** property to **none** to hide it both on the screen and for screen readers:

```
.collapsible-content-collapsed {
  display: none;
}
```

To keep the **span** before the heading ("Hide" or "Show") in place to be read by screen readers but hidden on screen, we position it far off-screen:

```
.collapsible-heading-status {
  position: absolute;
  left: -99999px;
}
```

Finally, we'll apply formatting and style to the collapsible widget content to make it appear closer to our target design. This portion of the visual design is tied to specific elements (**h2**, **ul**), so we'll specify them in our selectors:

```
h2.collapsible-heading {
  font-size: 1.5em;
  font-weight: normal;
}


h2.collapsible-heading .collapsible-heading-toggle {
  color: #333;
}


ul.collapsible-content {
  border-top: 1px solid #aaa;
  padding-left: 0;
  margin-left: 16px;
}


ul.collapsible-content li {
  line-height: 1;
```

```
  font-size: 1.3em;

  color: #000;

  border-bottom: 1px solid #aaa;

  padding: .5em 0;

  list-style: inside url(../images/icon-file-warning.png);
}


ul.collapsible-content li em {

  color: #666;

  font-style: italic;

  float: right;

  margin-right: 40px;

  font-size: .9em;
}
```

We now have the foundation markup structure and styles for the fully accessible expanded and collapsed states of our widget.

Figure 8-6 Collapsed (top) and expanded (bottom) states of the widget

Collapsible enhancement script

The enhancement script will transform foundation markup into the enhanced widget by automating the addition of new markup and classes, and attaching the click behavior to the heading to toggle the state classes.

GENERATING THE ENHANCED MARKUP

First, we'll create variable references to our heading and content elements so we can manipulate them with the script:

```
//find the h2 using jQuery
var collapsibleHeading = $('h2');
```

```
//jQuery's next() method finds the next sibling element
var collapsibleContent = collapsibleHeading.next();
```

For the heading, we'll attach the **collapsible-heading** class, add the status **span** with show/hide text, and wrap the link tag around the heading text:

```
collapsibleHeading
  .addClass('collapsible-heading')
  .prepend('<span class="collapsible-heading-status"></span>')
  .wrapInner('<a href="#"
➥class="collapsible-heading-toggle" role="button"></a>')
```

The content list is assigned the **collapsibleContent** class:

```
collapsibleContent
  .addClass('collapsible-content');
```

APPLYING BEHAVIOR TO THE ENHANCED MARKUP

Next, the script will assign events to the heading to expand and collapse the content. We'll use custom events here, which will allow us to programmatically trigger expand and collapse behavior from a mouse click on the header.

First, we'll create a custom collapse event that assigns the collapsed classes to the heading, changes the status text to say "Show ", and adds the collapsed class and **aria-hidden** attribute to the content:

```
collapsibleHeading.bind('collapse', function(){
  //in this context, $(this) refers to the heading
  $(this)
      //add collapsed class, making arrow icon point to the right
      .addClass('collapsible-heading-collapsed')
      //change the text of the accessible context span to "Show "
      .find('.collapsible-heading-status').text('Show ');


  collapsibleContent
      //add collapsed class to content container
      .addClass('collapsible-content-collapsed')
```

```
    //set aria-hidden attr to true
    .attr('aria-hidden',true);
});
```

We'll also create a custom event to expand the content, which follows the same general procedure as the collapse in reverse—removing and toggling attributes and changing the text to reflect the expanded state:

```
collapsibleHeading.bind('expand', function(){
  //in this context, $(this) refers to the heading
  $(this)
    //remove collapsed class, making arrow icon point down
    .removeClass('collapsible-heading-collapsed')
    //change the text of the accessible context span to "Hide "
    find('.collapsible-heading-status').text('Hide ');


  collapsibleContent
    //add collapsed class to content container
    .removeClass('collapsible-content-collapsed')
    //set aria-hidden attr to false
    .attr('aria-hidden',false);
});
```

TRIGGERING THE CUSTOM EXPAND/COLLAPSE EVENTS

Now that we've created custom events, we just need to trigger them at the appropriate times. The enhancement script will trigger the collapse event immediately at page load, to automatically collapse the content by default:

```
collapsibleHeading.trigger('collapse');
```

We'll also write logic to trigger the appropriate event when the user clicks the heading (expand if the content is collapsed, collapse if the content is expanded). We can do this with a simple if/else statement. When the click occurs, we'll check to see if the collapsed class is present on the heading, and then trigger the appropriate event. We'll finish the click event by returning it **false** to make sure the native link behavior doesn't follow through (if it did, a # character would be appended to the URL, and most browsers would scroll to the top of the page):

```
collapsibleHeading.click(function(){
    //if the heading has a collapsed class, expand it
    if( $(this).is('.collapsible-heading-collapsed') ){
        $(this).trigger('expand');
    }
    //otherwise, collapse it
    else {
        $(this).trigger('collapse');
    }
    //return false to prevent default anchor click
    return false;
});
```

We now have a fully functioning collapsible content widget that is entirely accessible with the keyboard and for screen readers.

Using the collapsible script

The demo and downloadable code that accompanies this book (available at www.filamentgroup.com/dwpe) includes a script, **jQuery.collapsible.js**, that wraps all of the principles in this chapter in an easy, reusable function you can apply to any element on the page.

To use this script, download and reference the same files listed in the collapsible demo page. To make a heading on your page act as a collapsible widget, simply call the **collapsible** method on it by specifying the jQuery selector:

```
$('h2').collapsible();
```

In this example, the collapsible script will apply the collapsible behavior to every **h2** on the page. There is no need to specify which content block the plugin should expand and collapse, because it assumes that the very next element—the one *immediately* following the markup on which you call the **collapsible** method (the unordered list, in our example)—is the content.

Applying this behavior to every **h2** may be a little too broad for real-world applications, so you could use jQuery's selectors to find collapsible elements within a tighter scope, perhaps with an ID or class attribute, or a descendent selector like the following (which would apply collapsible behavior to all **h2** elements within a specific **div**):

```
$('#main h2').collapsible();
```

* * *

We frequently use the techniques described in this chapter to show and hide content—both visually and for screen readers—in many enhanced experiences; they let us responsively target content and functionality to the appropriate audience.

These basic ideas and principles—for classing, applying keyboard access, adding useful instructional language, and hiding and showing—can be applied to any content on the page. They can be used to build more complex components, or create forms that interactively hide and show form elements based on user selections in an accessible way.

chapter nine

tabs

Tabs neatly organize content into a set of logical sections, and save space in a layout by showing only one section at a time. The tab metaphor is instantly recognizable and intuitive because it mimics the appearance and behavior of models in the physical world, like tabbed manila file folders, or the tabbed sections of an address book.

There are numerous ways to use tabs in a website or application interface, including:

▶ Presenting a compact content module, like a set of most-emailed/popular/discussed stories on a news site or a set of features that cycle like a slideshow

▶ Acting as the local navigation or primary view switcher where each tab swaps out large portions of a page, like edit and preview modes in a publishing application

▶ Visually grouping a set of form elements associated with a radio-button element, like the checkout payment example in Chapter 2 on the x-ray perspective

The primary function of a tab set is to selectively hide and show content visually; it's important to ensure that each block of content is hidden in a way that is still accessible to screen readers. To further improve accessibility, it's essential to implement ARIA attributes, and add scripting to ensure that screen-reader users can both navigate and select tabs with the keyboard.

In this chapter, we'll show you how to build a set of tabs so the content is organized and usable in the basic experience, and how to transform the foundation markup into accessible tabs that that will be satisfying and usable for everyone.

X-ray perspective

Let's say we're building a news site with a small block of featured content embedded in the home page that displays tabbed sections for breaking news stories, top sports stories, and the five-day weather forecast.

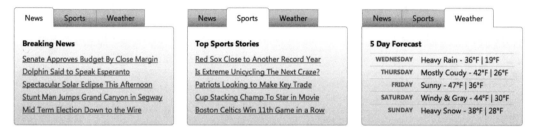

Figure 9-1 Target news design for the enhanced experience

There are two ways we could write the foundation markup for a tab widget that would make sense semantically:

▶ Code the three tab sections as sequential blocks, each with a heading immediately followed by its content, and style the headings as tabs

▶ Create an unordered list of anchor links that map to related blocks of content; when a user clicks a link, the page scrolls to a specific content block

Either markup choice is valid and usable in the basic experience. In the case of our news example, the individual blocks of content include descriptive headers, which we could use as a heading in the tab in the enhanced experience. This approach can work quite well, and is very simple to implement.

But the text in those headers is a little long for the available space dedicated to tabs in our compact feature block. And on a mobile device, the stacked content blocks could run long and push down on the page, meaning the second and third blocks won't be immediately visible and available to those users.

Using a list of anchor links for the tabs offers us the option to use abbreviated names for the three tab sections, and also serves as a compact jump navigation, displaying all options at the very top of the page. Anchor links also provide an added benefit: they let users bookmark a specific content block in the basic experience because the anchor's **href** value, or hash, is automatically added to the browser's address bar (e.g., **index.htm#sports**)—a feature that isn't possible with static heading tagsd. Finally, an anchor link and its associated content don't have to be listed sequentially in the markup; we can tie them together with HTML semantics by matching each link's **href** value (**href="#sports"**) and an ID set on the specific content block (**div id="sports"**).

For these reasons—compactness, easy jump navigation, bookmarking, and flexibility to structure the page as we like—we'll use anchor links for our tabs.

With this markup structure in place, the basic experience is clearly organized and usable in the absence of CSS or JavaScript. This foundation markup structure is also inherently accessible by keyboard and should work with any screen reader, because it uses semantic HTML.

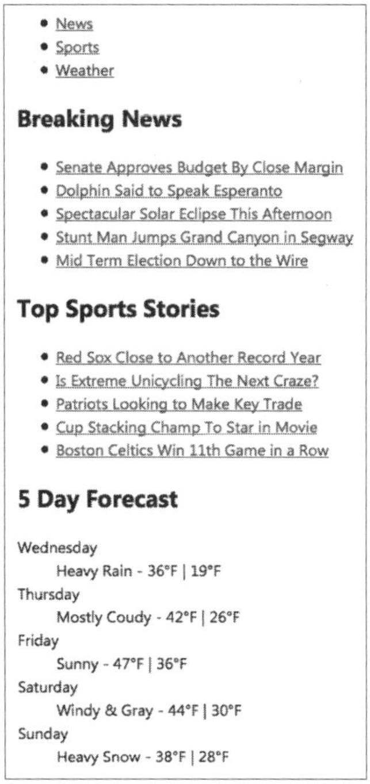

Figure 9-2 Tab content in the basic experience

- News
- Sports
- Weather

Breaking News

- Senate Approves Budget By Close Margin
- Dolphin Said to Speak Esperanto
- Spectacular Solar Eclipse This Afternoon
- Stunt Man Jumps Grand Canyon in Segway
- Mid Term Election Down to the Wire

Top Sports Stories

- Red Sox Close to Another Record Year
- Is Extreme Unicycling The Next Craze?
- Patriots Looking to Make Key Trade
- Cup Stacking Champ To Star in Movie
- Boston Celtics Win 11th Game in a Row

5 Day Forecast

Wednesday
    Heavy Rain - 36°F | 19°F
Thursday
    Mostly Coudy - 42°F | 26°F
Friday
    Sunny - 47°F | 36°F
Saturday
    Windy & Gray - 44°F | 30°F
Sunday
    Heavy Snow - 38°F | 28°F

For browsers capable of rendering the enhanced experience, we'll layer additional styles and behavior to transform this structured content into a tab widget, and add ARIA attributes and keyboard behavior to ensure accessibility for screen readers.

The ARIA specification provides a detailed set of attributes to properly describe the roles and states of the components in a tab widget for screen readers; our enhancement script will apply these to the enhanced markup. ARIA also recommends specific interaction behaviors for keyboard navigation in tab components: specifically, it recommends that the individual links in the tab strip (News, Sports, Weather) behave as a single UI control. When a tab strip receives focus, the arrow keys should toggle back and forth among the tabs. When the user focuses on a tab, pressing the Tab key should jump focus away from the tab strip to the next focusable element on the page—this could be content within the currently open tab if there is a focusable link or form element; or an element outside the tab widget if not. This behavior will need to be scripted, because the Tab key would normally move focus through each link in the tab strip, and the arrow keys would natively scroll the browser window.

We'll also have to make a decision about how to address the URL hash in the enhanced experience. As we mentioned, in the basic experience, bookmarking and Back button support is natively built into the internal anchor links (i.e., those that reference content within the same page)—when the user clicks an anchor link, the page URL (**index.htm**) is automatically updated with the "hash" with the anchor's target (**index.htm#sports**), which can then be bookmarked. Clicking the Back button will return the page to its previous hash and scroll location.

If the tab widget controls a very large portion of the page, users may consider the tab a page-level navigation element, and could expect to bookmark specific tab views or step them by using the Back button. To enable this, additional JavaScript logic must be added to programmatically update the URL hash when a user clicks a tab link and also look for presence of (and changes to) the hash in the URL to show the appropriate tab content to match the current hash value.

In the case of our particular target design, however, the tabbed component is a very small widget embedded in a larger page. It would likely be confusing and inconvenient for interactions within it to influence the browser history and Back button behavior—for example, if a user tabs to the Sports and then the Weather tab sections, they would need to click the Back button three times to go the previous page (**index.htm #weather** > **index.htm #sports** > **index.htm** > previous page). For this reason, we don't want to update the URL hash each time a user clicks on a tab. JavaScript can be used to suppress the anchors' default behavior of updating the hash in URL for small tab widgets like this.

We'll first cover how to create a simple news tab widget—from constructing its foundation markup to adding enhancements—then provide an overview of how to extend a tabs widget to include bookmark and history tracking (Back button) support.

Creating the tabs

To build our news tabs widget, we'll start by writing well-structured foundation markup that starts with a list of anchor links and organizes the content as clearly as possible, and then apply style and script enhancements for capable browsers.

Foundation markup and style

We'll mark up the tabs as a set of anchor links in an unordered list; each link points to a specific content block by referencing its ID. In the basic experience, clicking a link will scroll to the associated content block and update the URL with the appropriate hash (e.g., **index.htm#news**):

```
<ul>
  <li><a href="#news">News</a></li>
  <li><a href="#sports">Sports</a></li>
  <li><a href="#weather">Weather</a></li>
</ul>
```

Below the list, each block of tab content is coded as a **div** with a unique ID that's associated with an anchor link above:

```
<div id="news">...</div>
<div id="sports">...</div>
<div id="weather">...</div>
```

In the first two tabs, News and Sports, we'll use an **h2** heading for the title, followed by an unordered list with story links. In the basic experience, the links will display in a bulleted format that's easy to read:

```
<div id="news">
<h2>Breaking News</h2>
  <ul>
      <li><a href="senate.htm">Senate Approves Budget By Close
      Margin</a></li>

      ...

  </ul>
</div>
```

The Weather content block will also start with an **h2** for the title, and then use a definition list (**dl**) to present each day of the week and its associated forecast. In the basic experience, most browsers will render this markup by default with a clear distinction between the day of the week (**dt**) and forecast (**dd**):

```
<div id="weather">
  <h2>5 Day Forecast</h2>
  <dl>
      <dt>Wednesday</dt>
```

```
        <dd>Heavy Rain - 36&#176;F | 19&#176;F</dd>

        ...

    </dl>

</div>
```

A container **div** with an ID of **featured** is wrapped around the entire tab structure (list of links and content blocks) to describe the content's purpose. The unordered list inside is assigned the ID of **featured-links** and all of the content blocks—for news, sports, and weather—are grouped into a container **div** with the ID **featured-content**. Though we'll use these containers primarily in the enhanced experience to style the tab components, they also help to group and organize content in the basic experience:

```
<div id="featured">

    <ul id="featured-links">

        <li><a href="#news">News</a></li>

        <li><a href="#sports">Sports</a></li>

        <li><a href="#weather">Weather</a></li>

    </ul>

    <div id="featured-content">

        <div id="news">...</div>

        <div id="sports">...</div>

        <div id="weather">...</div>

    </div>

</div>
```

We don't need much CSS to style the basic experience, because we're using very descriptive markup like headings, lists, and anchor links that will format the content in a clear and usable way. To keep things simple, we'll add a single rule to the basic style sheet to set our base font preferences, and we'll leave the remaining styles up to browser defaults:

```
body { font-family: "Segoe UI", Arial, sans-serif; }
```

We now have the foundation markup and safe styles applied to create our basic experience (as seen in Figure 9-2).

Enhanced markup and style

When the tab enhancement script runs, it will add a number of classes and IDs to the markup to apply the tab widget styles and scripting behavior.

We'll assign the class **tabs-nav** to the unordered list of anchor links, and assign a script-generated ID to each list item that is built by taking the anchor ID and prefixing it with **"tab-"**. We'll also assign the class **tab-selected** to the currently selected tab, and later apply style rules to make it appear highlighted and visually connected to the tab's content container.

We'll add the class **tabs-body** to the outer tab content container, and assign each tab content **div** within it a class of **tab-panel**. The currently selected tab panel is also assigned a class of **tabs-panel-selected**, which will be used to toggle the visibility of the tab content:

```
<div id="featured">
  <ul id="featured-links" class="tabs-nav">
      <li class="tab-selected" id="tab-news"><a href="#news">News</a></li>
      <li id="tab-sports"><a href="#sports">Sports</a></li>
      <li id="tab-weather"><a href="#weather">Weather</a></li>
  </ul>
  <div id="featured-content" class="tabs-body">
      <div id="news" class="tabs-panel tabs-panel-selected">
          ...
      </div>
      <div id="sports" class="tabs-panel">
          ...
      </div>
      <div id="weather" class="tabs-panel">
          ...
      </div>
  </div>
</div>
```

For accessibility support in the enhanced experience, we'll add several ARIA and **tabindex** attributes. We'll start by applying the ARIA **role** of **application** to the **body** element to instruct the screen reader to recognize this as an application-style widget, not as standard web content:

```
<body role="application">
```

We'll assign the **role** of **tablist** to the anchor links, and the **role** of **tab** to each list item, to inform screen-reader users that these links make up the clickable tab strip. Each content **div** gets the ARIA **role="tabpanel"** to indicate that it's a content block for a tab, and the **aria-labelledby** attribute to associate it with its tab's **id**. An additional **aria-hidden** attribute set to **false** indicates the currently visible tab panel; we'll set a **true** value for all others. And we'll apply a **tabindex** attribute to each of the tabs, with a value of **0** for the active tab, and **-1** to the others:

```
<div id="featured">

  <ul id="featured-links" role="tablist" class="tabs-nav">

    <li role="tab" class="tabs-selected" id="tab-news">
    <a href="#news" tabindex="0">News</a></li>

    <li role="tab" id="tab-sports"><a href="#sports"
    tabindex="-1">Sports</a></li>

    <li role="tab" id="tab-weather"><a href="#weather"
    tabindex="-1">Weather</a></li>

  </ul>

  <div id="featured-content" class="tabs-body">

    <div id="news" role="tabpanel" aria-labelledby="tab-news"
    aria-hidden="false" class="tabs-panel tabs-panel-selected">

    ...

    </div>

    <div id="sports" role="tabpanel" aria-labelledby="tab-sports"
    aria-hidden="true" class="tabs-panel">

    ...

    </div>

    <div id="weather" role="tabpanel" aria-labelledby="tab-weather"
    aria-hidden="true" class="tabs-panel">

    ...

    </div>

  </div>

</div>
```

With the **tabindex** attributes applied to the anchor links in this way, we can override their native behavior as individual focusable elements, and instead treat them as a single component with one element that can receive focus. As focus shifts between the tabs, we'll use JavaScript to move the value **tabindex="0"** (focusable) to only the currently selected tab, and **tabindex="-1"** to the others. Changing this value dynamically ensures that each time the component receives Tab focus in the page, the focus returns to the active tab. This technique is known as the *roving tab index* technique.

With the markup complete, we can move on to styling the tabs to match our target design. In the enhanced style sheet, we'll start by styling the unordered list for the tab strip by shifting it down by one pixel to overlap the panels, removing the bullets, floating the list items so they sit side by side, and styling the link with a background image and border:

```
.tabs-nav {
  height:2em;
  margin:0;
  padding:0;
  padding-left:1px;
  bottom:-1px;
  list-style:none;
  position:relative;
}
.tabs-nav li {
  float:left;
  margin:0;
  padding:0;
}
.tabs-nav li a {
  float:left;
  padding:.3em 1.4em .4em;
  text-decoration:none;
  font-size:1.4em;
  border:1px solid #aaa;
  border-bottom:0;
  background:#ddd url(../images/bg-tab.png) 50% 50% repeat-x;
```

```
margin-right:-1px;
color:#222;
}
```

Figure 9-3 Tab strip styles
applied to the list of links

Next, we'll write a few CSS rules to change the appearance of the tabs' hover state:

```
.tabs-nav li a:hover {
  background:#eee url(../images/bg-tab-hover.png) 50% 50% repeat-x;
  color:#000;
}
```

Then we'll apply the styles for the selected state. The selected tab has a bottom white border to visually connect it with the tab panel and rounded top corners. We'll also add the CSS3 **border-radius** property to round the top two corners of the selected tab (don't worry, browsers that don't support this property will simply show squared corners). By default, **border-radius** applies to all four corners of an object; to round a specific corner, each corner needs three properties set to accommodate the various browser implementations—for example, to round just the upper right corner, we need to set the standard **border-top-right-radius** property, and two browser-specific **-moz** and **-webkit** versions of this property:

```
.tabs-nav li.tabs-selected a {
  position:relative;
  background:#fff;
  padding-top:.5em;
  margin-top:-.2em;
  border-bottom:1px solid #fff;
  -moz-border-radius-topright:5px;
  -webkit-border-top-right-radius:5px;
  border-top-right-radius:5px;
  -moz-border-radius-topleft:5px;
  -webkit-border-top-left-radius:5px;
  border-top-left-radius:5px;
}
```

```
.tabs-nav li.tabs-selected {
  margin-left:-1px;
}
```

Figure 9-4 Tab interaction states (left to right): selected, hover, and default

The container that groups the tab content panels (**tabs-body**) is set to a fixed width and given a border and background image to add a bit of definition and texture, and all corners are rounded except the top left (which we keep squared off to connect it to the tab above it). Each tab content **div** (**tabs-panel**) is set to **display:none** to hide it by default. When a tab is selected, the script will add the **tabs-panel-selected** class to the associated tab content panel, which sets it to **display: block** and makes it visible:

```
.tabs-body {
  clear:both;
  overflow:auto;
  border:1px solid #aaa;
  width:300px;
  background:#ddd url(../images/bg-tab-body.png) 50% bottom repeat-x;
  -moz-border-radius-topright:5px;
  -webkit-border-top-right-radius:5px;
  border-top-right-radius:5px;
  -moz-border-radius-bottomright:5px;
  -webkit-border-bottom-right-radius:5px;
  border-bottom-right-radius:5px;
  -moz-border-radius-bottomleft:5px;
  -webkit-border-bottom-left-radius:5px;
  border-bottom-left-radius:5px;
}
.tabs-body div.tabs-panel {
  padding:15px;
  overflow:auto;
  display:none;
```

```
  font-size:1.4em;
}
.tabs-body div.tabs-panel-selected {
  display:block;
}
```

Figure 9-5 Completed tab styles for the enhanced experience

Tabs script

With the markup roughed out and styles in place, we can now write the enhancement script that transforms the foundation markup into the tabs widget for browsers that pass the capabilities test.

First, we'll define variables for referencing the important elements in the tabs control, including the outer container, list of anchor links, and container for the tab content. The ID prefix (**tabs-**) that will be used to generate unique IDs and the ARIA application mode are all defined here, up front:

```
//reference to tabs container
var tabs = $('div#featured);


//set app mode
$('body').attr('role','application');


//nav is first ul
var tabsNav = tabs.find('ul:first');
```

```
//body is nav's next sibling
var tabsBody = tabsNav.next();


//prefix for creating the tab's IDs based on the corresponding div's ID
var tabIDprefix = 'tab-';
```

Next, all classes, IDs and ARIA and **tabindex** attributes are added to the foundation markup to match our enhanced markup.

```
//add class, aria to nav
tabsNav
  .addClass('tabs-nav')
  .attr('role','tablist');


//add class to tabs body
tabsBody.addClass('tabs-body');


//find tab panels, add class and aria attributes
tabsBody.find('>div').each(function(){
  $(this)
     .addClass('tabs-panel')
     .attr('role','tabpanel')
     .attr('aria-hidden', true)
     .attr('aria-labelledby', tabIDprefix + $(this).attr('id'));
  });


//set role of each tab
tabsNav.find('li').each(function(){
  $(this)
  .attr('role','tab')
  .attr('id',
  tabIDprefix +$(this).find('a').attr('href').split('#')[1] );
});
```

```
//set tabindex on all tabs to -1
tabsNav.find('a').attr('tabindex','-1');
```

When the user selects a tab, classes are added and removed to highlight the correct tab with the selected state, adjust the **tabindex** values for the tabs, set focus on the selected tab, and show the associated tab content block. We'll need a generic, reusable way to select tabs programmatically, because they can be chosen in a number of ways—with mouse clicks, keyboard events, and when the page first loads:

```
//generic function for selecting a tab
function selectTab(tab){
  //deselect active tab
  tabsNav
      .find('li.tabs-selected')
          .removeClass('tabs-selected')
          .find('a')
              .attr('tabindex','-1');
  //select new tab
  tab
      .attr('tabindex','0')
      .parent()
          .addClass('tabs-selected');
  //deselect active panel
  tabsBody
      .find('div.tabs-panel-selected')
          .attr('aria-hidden',true)
          .removeClass('tabs-panel-selected');

  //select new panel
  $( tab.attr('href') )
      .addClass('tabs-panel-selected')
      .attr('aria-hidden',false);
```

```
//update url hash and focus tab, unless told otherwise
window.location.hash = tab.attr('href').replace('#','');


//direct the focus to the newly selected tab
tab[0].focus();
};
```

With this in place, we can call the **selectTab** function with the tab anchor element we want to select as an argument. Now we're ready to apply the mouse, keyboard, and other events to tie it all together.

First, we'll apply events to the tab links. When the user clicks a tab with a mouse, we'll pass that tab to the generic **selectTab** function. When binding this event, we'll **return false** to prevent the native anchor link behavior (i.e., updating the URL hash, and jumping focus away from the tab link into the content block) from happening:

```
tabsNav.find('a')
  .click(function(){
      selectTab( $(this) );
      return false;
  });
```

The next point of interaction to consider is the keyboard. We'll track any **keydown** events that fire when a tab is focused, and map specific keys to shift focus to another tab—the Left Arrow and Up Arrow keys will select the previous tab, while Right Arrow and Down Arrow select the next tab. The Home and End keys select the first and last tabs, respectively. We'll associate keyboard events by binding logic to specific key codes (for example, 36 is the Home key):

```
tabsNav.find('a')
  .keydown(function(event){
      var currentTab = $(this).parent();
      switch(event.keyCode){
          case 37: // left arrow
          case 38: // up arrow
              if(currentTab.prev().size() > 0){
              selectTab( currentTab.prev().find('a'));
              }
```

```
            break;
        case 39: // right arrow
        case 40: // down arrow
            if(currentTab.next().size() > 0){
            selectTab( currentTab.next().find('a') );
            }
            break;
        case 36: // home key
            selectTab( tabsNav.find('li:first a') );
            break;
        case 35: // end key
            selectTab( tabsNav.find('li:last a') );
            break;
        }
    });
```

Finally, we'll open the first tab panel at page load. We'll do this by passing a reference to the first tab to our **selectTab** function:

```
selectTab( tabsNav.find('a:first') );
```

Taking the tabs further

This chapter has described the steps involved in creating a simple tabs component, but there are additional ways in which the tabs could be modified or extended, depending on the needs of your implementation. These include bookmark and history tracking support, creating an auto-rotating effect, referencing external tab content, and displaying tabs as an accordion widget.

Bookmarking and history (Back button) tracking

When a tab strip is used in the enhanced experience to control larger portions of the screen, users may expect it to act as a navigation component, where the browser's Back button will traverse through each tab click and return them to the previous tab. The ability to bookmark and restore a specific tab view, often referred to as *deep linking*, is a complementary feature that is usually included when supporting history and Back button support.

SUPPORTING BOOKMARKS AND DEEP LINKING

In order to implement deep linking in a tab widget, we'll need to check the URL hash at page load; if it corresponds with the ID of one of our tabs, the script will automatically select and show that tab.

Figure 9-6 Hash in the URL

The URL hash value can be captured in a variable using the JavaScript property, **window.location.hash**, which we'll use to look for a tab with an **href** attribute matching that hash's value. If a tab exists, then we can pass it to our **selectTab** function. If no match is found—either because there is no URL hash present, or there's a hash but it doesn't match any of our tabs—we'll select the first tab in the list as a fallback:

```
//find a tab with an href matching the URL hash
var hashedTab = tabsNav.find('a[href='+ window.location.hash +']');


//if that tab exists, select it
if( hashedTab.size() > 0){
  selectTab(hashedTab);
}


//if it doesn't exist, select the first tab
else {
  selectTab( tabsNav.find('a:first') );
}
```

Now our tabs support the ability to load the correct tab when a hash is specified. Of course, this will only be useful if our tabs update the hash when they are selected. To do that, we'll add a line to the end of our **selectTab** function that updates the URL hash with the tab anchor element's **href** (which corresponds to the **id** of its tab panel):

```
function selectTab(tab){
  tabsNav
      .find('li.tabs-selected')
          .removeClass('tabs-selected')
          .find('a')
              .attr('tabindex','-1');

  tab
      .attr('tabindex','0')
      .parent()
          .addClass('tabs-selected');

  tabsBody
      .find('div.tabs-panel-selected'')
          .attr('aria-hidden',true)
          .removeClass('tabs-panel-selected');

      $( tab.attr('href') )
          .addClass('tabs-panel-selected')
          .attr('aria-hidden',false);

  // Update the hash to the match the selected tab
  window.location.hash = tab.attr('href').replace('#','');

  tab[0].focus();
};
```

By adding this line of code just before directing focus to the tab, we can make sure that after the hash is updated, focus returns to the tab itself (which is necessary for giving context to keyboard events).

Now our tabs report their state to the URL hash, allowing any tab to be bookmarked or emailed. But by implementing this feature, we've introduced some new problems: first, the browser now scrolls to the tab panel whenever the user clicks a tab, and second, we've broken the Back button—it won't navigate users to a previously selected tab!

To fix the scrolling problem, we recommend using JavaScript to modify the **id** attributes of each of the tab panels so that they no longer correspond with the tab anchor's **href** values. This way, when the URL hash changes, there will no longer be an element on the page with an ID matching that hash, and the browser won't scroll. Of course, when these IDs are modified, the tabs script will also need to be modified to look for those new IDs when a tab is clicked. This could be handled by making a simple adjustment to the **selectTab** function, setting it to look for a tab panel that has an **id** equal to the hash value plus whatever predefined prefix you decide.

Fixing the back button however, requires some additional work.

SUPPORTING THE BACK BUTTON

Currently, each time the user selects a tab, the URL changes and the browser stores that change in its history menu. Despite that, the Back button won't lead users back to the last page they visited, or even the last tab. In fact, it seems to do nothing at all, because the browser doesn't automatically refresh to the state associated with the last hash.

When creating components that manipulate the URL hash, we recommend building in logic to update the component whenever the hash changes, whether it's changed with the browser's Back button, Forward button, or history menu. Here are some scenarios where it makes sense to track state in the URL hash:

▶ When the tabs contain a large portion of the page content (because the user may expect that each tab is actually a new page)

▶ When it would be common for users to save (or bookmark) links to a particular tab state

Supporting components that update when the hash changes should be straightforward, but unfortunately, it isn't, because of spotty browser support. As of this writing, only Internet Explorer 8 and Firefox 3.6 support the HTML5 **hashchange** event, which is a clean and reliable way to detect when the URL hash changes; in all other browsers, there's no native support for this event, and therefore no way to know when the hash has changed.

To support other browsers, we can emulate the native **hashchange** event by setting a JavaScript function that checks the URL hash on a time interval and compares it to the value last time it checked. If the value is different, the hash has changed, and the script can call a function to update our tabs based on the new hash:

```
//get current hash
var hash = window.location.hash;

//function to check for hash changes and set tabs when they happen
function checkHash(){
  if(hash != window.location.hash){

      //hash has changed, set tab accordingly
      alert('THE HASH CHANGED!');

      //reset hash var
      hash = window.location.hash;
  }
}
//run checkHash function every 1/2 second
setInterval(checkHash, 500);
```

In Internet Explorer versions 7 and earlier, when a user presses the Back button, the browser will always report to JavaScript the original URL hash value it had at page load, despite the fact that it visibly changes in the address bar, so the hash value is unreliable in these popular browsers. In order to support the Back button in these versions of IE, developers usually inject an **iframe** into the page and use its **src** attribute to track hash changes, since the **iframe**'s hash changes reliably when the Back/Forward buttons are clicked.

The actual scripting involved to achieve this *way*-behind-the-scenes method of supporting the Back button is beyond the scope of this chapter, but several JavaScript libraries exist that serve this purpose. One such library is called jQuery History (available at www.mikage.to/jquery/jquery_history.html). This plugin is fairly simple to use and provides support for both the Back button and bookmarking in a convenient package that handles all the various browser quirks and bugs. The script included with this book incorporates this plugin as an option. We'll cover how to use it in "Using the tabs script" later in this chapter.

Auto-rotating tabs

Another feature commonly seen on the web is auto-rotating tabs, where each panel displays for a length of time before shuffling to the next tab panel. This popular feature is used on the home pages of news websites that rotate through a set of top stories for the day.

The tabs in this chapter could be extended to implement auto-rotate with a minimal amount of work. The script would simply select the initial tab, and then set an interval loop that shuffles to the next tab after five seconds or so, depending on the length of the tab content.

Using jQuery, that loop could look something like this:

```
//start an interval for auto-rotating the tabs.
var tabRotator = setInterval(function(){
  //get the current selected tab
  var currentTabLI = tabsNav.find('li.tabs-selected');


  //get the selected tab's next sibling
  var nextTab = currentTabLI.next();


  //if the sibling exists, select it
  if(nextTab.length){
      selectTab(nextTab.find('a'));
  }
  //if not, we're at the end of the tab strip. Select the first
  else{
      selectTab( tabsNav.find('a:first') );
  }
//re-run this every 5 seconds (5000ms)
}, 5000);
```

This feature could be annoying to users if there's no way to stop rotating the tabs. Stopping the auto-rotation is as simple as clearing the interval that was set, with the statement **clearInterval(tabRotator)**. We recommend running this code as soon as the user clicks, focuses, or presses a key anywhere within the tabs control, such as the following example:

```
tabs.bind('click keydown focus',function(){
  clearInterval(tabRotator);
});
```

The plugin included with this chapter includes this feature as an option. For details, be sure to check out "Using the tabs script" below.

Referencing external tab content

Our example news tab widget could be extended to use Ajax to fetch external content for the panels. This is particularly useful when converting a website's top navigation into a tabs component that allows users to peruse the content of each section without requiring them to refresh the entire page. (This would be a good example of where supporting history tracking might make a lot of sense).

The markup for an Ajax-populated tab widget could be similar to the foundation markup discussed earlier in this chapter, except that the links within the unordered list would each reference external pages, rather than local content anchors (with the caveat that we would generally recommend that the content for at least the active tab be delivered with the page along with those links, so users in the basic experience can access it). When a tab is clicked, the script formulates an Ajax request based on the link's **href** attribute to pull the external content into a tab panel.

For a great example of a jQuery plugin that already supports this behavior, we highly recommend the jQuery UI tabs component. In addition to Ajax support, jQuery UI tabs include the ability to collapse tab panels, and can be styled with the ThemeRoller tool. You can download the tabs plugin at jQueryUI.com/download.

Displaying tabs as an accordion

Due to their differing visual layouts, it may not be obvious that tabs and accordion controls have much in common, but they're nearly identical in behavior. Both allow for toggling the display of content panes, and allow only one pane to be viewed at a time.

Technically, the markup behind each control could be quite similar as well, but the source order may vary depending on the implementation. For example, while the foundation markup presented in this chapter included an unordered list of tabs, followed by all of the tab panels, an accordion's source order might alternate between headers and blocks of content, reflecting the order in which they're presented visually. Source order aside, the accordion's HTML attributes could be identical to the tabs described in this chapter, *including* the ARIA roles and states. In fact, because the accordion is so similar to tabs, the ARIA spec doesn't even include a role for it; using the tabs role(s) is actually the recommended W3C approach for implementing an accordion.

For a good example of an accordion control that follows the principles in this chapter, visit http://test.cita.uiuc.edu/aria/tabpanel/tabpanel2.php.

Using the tabs script

The tabs demo and code that accompanies this book (available at www.filamentgroup.com/dwpe) includes a reusable, easy-to-use plugin, **jQuery.tabs.js**, that packages the script outlined in this chapter for use in your projects.

To use this script in your page, download and reference the files listed in the tabs demo page, and simply call the **tabs** method on the parent container for the tab content. For example, using the foundation markup provided in this chapter, you could simply call the **tabs** method on the **div** with an ID of **featured**:

```
$('#featured).tabs();
```

The tab content markup needs to follow the same structure of the example in this chapter: a parent tab container that holds an unordered list of anchor links followed by a wrapper **div** that contains the set of corresponding tab content panels.

The tabs plugin also has two configurable options for supporting bookmark-able tab URLs and the Back button. To use these features, you'll need to include a reference to the jQuery History plugin script. See the history tab example page to see how to properly reference all the necessary script files.

In our tabs plugin, state-tracking features are disabled by default, but you can enable them with the **trackState** option, which accepts a **true**/**false** value:

```
$('#featured).tabs({
  trackState: true
});
```

With state-tracking enabled, you'll also need to provide a URL to the blank page on your server to be used in history tracking (learn more about this in the jQuery History plugin documentation). The **srcPath** option defaults to **jQuery.history.blank.html** and can be overridden with a path to a blank filename of your choice:

```
$('#tabs').tabs({
  trackState: true,
  srcPath: 'blank.html'
});
```

Our tabs plugin also supports auto-rotation, which is disabled by default, but can be activated by setting the **autoRotate** option to a desired interval in milliseconds:

```
$('#featured).tabs({
  autoRotate: 5000
});
```

* * *

Now that you understand how to create a fully functional and accessible tabs component, you can see just how to structure the content and include key ARIA attributes and keyboard navigation behavior that make it truly usable to everyone. Tab components can be used for small and large content blocks, so considering user expectations of bookmark support and Back button behavior can dramatically improve the user experience. The core techniques and principles we discussed in this chapter for tracking hash states and preserving Back button support are applicable to a wide range of interactive and Ajax-powered widgets.

chapter ten

tooltips

Tooltips are used to present content "on demand" in an interface—typically, secondary content like a simple text description for an icon button, detail for a data point on a chart, or helpful field-level instruction in a form—so that users can gain greater context without having to interrupt what they're reading or doing. Tooltip content generally displays as a small overlay that appears when the user places their cursor over an element.

Most browsers include a standard tooltip feature by default: any content in a **title** attribute assigned to an HTML tag will render as a tooltip when the user hovers the cursor over an element for about a second. However, these standard browser tooltips have a fixed appearance (usually a fixed text size in a yellow box, positioned to the right of the cursor) that can't be changed with CSS. And their content is limited to a string of text—no HTML tags, images, background images, or other formatting can be used to introduce style, structure, or hierarchy. They don't even support line breaks! In some browsers, tooltips don't support wrapping, so all text is displayed in a single line; if the text is long, it may bleed beyond the visible browser window.

There are a number of situations where a more robust tooltip would be useful, including:

▶ Sites with distinctive branded designs that include advanced CSS formatting such as rounded corners, drop shadow, borders, and backgrounds, where the tooltip should reflect that established design

▶ Ecommerce sites that show product images, richly formatted text, or a complex layout—like Netflix's movie tooltips, for example, which contain a photo, a short plot description, and a table listing the director, actors, format, genre, and user rating

▶ Websites that cater to older or younger target audiences, or to users with impaired vision, where it would help to display tooltips with larger text sizes and higher contrast than a native tooltip

In this chapter, we'll explore techniques for creating custom tooltips using progressive enhancement techniques that allow for a wide range of customized appearance and behavior, and incorporate the semantic markup structure required for accessibility. Specifically, we'll discuss how to style and show a simple tooltip based on a **title** attribute's value, and then a more complex tooltip with hierarchical structure based on content within the page or pulled in from an external page via Ajax.

X-ray perspective

For our target tooltip design, we'll consider a case where tooltips are very common: a registration form.

To keep the form's appearance simple and uncluttered, we'll use tooltips to selectively provide all the information a registrant needs for an error-free registration when they hover the cursor over labels and links. Here's our target design (at right):

Two different types of content in this form lend themselves to tooltips:

▶ Brief field-level instructions, like formatting guidelines, or information about how the data is used for each text input

▶ Privacy Policy and Benefits of Registering content, which the user may choose to review before moving on to the next step (see links at the bottom of the form)

Figure 10-1 Form field tooltips in the enhanced experience

In the enhanced experience, instruction for each text input will be placed in tooltips that appear when the user hovers the cursor over the field's label. The design also includes a small "i" icon to the right of each label as a visual indicator that additional information is available; the tooltip will also appear if the user hovers the cursor over that icon. The tooltips will also be read aloud to screen-reader users when they focus on an associated field. The instructions are text-only and don't require any special functionality or behavior; in short, they'll behave just like a standard tooltip that appears when a **title** attribute is specified. So in our foundation markup, we'll simply add a **title** attribute to each **label** element, and then write a short script for the enhanced experience that will parse the contents of each **title** attribute and present it in a custom-styled tooltip—with nicer typography and design.

The Privacy Policy and Benefits of Registering links at the bottom of the form will reveal, respectively, a short privacy policy statement and a longer block of content to explain the benefits of registering. We'll display both of these content blocks as tooltips because they are supplemental information that is not required for filling out or submitting the form.

The privacy policy content is an introductory paragraph followed by a simple bulleted list:

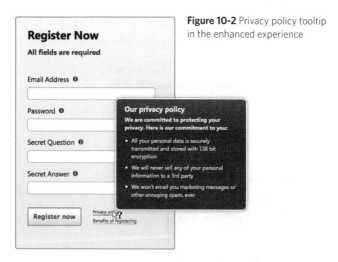

Figure 10-2 Privacy policy tooltip in the enhanced experience

Since this privacy information is both brief and important to communicate to the majority of the audience at the time of registration, in the basic experience we'll keep it in the page in the foundation markup, right below the form:

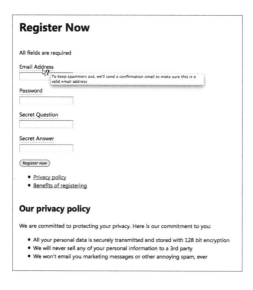

Figure 10-3 Basic experience with privacy policy content displayed below the form

The Privacy Policy link in the basic experience will be an anchor link that scrolls users down to the policy content when clicked; to do that, we'll set the link's **href** attribute to match the privacy content block's ID preceded by a pound sign (**href="#privacy"**). In the enhanced experience, we'll use a script to find the anchor link's **href** attribute and its associated content, and then display that content as a tooltip when a user hovers the cursor over the link.

Last but not least, the Benefits of Registering content consists of a fairly long set of features and benefits along with a graphic image ("Free to Join"):

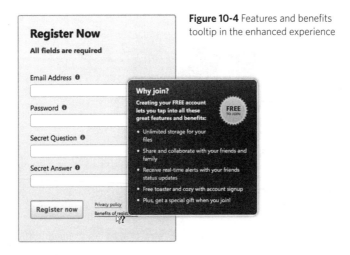

Figure 10-4 Features and benefits tooltip in the enhanced experience

While it's helpful and may be interesting to many people, it's not as essential to complete the form as, say, the privacy information. For that reason, in the basic experience we will place the benefits content in a separate page (**benefits.html**) that the user can access by clicking the Benefits of Registering link. And because we don't want to dead-end our users, we make sure that the separate benefits page links back to the registration form.

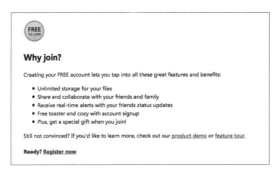

Figure 10-5 Features and benefits content in a separate page

In the enhanced experience, a script will find the link's **href** value (**benefits.html**) and build an Ajax request to pull that page's content into the registration form and display it as a tooltip.

Happily, we can use a great deal of the same markup, styles, and scripts for all three tooltip types. We'll first look at the simple **title**-based tooltip, follow that with a summary of the modifications to make in order to create a tooltip from an anchor link, and then discuss how to create a tooltip from content in an external source.

Creating a tooltip from title content

We'll start with the simplest of our tooltips—the field-level instructional text that appears next to each label in the form.

Foundation markup and style

Each field in the registration form consists of a **label** and **input** pair, with the **label**'s **for** attribute pointing to the input's **id** to properly associate them. The **input** also has a class of **text**, which we can use to apply style rules:

```
<label for="email">Email Address</label>

<input type="text" name="user" id="email" class="text" />
```

We'll add a **title** attribute to each **label** with instructions that explain how to fill out the field correctly, or provide feedback about how the data will be used:

```
<label for="email" title="To keep spammers out, we'll send a confirmation
email to make sure this is a valid email address">Email Address</label>

<input type="text" name="user" id="email" class="text" />
```

In most browsers, the title attribute will display as a simple tooltip when the mouse is placed over the label:

Figure 10-6 Native browser tooltip displayed below label on cursor hover

There are a number of safe styles we can add to our foundation markup in the basic experience. To make the form easier to read (and a bit more attractive), we'll set the global font style:

```
body { font-family: "Segoe UI", Arial, sans-serif; }
```

Next, we'll provide a couple of visual cues to indicate that the label has a tooltip. We'll set the **cursor** style property to **help**, which makes it look like a question mark (?) when the user hovers the cursor over the label; and we'll add a dotted underline to the label text, which is a fairly common web convention to indicate the presence of a tooltip:

```
label { cursor: help; border-bottom: 1px dashed #777; }
```

To make the form easier to scan, we can stack the label over the input by setting it to **display: block,** and add a little top margin:

```
input.text { display: block; margin: .5em 0 0; }
```

Figure 10-7 Foundation markup with safe styles applied

Enhanced markup and style

For our enhanced experience, we'll create styles for both the form and the tooltip content, which we can leverage for all three tooltip types.

To show that a tooltip is available in the form, we'll add a small "i" icon background image to the right of the **label** (instead of the simple underline we use in the basic experience). We'll remove the bottom border style property from each label, specify a background image for the icon, and add right padding to ensure that the text (e.g., "Email Address") doesn't obscure the icon:

```
label {
    font-size:1.5em;
    text-align:left;
    margin-top:.8em;
    margin-bottom: .3em;
    border-bottom: 0;
    display: block;
    float: left;
    background: url(../images/icon-info.png) right 3px no-repeat;
    font-size:1.5em;
    padding-right:20px;
```

```
text-align:left;
}
```

The form fields now look like our target design:

Figure 10-8 Enhanced styles applied to the email form field

For the custom tooltip content in the enhanced experience, we'll need to generate a new snippet of HTML and style it to look like our target tooltip design. The markup will be a simple **div** with a class of **tooltip**:

```
<div class="tooltip">To keep spammers out, we'll send a confirmation email
to make sure this is a valid email address</div>
```

The tooltip **div** is styled with a background image, border and padding, and opacity set to 90% to create a semi-transparent effect (this property won't be recognized in current versions of Internet Explorer, but will cause no harm). We'll position the tooltip absolutely on the page, so that later we can dynamically set the top and left coordinates with the script:

```
.tooltip {
  position:absolute;
  background:#252122 url(../images/bg-tooltip.gif) top repeat-x;
  padding:12px 18px;
  font-size:1.2em;
  line-height:1.4;
  border:2px solid #fff;
  width:250px;
  color:#fff;
  opacity:.9;
}
```

To give this tooltip even more visual polish (without requiring multiple background images), we'll add some vendor-specific and standards-based CSS3 properties: **border-radius** for rounded corners, and **box-shadow** for a drop shadow behind the tooltip. These properties will display in newer versions of Firefox, Safari, and Opera;

in other browsers, the tooltip will display all other style rules, but with squared corners and no shadow:

```
.tooltip {
  position:absolute;
  background:#252122 url(../images/bg-tooltip.gif) top repeat-x;
  padding:12px 18px;
  font-size:1.2em;
  line-height:140%;
  border:2px solid #fff;
  width:250px;
  color:#fff;
  opacity:.9;
  -moz-border-radius: 5px;
  -webkit-border-radius: 5px;
  border-radius: 5px;
  -o-box-shadow: 0 0 5px #aaa;
  -moz-box-shadow: 0 0 5px #aaa;
  -webkit-box-shadow: 0 0 5px #aaa;
  box-shadow: 0 0 5px #aaa;
}
```

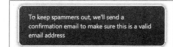

Figure 10-9 Enhanced tooltip markup with styles applied

To show and hide the tooltip, we'll also add a class called **tooltip-hidden** that will set the tooltip's **display** property to **none**, and conditionally toggle it on and off by the script:

```
.tooltip-hidden { display: none; }
```

Enhanced tooltip script

Now that the foundation and enhanced markup and styles are complete, we'll address the enhancement script that creates and displays the tooltips. As with the styles, much of the behavior—including the container definitions and the mouse events to position them properly—can be written once and reused for all three tooltip types.

First, we'll create a few variables that we'll use to generate the enhanced tooltip: the **label** element that's associated with the email text **input**, the value of the label's **title**, and a unique ID for the tooltip **div** to associate the label with the custom tooltip for screen-reader users:

```
var label = $('label[for=email]'); var tooltipContent =
label.attr('title'); var tooltipID = "email-tooltip";
```

Now we can generate the tooltip markup: a new **div** element with an **id** of **email-tooltip** and content drawn from the label's **title** (stored in the variable **tooltipContent**). We'll assign the **tooltip** and **tooltip-hidden** classes so that we can style the **div** with CSS, and make sure it is hidden by default. We will also add an ARIA **role** of **tooltip** to describe its purpose to screen-reader users, and an **aria-hidden** attribute to let screen readers know that it's currently hidden:

```
var tooltip = $('<div class="tooltip tooltip-hidden" role="tooltip"
id="'+ tooltipID +'" aria-hidden="true">'+ tooltipContent +'</div>');
```

Then, we'll append the tooltip to the end of the page body:

```
tooltip.appendTo('body');
```

In order to enable screen readers to recognize the tooltips, we'll add the ARIA **role** of **application** to the **body** element:

```
$('body').attr('role','application');
```

Now that we've generated the tooltip markup, we should remove the **title** attribute from the **label** to prevent the now-duplicative native tooltip from appearing. To make a new custom tooltip that's related to the **label** accessible to screen readers, we'll associate it by assigning an ARIA attribute, **aria-describedby**, set to the same value as the tooltip's **id**:

```
label.removeAttr('title').attr('aria-describedby', tooltipID);
```

Next, we'll make the tooltip show on **mouseover** and hide on **mouseout**. We'll bind a **mouseover** event to the **label** that shows the tooltip on hover by removing the **tooltip-hidden** class, setting its **aria-hidden** attribute to **false**, and positioning the tooltip's coordinates relative to the cursor's location in the page. We can also retrieve information about the **mouseover** event by passing a variable argument (**e**) to the **mouseover** event's callback function—for example, finding the x and y coordinates of the mouse, as we do with the argument shown below as **e.pageY** and **e.pageX**:

```
label.mouseover(function(e){
  tooltip .removeClass('tooltip-hidden')
      .attr('aria-hidden',false)
      .css({
          top: e.pageY - tooltip.outerHeight(),
          left: e.pageX + 20
      });
})
```

We'll bind a **mouseout** event so that when a user moves the cursor off the label, the **tooltip-hidden** class is reapplied, and the **aria-hidden** attribute is set back to **true**:

```
label.mouseout(function(){
  tooltip.addClass('tooltip-hidden')
      .attr('aria-hidden',true);
});
```

There's a final step that's necessary to make the tooltip fully accessible to screen-reader users: we need to make sure the text **input** associated with the **label** has the **aria-describedby** attribute. With this attribute applied, screen-reader users gain access to the additional descriptive information. Depending on the screen reader, the tooltip may be read aloud whenever a screen-reader user focuses on the **input**, or the user may hear the tooltip spoken after pressing a key combination.

```
$('#' + $(this).attr('for')).attr('aria-describedby', tooltipID);
```

Now we have a fully functional enhanced custom tooltip based on the native **title** attribute:

Figure 10-10 Tooltip in the enhanced experience

This **title**-based approach is perfect for simple text-based tooltips, but won't work for content with richer text formatting. The next two methods we discuss will demonstrate how to create enhanced tooltips with structured content, either from a different section of the page or from an external resource.

Creating a tooltip from an anchor link

We often use local anchor links to provide quick navigation from one area of a page to another; to do this, we just set the anchor element's **href** value to the pound sign plus the **id** of the destination element on the page. When the **href** is set up this way, clicking the anchor directs focus to the referred element, and the browser immediately scrolls to that focused element (as page height allows). We can use JavaScript and the link's **href** value to find the relevant content on the page and use it to populate a tooltip in the enhanced experience.

To start, we write the Privacy Policy content into the foundation page markup below the registration form and assign an **id** with the value **privacy**:

```
<div id="privacy">

    <h2>Our privacy policy</h2>

    <p>We are committed to protecting your privacy. Here is our commitment
    to you:</p>

    <ul>

        <li>All your personal data is securely transmitted and stored with
        128 bit encryption</li>

        <li>We will never sell any of your personal information to a 3rd
        party</li>

        <li>We won't email you marketing messages or other annoying spam,
        ever</li>

    </ul>

</div>
```

The related link will act as a standard local anchor in the basic experience, scrolling the user to that section of the page. To do this, we'll set the Privacy Policy link's **href** to reference the privacy content:

```
<a href="#privacy">Privacy policy</a>
```

In the basic experience, this link will scroll the browser window down to the privacy policy content block:

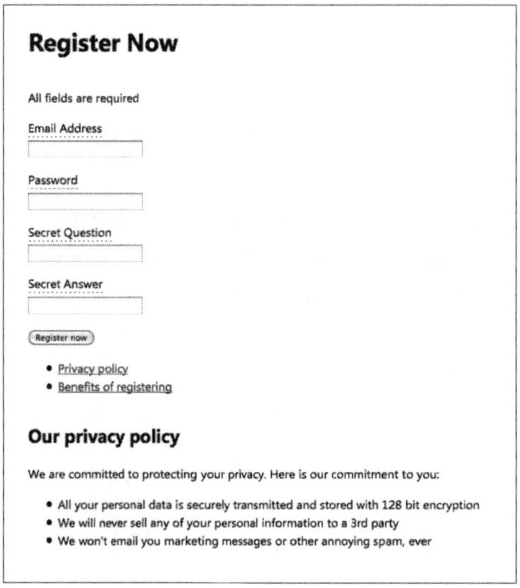

Figure 10-11 Privacy policy content placed below the form in the basic experience

Once the content is in the page and the anchor and its related content block are associated, we can modify the JavaScript from the previous **title**-based tooltip example, and use the link's **href** value to find the relevant content on the page and populate a tooltip. We just need to amend the script to change the way we insert content into the tooltip.

To start, we'll create a new, empty tooltip **div**, using the **tooltipID** variable:

```
var tooltip = $('<div class="tooltip" role="tooltip"
id="'+ tooltipID +'"></div>');
```

Since the **href** of the any local anchor—the pound sign (**#**) plus the value of the **id** attribute—is the same syntax as the selector jQuery needs to find the tooltip content on the page (in this case, **#privacy**), the script can simply reference the entire **href** value to find the tooltip **content:$(this).attr('href')**.

All that's left to do is append the privacy content into the empty tooltip:

```
tooltip.append( $(this).attr('href') );
```

■ Note

When content is appended this way—with either the jQuery append method, as shown, or the standard JavaScript appendChild method—it's actually moved from its original location in the markup to the tooltip container, so no markup "cleanup" is necessary.

To complete the process, we leverage the existing styles and script logic to display the new custom tooltip when the user hovers the cursor over the Privacy Policy link:

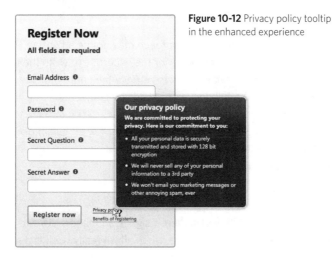

Figure 10-12 Privacy policy tooltip in the enhanced experience

Creating a tooltip from an external source

We've shown how to grab tooltip content from a **title** attribute and leverage the **href** value of a local anchor link. Now we'll review how to get content from a separate linked page.

At the bottom of the registration form is a link to the Benefits of Registering page, benefits.html:

```
<a href="benefits.html">Benefits of registering</a>
```

In the enhanced experience, we'll use Ajax to request this page's content from the server to populate the tooltip. Ideally, the web server would be smart enough to decide whether to send the full HTML page or, if the request is made using Ajax, send only the light-weight snippet of markup needed to populate the tooltip. If we have a smart server that is configured to handle requests differently if they're coming from Ajax, we can utilize jQuery's **load** method to request the benefits page with Ajax and the server will know to return only a subset of the page's content. The **load** method provides an extremely simple interface for loading external content with Ajax and needs only a single argument for the URL to load.

Our enhancement script can grab the URL from the link's **href** and append it to our tooltip **div**:

```
tooltip.load( $(this).attr('href'));
```

There may be cases where the smart server approach may not be an option, either because you don't have full access to the server or the expertise to write the scripting logic. For these situations, you can use Ajax to retrieve the entire Benefits page referenced in the **href**—including the full document **head** and **body**—and write JavaScript logic to parse out the relevant portion of the document and insert it into the tooltip **div**. The **load** method provides a slick way to grab the markup we want by simply specifying the selector (**#content**) of the tooltip content we want inside the full page, and jQuery will insert the relevant snippet into our tooltip:

```
tooltip.load( $(this).attr('href') +' #content');
```

While this JavaScript-only approach works, there's significant bandwidth and processor overhead involved in requesting the entire page, when all we really want is a small portion of it. If possible, the smart server approach will always be the first choice for speed and efficiency in Ajax situations like this.

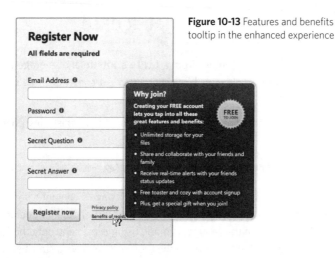

Figure 10-13 Features and benefits tooltip in the enhanced experience

Using the tooltip script

We've created a jQuery plugin, **jQuery.tooltip.js**, that automates the process of creating tooltips and works with a range of content sources (**title**, anchor, or external page). The script and example code is available for download at www.filamentgroup.com/dwpe.

To use the tooltip script, simply find one or many elements in the page using a jQuery selector and call the **tooltip** method on them. For example, to assign tooltip behavior to all links inside a paragraph in a container with an ID of **#content**, use the following reference:

```
$('#content p a').tooltip();
```

From this single method, the script will automatically generate a tooltip and populate it with the appropriate content.

The script is smart enough to look for the three possible content sources we've described in this chapter—**title** attribute, local **href** anchor, and Ajax external resource—and will then populate the tooltip according to the following logic:

1   It first looks to see if a custom HTML5 **data-hrefpreview** attribute is present on the element and, if so, pulls the external content source referenced in that attribute into the tooltip with Ajax. The **data-hrefpreview** attribute is custom to this plugin, and doesn't have any semantic value beyond the context of this script.

2   If the **data-hrefpreview** attribute isn't found, the script will then look for a local **href** reference (**href="#privacy"**) and populate the tooltip with the contents of the ID referenced in the anchor link.

3   If neither of these sources is found, the script will use the **title** attribute to populate the tooltip.

The logic order is structured to cascade: the **data-hrefpreview** attribute takes precedence over the **href** reference, which in turn takes precedence over the **title** attribute. For example, if all three content sources are populated within a link, the script will populate the tooltip using the content referenced in the **data-hrefpreview** attribute:

```
<a href="#privacy" data-hrefpreview="privacy.txt" title="We respect your
privacy but won't tell you specifics">Privacy policy</a>
```

The script degrades gracefully: in cases where **tooltip** is called on an element but none of these sources is populated with content, the script simply won't display a tooltip for the element in question, but will not throw an error.

* * *

By applying progressive enhancement, we were able to build upon native **title** attributes, anchor links, and HTML 5 **data** attributes to turn content stored within the semantic markup of the page into richly formatted and styled tooltips. This approach gives us the design flexibility we need for effective user experiences, without sacrificing the quality of the basic user experience or negatively impacting usability.

chapter eleven

tree control

Tree controls are one of the most popular ways to represent hierarchical information in web interfaces—they provide a means to deliver deeply nested, multi-level content in a compact space, and allow users to selectively expand and collapse nodes to control which parts of the tree structure to display. A tree control is often used as:

▶ A navigation component for websites with deeply nested structures, like ecommerce sites with a wide range and depth of product organization

▶ A data table with rows that can be expanded or collapsed, like in the project management tool Microsoft Project

▶ Navigation for a web application with hierarchical folders, like an email system or RSS reader.

A tree is essentially a series of nested, collapsible containers, where each parent (or branch) node expands to reveal a list of child nodes. Tree designs often indicate nodes that contain child nodes by identifying them with a folder, a plus (+) icon, or an arrow icon to the left of the container node label.

The key factor that distinguishes a tree is its installed application-like interaction norms—specifically, a tree component follows the traditional desktop behavior in which focus moves from one component to the next with the Tab key, and movement within a single component is managed with arrow keys. (This behavior stands in contrast to the standard web interaction of navigating sequentially among individual focusable elements with the Tab key, and reserving arrow key movements for screen scrolling.)

As more complex applications migrate to the web, we see the line between web behavior and traditional desktop behaviors blurring. Power users and screen-reader users are accustomed to navigating trees and expand or collapse nodes with the keyboard—so any custom tree built for the enhanced experience should incorporate standard keyboard navigation conventions for trees.

In this chapter, we'll show how to build a tree control that uses semantic HTML for the basic experience, and then transform it into an interactive tree control that's accessible to screen readers and can be controlled with keyboard commands.

■ Note

Many websites use multi-level hierarchical navigation structures that follow traditional web behavior, where the user can press the Tab key to shift focus from one link to the next. To create this type of hierarchical navigation, consider a series of collapsible content widgets with associated lists of links, which we describe in Chapter 8, "Collapsible content."

X-ray perspective

Our target tree design is a navigation pane in a web-based document-editing tool that lists the user's files:

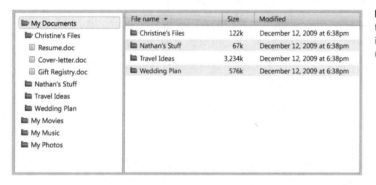

Figure 11-1 Target design for the tree control in a document-editing interface with a navigation tree (left) and a preview pane (right)

The tree component is part of a two-pane interface, and controls the display of data in the companion detail pane to its right. For the purposes of x-ray analysis and the rest of the chapter, we'll focus specifically on the tree component.

The tree nodes fall into two categories: containers for organizing content, represented with folder icons; and read-only or editable files, represented with page icons. To provide visual feedback, each folder icon is closed by default, and changes to an open folder when the node is expanded.

In the enhanced experience, users can select nodes in the tree control by using mouse clicks or keyboard commands—much like a desktop finder window:

▶ Clicking a folder with the mouse expands or collapses it in the tree structure, and displays a preview of the folder's contents in the right pane; clicking a file would open it for view and editing.

▶ Using the Up and Down Arrow keys traverses the tree structure and updates the preview pane with information about each node; for example, focusing on a folder node with an arrow key would update the preview pane with that folder's contents.

▶ Once a folder or file is focused with an arrow key, pressing the spacebar or Enter key expands or collapses the folder, or opens the file; pressing the Right or Left Arrow key could also expand or collapse a folder, respectively.

For the key commands to work properly, logic for the enhanced experience must be scripted so that the tree receives focus at the currently selected node. That way it will behave more like a desktop application, where a user can focus on the tree by tabbing to it (using the Tab key), and then shift focus among individual tree nodes using the arrow keys.

In the basic experience, without JavaScript or advanced CSS, the tree control is presented as a simple list of links:

Figure 11-2 Basic experience for the tree control

Users of the basic experience can also browse the tree with mouse clicks and keyboard controls, but in a slightly different way: without JavaScript, the basic tree follows standard browser behavior. They can click on a file or folder link to open it, or use the Tab (or Shift+Tab) key to traverse the list, and then open a link by pressing the Enter key or spacebar. When the user opens a folder link, the page refreshes with a snapshot of that folder's contents and an abbreviated segment of the tree for quick navigation back to the full list:

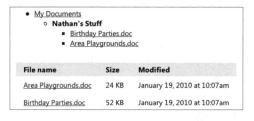

Figure 11-3 Viewing a segment of the tree in the basic experience

From an x-ray perspective, the markup choice for both file and folder links is obvious: the anchor link (**a**), with each pointed to a specific file or a folder snapshot page. To create the multi-level organizational structure, an unordered list provides a good basis, because it can contain child unordered lists to represent additional nodes in the hierarchy.

So we'll code the tree control's foundation markup as an unordered list of links. For the basic experience, we'll apply minimal styles and display the full list of links without any expand/collapse behavior. The page will be fully usable and accessible by keyboard users and screen-reader users, as they'll simply interact with the tree as a standard list of links.

For the enhanced experience, we'll style list items to look like tree nodes by adding appropriate icons, and use JavaScript to hide all but the top-level nodes by default. The script will also apply logic to direct browser focus so that arrow keys can be used to traverse the tree control, and expand and collapse folder nodes when they're clicked.

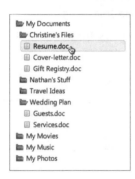

Figure 11-4 Navigation tree in the enhanced experience

We'll assign ARIA attributes to help screen readers in the enhanced experience understand that this is a tree control that behaves like a desktop finder tool, and is not just a collection of links in an unordered list. The enhancement script will also properly assign and manage ARIA attributes as a user interacts with the tree.

Creating the tree control

We'll start by writing foundation markup for the tree control using a set of nested unordered lists to create the proper hierarchy for folders and files. Then we'll apply style enhancements to transform the list into our tree control with feedback icons, and apply mouse and keyboard behavior with JavaScript to browse the tree.

Foundation markup and style

Our foundation markup consists of nested unordered lists (**ul**) that contain links to files and folders stored on the server.

The outermost list has an **id** of **files** and contains four top-level nodes (list items) that we'll use as folders to organize files. Inside each list item, the folder name is linked, which allows the user to see a page in the basic experience with only the files inside that folder:

```
<ul id="files">
  <li><a href="documents/">My Documents</a></li>
  <li><a href="movies/">My Movies</a></li>
  <li><a href="music/">My Music</a></li>
  <li><a href="photos/">My Photos</a></li>
</ul>
```

Within the My Documents folder node, and after the link, we'll insert another unordered list for second-level folders:

```
<ul id="files">
  <li><a href="documents/">My Documents</a>
    <ul>
    <li><a href="documents/Christines_Files/">Christine's Files</a></li>
    <li><a href="documents/Nathans_Stuff/">Nathan's Stuff</a></li>
    <li><a href="documents/Travel_Ideas/">Travel Ideas</a></li>
    <li><a href="documents/Wedding_Plan/">Wedding Plan</a></li>
    </ul>
  </li>
  <li><a href="movies/">My Movies</a></li>
  <li><a href="music/">My Music</a></li>
  <li><a href="photos/">My Photos</a></li>
</ul>
```

We'll fill out the remaining tree levels the same way, by nesting unordered lists inside folder nodes, and linking each node to its folder or file path.

To complete the foundation markup, we'll apply a global font to the basic style sheet:

```
body { font-family: "Segoe UI", Arial, sans-serif; }
```

For all other styles, we'll let each device render the links and nested lists according to its default browser style sheet.

At this stage, we have a perfectly usable navigation system in the basic experience, which takes advantage of nested lists' default indentation styles, and displays the hierarchy of contents in a clear, structured manner.

Figure 11-5 Full navigation tree in the basic experience

Enhanced markup and style

We'll add several attributes to the markup to apply visual styles for each type of node (folder or file) and its state (open or closed, hovered or focused), and assign ARIA attributes to help communicate the role and status of the tree control and its components to screen readers.

To start, we'll add an ARIA **role** attribute with a value of **application** to the **body** element, to allow screen readers to recognize the application controls in our enhanced markup and allow us to take advantage of custom keyboard behavior:

```
<body role="application">
```

We'll apply a **class** of **tree** to the outermost **ul**. To keep the markup simple, we'll style every node link as a file by default; later, the script will identify which nodes link to folders—they contain child lists—and add a class of **tree-parent** to their links to assign the folder icon:

```
<ul id="files" class="tree">
  <li>
    <a class="tree-parent" href="documents/">My Documents</a>
```

```
<ul>
<li><a href="documents/Christines_Files/" >Christine's Files</a>
    <ul>
    <li><a class="tree-parent" href="documents/Christines_Files/
    Resume.doc">Resume.doc</a></li>
```

...

We want screen readers to treat this collection of lists and links like a tree component, not a plain list of links, so we'll add the ARIA attributes that identify it as a tree widget (for a complete reference to the tree roles and states, visit www.w3.org/TR/wai-aria/roles#tree). We'll add the **role** of **tree** to the outermost unordered list, the **role** of **group** to each nested list, and the **role** of **treeitem** to every list item:

```
<ul id="files" class="tree" role="tree">
  <li role="treeitem">
    <a class="tree-parent" href="documents">My Documents</a>
    <ul role="group">
      <li role="treeitem"><a href="documents/Christines_Files/">
      Christine's Files</a>
        <ul role="group">
          <li role="treeitem"><a class="tree-parent" href="documents
          /Christines_Files/Resume.doc">Resume.doc</a></li>
```

...

The **aria-expanded** attribute identifies whether a node is expanded or collapsed; by default, each node is collapsed, so we'll assign this attribute with the value **false**. We'll also add classes to style the collapsed state. At page load, each folder link (**tree-parent**) will have the **class tree-parent-collapsed**, and each nested list will have the **class tree-group-collapsed**; we'll toggle these classes on and off to provide visual feedback and hide and show the nodes.

Markup for a collapsed (hidden) node looks like this:

```
<li role="treeitem" aria-expanded="false">
  <a class="tree-parent-collapsed" href="documents/" tabindex="-1">My
  Documents</a>
  <ul role="group" class="tree-group-collapsed">......</ul>
</li>
```

When expanded, the enhanced script will update the ARIA attribute and class values:

```
<li role="treeitem" aria-expanded="true">
  <a class="tree-parent" href="documents/" tabindex="0">My Documents</a>
  <ul role="group">...</ul>
</li>
```

We'll also add a **tabindex** attribute to each node link in the tree. By default, all links on a page can receive focus by navigating to them with the Tab key; subsequent Tab keypresses shift focus to the next link (or other focusable element). In this case, however, we want to treat the tree as a single component, not as a list of links, so we'll remove each node link from the tab order by assigning a **tabindex** value of **-1**. Then, to ensure that users can tab to and from the tree widget, we'll dynamically assign a **tabindex** of **0** to a single node link in the tree (by default, the first), which brings that node link back into the tab order; as the user browses through the tree using arrow keys, the next focused node link will gain the **tabindex** value of **0**, while the previously focused link reverts to **-1** to once again prevent it from receiving tab focus. (We'll return to the discussion of this technique, called the *roving tab index*, later in this chapter, when we review the enhancement script.)

Next, we'll style the tree by setting font sizes; removing the default list bullets, margin, and padding; and setting an 8-pixel left margin on each list nested inside the tree to indent each level:

```
body {
  font-size: 62.5%;
}
.tree {
  overflow:auto;
  font-size:1.5em;
}
.tree,.tree ul,.tree li {
  list-style:none;
  margin:0;
  padding:0;
}
.tree ul {
  margin-left:8px;
}
```

All node links in the tree are assigned the file-icon background image and styled with enough left padding to ensure that the link text doesn't obscure the background image; the enhancement script will assign the **tree-parent** class specifically to folder nodes, which are assigned the folder-icon background image:

```
.tree li a {
  color:#555;
  padding:.1em 7px .1em 27px;
  display:block;
  text-decoration:none;
  border:1px dashed #fff;
  background:url(../images/icon-file.gif) 5px 50% no-repeat;
}
.tree li a.tree-parent {
  background:url(../images/icon-folder-open.gif) 5px 50% no-repeat;
}
```

When a folder link is closed, it's assigned the **tree-parent-collapsed** class, which changes the background image to a closed folder icon, and the associated child list is set to **display:none** to hide it:

```
.tree li a.tree-parent-collapsed {
  background:url(../images/icon-folder.gif) 5px 50% no-repeat;
}
.tree ul.tree-group-collapsed {
  display:none;
}
```

Figure 11-6 Collapsed (top) and expanded (bottom) states of the folder node

We also want to build in good visual feedback so that mouse and keyboard users know which node is focused; for mouse users in particular, we'll also provide a hover state to identify the node their cursor is over.

Users can focus on a node by clicking it, or by tabbing into the tree control and traversing the list with arrow keys—the clicked or currently selected node is focused, and thereby provides the necessary focus the system needs to understand how to implement subsequent keyboard commands, like the Enter key to open it. For this reason, the focused style has a darker outline and background color than the hover state.

When a user hovers over a node with their cursor, we also provide a lighter hover state for feedback:

```
.tree li a:hover,

.tree li a.tree-parent:hover,

.tree li a:focus,

.tree li a.tree-parent:focus,

.tree li a.tree-item-active {

  color:#000;

  border:1px solid#eee;

  background-color:#fafafa;

  -moz-border-radius:4px;

  -webkit-border-radius:4px;

  border-radius:4px;

}

.tree li a:focus,

.tree li a.tree-parent:focus,

.tree li a.tree-item-active {

  border:1px solid #e2f3fb;

  background-color:#f2fafd;

}
```

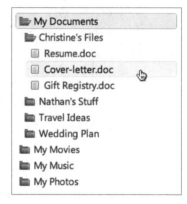

Figure 11-7 The My Documents folder node is focused; Cover-letter.doc displays the hover state.

Enhanced tree script

Our enhancement JavaScript will add the default ARIA **role** and **class** attributes to the foundation markup; create custom events for expanding, collapsing, and traversing up and down the tree; and then trigger these events when a user interacts with the tree using a mouse or keyboard commands.

ASSIGNING ENHANCED TREE ATTRIBUTES

The first step in the script is to reference the unordered list we're enhancing into a tree and store it in a **tree** variable:

```
var tree = $('ul#files');
```

Next, the script will add the appropriate ARIA **role** attributes and state classes, and set the nodes' **tabindex** in the markup:

```
//add role and class of tree
tree.attr({'role': 'tree'}).addClass('tree');


//set first node's tabindex to 0
tree.find('a:eq(0)').attr('tabindex','0');


//set all others to -1
tree.find('a:gt(0)').attr('tabindex','-1');


//add group role and tree-group-collapsed class to all ul's
tree.find('ul').attr('role','group').addClass('tree-group-collapsed');


//add treeitem role to all li children
tree.find('li').attr('role','treeitem');


//find "folder" tree items, collapse them and add tree-parent classes
tree.find('li:has(ul)')
  .attr('aria-expanded', 'false')
  //find that li's immediate child anchor
  .find('>a')
  .addClass('tree-parent tree-parent-collapsed')
```

At this stage, the static attributes on the tree nodes are complete, so we can add user interaction behavior to the script.

APPLYING TREE BEHAVIOR

We'll create custom jQuery events to expand and collapse nodes within the tree, and bind them to the tree itself (the outermost **ul**) to take advantage of JavaScript's native event-delegation behavior. For example, when a user clicks anywhere on the tree, the script will figure out which node was clicked, and then expand or collapse it based on its current state. Binding behavior this way—attaching logic to a single container element—is more efficient, and will perform faster, than binding events to each tree node separately; it would also let us dynamically add nodes, if needed, because each new node would automatically inherit the behavior assigned to the tree.

First we'll create the **expand** event:

```
//bind custom expand event to tree UL
tree.bind('expand',function(event){
  //save reference to the click target link
  var target = $(event.target);


  //remove collapsed class, changing the folder icon
  target.removeClass('tree-parent-collapsed');


  //get the target's sibling UL
  target.next()
      //hide the UL with display:none and remove hidden class
      .hide().removeClass('tree-group-collapsed')


      //slide the UL down to expand it
      .slideDown(150, function(){
          //find the parent LI, set its expanded attribute
          target.parent()
              .attr('aria-expanded', 'true')


          //remove inline style from animation
          $(this).removeAttr('style');
      });
});
```

Now we can expand any folder node by triggering its **expand** event:

```
tree.find('a.tree-parent').trigger('expand');
```

Next, we'll create a **collapse** event, which reverses the actions of the **expand** event:

```
//bind custom collapse event to tree UL
tree.bind('collapse',function(event){
  //save reference to the click target link
  var target = $(event.target);

  //add collapsed class, changing the folder icon
  target.addClass('tree-parent-collapsed');

  //get the target's sibling UL
  target.next()

      //slide the UL up to collapse it
      .slideUp(150, function(){
          //find the parent LI, set its expanded attribute
          target.parent().attr('aria-expanded', 'false');

          //add hidden class to UL and remove inline style
          $(this).addClass('tree-group-collapsed')
              .removeAttr('style');
  });
});
```

And we'll collapse an open tree node by triggering its **collapse** event:

```
tree.find('a.tree-parent').trigger('collapse');
```

With these events at our disposal, we can make the tree expand and collapse in reaction to a mouse click. To be sure that the tree expands or collapses the correct node, we'll check if the clicked element is a link with the class **tree-parent** and whether its parent list item has an **aria-expanded** attribute set to **true** or **false**:

```
//bind click event to the tree
tree.click(function(event){
    //save reference to the target (the element that was clicked)
    var target = $(event.target);

    //check if target is a tree node
    if( target.is('a.tree-parent') ){

        //check if tree node's parent LI is collapsed
        if( target.parent().is('[aria-expanded=false]') ){
            //call expand function on the target
            target.trigger('expand');
        }

        //otherwise, parent must already be expanded
        else{
            //collapse the tree node
            target.trigger('collapse');
        }

        //direct focus to the target node
        target[0].focus();

        //prevent browser from following the link
        return false;
    }
});
```

■ Note

When the user clicks a link within the tree that doesn't have a class of tree-parent—in other words, a file node—we won't take any action. Instead, we'll let the browser handle the click natively and open the selected file.

When the tree is clicked, or when the user tabs to the tree control using the Tab key, a tree node gains focus. Once a node in our tree gains focus, we'll manage the focused state in a few ways:

▶ As the user navigates and moves focus among tree nodes, we'll dynamically move the **0 tabindex** to the focused item, using the roving **tabindex** technique.

▶ We'll use the focused state to identify which node is acted upon when the user presses keys, so that the script will know which node to expand or collapse.

▶ We'll control the order in which nodes gain focus, so that users can traverse up and down the tree structure using the Up and Down Arrow keys.

To start, we'll set the **tabindex** of the focused node to **0** so that it (and the tree widget, by proxy) is accessible with the Tab key:

```
//bind focus event to tree
tree.focus(function(event){
  //set tabindex to -1 on previously focused tree node, if one exists
  //and remove the active class
  tree.find('[tabindex=0]')
      .attr('tabindex','-1')
      .removeClass('tree-item-active');

  //assign 0 tabindex to focused item
  //and add the active class
  $(event.target)
      .attr('tabindex','0')
      .addClass('tree-item-active');
});
```

■ Note

An alternate approach for managing tab focus is to leverage the ARIA attribute called aria-activedescendent, which handles focus for the newest screen readers that understand ARIA. The downside to this approach is that it works only for the newest screen readers, while the roving tabindex technique works for all screen readers and for all keyboard users.

We'll create a **keypress** event to expand and collapse a focused folder node with the Left and Right Arrow keys, and bind it to the tree **ul**. The associated function will check which key was pressed based on the event's **keyCode** property (**37** is Left Arrow, **39** is Right Arrow). When the Left or Right Arrow key is pressed, the script will trigger the **expand** or **collapse** event, respectively, on the focused item:

```
//bind a keydown event handler to tree UL
tree.keydown(function(event){
  //save reference to the focused item
  var target = $(event.target);

  //if key is left arrow and list is collapsed
  if(event.keyCode == 37
      && target.parent().is('[aria-expanded=true]')){
        //trigger the collapse event
        target.trigger('collapse');


        //return false to prevent browser scroll
        return false;
  }


  //if key is right arrow and list is collapsed
  if(event.keyCode == 39
      && target.parent().is('[aria-expanded=false]')){
        //trigger the expand event
        target.trigger('expand');


        //return false to prevent browser scroll
        return false;
  }
});
```

To allow navigation with the Up and Down Arrow keys, we'll bind two more custom events, **traverseUp** and **traverseDown**, which will move the focus up or down in the tree.

When the user navigates up or down the tree, we want the very next visible node to gain focus, regardless of whether it sits within the same hierarchical level of the tree. For example, if the current focus is on "Travel Ideas," each line above in the tree will be successively focused as the user presses the Up Arrow key:

The logic for traversing up must handle a few scenarios: users should be able to traverse between sibling nodes, climb up to parent nodes, and traverse deeper into the tree structure:

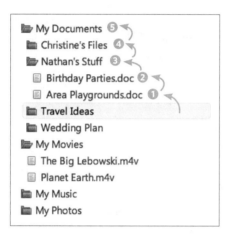

Figure 11-8 Diagram of traversing up the tree structure

```
//bind custom traverseUp event to tree
tree.bind('traverseUp',function(event){


  //save reference to target of event, the focused item in tree
  var target = $(event.target);


  //save reference to target's parent li
  var targetLi = target.parent();


  //check if the target list item has a previous sibling
  if( targetLi.prev().length ){
      //if it does, check if the sibling is expanded
      if( targetLi.prev().is('[aria-expanded=true]') ){
```

```
            //dive in. direct focus to its last visible child
            targetLi.prev()
                .find('li:visible:last a')[0].focus();
        }


        //otherwise, if the previous is collapsed
        else{
            //focus on the previous sibling itself
            targetLi.prev().find('a')[0].focus();
        }
    }
    //otherwise, no previous sibling exists.
    //item in its tree group.
    else {
        // Move up a level and try to focus on a parent node
        targetLi.parents('li:eq(0)').find('a')[0].focus();
    }
});
```

With that, we can trigger the **traverseUp** event when the user presses the Up Arrow key while focused within the tree:

```
//bind a keydown event to the tree UL
tree.keydown(function(event){
    //if the key is the up arrow
    if(event.keyCode == 38){
        //trigger traverseUp on the focused item
        $(event.target).trigger('traverseUp');

        //return false to prevent browser scroll
        return false;
    }
});
```

We'll also create a **traverseDown** event, which is, not surprisingly, essentially the opposite of **traverseUp**. We'll check if the focused element is expanded, and if so, the focus should jump to its first child tree item. If it's not expanded, we'll check if it has a next sibling item to direct focus to. If that condition is **false**, the currently focused item is the last one in its tree group. We'll try to find a parent list item with a next sibling; if we find one, we'll direct focus there.

If none of these conditions is true because the user has traversed to the end of the tree, **traverseDown** simply won't move focus away from the currently focused item.

```
//bind the traverseDown event to the tree UL
tree.bind('traverseDown',function(event){

  //save reference to target of event, the focused item in tree
  var target = $(event.target);


  //save reference to target's parent li
  var targetLi = target.parent();


  //check if the target's parent LI is expanded
  if(targetLi.is('[aria-expanded=true]')){
    //it's expanded. Dive in and focus on the first child
    target.next().find('a')[0].focus();
  }


  //if it's not expanded, see if it has a next sibling
  else if(targetLi.next().length) {
    //focus on that next sibling
    targetLi.next().find('a')[0].focus();
  }


  //if it's not expanded and has no next sibling, it's the
  //end of the that tree group list
  else {
```

```
    //try to find any parent li with a next sibling
    //and direct focus there
    targetLi.parents('li').next().find('a')[0].focus();
  }
});
```

Now we can trigger the **traverseDown** event on a Down Arrow keypress:

```
//bind a keydown event to the tree UL
tree.keydown(function(event){
  //if the key is the down arrow
  if(event.keyCode == 40){
      //trigger traverseDown on the focused item
      $(event.target).trigger('traverseDown');

      //return false to prevent browser scroll
      return false;
  }
});
```

With the enhanced scripting complete, the tree is now fully functional, ARIA-compliant, and keyboard accessible.

Using the tree script

The demo and code that accompanies this book (available at www.filamentgroup.com/dwpe) includes a script, **jQuery.tree.js**, that uses the principles outlined in this chapter in an easy-to-use method.

To use this script in your page, download and reference the files to match those shown in the tree example page, and call the **tree** method on any list element on the page when the DOM is ready. For example, to create a tree control based on the foundation markup in this chapter, find the **ul** element with an **id** of **files**, and call the **tree** method on it:

```
$('#files').tree();
```

You can also call the **tree** method on several multi-level hierarchical lists at once to change them all into tree controls. For example, this will turn any **ul** in the **#content** container into trees:

```
$('#content ul').tree();
```

This plugin is very simple by design, and includes a single option for setting a node (or nodes) open by default. Simply pass in one or more list item selector(s) to the expanded option. For example, to open the first node by default:

```
$('#files').tree({
  expanded: 'li:first'
});
```

Or to expand a list item with an ID of **wedding**:

```
$('#files').tree({
  expanded: '#wedding'
});
```

It's possible to open several nodes by assigning a **class** to several list items and referencing that **class** with the expanded option:

```
$('#files').tree({
  expanded: '.default-expand'
});
```

★ ★ ★

The tree control enhanced widget can be very clearly described by simple HTML semantics in the foundation markup. The advantage of this approach is that the enhanced experience can be built by simply layering additional ARIA attributes, CSS styles, and JavaScript behaviors on top of solid foundation markup—a textbook example of progressive enhancement.

The **tabindex** attribute and keyboard navigation are important features that make the tree efficient for all users and accessible to screen readers. The extra time it takes to write scripting required to support these behaviors is essential, because relying solely on mouse input won't work for everyone, and may even frustrate users who expect the tree to behave like a native OS control.

chapter twelve

charts with html5 canvas

Presenting complex data graphically—as a pie, line, area, or bar chart—is a powerful way to convey information and illuminate patterns and trends that would be much harder to spot poring over large tables of numbers. More and more on the web, we see charts and graphs used to deliver key information, including:

▶ Comparisons of statistical numbers or percentages, like voting or opinion poll results

▶ Tracking simple activity or performance information over time, like the number of users accessing a website, instances of news stories about a topic, or stock share prices

▶ Displays of complex financial or scientific trend data with moving averages, minimum and maximum values visualized to correlations, and other enhanced analyses in visual form

The two most common approaches to presenting visual chart and graph data have been to embed static chart images generated by a web server or to require plugins like Flash, Java, or Silverlight that generate charts within the browser. Unfortunately, neither of these approaches is ideal: static images are a problem because, being simply pictures, they don't contain any actual data values. (The only way to summarize data from "pictures" for users without access to visuals is to populate the **title** attribute, which is difficult to manage for even very simple data sets.) And while plugin-based charting solutions can be made accessible in a subset of desktop browsers, many mobile devices, older browsers, or corporate environments that impose customized browser settings for security reasons may not support the specific plugin version required, leaving users with either a notice to upgrade or a blank block where the chart should be.

In the summer of 2004, the Safari browser development team put another option on the table when they introduced a new HTML element called **canvas**. The **canvas** element provides a native JavaScript drawing API for generating visuals on the front-end. In 2009, the HTML 5 specification added **canvas** as a standard element, which already has broad support in newer versions of Firefox, Safari, Chrome, Opera, and Webkit-powered mobile devices like the iPhone, Android, and Palm Pre. With relatively easy workarounds for Internet Explorer (which we'll discuss in this chapter), **canvas** can be used safely in all popular modern browsers.

The visualization capabilities of the **canvas** element are not limited to charts and graphs—**canvas** can draw any type of image, and even supports animation. However, it's important to note that on its own it is not a fully accessible solution—just like the **image** element, it's a purely visual format, and offers very little means of communicating its content in a way that is accessible to users with disabilities such as blindness, or to non-human data parsers such as search engines.

But **canvas** does have the ability to read structured data (in the form of an HTML **table**) and visually render it to create chart visualizations in the browser client-side—providing a new way to present content that's both visually rich and fully accessible to all users. It provides an enhanced visual representation of the data, without leaving any users in the dark about the information being conveyed.

In this chapter, we'll demonstrate how to use the **canvas** element to generate a line chart from an HTML **table**, highlighting key concepts you'll need to understand in order to use **canvas** effectively. Then, in the "Taking canvas charts further" section at the end of the chapter, we'll discuss some of the more advanced logic required to create several other types of charts—including line, pie, bar, stacked bar, and area charts—with relative ease.

Note

The markup and scripts in the narrative below are representative to illustrate key ideas and principles for properly implementing accessible charting using the canvas element, but as is don't include the full framework required for a working accessible charting implementation. In order to implement a working solution, we recommend that you download the visualize.js plugin at www.filamentgroup.com/dwpe, and then use the guidelines below to customize it as you like.

X-ray perspective

Let's say we have a corporate dashboard that keeps track of employee sales performance data. We'd like to be able to show the sales data as a line chart so users can see how each person is selling in the various product categories, spot trends, and easily compare performance. We'd like the data chart to look something like this:

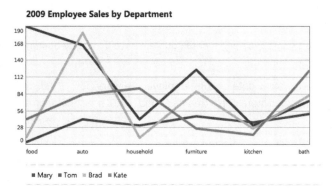

2009 Employee Sales by Department

Figure 12-1 Sales performance target chart design

When we put the x-ray to our chart, the colors or the line weights in the image aren't the important "bones" users need to see—it's the data that matters. So instead of embedding an image of a chart into our page, we'll start with a simple HTML table containing all our sales information:

2009 Employee Sales by Department

Figure 12-2 Performance data in chart form

	food	auto	household	furniture	kitchen	bath
Mary	190	160	40	120	30	70
Tom	3	40	30	45	35	49
Brad	10	180	10	85	25	79
Kate	40	80	90	25	15	119

Because the table is coded with well-structured HTML, this data is accessible to anyone, including mobile devices, screen readers, and search engines.

Creating accessible charts takes a few more steps than some of the other widgets in this book, but still follows the same basic model: start with foundation markup that includes all relevant information a user needs in a fully accessible format; then apply the advanced CSS and JavaScript to transform that basic data into a visual image in the enhanced experience.

To create a chart from this table, we'll parse the HTML **table** to extract all the data values, and use this data to create our chart in the browser using the **canvas** element. We'll walk through the steps involved in generating a line chart from this table, and then, at the end of the chapter, we'll discuss how to use our jQuery Visualize plugin, a full-featured charting script available on the book website.

Foundation markup

Before we can make a chart, we need a data source, so we'll start by building an HTML **table** in our foundation markup.

The table contains retail sales data on four employees—Mary, Tom, Brad, and Kate—and their recent sales in various store departments—food, auto, household, furniture, kitchen, and bath.

Tables can have many child elements and attributes that add semantic value for both visual and non-visual users. We'll make use of all the structure and meaning we can encode into the basic version of our page. Marked up, the table of sales data looks like this:

```
<table>
  <caption>2009 Employee Sales by Department</caption>
  <thead>
    <tr>
      <td></td>
      <th scope="col">food</th>
      <th scope="col">auto</th>
      <th scope="col">household</th>
      <th scope="col">furniture</th>
      <th scope="col">kitchen</th>
      <th scope="col">bath</th>
    </tr>
  </thead>
  <tbody>
    <tr>
      <th scope="row">Mary</th>
      <td>190</td>
```

```
    <td>160</td>

    <td>40</td>

    <td>120</td>

    <td>30</td>

    <td>70</td>

</tr>

<tr>

    <th scope="row">Tom</th>

    <td>3</td>

    <td>40</td>

    <td>30</td>

    <td>45</td>

    <td>35</td>

    <td>49</td>

</tr>

<tr>

    <th scope="row">Brad</th>

    <td>10</td>

    <td>180</td>

    <td>10</td>

    <td>85</td>

    <td>25</td>

    <td>79</td>

</tr>

<tr>

    <th scope="row">Kate</th>

    <td>40</td>

    <td>80</td>

    <td>90</td>

    <td>25</td>

    <td>15</td>
```

```
            <td>119</td>
        </tr>
    </tbody>
</table>
```

The table markup consists of three main sections: **caption** (a table-specific element that provides a short description of the tabular data to follow); **thead** (the top, horizontal header row of the table); and **tbody** (the rows containing the body of the table content). We mark up the first item in each column and row with the **th** element, denoting that the content serves as a heading for its column or row by applying a **scope** attribute with a value of either **col** or **row**, respectively. The **scope** attribute is recognized by newer screen readers, like the latest version of JAWS; however, support for this attribute is inconsistent across a wider range of screen readers. We find it's still helpful to include for anyone who reads the markup, including screen readers and developers alike.

■ Note

For more complex tables, where headers and cells span multiple rows or columns, use the headers attribute to associate headers to their data cells. We describe how to use this attribute in Chapter 3, "Writing Meaningful Markup." It's also worth noting that the script described in this chapter would need to be modified to accommodate such a complex table structure.

While it's semantically rich, in most browsers the default appearance of a table element leaves much to be desired. In a newer browser like Firefox 3, tables don't have borders or much cell padding, making it difficult to read the data.

2009 Employee Sales by Department					
food	**auto**	**household**	**furniture**	**kitchen**	**bath**
Mary 190	160	40	120	30	70
Tom 3	40	30	45	35	49
Brad 10	180	10	85	25	79
Kate 40	80	90	25	15	119

Figure 12-3 Unstyled foundation table markup

To improve the legibility of the basic table, we'll add some "safe" styles to the basic style sheet that are supported by most older and mobile browsers, and will safely degrade in browsers that don't support them. First, we'll collapse the borders of the table, leaving a single stroke between the cells, and apply light gray borders and some padding to the cells to make the rows easier to scan. The **caption** element also acts as a visual heading for the table, so we'll bold the text and add bottom margin to make it stand out. We'll also add a **font-family** stack to make the typeface look consistent with the rest of the site, but we'll leave font sizes undefined to let each device use its defaults:

```css
body {
  font-family: "Segoe UI", Arial, sans-serif;
}


table {
  border-collapse: collapse;
}


caption {
  margin: 0 0 .5em; font-weight: bold;
}


td, th {
  text-align: center;
  border: 1px solid #ddd;
  padding:2px 5px;
}
```

With these small style tweaks added to our basic CSS, the data table is now easier to read.

2009 Employee Sales by Department

	food	auto	household	furniture	kitchen	bath
Mary	190	160	40	120	30	70
Tom	3	40	30	45	35	49
Brad	10	180	10	85	25	79
Kate	40	80	90	25	15	119

Figure 12-4 Foundation table markup with "safe" basic styles added

Creating an accessible chart

Creating a chart from the data table in our foundation markup takes a few steps: parse the data from the basic markup to make it usable for visualization; initialize the canvas element and write instructions to draw the image that represents the data values, legends, and labels within it; if keeping the data table on the page is desired, add enhanced styles to improve its presentation; and, lastly, add a couple of instructions and shortcuts to support accessibility.

Parsing the table data

Now that we have the HTML table set up and styled, we'll use JavaScript to mine its information and structure it in a format that can be used to generate a chart that shows a comparison of each person's sales by department.

First, we'll create a JavaScript object called **tableData** to neatly hold all the information:

```
var tableData = {};
```

The **tableData** variable can be used as a namespace for additional variables, acting as a clean container for data parsed from the table. For example, we could add a property to this object by stating **tableData.myNewProperty**, and set that property's value to whatever we like. In preparation for generating our line chart, we'll gather the necessary data from the HTML table and store it in the **tableData** object.

For convenient referencing, we'll also store our table element in a variable **table**:

```
var table = $('table');
```

X-AXIS LABELS

The first property in the **tableData** object will be named **xLabels**. As the name suggests, it will contain values for the labels along the bottom x-axis that identify the data points charted above them.

For this graph, we'll chart the "departments" data from left to right, so that the x-axis labels map to the top of the table in the **thead**.

2009 Employee Sales by Department

THEAD		food	auto	household	furniture	kitchen	bath
	Mary	190	160	40	120	30	70
	Tom	3	40	30	45	35	49
	Brad	10	180	10	85	25	79
	Kate	40	80	90	25	15	119

xLabels = ['food','auto', 'household','furniture', 'kitchen','bath']

Figure 12-5 X-axis labels are read from the table headers in THEAD.

We'll define **xLabels** as an empty array, and then use jQuery's **each** method to loop through each **th** element in the **thead** and push its text value into the **xLabels** array:

```
//define xLabels array
tableData.xLabels = [];
```

```
//loop through each th element in the table's thead
table.find('thead th').each(function(){
  //push each th's text value into the xLabels array
  xLabels.push( $(this).html() );
});
```

LEGEND LABELS

The data from the left column of the table (employee names) will serve as the chart's legend.

2009 Employee Sales by Department

	food	auto	household	furniture	kitchen	bath
Mary	190	160	40	120	30	70
Tom	3	40	30	45	35	49
Brad	10	180	10	85	25	79
Kate	40	80	90	25	15	119

TBODY TH

Legend = ['Mary','Tom','Brad','Kate']

Figure 12-6 Chart legend labels are fetched from the THs in the table's TBODY.

To capture that, we'll add another property to the **tableData** object called **legend**:

```
//define legend array
tableData.legend = [];
```

```
//loop through each th in the table's tbody
table.find('tbody th').each(function(){
  //push each th's text value into the legend array
  legend.push( $(this).html() );
});
```

As you can see, the process of generating the legend array is very similar to the loop used to create the **xLabels** array, except that it references the **th** elements within **tbody** rather than in **thead**.

Y-AXIS LABELS

Next come the chart's numeric y-axis labels, which we calculate by finding the highest and lowest values in the data set in the body of the table using the following logic:

```
//define topValue and bottomValue properties with initial value of 0
tableData.topValue, tableData.bottomValue = 0;

//loop through each td element in the tbody
table.find('tbody td').each(function(){

  //define thisValue variable, with td text converted to a number
  var thisValue = parseFloat( $(this).text() );

  //check if thisValue is greater than the current topValue
  if( thisValue > tableData.topValue ) {
    //thisValue becomes the new topValue
    tableData.topValue = thisValue;
  }
  //check if thisValue is less than the bottom value
  if( thisValue < tableData.bottomValue ){
    //thisValue becomes the new bottomValue
    tableData.bottomValue = thisValue;
  }
});
```

2009 Employee Sales by Department

	food	auto	household	furniture	kitchen	bath
Mary	190	160	40	120	30	70
Tom	3	40	30	45	35	49
Brad	10	180	10	85	25	79
Kate	40	80	90	25	15	119

topValue = 190

bottomValue = 3

Figure 12-7 Y-axis is calculated by establishing the top and bottom data values.

We've now defined two new values in our **tableData** object: **topValue** and **bottomValue**, for the highest and lowest data points, respectively. We'll use these to calculate our y-axis labels. In this case, the y-axis for a bar or line chart will need to cover from 3 (**bottomValue**) to 190 (**topValue**), so the script will set the axis to 0–190 with as many tick marks between that will comfortably fit within the chart height.

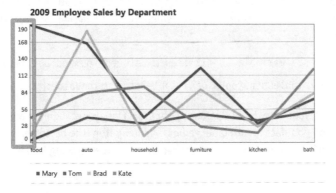

Figure 12-8 Y-axis displayed on the line chart

To complete the information required to generate the y-axis labels, we'll need to determine a few pieces of data:

▶ The height of the chart

▶ A preferred pixel distance between each of the labels on the y-axis

▶ The range between the lowest to the highest value in our data set

We'll base the dimensions of our chart on the width and height of the table:

```
//define chartHeight variable from height of table element
var chartHeight = table.height();
```

```
//while we're at it, let's define the chartWidth as well, for later
var chartWidth = table.width();
```

Then, we'll figure out the number of labels that will display on the y-axis. We'll divide the **chartHeight** by a number that represents the pixel distance between the labels. In this case, we'll specify 30 pixels as our preferred label spacing, as that will create a comfortable distance given their font size. The rounded result gives us the number of labels that will be displayed on the y-axis:

```
//define chartHeight variable from
var numLabels = Math.round(chartHeight / 30);
```

Now that we know the number of labels to display, we'll find the total range of our data set, and iterate through it to generate the value of each label. We'll define the variable **totalRange** as the difference between the top and bottom values. In our sample data, **totalRange** will equal **topValue**; however, this calculation is still necessary because it ensures that data sets containing negative values will be properly represented in the total range:

```
//define totalRange variable as difference between top and bottom values
var totalRange = tableData.topValue - tableData.bottomValue;
```

Now that we have adequate data to generate our y-axis labels, we'll define a new **yLabels** array and populate it with label values, spanning from the bottom value to the top value, and include as many values as we can fit in between (taking into account the chart's height):

```
//define yLabels array
tableData.yLabels = [];


//find our increment amount, rounding any remainder up
var yIncrementAmt = Math.ceil(totalRange / numLabels);


//start an incrementing variable at the bottom value
var currentValue = tableData.bottomValue;


// while currentValue is still less than the top value minus an increment
while( currentValue < tableData.topValue - yIncrementAmt){
  //add the currentValue to the yLabels array
  tableData.yLabels.push(currentValue);


  //increase the currentValue by the incrementAmt
  currentValue += yIncrementAmt;
}
//lastly, add the top value as the last label
tableData.yLabels.push(tableData.topValue);
```

DATA GROUPS

The next property we'll create is called **dataGroups**–a two-level array that aggregates the values from each table cell (**td**), organized by columns or rows depending on the direction we choose to display the data in the chart. Here we'll go from left to right, grouping the values by each containing **tr** row.

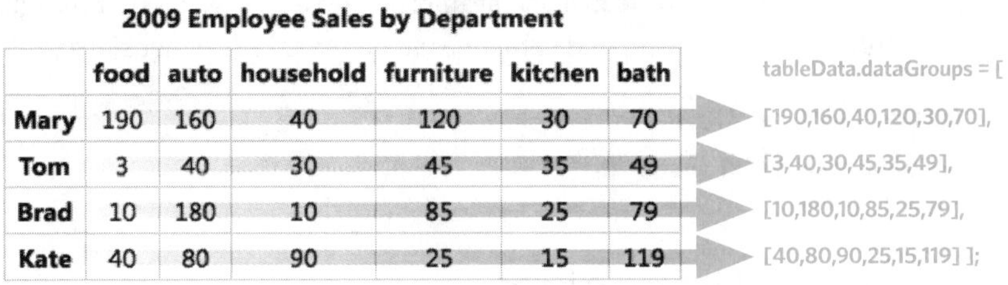

2009 Employee Sales by Department

	food	auto	household	furniture	kitchen	bath	
Mary	190	160	40	120	30	70	[190,160,40,120,30,70],
Tom	3	40	30	45	35	49	[3,40,30,45,35,49],
Brad	10	180	10	85	25	79	[10,180,10,85,25,79],
Kate	40	80	90	25	15	119	[40,80,90,25,15,119]];

tableData.dataGroups = [

Figure 12-9 Data groups are created from parsing each row's data values into an array.

We'll need to parse the table data to arrive at the array shown above. To do that, we'll define the dataGroups array, and then loop through each row of the table, adding each row's array of text values as an item in **dataGroups**:

```
//define dataGroups array
tableData.dataGroups = [];


//loop through each tr in the tbody
table.find('tbody tr').each(function(i){
  //define next item in dataGroups as a new array
  tableData.dataGroups[i] = [];


  //loop through each td in this tr
  $(this).find('td').each(function(){
      //convert the td text into a number
      var tdNumberValue = parseFloat( $(this).text() );


      //add the value to the dataGroups[i] array
      tableData.dataGroups[i].push( tdNumberValue );
  });
});
```

We now have a programmatically generated array matching the content rows in the table, and can move on to the fun part: drawing the chart.

Using canvas to visualize data

We have the necessary data to begin drawing a chart. The first step is to create the **canvas** element and set its **width** and **height** attributes using the **chartHeight** and **chartWidth** variables we created earlier based on the table's dimensions:

```
//create new canvas element
var canvas = $('<canvas />');


//set width and height attributes
canvas.attr({
  height: chartHeight,
  width: chartWidth
});
```

■ **Note**

It's important that we set the size of the canvas using HTML width and height attributes, rather than CSS. While it's possible to use CSS to style the canvas element, the canvas drawing API corresponds only to the element's width and height attributes.

Now that we've created a blank **canvas**, we'll append it to the page inside a wrapper **div,** which neatly contains the elements associated with the chart, including headings, captions, and axis labels. We'll create this wrapper **div**, set its dimensions to match the canvas, inject the canvas into it, and then append it to the page just after the table:

```
//create canvas container div
var canvasContain = $('<div class="chart"></div>')
  //set its width and height css properties
  .css({width: chartWidth, height: chartHeight})

  //append the canvas element to it
  .append(canvas)
```

```
//insert it after the table element
.insertAfter(table);
```

BRINGING IE UP TO SPEED

We're almost ready to draw the chart. Before we do that, we'll need to account for the fact that Internet Explorer (through version 8) doesn't support the **canvas** element and its drawing API. For our charts to work in Internet Explorer, we'll need a workaround. Fortunately, Google developed a library called **exCanvas**, which translates **canvas** commands into VML—a proprietary drawing language supported exclusively by Internet Explorer. To use **exCanvas**, we need to reference the **excanvas.js** script from the **head** of our page, before any other scripts that use **canvas** commands. We can reference the script using a conditional comment to make sure only IE sees and downloads the script:

```
<!--[if IE]><script src="excanvas.js"></script><![endif]-->
```

With **exCanvas** attached, we just need to initialize our **canvas** in IE by calling the **G_vmlCanvasManager.initElement** method. We'll wrap this in an **if** statement that checks if **exCanvas** is defined, so that it's applied only to the relevant browser (Internet Explorer):

```
//check if the browser is IE by checking for excanvas object
if( typeof(G_vmlCanvasManager) != 'undefined' ){
  //if so, initialize the canvas so we can draw in IE
  G_vmlCanvasManager.initElement( canvas[0] );
}
```

Now we can start drawing our chart onto the **canvas**.

DRAWING THE CHART LINES

We'll use the canvas 2D drawing API for our chart, so the first step is to call the **getContext** method to define the context of the canvas as 2D. We'll save a variable, **ctx**, to store a reference to that context, which will be used to send drawing instructions to the canvas:

```
//define ctx var as our canvas 2d context object
var ctx = canvas[0].getContext('2d');
```

We want the lines on the chart to be distinguishable from one another, so we'll set up an array of hexadecimal color values. To keep things simple, we'll call it **colors**:

```
var colors = ['#be1e2d', '#666699', '#92d5ea', '#ee8310'];
```

■ Note

When selecting colors to use in charts, choose ones that are distinguishable for the 5% of users (mostly male) who may have color blindness. Avoid picking red, green, and yellow hues that have the same value (level of darkness), and test your color choices in a color-blindness simulator such as Color Oracle (http://colororacle.cartography.ch).

Moving on to the lines: By default, the canvas drawing API orients its coordinates to start at the top-left corner and move down and right with positive values. In a chart, however, the coordinates start from the *bottom*-left corner and move right and up, so we need to reset the default starting point. We'll use the canvas **translate** method to reset the y-axis value to the height of our canvas, again using the **chartHeight** variable:

```
ctx.translate( 0, chartHeight );
```

Now the starting point for drawing is in the bottom-left corner of the chart.

Earlier, we created a **dataGroups** property of the **tableData** object, which contains the data from the table, grouped by row. Now, we'll use a **for** loop to iterate through the **dataGroups** array and plot lines on the chart. To prepare for running the loop, we'll calculate the increment at which points should be plotted across the canvas, and divide its width by the number of points per line; we'll store that quotient in a variable called **xIncrementAmt**. We'll also define the width of the chart lines to 2 pixels using the **lineWidth** property:

```
//define xIncrementAmt as distance between points in line graph
var xIncrementAmt= chartWidth / (tableData.xLabels.length -1);


//set the lineWidth of the canvas context to 2px
ctx.lineWidth = 2;
```

With these variables defined, we're ready to loop through the data array and actually draw the lines. We'll start by moving the drawing tool to the first data point in the current group, using **ctx.moveTo(0,-points[i])**, and then match the line color to the item in the colors array that corresponds to this group using the iterating **i** variable. Next, we'll press the drawing tool onto the canvas with the **beginPath** method, and run a loop through each point in the group, drawing a line from the previous point to the current one, incrementing the left offset by the amount of the **xIncrementAmt** variable.

After the loop is finished, the line is plotted. We'll apply color and width to the line, and then close the path to end it (otherwise it would connect to the next line when the loop continues).

```
//begin for...in loop on the dataGroups array
for(var i in dataGroups){
  //define points as the current child array of dataGroups
  var points = dataGroups[i];

  //move the pencil to the first data point of this array
  //y value is negative to move upward from bottom left corner
  ctx.moveTo(0,-points[i]);

  //set the line color to the corresponding color in the colors array
  ctx.strokeStyle = colors[i];

  //press the pencil down and begin to draw
  ctx.beginPath();

  //define currentXvalue to store incrementing value
  var currentXvalue = 0;

  //begin for loop through points array, for plotting each point
  for(var j in points){
      //draw a line to the next point from the current location
      ctx.lineTo(currentXvalue,-points[j]);

      //increase the currentXvalue by the increment amount
      currentXvalue += xIncrementAmt;
  }
  //stroke the line, making it visible
  ctx.stroke();
```

```
//done with this line, pick up the pencil
ctx.closePath();
}
```

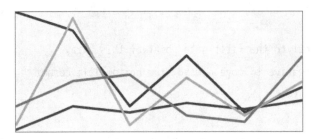

Figure 12-10 Canvas chart with a line plotted for each data set in a unique color

ADDING AXIS LINES AND LABELS

The hard part is finished: our chart is drawn!

Next, we'll add text labels to the axes so users can make sense of the charted lines. Earlier we created properties in the **tableData** object for **xLabels** and **yLabels**, and we'll use them now to set labels along the axes of the chart.

From a technical standpoint, we could create these labels in several ways. Perhaps the cleanest way would be to write the text labels directly onto the canvas, using the native canvas text methods. Unfortunately, the canvas text methods aren't supported as broadly as the canvas drawing methods, so canvas text won't meet our needs.

Instead of writing the labels into the canvas, another valid approach is to add HTML markup for any text needed, and position it with CSS inside the chart **div**. For each set of labels, we'll create an unordered list (**ul**), and loop through each property to append list items for each label. To style and position the labels, we'll use a blend of external and inline CSS. As with any CSS layout, we'll keep as much of the CSS in external style sheets as possible, but in the case of labels, which are dynamically positioned with JavaScript, it makes much more sense to set the coordinates inline than to attempt to guess their potential locations and apply classes. We'll position the labels absolutely and set only the left or bottom values for each list item inline, depending on the axis.

We'll use JavaScript to generate this list, iterating through the **xLabels** array and setting each list item's **left** and **width** inline styles programmatically to divide them evenly along the x-axis. Our generated HTML for the x-axis labels looks like this:

```
<ul class="labels-x">
    <li style="left: 0px; width: 83px;">food</li>
```

```
<li style="left: 83px; width: 83px;">auto</li>

...

</ul>
```

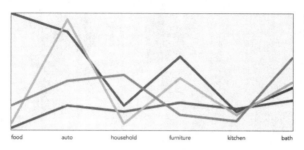

Figure 12-11 Chart with x-axis labels added

The y-axis labels are slightly more complicated, because the horizontal lines should span the graph at each label increment to make it easy to associate lines with their data points. We'll use the following markup for the y-axis labels:

```
<ul class="labels-y">
    <li style="bottom: 199px;">
        <span class="line"></span>
        <span class="label">190</span>
    </li>
    <li style="bottom: 166px;">
        <span class="line"></span>
        <span class="label">145</span>
    </li>

    ...

</ul>
```

As you can see, the y-axis markup contains two spans per list item: one for a chart line and one for the text label. This time, we're positioning the list items with **bottom** instead of **left**, so the items stack vertically from bottom to top.

The rest of the styling for the labels and lines can be handled through the following styles:

```
.chart { position: relative; }
.labels-x,
```

```css
.labels-y {
  position: absolute;
  left: 0;
  top: 0;
  list-style: none;
  margin: 0;
  padding: 0;
  width: 100%;
  height: 100%;
}
.labels-x li,
.labels-y li {
  position: absolute;
  bottom: 0;
  color: #555;
}
.labels-y li span.line {
  position: absolute;
  border: 0 solid #ccc;
}
.labels-x li {
  margin-top: 5px;
}
.labels-y li {
  width: 100%;
}
.labels-y li span.label {
  right: 100%;
  position: absolute;
  margin-right: 5px;
}
```

```
.labels-y li span.line {
  border-top-width: 1px;
  width: 100%;
}
```

We set the dimensions of each label **ul** to 100% of the chart container **div**'s **width** and **height** so that we can position the list items around the chart easily using **top**, **right**, **bottom**, and **left** properties. We can then absolutely position the list items (and labels, in the y-axis), and set either their top or right values to 100%, depending on the axis.

We also set the width of the y-axis list items (as well as their child **line** spans) to 100%, so that we can add a top border to those spans to make lines that correspond to each label on the y-axis.

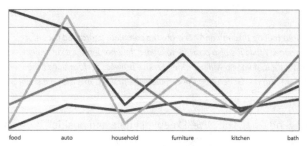

Figure 12-12 Chart with x- and y-axis labels and horizontal lines

ADDING A COLOR LEGEND

Our line chart is almost complete: we need a legend to associate each line with an employee.

The legend will simply be another unordered list, where each item contains a span to serve as a color icon next to the employee's name. We'll loop through the **legend** array and generate a list using the following script (note that we're referencing a parallel item in our **colors** array to obtain the appropriate color for each employee):

```
//create the legend UL
var legendList = $('<ul class="legend"></ul>');

//loop through the items in the legend
for(var i in tableData.legend){
  //create list item with text of legend item
  $('<li>'+ tableData.legend[i] +'</li>')
```

```
    //prepend span for color key box

    .prepend('<span style="background: '+
    ➥tableData.colors[i] +'" />')


    //append the list item to the legend list

    .appendTo(legendList);

}
//append legend UL to chart container div

legendList.appendTo(canvasContain);
```

When the legend list is complete, we'll append it to the **canvasContain div**.

◆ Tip

The script above is structured to loop through and generate the complete unordered list before it injects anything into the page. While it's also possible to create the unordered list and inject it to the page and then populate it, doing so will potentially cause browser performance problems, particularly for very large tables. Generating the complete list first ensures that the script acts quickly.

Now we'll style the legend using CSS. We'll keep it simple and position it below the chart in a flattened list format. The following CSS is all we need:

```
ul.legend {
  list-style: none;
  position: absolute;
  border: 1px solid #000;
  padding: 10px;
  left: 100%;
  margin-left: 10px;
}
ul.legend li span {
  width: 6px;
  height: 6px;
  float: left;
  margin: 3px;
}
```

The styled legend now sits below the chart:

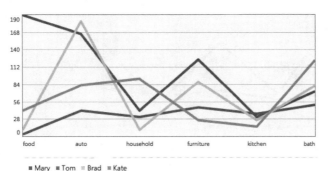

Figure 12-13 Chart legend with color-coded squares to identify each line

ADDING A CHART TITLE

The last step in visualizing the table data is to copy and style the text from the table's **caption** element to use as a title for the chart:

```
//create chart title div
$('<div class="chart-title">'+ table.find('caption').html() +'</div>')
  //prepend it to the chart wrapper div
  .prependTo(canvasContain);
```

Then we'll style the title to coordinate with the chart:

```
.chart-title {
  font-size: 14px;
  font-weight: bold;
  position: absolute;
  bottom: 100%;
  margin-bottom: 10px;
  width: 100%;
}
```

Our final **canvas** chart, with all styles applied:

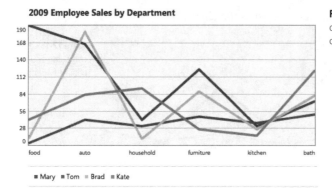

Figure 12-14 Complete chart, including a title based on the table's caption

Adding enhanced table styles

Though we have a fancy new chart, there may be cases where it makes sense to also keep the original table on the page—to provide additional numeric data for easy scanning, for example. In this case, we'll add a few rules to the enhanced style sheet to improve its presentation.

Building on the styles we created for the foundation markup, we'll style the **caption** element to be larger and bold, and add a very light gray background color to the table headers to help distinguish them from the table data cells.

2009 Employee Sales by Department

	food	auto	household	furniture	kitchen	bath
Mary	190	160	40	120	30	70
Tom	3	40	30	45	35	49
Brad	10	180	10	85	25	79
Kate	40	80	90	25	15	119

Figure 12-15 Styled data table and final line chart both visible and stacked

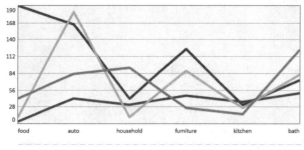

Keeping the data accessible

As we mentioned early in this chapter, our page started out with an accessible data table, and since we've done nothing to prevent a user's ability to access that table, our data remains accessible alongside its supplemental **canvas** chart. But now that we have both a table and a chart on the page, we might want to hide one or the other from view, perhaps to free up some space in the layout on a small screen, or simply to reduce redundancy on the page.

HIDING THE TABLE FROM VIEW

A common approach to hiding the data table from view might be to either use the CSS property **display: none;** or to remove it from the page entirely using JavaScript. Unfortunately, and perhaps obviously, both of these techniques not only hide the content visually, but also hide it from screen-reader users, which effectively defeats the point of our table-generated approach—accessiblity.

Fortunately, there are other methods of hiding content that don't affect accessibility. We recommend simply positioning the table absolutely and placing it far off the left edge of the page. This successfully hides it from visual users, yet preserves it in the document flow so that it's accessible to screen readers:

```
table { position: absolute; left: -99999px; }
```

HIDING THE CHART FROM SCREEN READERS

The chart we generated serves a purely visual purpose, so it provides little value for visually impaired users; therefore, it would be helpful to hide this portion of the content from users with screen readers.

The W3C's WAI-ARIA draft specification provides the **role="img"** attribute, which is perfect for just this purpose, because it informs a screen reader that the element is playing the role of an image.

Just like an image's **alt** attribute, the **img** role can be paired with an **aria-label** attribute to describe the image in plain text. We'll add these attributes to our chart wrapper **div**, which contains the **canvas** and other lists:

```
<div class="chart" role="img" aria-label="line chart representing data
from: 2009 Employee Sales by Department">
  <!—canvas and the extra lists go here -->
</div>
```

And these attributes could be easily added using jQuery:

```
//set role and aria-label attributes on our wrapper div
canvasContain.attr({
  'role': 'img',
  'aria-label': 'Chart representing data from: ' +
  ➥table.find('caption').text()
});
```

Many screen-reader users are still using versions that don't support ARIA very well, or even at all, so we'll provide fallback text to alert these users that the content contained in the element is purely for visual purposes, and provide a link to allow the user to skip the element. This message will be contained within a **div** with an **img** role, so users on newer screen-reader versions will know that the **div** is purely visual, and they won't see this message contained within it.

First, we'll insert a paragraph element to the chart **div** that contains a message describing the visual nature of the content:

```
$('<p class="chart-access-message"><strong>Note:</strong> The following
block of content contains HTML used to visually represent a data table
elsewhere on this page. <a href="#endOfChart">Skip this chart</a></p>')

   .prependTo(canvasContain);
```

As you can see, we've added a "skip" link that references an element with an **id** attribute of **endOfChart**. For this skip link to work, we'll create that corresponding element and append it to the end of the chart container. We'll also set the element's **tabindex** attribute to **-1**, which allows it to receive programmatic focus and prevent a bug in Internet Explorer that breaks jump scrolling:

```
$('<div id="endOfChart" tabindex="-1"/>').appendTo(canvasContain);
```

Now we'll hide that message from visual users, because it's relevant only to those browsing with screen readers:

```
.chart-access-message {
  position: absolute;
  left: -99999px;
}
```

With this quick addition to the chart styles and scripts, screen-reader users will now either recognize the chart as an image, or be warned of the visual-only content with a way to skip it.

Taking canvas charts further: the visualize.js plugin

We've extended the high-level ideas discussed in this chapter into a jQuery plugin called **visualize**. This plugin is more full-featured than the line chart example; it covers additional chart types like bar, area, and pie; includes two visual theme styles (the light white background style as shown, and an additional dark chart theme shown in the charts to follow); and is constructed with a clear API for generating charts with plenty of configuration options like width, height, colors, parse direction, and a lot more. You can use it to generate the chart described in this chapter by simply linking to the jQuery library and the plugin script and calling the **visualize** method on any table in the page.

To call the visualize.js plugin on a table, set the chart **type** to **line**, **area**, **bar**, or **pie**. If you don't specify a chart type, a line chart will be created by default.

```
$('table').visualize({type: 'line'});
```

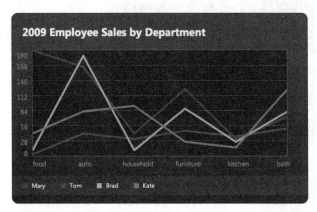

Figure 12-16 Line chart created from the visualize.js plugin

To create an area chart with semi-transparent filled areas under each line, simply pass in the **area** chart **type**:

```
$('table').visualize({type: 'area'});
```

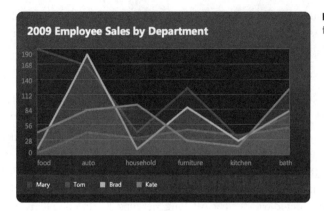

Figure 12-17 Area chart created
from the visualize.js plugin

For a bar chart, pass in the **bar** chart **type**:

```
$('table').visualize({type: 'bar'});
```

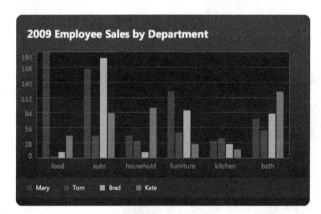

Figure 12-18 Bar chart created
from the visualize.js plugin

As you might expect, you can also summarize data into a pie chart by specifying the **pie** chart **type**. Pie charts created with **visualize.js** automatically constrain their dimensions to fit within the rectangular **canvas**. This size works well for bars and lines, but feels restrictive for the round pie; we can give it extra space by passing in an optional **height** argument to make the **canvas** a bit taller and let the pie scale:

```
$('table').visualize({type: 'pie', height: '300px'});
```

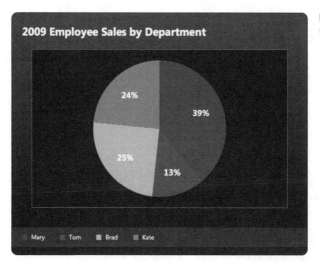

Figure 12-19 Pie chart created from the visualize.js plugin

The **visualize** method returns a new chart container **div** and automatically inserts it on the page just after the table. To display multiple visualizations of a single table, just call **visualize** multiple times:

```
$(function(){
    $('table').visualize({type: 'pie', height: '300px'});
    $('table').visualize({type: 'bar'});
    $('table').visualize({type: 'area'});
    $('table').visualize({type: 'line'});
});
```

■ Note

The visualize.js plugin referenced in this section is available for download at www.filamentgroup.com/dwpe. For more information on how to use the visualize.js plugin, read our article at www.filamentgroup.com/lab/ jquery_visualize_plugin_accessible_charts_graphs_from_tables_html5_canvas.

* * * * *

The **canvas** element provides a rich API with robust drawing capabilities, compatibility with a wide range of browsers and devices, and the added benefit of allowing you to use data from within the page, which maximizes accessibility. There are just a few things to keep in mind when using **canvas** in your own work:

▶ Start with a well-structured, semantic data table that encodes as much meaning as possible.

▶ When referencing the **canvas**, also remember to reference the exCanvas library, to ensure that Internet Explorer users will see your charts.

▶ Set the **canvas** size with HTML **width** and **height** attributes—don't rely on CSS to set dimensions.

▶ If your chart coordinates need to start at the bottom (as ours did) rather than the native canvas top-left, use the **translate** method to set the context.

▶ If you choose to hide the data table from sighted users, do so in a way that preserves it in the source for screen readers and search engines.

▶ As a service to screen-reader users, provide a "skip" link so they may move quickly past the chart markup and on to more meaningful data in the page.

chapter thirteen

dialogs and overlays

Dialogs and overlays present content that appears to float over the page. Dialogs usually offer richer interactive content like embedded form elements, buttons, and links, and require a decision or input from the user; overlays typically present read-only content. The wide range of uses for dialogs and overlays include:

▶ Presenting system error messages and confirmations that require user interaction to dismiss

▶ Collecting user input in a form or multi-step wizard

▶ Displaying large version of a photo in a "lightbox" when a thumbnail image is clicked on the page

▶ Creating floating palettes and UI inspector windows in a web application, like a document editor

▶ Opening a "sticky" tooltip or mini-overlay to offer content and functionality in a compact format

Both dialogs and overlays can adopt two broad interaction patterns: *modal* and *non-modal*:

▶ A modal dialog or overlay prevents any interaction with the underlying page while it's open, which focuses and constrains the user to completing the current interaction. To make this relationship clear, many designs call for a semi-transparent layer—either dark or light—between the dialog and page body to make the page look temporarily disabled and help the overlay stand out visually. Modal dialogs and overlays are useful for confirming user interactions, providing important error or system messages, collecting user input with a form, or simply focusing attention on specific content.

▶ A non-modal dialog or overlay allows a user to continue to interact with the base page while it's open. It's useful for situations where the dialog's content updates the page dynamically based on the user's interaction with it, like a floating color palette, Help content pane, search box, or chat window.

Dialogs and overlays can have fixed size and placement, or can be developed to be moveable and resizable to help them feel like tool palettes or application windows on a desktop PC. Both are relatively easy to build with modern web technologies, but they can present issues for screen readers if accessibility features like keyboard access, focus management, and ARIA attributes aren't built in. It's also important to consider how to make the content and functionality available to users in the basic experience, especially when Ajax is used to pull the overlay content into the enhanced page.

In this chapter, we'll discuss how to build accessible dialogs and overlays with a progressive enhancement approach. We'll focus specifically on a dialog, because it includes all the complexity you'd need to address in a simpler overlay; our example will use Ajax to update dialog content to highlight the specific techniques that need to be addressed for this more complex scenario.

X-ray perspective

Our target design is a common case in which dialogs are employed: a site with login and registration links in the global header that open mini forms over the page to keep the user in their place on the site. For the purposes of this discussion, we'll focus on the login form, but the registration form would use the same principles and coding approach.

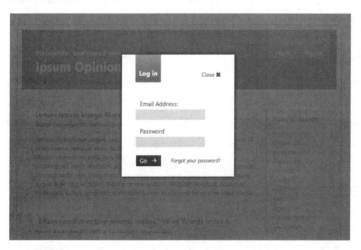

Figure 13-1 Target design for the login modal dialog

Looking at the login dialog design from an x-ray perspective, we clearly see that the dialog is modal, and a fixed size. Within it, the form fields can be easily coded as a simple

HTML form that will work on any device. The big question is: *where* should the form code be included in the markup?

We have two options: either add the login form to the foundation markup in every page on the site, or link to a separate login page.

If we include the login form in the foundation markup, the login link at the top would be an internal anchor link that, when clicked, would scroll the user to the form block on the page. The upside of this approach is that the content is immediately available and fully accessible. The downside is that this form markup needs to be included on every page of the site, adding page weight and visual clutter in the basic experience, especially if both the login and registration forms are included.

The other option is to create a separate HTML page for the login form and link to that page in the foundation markup. This keeps the page weight and visual clutter to a minimum in the basic experience.

Either approach is valid. The choice will depend on the importance and frequency of use of the dialog for the site in question, and markup size of the content in each dialog. In this situation we want to keep our pages as lightweight as possible, so we'll use the separate linked page approach.

In the basic experience, the Login link in the global header will navigate the user to a separate login page. If the user clicks the "forgot your password?" link from this login page, they navigate to a separate password retrieval page. If the user doesn't fill out either form correctly, the server reloads the form with the incorrect fields highlighted and a corresponding error message. Once either form is completed successfully, the user returns to the page he was on, and the header will update to reflect their login status. These individual linked pages will be fully accessible and navigable with the keyboard—as long as we use semantic HTML markup for our links and forms.

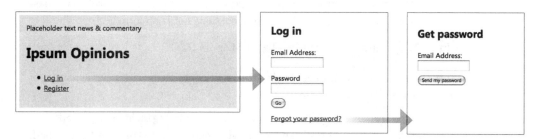

Figure 13-2 Multiple linked pages of the basic experience login sequence

All the server-generated pages and logic required for the basic experience will be reused in the enhanced experience.

There is no native dialog HTML element; the enhanced experience will use a **div** as the container for the form content, and use Ajax to load and display it in a dialog:

Figure 13-3 The enhanced experience brings the login sequence into the dialog using Ajax.

We will need to add ARIA attributes to the container **div** to tell screen readers that it's playing the role of a dialog. We also need to use JavaScript to programmatically move the tab focus into the body of the dialog to ensure that it's usable and accessible without a mouse.

Creating the dialog

Now that we have an approach outlined for our login dialog, we can write the foundation markup for the basic screens, and the enhanced styles and scripts to create the enhanced modal dialog presentation.

Foundation markup and style

Our foundation markup consists of two components: a standard anchor link in the base page that points to the **login.html** page that contains our login form:

```
<a href="login.html" id="option-login">Log in</a>
```

...and a fully formed HTML page, **login.html**, that contains the site's global navigation elements and all login form content.

In the enhanced experience, we'll need only a subset of the **login.html** page markup—just the part that contains the title and form. We'll request the full page using Ajax, and filter its contents to the portion of content that we want to appear in the enhanced dialog.

To prepare that subset of content for the Ajax request, we'll wrap it in a **div** container with an **id** of **login**, and create a heading describing the page content, a login form with pairs of **labels** and text **inputs**, and a Go button to submit the form data. After the form elements, a "forgot your password?" link points to a separate password-retrieval page:

```
<div id="login">

  <h1>Log in</h1>

  <form action="login.php" method="post" id="login-form">

      <label for="email">Email Address:</label>

      <input type="text" class="type-text" name="email" id="email" />

      <label for="email">Password</label>

      <input type="password" class="type-text" name="password"
      id="password" />

      <input type="submit" id="submit-login" name="submit-login" value="Go" />

      <a href="forgot_pass.html" class="alt-option">Forgot your password?</a>

  </form>

</div>
```

The form's foundation markup is fully functional without any CSS applied, but it looks a bit clunky with the labels, inputs, button, and links all running together on one line.

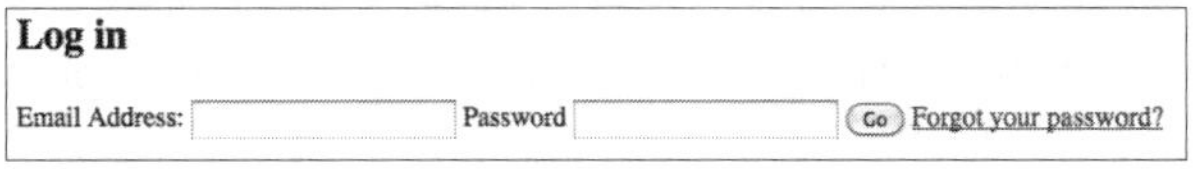

Log in	
Email Address: _____ Password _____ (Go) Forgot your password?	

Figure 13-4 Unstyled foundation markup in login.html

To remedy this, we'll add a few safe styles to the basic style sheet to set a default font for the page, and set the **label** and **input** elements to **display:block** so they sit on separate lines. The input elements are styled with **1em** of bottom margin to provide more vertical spacing between the form fields:

```
body, input { font-family: "Segoe UI", Arial, sans-serif; }

label, input { display:block; }

input { margin-bottom:1em; }
```

These simple, safe CSS rules make our form much clearer and easier to read in the basic experience:

Figure 13-5 Foundation markup with safe styles applied

Enhanced markup and style

In the enhanced experience, we want users to focus on and complete the login action, and don't want to support simultaneous interaction with the base page. To accomplish this, we need to create markup for two separate components: the semi-transparent screen that covers the base page content and disables its functionality; and the dialog container that floats over it and presents the form content.

To accomplish the modal screen effect, the enhancement script needs to inject two elements into the enhanced markup at the end of the **body** element: a **div** that will receive the background color and opacity shift, and an **iframe** nested inside it to apply the protective behavior that keeps users from interacting with the page below. The **iframe**'s **src** must be set to avoid security warnings in some browsers, so we'll set it to **javascript:false;** which acts as a null value, preventing it from making an unnecessary HTTP request:

```
<div class="modal-screen"><iframe src="javascript:false;"></iframe></div>
```

The **div** is styled with height and width of 100% to fill dimensions of the screen, a dark gray gradient background image, **opacity** of 90% to allow the page content to subtly show through the layer in browsers that support CSS opacity, and a high **z-index** value to ensure it stacks in front of other elements on the page that have **z-index** properties set:

```
.modal-screen {
    background:#717174 url(../images/bg-modal-screen.png) top repeat-x;
    position:absolute;
    width:100%;
    overflow:hidden;
    height:100%;
    top:0;
    left:0;
    opacity:.9;
    z-index: 9999;
}
```

The **iframe** inside this **div** is used as a workaround for **z-index** (i.e., CSS stacking order) issues in some browsers that cause them to incorrectly display page elements—including select menus and elements with scrollbars—in front of the screen layer and dialog, regardless of the **z-index** stacking order set in the style sheet. The **iframe** will consistently and reliably stack above every element in the page, so it acts as a protective layer for the modal screen and dialog. We'll set it to 100% height and width to fill the dimensions of the modal screen **div**, and with **opacity** set to **0** (we'll reinforce this property with JavaScript so that it works in Internet Explorer 6, which doesn't natively support the **opacity** CSS property). Even though it's transparent, it will still prevent any z-index issues from occurring.

```
.modal-screen iframe {
  height:100%;
  width:100%;
  position:absolute;
  top:0;
  left:0;
  padding:0;
  margin:0;
  opacity: 0;
}
```

To complete the screen effect, the script will add a **class** to the **body** element when the dialog is present to remove any scrollbars on the browser window, preventing the user from being able to scroll the dialog out of view:

```
body.blocked {
  overflow:hidden;
}
```

Figure 13-6 Modal screen covering the entire page content

Now that the modal screen's markup and styles are roughed out, we can move on to the dialog code. First, we'll add a **role** of **application** to the **body** element so that screen readers will properly recognize the dialog widget and allow us to define custom keyboard behavior:

```
<body role="application">
```

To create a container for the dialog, the enhancement script will generate a **div** with an ID of **dialog**:

```
<div id="dialog"></div>
```

For accessibility support, we'll add an ARIA **role** attribute of **dialog** to the **div** to tell screen readers that it is acting as a dialog UI widget instead of a standard **div**. We'll also assign a unique **id** to the **div**, which will be referenced by the Close link, and an **aria-hidden** attribute set to **false**, to tell screen readers that the dialog is currently visible:

```
<div id="dialog" role="dialog" aria-hidden="false"></div>
```

The enhancement script will load the full **login.html** page with Ajax, find the contents of the login form content **div** (**#login**) in the basic page, and add this block of markup into the dialog **div**:

```
<div id="dialog" role="dialog" aria-hidden="false">

  <div id="login">
      <h1>Log in</h1>
      <form action="login.php" method="post">
      <label for="email">Email Address:</label>
      <input type="text" class="type-text" name="email" id="name" />
      <label for="email">Password</label>
      <input type="password" class="type-text" name="password"
      id="password" />
      <input type="submit" id="submit-login" name="submit-login" value="Go" />
      <a href="forgot_pass.html" class="alt-option">Forgot your password?</a>
  </form>
  </div>
</div>
```

To allow for styling consistency, the script will wrap a container **div** with a class of **dialog-content** around all the dialog content:

```
<div id="dialog" role="dialog" aria-hidden="false">
  <div class="dialog-content">
    <div id="login">
      <h1>Log in</h1>
      ...login form markup...
    </div>
  </div>
</div>
```

The ARIA specification stipulates that when using the **role** of **dialog**, the markup should add the **aria-labelledby** attribute to point to the **id** of an element acting as the label for the dialog. To support this, the enhancement script will assign an **id** of **dialog-title** to the **h1** element within the dialog content for this attribute to reference. With this connection in place, a screen reader will know the "Log in" heading describes the dialog's purpose, and may speak "Log in dialog" when the dialog appears.

```
<div id="dialog" role="dialog" aria-hidden="false" aria-labelledby=
"dialog-title">
  <div class="dialog-content">
    <div id="login">
      <h1 id="dialog-title">Log In</h1>
      ...login form markup...
    </div>
  </div>
</div>
```

■ Note

If there isn't a descriptive element like a heading already in the markup that can be associated, the aria-label attribute can be used to title the dialog for a screen reader.

The enhancement script will append a link after the heading element that will have behavior attached to close the dialog when clicked. We can tell screen readers that this link is acting as a Close button that controls the dialog by assigning the ARIA attribute **aria-controls** to reference the ID of the dialog **div** and adding the **role=button** attribute to this link:

```
<div id="dialog" role="dialog" aria-hidden="false"
aria-labelledby="dialog-title">
  <a href="#" class="dialog-close" role="button" aria-controls="dialog">
  Close</a>
  <div class="dialog-content">
      <div id="login">
          <h1 id="dialog-title">Log In</h1>
          ...login form markup...
      </div>
  </div>
</div>
```

The enhanced CSS for the dialog **div** will set it to a fixed width and absolutely position it in the center of the screen. We'll do this by setting a **50% left** value, offset by a negative left margin equal to half the dialog's width (e.g., **125px**). We'll add a drop shadow effect in modern browsers that support the CSS3 box shadow property, and a **z-index** to position it in front of the modal overlay:

```
#dialog {
  background:#fff;
  position:absolute;
  width:250px;
  top:20%;
  left:50%;
  margin-left:-125px;
  -o-box-shadow:0 0 8px #111;
  -moz-box-shadow:0 0 8px #111;
  -webkit-box-shadow:0 0 8px #111;
  box-shadow:0 0 8px #111;
  z-index: 10000;
}
```

The title and Close button are both floated left so they sit side by side. The title has a background gradient image and a few rules to set a comfortable margin and padding on the text. The Close link has an "x" icon added as a background image to the left of the text and a rule to add an underline on hover:

```css
#dialog-title {
  background:#8c8c8d url(../images/bg-dialog-title.png) top repeat-x;
  font-size:1.4em;
  color:#fff;
  margin:0 0 20px 30px;
  padding:30px 8px 10px;
  float:left;
  text-decoration:none;
  outline:none;
}
.dialog-close {
  position:absolute;
  top:34px;
  right:30px;
  color:#888;
  font-size:1.2em;
  text-decoration:none;
  background:url(../images/icon-close.png) right 50% no-repeat;
  padding-right:15px;
}
.dialog-close:hover {
  text-decoration:underline;
}
```

The **div** wrapped around the dialog content clears the title and the Close link's floats so it always sits below them. The styles for the **form** element set basic font formatting, spacing, and colors for the labels, text inputs, and Submit button:

```css
.dialog-content {
  clear: both;
}
form {
  padding:10px 30px 20px;
  overflow:auto;
```

```
    clear:both;
}
form label {
  display:block;
  font-size:1.3em;
  color:#808080;
  margin:.6em 0 .3em;
  padding-left:10px;
}
form input.type-text {
  margin:.3em 0 1.2em;
  display:block;
  border:1px solid #fff;
  background:#E6E6E6;
  padding:.3em .4em;
  font-size:1.3em;
}
```

The **:focus** pseudo-class allows us to specify a darker stroke color when the user focuses into the text **input**. Some browsers will add additional visual feedback for a focused element—for example, a blue glow in Apple's Safari. Although this can be overridden by setting the **outline** CSS property on the input, we recommend letting each browser handle outline focus styling in their internally consistent way, if possible:

```
form input.type-text:focus {
  border-color:#aaa;
}
```

Figure 13-7 Styled login form markup for the enhanced experience

Enhanced dialog script

Now that we've created our foundation markup and planned the enhanced markup and styles for the dialog, we'll write the JavaScript that will generate the dialog markup and assign behavior in browsers that pass the capabilities test.

We'll start by adding the **role** of **application** to the **body** element:

```
$('body').attr('role','application');
```

Whenever the Login link is clicked in the enhanced experience, it will open the login dialog. To do this, we'll start by binding a click event to the link:

```
$('#option-login').click(function(){
  //...click event scripting goes here
});
```

GENERATING THE ENHANCED MARKUP FROM AJAX

Once the link is clicked, the script will request the dialog content from the web server using Ajax. We'll use the jQuery **$.get** utility method to load the page with Ajax by passing the login link's **href** attribute as the URL we'd like to request:

```
$('#option-login').click(function(){
  $.get( $(this).attr('href') );
});
```

The **$.get** Ajax utility provides a callback function that will execute when the server response returns the **login.html** page. This response (provided in the **response** variable below) is the full text of the HTML page source, so we'll need to search within it to find the specific markup we need for the dialog. From the full Ajax response, the **dialogContent** variable references the login **div** element in the login page:

```
$('#option-login').click(function(){
  $.get($(this).attr('href'), function(response){
    //get the ajax response text, reference it in a $()
    var response = $(response);
    //find the login div within response, for dialog content
    var dialogContent = response.find('#login');
  });
});
```

Now that we have the content, our script can generate the dialog according to the enhanced markup template we planned earlier:

```
$('#option-login').click(function(){
  $.get($(this).attr('href'), function(response){
    // get the ajax response text, reference it in a $()
    var response = $(response);

    // find the login div within response, for dialog content
    var dialogContent = response.find('#login');

    // find the element that will act as the dialog's title
    var dialogTitle = dialogContent.find('h1');

    //add ID attr to the title, for ARIA reference
    dialogTitle.attr('id', 'dialog-title');

    // create the modal screen:
    var modalScreen = $('<div class="modal-screen">
➥<iframe src="javascript:false;"></iframe></div>');

    //set modal screen's opacity to fix Internet Explorer
    modalScreen.children(0).css('opacity',0);

    // create the dialog wrapper
    var dialog = $('<div id="dialog" role="dialog"
➥aria-hidden="false" aria-labelledby="dialog-title"></div>');

    // create the close link
    var close = $('<a href="#" class="dialog-close"
➥role="button" aria-controls="dialog">Close</a>')
      .appendTo(dialog);
```

```
    // create the content div
  var content = $('<div class="dialog-content"></div>')
      .append(dialogContent)
      .appendTo(dialog);
  });
});
```

At this stage, the script has pulled in the full login page with Ajax, parsed out the relevant content needed for the form, and assembled the full enhanced markup for the overlay screen and dialog, so it's ready to apply events to the dialog markup.

APPLYING BEHAVIOR TO THE ENHANCED MARKUP

For the script to apply events to the dialog markup, first a custom **close** event is created that lists everything that must happen when the dialog closes: removing the modal screen, dialog markup, and the **blocked** class from the body that prevents the window from scrolling. This event can be triggered from a range of situations: clicking the Close button, pressing the Esc key, or successfully logging in. For context and clarity, the rest of the code examples will collapse a portion of their previous code in ellipses.

```
$('#option-login').click(function(){
  $.get($(this).attr('href'), function(response){
      ...previous dialog code...
      //bind a custom close event to the dialog div
      dialog.bind('close',function(){
          //remove modal screen from page
          modalScreen.remove();

          //remove dialog div from page
          dialog.remove();

          //remove blocked class from body
          $('body').removeClass('blocked');
      });
  });
});
```

We'll trigger the **close** event when the Close link is clicked, and return the **click** event **false** to prevent the URL hash from updating with the link's **href** value:

```
$('#option-login').click(function(){
  $.get($(this).attr('href'), function(response){
      ...previous dialog code...
      //bind click event to the close button
      close.click(function(){
          //trigger the dialog's close event
          dialog.trigger('close');

          //prevent link's href # from populating url
          return false;
      });
  });
});
```

The **close** event will also be triggered any time the user presses the Esc key by looking for the **keydown** event for that key's **keyCode** (**27**):

```
$('#option-login').click(function(){
  $.get($(this).attr('href'), function(response){
      ...previous dialog code...

      $(document).keydown(function(ev){
          if(ev.which == 27){
              dialog.trigger('close');
          }
      });
  });
});
```

APPENDING AND SHOWING THE DIALOG

Now that the dialog markup is generated and events are bound, the enhancement script will add the class of **blocked** to the body element to prevent it from scrolling, and inject the completed dialog widget into the page to make it visible:

```
$('#option-login').click(function(){
  $.get($(this).attr('href'), function(response){
    ...previous dialog code...
    //find body element, add class, append dialog
    $('body')
        .addClass('blocked')
        .append(modalScreen)
        .append(dialog);
  });
});
```

MANAGING FOCUS

Managing keyboard focus to optimize navigation and accessibility is a crucial step in building a dialog that is fast and efficient to use. The ARIA spec recommends directing cursor focus into the dialog so the user can start interacting with the content within; otherwise the dialog would open but the focus would remain on the page below, which would be very confusing.

In our login form, even though the Close link is technically the first focusable element inside the dialog, the first text input is the most *useful* element to receive focus when the dialog opens, so users can immediately start entering their email address. We'll direct focus there by using jQuery to find the first **input** inside **dialogContent**:

```
$('#option-login').click(function(){
  $.get($(this).attr('href'), function(response){
    ...previous dialog code...
    //focus first input in login form
    dialogContent.find('input')[0].focus();
  });
});
```

Once focus is placed in the first text **input**, the user can use the Tab key to navigate to the next password **input**, the submit button, and finally, the "forgot your password" link.

Pressing the Tab key one more time will natively move focus out of the dialog and onto the next focusable item in the source order of the page beneath it. This would be confusing for a user, because the dialog is designed to be modal. The script will programmatically constrain focus within the dialog, starting with the Close link, and then moving on to the form fields. We'll apply this constraint by binding a **focus** event to the entire **document** that triggers whenever a change in focus occurs; when that change happens, the script checks if the newly focused element is outside of the dialog **div**, and if so, sends focus back to the first focusable element in the dialog:

```
$('#option-login').click(function(){
  $.get($(this).attr('href'), function(response){
     ...previous dialog code...


  //list of native focusable elements, or with a tabindex
  var focusable = 'a,input,button,textarea,select,[tabindex]';


     //bind a focus event to the document
     $(document).bind('focus', function(ev){


        //if a dialog is present on the page and the
        //the focused element is not inside that dialog
        if($('#dialog').length &&
           !$(ev.target).parents('#dialog').length){
           //direct focus to the first
           //focusable element in dialog
           dialog.find(focusable)[0].focus();
        }
     });
  });
});
```

Taking dialog further

The summary above covers all markup, style, and script cases to create a single fixed-size modal dialog, but there are a host of other dialog and overlay features and scenarios you may want to implement, including non-modal dialogs to provide tool palettes, simple overlays like photo slideshows that display images, and resizable helper text overlays to show supplementary content over a page.

The jQuery UI dialog plugin includes an expanded feature set for these dialog and overlay cases—including modal and non-modal capabilities, resizing, dragging, and placement, as well as the ability to support multiple dialogs on a page at one time—and also factors in ARIA support. In addition, jQuery UI dialog can be styled with the ThemeRoller tool. You can access the jQuery UI dialog plugin demo and documentation at jqueryui.com/demos/dialog, and download the dialog plugin at jqueryui.com/download.

Using the dialog script

The demo and code that accompanies this book (available on the book website, www.filamentgroup.com/dwpe) includes a script, **jQuery.dialog.js,** that wraps the techniques to create a single modal dialog as presented in this chapter into a convenient jQuery plugin for use in your projects.

To use this script in your page, download and reference the files listed in the dialog example page. Then, simply find an element on the page (or even a string of HTML wrapped in a jQuery function) and call the dialog method on it. For example, let's assume there's a form on the page with an **id** of **login**. To display that form in a dialog, find it with a jQuery selector and call the **dialog** method on it:

```
$('form#login').dialog();
```

The **dialog** method will automatically generate a dialog wrapper for the content that includes all the markup and behavior specified in this chapter, such as the modal protector screen, and a Close link. When called, it will first close any existing dialogs on the page, ensuring only one dialog is visible at a time. The **dialog** method also includes configurable options for **title**, **buttons,** and **focus**, which are passed as an object containing key/value pairs.

The **title** option is used for specifying a particular element within the dialog to serve as the title for screen-reader users, and the plugin will automatically apply an **id** of **dialog-title** to this element. The **title** option accepts a jQuery selector as its value, and if no **title** option is specified, the plugin will default to the first occurrence of the following elements: **h1**, **h2**, **h3**, **h4**, **h5**, **h6**, **legend**, **label**, and **p**. For example, the following code sets the **title** option to the first **span** element within the dialog's content area:

```
$('form#login').dialog({
  title: 'span'
});
```

The **buttons** option allows you to generate buttons that will be appended to the bottom of the dialog. This is helpful in situations when the dialog is acting as a prompt that the user must either confirm or cancel. The **buttons** option accepts its own object of key/value pairs, generates **button** elements for each pair, and appends them to a **div** with a class of **dialog-footer**, which is placed at the end of the dialog markup. Within the key/value pairs, the key serves as the HTML text within the button itself, and its value serves as a function that will execute when that button is clicked. For example, the following script generates a dialog with two buttons, each triggering a different alert when clicked:

```
$('div#documentUnsavedPrompt').dialog({
  buttons: {
      'Okay': function(){
         alert('You clicked Okay.');
      },
      'Cancel': function(){
         alert('You clicked Cancel.');
      },
  }
});
```

The **focus** option lets you specify a particular element that should receive focus when the dialog opens. By default, the plugin will attempt to focus on the first natively focusable element (such as an anchor, a form element, or anything with a **tabindex** attribute) in the dialog content **div**; if it doesn't find any, it falls back to any buttons generated by the **buttons** option, and then to the dialog's Close link as a last resort. You can override the **focus** option by specifying a jQuery selector to a specific element within the dialog. This might be useful in cases like a confirmation prompt, where you may want to direct focus to the Okay button, regardless of the content in the dialog:

```
$('div#documentUnsavedPrompt').dialog({

  buttons: {

      'Okay': function(){

          alert('You clicked Okay.');

      },

      'Cancel': function(){

          alert('You clicked Cancel.');

      },

  },

  focus: '.dialog-footer button:first'

});
```

The dialog plugin also comes with a utility function (with the same name as the **dialog** method) that's designed to create dialogs from external content. The **dialog** utility function requires a URL argument that specifies the location of the dialog content. For example, the following script will create a dialog with the content of the page **login.html**:

```
$.dialog('login.html');
```

The dialog will open immediately, displaying a "loading..." message while the Ajax request is made. Once the request returns, the dialog will rebuild itself using the content of **login.html** and any configuration specified in the **options** argument. The loading message can be configured by passing any string of text to the **loadingText** option, via the **options** argument:

```
$.dialog('login.html',{

  loadingText: 'Please wait...'

});
```

Assuming **login.html** is a full web page, including **html**, **head**, and **body** elements, as well as references to JavaScript and CSS files, you'd probably want only a subset of that page's content to appear in the dialog. The **dialog** utility function makes this simple: just add a space after the URL path and include any jQuery selectors you'd like. For example, the following script will create a dialog from the content of a **div** with an **id** of **login** on the page **login.html**:

```
$.dialog('login.html #login');
```

This approach could be used to easily produce the example described in this chapter, by binding a **click** event to the Login link that generates a dialog based on the page referenced in the link's **href** attribute:

```
//assign click event to login link
$('#option-login').click(function(){

  //create dialog out of the #login div located in the page
  //referenced in the link's href attribute
  $.dialog( $(this).attr('href') +' #login' );


  //prevent browser from refreshing
  return false;
});
```

The **dialog** utility plugin also accepts an **options** argument that accepts any of the configurable dialog options specified above (e.g., **title**, **buttons**, **focus**), as well as an additional option, **complete**. The **complete** option accepts a callback function that executes after the Ajax response returns and the dialog is populated with its content. By passing a variable argument to the **complete** function, you can reference the Ajax response's HTML, which can be used for further modification, such as adding events to the markup contained in the dialog. The following example extends the previous script by specifying a **complete** callback function that digs into the response content to find the "forgot your password" link, and binds a click event to request its content in a new dialog:

```
//assign click event to login link
$('#option-login').click(function(){

  //create dialog out of the #login div located in the page
  //referenced in the link's href attribute
  $.dialog( $(this).attr('href')+' #login', {


    //specify complete callback function, w/ response argument
    complete: function(response){


      //find forgot password link, bind click event
      response.find('a.alt-option').click(function(){
```

```
        //create dialog with #forgot div, located in
        // the page referenced in the link's href

        $.dialog($(this).attr('href')+' #forgot');
        //prevent browser from refreshing
        return false;
      });
    }
  });
  //prevent browser from refreshing
  return false;
});
```

* * *

Creating accessible dialogs and overlays is pretty easy, as long as you remember to include the appropriate ARIA attributes, and manage focus to ensure proper keyboard support. The same basic coding principles illustrated here can be used to build a wide range of different widgets, from photo lightbox overlays to draggable and resizable panels, inspectors, and palettes.

chapter fourteen

buttons

Buttons are ubiquitous in websites and application interfaces—to submit data and initiate actions in toolbars, forms, and navigation controls—and designers frequently customize their appearance. We typically design custom-styled buttons for projects that must:

▶ Match the branding and presentation of the overall site or application

▶ Use color, texture, and dimension to convey button hierarchy—for instance, visually distinguishing primary and secondary actions

▶ Include icons to make them more uniquely identifiable and easier to scan, or compact, icon-only buttons, like those used in text-editing toolbars

▶ Introduce custom interaction states to provide better feedback, like a pressed state for touch-screen buttons

Virtually any HTML element can be made to look and behave like a button with a bit of CSS and JavaScript—for example, Google's Gmail web application uses **div**-based buttons throughout the interface. But relying on JavaScript events to handle form submission is risky; when scripting is disabled or not fully supported, all related functionality is rendered unusable.

For foundation markup that reliably works everywhere, we need to start with either an **input** element with a **type** of **button**, or the **button** element. Which of these elements to choose depends on the styling and functionality needs of the particular situation.

In this chapter, we'll walk through two target designs and discuss the criteria for deciding when to use **input** or **button** elements in the foundation markup, and then review how to transform them into richly formatted buttons in the enhanced experience.

X-ray perspective

Let's say we have a social networking site with a page that lists friend invitations, which can be accepted or ignored. Our design introduces a visual hierarchy for the buttons that emphasizes the positive Add Friend action over the negative Ignore action. Let's consider two possible target designs that illustrate the key factors that will help us decide which native element to use: a simpler one with buttons styled distinctly to show a difference in emphasis:

Figure 14-1 The target button design has a visual style that distinguishes primary and secondary buttons.

...or a more complex design that calls for icons inside each button and mixed font weights for the text formatting (the *Add John* is bold):

Figure 14-2 Target design with complex button formatting

There are two native elements we could use to code the foundation markup for our custom buttons: an **input** element with its **type** attribute set to **submit**, **reset**, or **image**, or a **button** element. Of the two markup options, the **input** element has been part of the HTML specification longer than **button** (**input** was included in the HTML3 specification circa 1996, vs. the **button**'s inclusion in the HTML4 specification around late 1999), and tends to work correctly in a broader range of older and mobile browsers. Because it's universally functional, an **input** is our first choice for creating buttons in the foundation markup.

Designers have traditionally avoided using standard **input**-based buttons when a design calls for a styled button; there's a common misperception that the **input** can't be styled reliably with CSS. We tested this idea and were surprised to find it's possible to consistently style **input**-based buttons in all mainstream browsers (even Internet Explorer 5!) with various type styles, background images, borders, rounded corners, custom dimensions, margins, and padding.

There is, however, a key limitation with an **input**: this element consists of a single self-closing tag, so it can't contain another HTML element—like an image, **span**, **em**, **strong**, or any other HTML tag. This prevents us from using the **input** for complex text formatting, layering several background images, or adding multiple icons.

The **button** element, by contrast, has both opening and closing tags and can contain additional HTML elements. This allows us to accommodate all the design features of our more complex target design—we can wrap the *Add John* text in a **strong** tag for emphasis and add a **span** tag to apply the icon. However, the **button** has its own drawback: since it was absent from the earliest HTML specifications, some older browsers and mobile platforms don't recognize it, and will either fail to display the button at all or won't properly submit the form when it's clicked.

For this reason, we recommend that our foundation button markup always be an **input**, and that we use **button** elements *only* in the enhanced experience. For the first, simpler design, we'll style the **input** for the enhanced experience as we would any other element; for the more complex design with formatted text and icons, we'll "transform" the **input** into a **button** to achieve advanced formatting and retain the ability to natively submit form data.

We'll start by reviewing how to style an **input**-based button. Then, we'll walk through how to transform an **input** into a **button** element in the enhanced experience to accommodate the additional icons and text formatting of the second example.

Styling input-based buttons

We'll construct our first design with **input**-based buttons and style them with CSS for both the basic and enhanced experiences. The design (as shown in Figure 14-1 above) is simple enough for this approach to work in a wide range of browsers.

To apply a visual hierarchy between the primary and secondary buttons, we'll distinguish them in the markup with descriptive classes assigned to the **input** elements (**btn-primary** and **btn-secondary**) in the foundation markup. To be safe, we'll reserve much of the visual styling, such as the light-on-dark text of the Add button, for the enhanced experience, since older browsers may support styling only the text color (and not the background image or color), which may result in unreadable text.

We can, however, show visual emphasis in the basic experience by setting the font weight of the primary button to bold. (Though this style property is generally well supported, it may be ignored by some browsers when applied to an **input**.) In even very primitive browsers, our hint of primary and alternate actions will be communicated in the basic experience (as shown in Figure 14-2 above).

Foundation markup and style

The foundation markup for our social networking site starts with a **form** tag; within the form is a **fieldset** that contains a **legend**, a paragraph with the location and count of common friends, and two submit **input** elements for adding and ignoring friend requests:

```
<form action="friendForm.php">

  <fieldset>

      <legend>Friend request from John Smith</legend>

      <p>Boston MA - 16 friends in common with you</p>

      <input type="submit" name="add" value="Add John as a friend" />

      <input type="submit" name="ignore" value="Ignore" />

  </fieldset>

</form>
```

We'll add a class to each **input** element to identify its role as either primary or secondary:

```
<input type="submit" name="add" value="Add John as a friend"
class="btn-primary" />

<input type="submit" name="ignore" value="Ignore" class="btn-secondary" />
```

Our foundation markup now provides a usable experience on any device that supports basic HTML:

Figure 14-3 Unstyled foundation markup

The form is perfectly usable, but could use some visual polish, so we'll add a few safe CSS rules to the basic style sheet.

One style property that has a big impact on look and feel is **font-family**. Most elements on a page inherit **font-family** properties from their parent elements, but form controls are often an exception; many browsers specify a monospaced font for form controls regardless of other font styles set on the page. To fix this, we'll point our **font-family** rule at the **body** and **input** elements:

```
body, input { font-family: "Segoe UI", Arial, sans-serif; }
```

This simple rule makes our form look a lot better already!

Figure 14-4 Foundation markup with font style applied

To improve the form's legibility, we'll remove the **fieldset**'s border and adjust its margins, style the **legend** to be bold and green, and adjust the margins on the paragraph inside:

```
fieldset {
  margin-top: 1.2em;
  margin-bottom: 1.2em;
  border: 0;
}

legend {
  color: #339900;
  font-weight: bold;
}

fieldset p {
  margin: 0 0 1.2em;
}
```

Now the form block in the basic experience looks even closer to our target design:

Figure 14-5 Foundation markup with fieldset, legend, and paragraph styles applied.

Finally, we'll style the primary button with bold text and specify that the secondary button should have normal (not bold) text, to ensure a shift in visual emphasis in the basic experience:

```
.btn-primary { font-weight: bold; }

.btn-secondary { font-weight: normal; }
```

With these styles in place, the Add button takes visual precedence:

Figure 14-6 Foundation markup with bold text on the primary button for visual emphasis

Now that our foundation markup and styles are complete, we'll tackle the enhanced markup and styles that are applied to the page when the browser passes the capabilities test.

Enhanced markup and style

The buttons in our target design share a number of styles, so in our enhanced style sheet we'll write a single rule against both button selectors to apply shared styles. These rules define padding, font formatting and alignment, and set the cursor style to be the clickable hand icon over the **input**:

```
.btn-primary,

.btn-secondary {

  padding: .4em 1em;

  border: 1px solid #aaa;

  background-color: #eee;

  text-align: center;

  cursor: pointer;

  font-size: 1.2em;

}
```

■ Note

The buttons' font weight is inherited from the primary and secondary classes we wrote into the basic style sheet, so they don't need to be defined again in the enhanced style sheet.

Figure 14-7 Common styles applied to the **input** elements

◆ Tip

When setting button styles, using em units instead of pixels for properties like padding and margin, to ensure that the button (and the space it occupies) will expand and contract relative to its font size.

Older versions of Internet Explorer add extra width to **input** and **button** elements that can't be set with **padding** or **margin** values, but there is a fix: specify a **width** property and set the **overflow** property to **visible**. If the button doesn't require a specific **width**, you can set the value to **auto**:

```
.btn-primary,
.btn-secondary {
    padding: .4em 1em;
    border: 1px solid #aaa;
    background-color: #eee;
    text-align: center;
    cursor: pointer;
    font-size: 1.2em;
    width: auto;
    overflow: visible;
}
```

To give the buttons rounded corners, we'll apply the CSS3 **border-radius** property. At the time of this writing, only Mozilla- and Webkit-based browsers support the **border-radius** property (using vendor-specific property names), but it's still safe to use, because browsers that don't support it will simply display the buttons with square corners. We'll also append the standard **border-radius** property specified by the W3C, so that any browsers that implement this feature in the future will show rounded corners as well (both Opera and Internet Explorer have committed to supporting this property at the time of writing):

```
.btn-primary,
.btn-secondary {
    padding: .4em 1em;
    border: 1px solid #aaa;
    background-color: #eee;
    text-align: center;
```

```
    cursor: pointer;

    font-size: 1.2em;

    width: auto;

    overflow: visible;

    -moz-border-radius: 7px;

    -webkit-border-radius: 7px;

    border-radius: 7px;

}
```

Figure 14-8 Basic button styles with rounded corners

The primary and secondary button classes in the basic styles specify background images (green and silver, respectively), and text and border colors to match the design:

```
.btn-primary {

    background: #459e00 url(../images/button-green.gif) no-repeat left center;

    color: #fff;

    border-color: #2d7406;

}
```

```
.btn-secondary {

    background: #e7e8e9 url(../images/button-silver.gif) no-repeat left center;

    color: #555;

    border-color: #b3b3b3;

}
```

To help the text stand out against the background image, the **text-shadow** property adds a drop shadow on the button text. Like the **border-radius** property, **text-shadow** is supported by only a handful of browsers at this time (specifically, Firefox 3.5+, Safari 1.1+, and Opera 9.5+), but is harmless to include as long as the text has good contrast without the shadow.

```
.btn-primary {

    background: #459e00 url(../images/button-green.gif) no-repeat left center;

    color: #eee;
```

```
  border-color: #2d7406;

  text-shadow: -1px -1px 0 #37730e;

}


.btn-secondary {

  background: #e7e8e9 url(../images/button-silver.gif) no-repeat left center;

  color: #555;

  border-color: #b3b3b3;

  text-shadow: 1px 1px 0 #fafafa;

}
```

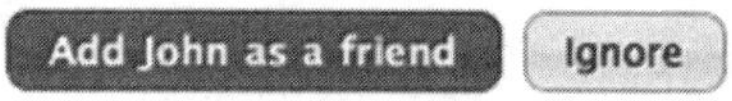

Add John as a friend   Ignore

Figure 14-9 Button styles applied

To provide good visual feedback when the user interacts with the button, a hover state is defined for each button type. Ideally, we would do this using the **:hover** pseudo-class, but Internet Explorer versions 6 and earlier don't support this on elements other than anchors (**a**). To remedy this, we'll use JavaScript to add and remove a hover class when the user moves the cursor onto or off of a button:

```
.btn-primary-hover {

  background-color: #57AF00;

  background-position: right center;

  color: #fff;

  border-color: #205b00;

}


.btn-secondary-hover {

  background-color: #F1F1F2;

  background-position: right center;

  color: #333;

  border-color: #777;

}
```

Figure 14-10 Secondary button hover state

Using image sprites

To reduce the number of server requests, we combine the primary and secondary buttons' default and hover background images into image sprites. An image sprite is a single image file that contains multiple background images; the appropriate background image is shown by positioning it with the CSS **background-position** property.

The button's default state is the left side, and the hover is the right, so we can simply shift the background position from left to right in the style sheet for each state. The sprite is 1,000 pixels wide (half default state, half hover state), so our buttons can be up to 500 pixels wide.

Figure 14-11 Primary and secondary button background image sprites

Lastly, we'll add font-size rules to the **legend** and paragraph to create appropriate visual weight for each:

```
legend { font-size:1.5em; }
fieldset p { font-size:1.3em; }
```

With these styles applied, the enhanced markup looks exactly like our target design:

Figure 14-12 Final enhanced styles

Enhanced hover state script

The scripting required for the **input**-based button is minimal: we'll use JavaScript to apply the **hover** class to the buttons when the user places their cursor over a button. This approach ensures that proper hover-state feedback will be displayed in all browsers that pass the capabilities test.

To start, we'll create two variables that capture our **input** elements, one each for all of the primary and secondary buttons on the page:

```
//find all input elements with primary and secondary btn classes
var primaryButtons = $('input.btn-primary');
var secondaryButtons = $('input.btn-secondary');
```

Then we'll add the **hover** class by binding a function to the input's **mouseover** event, and remove it using the **mouseout** event. As a convenience, jQuery provides a single **hover** method that lets you pass in functions for both the **mouseover** and **mouseout** events. The following example shows how to apply this hover-state toggle to primary buttons:

```
//apply the hover method
primaryButtons.hover(
    //first function argument applies the mouseover event
    function(){
        $(this).addClass('btn-primary-hover');
    },
    //second function argument applies the mouseout event
    function(){
        $(this).removeClass('btn-primary-hover');
    },
);
```

For secondary buttons, we'd construct a similar **hover** method that acts on the **secondaryButtons** variable, and use it to toggle the **btn-secondary-hover** class on and off.

Our **input** buttons now support the behavior and visual appearance specified in our initial target design. Next, we'll review how buttons with more complex visual formatting can be transformed from an **input** into a **button** in the enhanced experience.

Creating buttons with complex visual formatting

Our second target design builds on the first example, with a couple of additional features: icons for the Add and Ignore action buttons, and varying font weights to emphasize a portion of the primary button text.

Figure 14-13 Target design with complex button formatting

In this case we can't style the **input** element to match the target design, so we'll use an **input** element in the foundation markup, which we know will work reliably in all browsers and devices. In the enhanced experience, we'll run a script that replaces the **input** with a styled **button** element for a richer experience.

When swapping the **input** element with the **button**, we'll copy all of the **input** element's attributes and JavaScript events over to the **button** to ensure that the new element is a one-to-one match. The new **button** will completely replace all of the functionality of the **input** element, so when the script is complete, we'll remove the **input** from the page entirely.

Foundation markup and style

Like the first example, we'll start with **input** elements and assign primary and secondary classes, but we'll add an additional class to each **input** to identify the purpose of the buttons (**action-add** and **action-ignore**). These classes will be transferred to the **button** elements in the enhanced experience to apply specific icons to the buttons:

```
<input type="submit" name="add" value="Add John as a friend" class="btn-
primary action-add" />
```

```
<input type="submit" name="ignore" value="Ignore" class="btn-secondary
action-ignore" />
```

To identify the button text that should be styled with bold, we'll use an HMTL character as a delimiter; the script will look for this delimiter and apply the bold style to the words that precede it. A good choice for a delimiter is a punctuation mark or special character that makes sense when displayed in the basic experience and is unique enough to be detected by the script. In this button, there isn't a visible character that would read correctly, so the best choice for a delimiter is a non-breaking space character (** **), which is invisible in the basic experience:

```
<input type="submit" name="add" value="Add John as a friend"
class="btn-primary action-add" />
```

```
<input type="submit" name="ignore" value="Ignore" class="btn-secondary
action-ignore" />
```

The basic styles we created for the first example also apply here, with one slight modification: we'll add **button** to the **font-family** selector so that it inherits the correct font style:

```
body, input, button { font-family: "Segoe UI", Arial, sans-serif; }
```

With foundation markup and basic styles in place, we'll tackle the enhanced markup and styles that are applied to the page when the browser passes the capabilities test.

Enhanced markup and style

When the browser passes the capabilities test, we'll use JavaScript to replace each **input** with a **button** element that has the same attributes and JavaScript events:

```
<button type="submit" name="add" value="Add John as a Friend" class=
"btn-primary action-add">Add John as a Friend</button>

<button type="submit" name="ignore" value="Ignore" class="btn-secondary
action-ignore">Ignore</button>
```

Our enhancement script will remove the delimiter we inserted in the foundation markup—a non-breaking space (** **)—and wrap the text that precedes it in a **strong** element:

```
<button type="submit" name="add" value="Add John as a Friend" class="btn-
primary action-add"><strong>Add John</strong> as a Friend</button>
```

To apply an icon, the script will insert a **span** element with a **class** of **icon** to the markup, before the **button** text:

```
<button type="submit" name="add" value="Add John as a Friend" class=
"btn-primary action-add"><span class="icon"></span><strong>Add John
</strong> as a Friend</button>
```

As we did with the basic CSS, we'll build upon the enhanced CSS we created to style an **input** to specify styles required for the enhanced **button** element.

In our target design, a portion of the primary button's text is bold, while the rest is normal font weight. The **btn-primary** class applies a bold **font-weight** property to all primary buttons, so we'll need to make an exception for this particular primary button. We'll write a new style rule against the **action-add** class, specifically for the primary button in our target design; that way other primary buttons in the page will remain bold:

```
button.action-add { font-weight: normal; }
```

The input-to-button script will wrap **strong** tags around the emphasized text, *Add John*. By default, most browsers apply a bold font style to **strong** elements, but to ensure that the proper formatting is applied, we'll reinforce this style with a simple rule:

```
button strong { font-weight: bold; }
```

We'll also add styles for the icon **span**s that apply an **inline-block** property and dimension:

```css
button span.icon {
  display: inline-block;
  height: 12px;
  margin-right: 5px;
  width: 16px;
}
```

Finally, we'll set a background image for each icon **span**, based on the parent element's class:

```css
.action-add span.icon {
  background: url(../images/icon-add.png) 0 0 no-repeat;
}
.action-ignore span.icon {
  background: url(../images/icon-ignore.png) 0 0 no-repeat;
}
```

Now that our CSS supports complex button formatting, we'll move on to scripting the input-to-button conversion.

Enhanced input-to-button script

Our goal is to replace specific **input** elements in the foundation markup with custom-styled **button** elements when a browser passes the capabilities test. To start, we'll create a **buttoninputs** variable to store an array of references to all of the button-like **input** elements on the page:

```js
var buttoninputs = $('input.btn-primary, input.btn-secondary');
```

We'll loop through each item in the array using jQuery's **each** method and replace it with a new **button** element, including all of the **input** element's attributes and event bindings. The **each** method accepts an argument—a function—to execute on each item in the **buttoninputs** array:

```js
buttoninputs.each(function(){

  ...

});
```

In this function, we'll write the logic that grabs all of the input's attributes and events, assigns them to a new **button** element, and replaces the **input**.

First, we'll create a variable that acts as a template for the **button** markup, and use the **input** element's value for the **button** element's text label:

```
buttoninputs.each(function(){
  var button = $('<button>'+ $(this).val() +'</button>');
});
```

■ Note

Within the function we pass to the each method, the `this` keyword refers to the current `input` element. By wrapping `this` in parentheses and preceding it with a dollar sign, we turn it into a jQuery object reference, which allows us to apply jQuery methods to manipulate the element. For example, the statement `$(this).val();` returns the value of the input.

Next, we'll get all of the **input** element's attribute name/value pairs (**nodeName** and **nodeValue**, technically) and apply them to the new **button** using the **setAttribute** method:

```
buttoninputs.each(function(){
  var button = $('<button>'+ $(this).val() +'</button>');
  $.each(this.attributes, function(){
      button[0].setAttribute(this.nodeName, this.nodeValue);
  });
});
```

■ Note

At the time of writing, jQuery's `attr` method causes an error when it's used to set the type attribute in Internet Explorer 8. To avoid a conflict with Internet Explorer, we used the native JavaScript `setAttribute` method rather than jQuery's shortcut `attr` method; as with all native JavaScript attributes, `setAttribute` must reference the button variable using array notation, `button[0]`.

Now that we've reassigned the **input** element's attributes to the **button**, we'll do the same for all JavaScript events bound to the **input** element. Events bound using jQuery are stored in memory via the **data** method, which can be used to both get and set data values. We'll pass a single argument to that method—in this case, **events**—to retrieve all of the events tied to our input. And because each event, like **onload** or **onclick**, can have more than one binding, or function, associated with it, we'll also loop through those bindings to make sure we get them all:

```
buttoninputs.each(function(){
  var button = $('<button>'+ $(this).val() +'</button>');
  $.each(this.attributes, function(){
      button[0].setAttribute(this.nodeName, this.nodeValue);
  });
  if ($(this).data('events')) {
      $.each($(this).data('events'),
          function(eventname, bindings){
              $.each(bindings, function(){
                  button.bind(eventname, this);
              });
          });
  };
});
```

At this point, we've created custom buttons using the original **input** elements' attributes and events. Now we can safely remove the **input** elements from the markup. jQuery's **replaceWith** method gives us a tidy way to remove the **input** element and insert the new **button** element simultaneously:

```
buttoninputs.each(function(){
  var button = $('<button>'+ $(this).val() +'</button>');
  $.each(this.attributes, function(){
      button[0].setAttribute(this.nodeName, this.nodeValue);
  });
  if ($(this).data('events')) {
      $.each($(this).data('events'),
          function(eventname, bindings){
              $.each(bindings, function(){
                  button.bind(eventname, this);
              });
          });
  };
```

```
    $(this).replaceWith(button);
});
```

We've now converted the **input**s to **button** elements; next, we'll add the text formatting (**strong** tags) and icon spans. We'll reset the inner HTML of the **action-add** button by splitting its text at the non-breaking space character, and wrapping the first portion in a **strong** element:

```
//get a reference to the add button
var addButton = $('button.action-add');


//set the add button's html
addButton.html(
'<strong>'+addButton.html().split(' ')[0]+'</strong>'+
  addButton.html().split(' ')[1]
);
```

Finally, we'll add the icon **span** elements to all buttons using jQuery's **prepend** method, which inserts HTML at the beginning of an element:

```
$('button').prepend('<span class="icon"></span>');
```

Using the input-to-button script

The code that accompanies this book (available at www.filamentgroup/dwpe) includes a jQuery plugin that packages the principles shown in this chapter—specifically, in the second example—into a reusable script for use in your projects. To use the code, simply include all the files referenced in the button demo page, and call the **inputToButton** method on any **input** elements you'd like to convert to a **button**.

```
$('input#submitForm').inputToButton();
```

The **inputToButton** plugin will automatically transfer over any classes and events and apply hover classes to the buttons. You can safely call the **inputToButton** method on all **input** elements, as the script will make sure to not convert any non-button input types, like **text, radio**, or **checkbox**.

```
$('input').inputToButton();
```

To add the icon spans and non-breaking space-delimited text bolding (as we did for the Add button in this chapter), you can direct additional logic to look for the non-breaking space and inject the icon **span**:

```
$('input').inputToButton();


//split text at   character, removing it in the process
var splitText = addButton.html().split(' ');


//find button with action-add class and
//replace its content with a strong element wrapped around first segment
//of splitText, followed by text of second segment of splitText
$('button.action-add')
    .html('<strong>'+ splitText[0]+'</strong> '+ splitText[1]);


//add icon span to all buttons before the text
$('button').prepend('<span class="icon"></span>');
```

Taking the button further

In addition to submitting data, buttons are commonly used in applications as toggles for settings or preferences. Toggle buttons typically have an additional "pressed" state to make it appear selected.

Toggle buttons can either act alone, as a single on/off switch, or as part of a set that allows one selection at a time. If you think this sounds similar to another kind of HTML element, you're right—toggle buttons behave exactly like checkbox and radio button inputs.

For a detailed example of how to style checkbox and radio inputs like toggle buttons, check out Chapter 15, "Checkboxes, radio buttons, and star rating." The code that accompanies this book also includes a demo page with toggle buttons that resemble those shown in this chapter. Check out **toggle-buttons.html** in the accompanying code's **checkbox-radiobutton** folder.

On the use and styling of buttons

We found the following articles helpful in guiding our own work on customizing buttons:

www.456bereastreet.com/archive/200701/styling_form_controls_with_css_revisited/

http://jehiah.cz/archive/button-width-in-ie

http://allinthehead.com/retro/330/coping-with-internet-explorers-mishandling-of-buttons

www.filamentgroup.com/lab/
update_styling_the_button_element_with_css_sliding_doors_now_with_image_spr

www.filamentgroup.com/lab/styling_buttons_and_toolbars_with_the_jquery_ui_css_
framework

* * *

Custom-styled buttons can deliver enhanced visual sophistication and improve the usability of a site. When creating your own buttons, keep the following rules in mind to ensure a usable experience for all:

▶ Start with a universally functional **input** element with minimal, safe styles to ensure that all users have access to key functionality.

▶ For simpler button designs (without text formatting or icons), use the **input** element for both the basic and enhanced experience, and apply enhanced styles when the capabilities test passes.

▶ For more complex designs, convert each **input** element to a **button** to add style and visual feedback for capable browsers and devices.

▶ Style the button font size and padding with **em**s rather than pixels to preserve text-size scaling.

▶ To minimize server requests, use image sprites for button backgrounds. Just be sure that the image sprite is wide enough to accommodate your longest button at an enlarged font size.

chapter fifteen

checkboxes, radio buttons, and star rating

Thanks to widespread adoption of web standards and advanced CSS techniques, most interface components in modern web designs now have a customized look and feel, with rich color palettes and dimensional background images that tightly integrate with the overall visual style of the site.

Form checkboxes and radio buttons, however, are a stubborn exception to the rule. They've lagged behind, primarily because only a few browsers have built in support for styling these elements with CSS. To further complicate matters, browsers render checkboxes and radio buttons slightly differently in terms of size, spacing, and appearance.

For many, including most of our clients, the usability features inherent in the native checkboxes and radio buttons—including accessibility, keyboard support, label interactions, and universal browser compatibility—are significant enough that the benefits of custom styling pale by comparison. For this reason, we generally use the native elements in most situations and just accept that we can't control their appearance to match our design system.

But we've encountered a few design projects that genuinely required a custom-designed solution that involved changing the color, style, and/or size of checkboxes and radio buttons. A few examples include:

▶ A touch-screen mobile device or kiosk for which we created custom-styled, finger-friendly, larger-than-average toggles that still needed to capture user data input like native controls

▶ A charting application in which color-coded checkboxes acted as both the chart legend and the means to toggle each item on and off in the graph

▶ A search-results page containing a sort control, with links for date, relevance, and popularity, for example, where the user chose a single option for sorting data (analogous to a set of radio buttons)

▶ A simple checkbox or radio button that needed custom styling to match the branding and visual design of a site, especially one that uses a dark or colorful background color

When a custom-designed form element is required because the native element can't provide the level of visual control or functionality, we need to build a solution that is as accessible and easy to use as the one we're replacing.

In this chapter, we'll show how we use progressive enhancement to transform standard HTML checkboxes and radio buttons into custom-designed versions that are as light-weight as possible. We'll also walk through the process of building a custom star-rating widget, since it shares a lot of the same techniques and scripting.

X-ray perspective

One common application of custom input elements is in a survey, where questions with grouped checkbox and radio button options match the look and feel of a specific visual design. Our design looks something like this:

Figure 15-1 Survey design with custom checkbox and radio button styles applied

Analyzing the design with an x-ray perspective is very easy in this case: it's an obvious choice to use standard checkboxes and radio button inputs as our foundation markup. On their own, checkboxes and radio buttons capture data and display feedback, and the goal is to take advantage of that native functionality and not have to reinvent it using JavaScript.

We went in search of the best method to achieve custom styling without compromising the native element's rich functionality. A quick web search turned up several scripts that cleverly use a combination of JavaScript and CSS to create custom-styled checkboxes and radio buttons by hiding the original **input**, and insert replacement markup for the custom element that could be styled effectively. These scripts tended to be fairly complex to re-create all the functionality, behavior, state tracking, keyboard events, and accessibility features present in the native checkbox or radio button. In older screen readers that don't understand ARIA or if images aren't supported, these techniques would fail and leave the **input** unusable. Although replacement is sometimes necessary (we cover this in Chapter 17 for custom selects), it introduces code complexity, and we wanted to find a more elegant solution.

While exploring alternate ideas, we remembered a key feature that we could use to solve our problem: in all major browsers, when you click a **label** that's associated with a checkbox or radio button **input**, it has the same effect as clicking the form element itself—it will toggle the checked state on a checkbox or select the radio button.

In theory, this shouldn't work: The HTML specification says, "When a **label** element receives focus, it passes the focus on to its associated control." However, in every browser we tested, clicking the label passes focus *and the click event* to the associated checkbox or radio button. This browser behavior gave us a crucial hook to build a lightweight, but visually customized, checkbox and radio button for the enhanced experience that extensively leverages the native element.

We know we can rely solely on the **label** element to control the native checkbox or radio button state, without requiring the user to directly click on the actual **input** element. We can use this feature of the **label** to our advantage in the enhanced experience by applying styles to the **label** to make it look like a custom input and provide visual feedback.

With a bit of CSS positioning, we can stack the **label** element *over* the native checkbox or radio button. By adding a background image with our custom checkbox or radio button design to the **label**, we effectively mask the native input even though it's still visible. All that is required is that the **input**s and labels are paired with correct semantics in the foundation markup—in other words, matching the label's **for** attribute value with that of the **input**'s **id** value.

Figure 15-2 The label with its custom background image is placed over the native checkbox with CSS.

With this approach, we leave the native checkbox visible and in its normal position on the page, not positioned off-screen or hidden with CSS. When images are present, the background image is displayed on the label and the custom style is seen, masking the native input. As long as the background color of the label is set to transparent, when images aren't supported, the native input will be seen through the label so the control remains usable.

Figure 15-3 Enhanced version of the custom checkbox with images enabled (left) and disabled (left) in the browser

At this stage, we have a clear strategy for enhancing a set of HTML checkboxes and radio buttons. For every visitor who arrives at our site—even on the oldest browser, the most pared-down web-enabled device, or a system with selected functionality disabled—we'll serve up our simple, semantic HTML, confident that it will be accessible to all:

Figure 15-4 Checkboxes and radio buttons seen in the basic experience

Using the label to create the enhanced custom-styled checkbox or radio button preserves all the functionality, inherent keyboard support, and accessibility features of the native **input**. This eliminates the need to use ARIA attributes, since all users—including screen readers—are still interacting with the native form element. With this approach, very little additional markup is required for the enhanced experience, and the scripting can be simple and lightweight.

Creating the custom checkbox

With the target design and our end goal established, we'll review how to construct the foundation markup and how to enhance that markup into custom form controls with CSS and a short script.

Foundation markup

Let's start by creating the basic HTML markup for the checkbox section of our survey question.

We'll wrap the questionnaire in a **form** tag so it can be submitted. Inside, we'll wrap the checkbox controls in a **fieldset** to group them, and we'll use the **legend** tag for the question text.

It's critical to associate each **input** and **label** by setting the **for** attribute on the label to match the **id** of the checkbox **input**; these must be properly paired so the label can be clicked to toggle the state of the checkbox:

```
<form action="moviepoll.php" action="post">
  <fieldset>
      <legend>Which genres do you like?</legend>

      <input type="checkbox" name="genre" id="action" value="action" />
      <label for="action">Action / Adventure</label>

      <input type="checkbox" name="genre" id="comedy" value="comedy" />
      <label for="comedy">Comedy</label>

      <input type="checkbox" name="genre" id="epic" value="epic" />
      <label for="epic">Epic / Historical</label>

      <input type="checkbox" name="genre" id="science" value="science" />
      <label for="science">Science Fiction</label>

      <input type="checkbox" name="genre" id="romance" value="romance" />
      <label for="romance">Romance</label>

      <input type="checkbox" name="genre" id="western" value="western" />
      <label for="western">Western</label>
  </fieldset>
</form>
```

■ Note

In a screen reader, the `legend` text for the `fieldset` will be repeated before each input inside, so it's best to keep this concise but descriptive.

Without any CSS styling at all, each checkbox and label pair is clearly grouped with the question, which makes the survey usable to everyone:

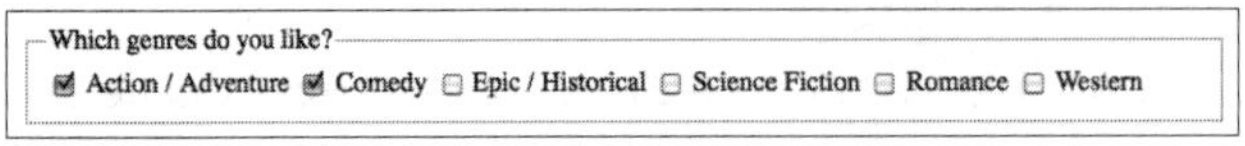

Figure 15-5 Unstyled foundation checkbox markup

To make this look more consistent with our site and add a hint of visual style, we'll apply some very simple CSS rules that are "safe" for pretty much any browser:

▶ A font-family stack on the **body** so it matches our site design

▶ A bold font-weight on the **legend** to introduce better visual hierarchy between the question and options

▶ A bit of margin around the legend, and to the right of each label, to better visually separate these options and increase the visual connection between each checkbox and its label, to help the page read better.

▶ Our "safe" styles look like this in the basic style sheet:

```
body { font-family: "Segoe UI", Arial, sans-serif; }


fieldset { margin-top: 1em; margin-bottom: 1em; border:1px solid #ddd; }
legend { font-weight:bold; }
label { margin-right:1.2em; }
```

▶ ... and like this on the page:

Figure 15-6 Foundation checkbox with safe styles applied

■ Note

We don't go too far with our basic safe styles because it's better to keep the CSS simple and let each device use its native rendering as much as possible. You'll see that we don't specify font sizes or dimensions on any of these elements; we want to let the browser decide how to best present the HTML. Also, we use margins sparingly and with intent because we believe it adds a lot to the usability of the page, but we understand that many older or mobile browsers may ignore margin rules.

Enhanced markup and style

Now that we have the foundation markup established, we can identify any markup changes and advanced styles that should be layered on by the enhancement script for browsers that pass the capabilities test.

The custom checkbox is quite simple, and requires only one markup enhancement: a wrapper **div** with the class **custom-checkbox** that will be added by the enhancement script:

```
<div class="custom-checkbox">

  <input type="checkbox" name="genre" id="check-1" value="action" />

  <label for="check-1">Action / Adventure</label>

</div>
```

This class will be used to apply our enhanced CSS styles. First, the div will be relatively positioned, which will allow us to absolutely position the **label** and checkbox inside this container:

```
.custom-checkbox { position:relative; }
```

Next, we'll absolutely position the **input**, and place it a few pixels in from the top-left corner of the wrapper to help it align with the label text. We'll also set the z-index on the label to ensure that it's on top:

```
.custom-checkbox input {
  position:absolute;
  left:2px;
  top:2px;
  margin:0;
}
```

Next, we'll write the CSS rule for the **label** to display it as a block-level element positioned in front of the input with a z-index of 1. We'll add 30 pixels of left padding to label to make room for our custom checkbox background image to sit to the left of the text label. We'll also add a rule to make sure the whole label looks clickable in all browsers by setting the **cursor** to **pointer**:

```
.custom-checkbox label {
  display:block;
  position:relative;
```

```
    font-size:1.3em;

    padding-right:1em;

    line-height:1;

    padding:.5em 0 .5em 30px;

    margin:0 0 .3em;

    cursor:pointer;

    z-index:10;

}
```

Then we'll add an image sprite for the custom-designed background images that represent the states on the label.

◆ Tip

Using a single image in place of many reduces the number of server requests, and pre-caches the various states so the page will load faster.

When taking this approach, there are two important requirements to keep in mind for the sprite to make sure it completely obscures the native checkbox:

▶ Sprite images must have an opaque background so they fully mask the native input.

▶ Each graphic in the sprite image must be large enough to fully cover the checkbox in all of its interaction states. For instance, when browsing in Firefox on a Mac, checkboxes "glow" with a 3-pixel blue border when they receive focus. The sprite graphics must be large enough to cover this effect.

Our image sprite stacks the four different checkbox states—unchecked, unchecked on hover, checked, and checked on hover—vertically from top to bottom. You can space your sprite images as you see fit, but they need to be far enough apart to keep the other states from showing through, as each label's height grows when text size increases or wraps to multiple lines. For the purposes of this example, the individual state images are spaced evenly apart at 100-pixel increments:

Figure 15-7
Checkbox image sprite, with visual treatments for all interaction states stacked, and plenty of space between states

We set a generic rule to assign the checkbox image sprite to the **label**:

```
.custom-checkbox label {

    background:url(../images/checkbox.gif) no-repeat;

}
```

We can now add in the CSS rules to shift the background position of the checkbox image sprite for the unchecked, unchecked on hover, checked, and checked on hover states. Each state is spaced apart evenly in the sprite, so we just need to adjust the **vertical position** by 100 pixels each time. Ideally, we would assign the hover states using the CSS **:hover** pseudo-class, but not all modern browsers support **:hover** on label elements, so we'll add a class called **hover** on **mouseover**, and remove it on **mouseout**:

```
.custom-checkbox label {
  background-position:-10px -14px;
}
.custom-checkbox label.hover, .custom-checkbox label.focus {
  background-position:-10px -114px;
}
.custom-checkbox label.checked {
  background-position:-10px -214px;
}
.custom-checkbox label.checkedHover, .custom-checkbox label.checkedFocus {
  background-position:-10px -314px;
}
```

At this point, all four checkbox states look as designed:

Figure 15-8 Enhanced checkbox design, with states created by changing the background position of the image sprite

While the visual shift of the hover states is helpful, it may not be discernable to all users. To make the focused state clearer for users who are navigating with their keyboards, for example, we'll add a light gray dotted outline on the currently focused option by adding a class of **focus** on the label:

```
.custom-checkbox label.focus { outline: 1px dotted #ccc; }
```

☐ Comedy

Figure 15-9 A dotted outline around the label aids in keyboard navigation.

Now that we've worked out the markup and styles for the various interaction states, we'll build the script that swaps the label's interaction states as the user hovers over and clicks the custom checkboxes.

Checkbox script

The script for enhancing the native checkbox is pretty simple. First, we'll gather all of the checkboxes by finding any **input** with a **type** of **checkbox**:

```
var checkboxes = $('input[type=checkbox]');
```

Then we'll loop through each checkbox using jQuery's **each** method, search for a **label** that has a **for** attribute matching the checkbox's **id**, and wrap both in a **div** with the **custom-checkbox** class. While we have the **label** handy, we'll assign **mouseover** and **mouseout** events to it to toggle a class of **hover** when the user hovers on it:

```
//loop through each checkbox input
checkboxes.each(function(){
    //find associated label element
    var label = $('label[for='+ $(this).attr('id') +']');
    //bind a mouseover event to label
    label.mouseover(function(){
        //add hover class
        $(this).addClass('hover');
        //check if checkbox has .checked class
        if( $(this).is('.checked') ){
            //add checkedHover class
            $(this).addClass('checkedHover');
        }
    });
    //bind mouseout event to label
    label.mouseout(function(){
        //remove all hover classes
        $(this).removeClass('hover checkedHover');
    });
    //wrap the checkbox and label in custom checkbox div
```

```
$(this).add(label).wrap('<div class="custom-checkbox"></div>');
});
```

Next, we'll create a custom **updateState** event that checks to see if the input is currently checked. If it's checked, the script adds the **checked** class to position the image sprite to the correct state. If it's not checked, we remove the **checked**, **checkedHover**, or **checkedFocus** class, if any are present, to make the custom checkbox look unchecked:

```
//bind custom updateState event to all the checkboxes
checkboxes.bind('updateState', function(){
    //find associated label element
    var label = $('label[for='+ $(this).attr('id) +']');
    //check if the checkbox is checked
    if ( $(this).is(':checked') ) {
        //add checked class to label element
        label.addClass('checked');
    }
    //if checkbox isn't checked
    else {
        //remove classes from label
        label.removeClass('checked checkedHover checkedFocus');
    }
});
```

Binding this custom event won't actually do anything on its own, since it's not a native event like **click**, or **mouseover**; in order for **updateState** to run, we'll have to trigger it ourselves. When the script first runs, we use jQuery's **trigger** method to run the **updateState** function and set all custom checkboxes to match the checked state of the native checkboxes:

```
//trigger updateState immediately at page load
checkboxes.trigger('updateState');
```

Then we'll bind a **click** event to each checkbox to run the **updateState** function every time a checkbox **input** or **label** is clicked. We'll bind the click event using jQuery's shorthand **click** method, which does the same thing as **bind('click')**:

```
//bind a click event to the checkboxes
checkboxes.click(function(){
  //trigger updateState whenever the checkbox is clicked
  $(this).trigger('updateState');
});
```

To add the dotted outline for our focus state, we'll assign the **focus** class when an **input** receives focus, again using the event's shorthand method:

```
//bind a focus event to the checkboxes
checkboxes.focus(function(){
  //find associated label element
  var label = $('label[for='+ $(this).attr('id') +']');
  //add class of focus to the label
  label.addClass('focus');
  //if the input is checked
  if( $(this).is(':checked') ){
      // add checkedFocus class
      $(this).addClass('checkedFocus');
  }
});
```

… and then remove the **focus** class when the **input** is blurred:

```
//bind a blur event to the checkboxes
checkboxes.blur(function(){
  //find associated label element
  var label = $('label[for='+ $(this).attr('id') +']');
  //remove focus classes from the label
label.removeClass('focus checkedFocus');
});
```

That's the complete basic-to-enhanced markup, style, and script for the custom check-boxes in our survey. The final design with these enhanced styles applied looks like this:

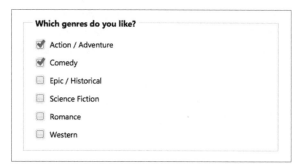

Figure 15-10 Final survey design with custom checkboxes

Creating custom radio buttons

The radio buttons will use very similar HTML markup to the checkboxes, and we'll follow a similar technique and reuse much of the styles and scripting to enhance them.

Foundation markup

As with the checkboxes, we'll use a **fieldset** with **legend** for the question and a list of radio button **input** and **label** pairs for each option:

```
<fieldset>

  <legend>Caddyshack is the greatest movie of all time, right?</legend>


  <input type="radio" name="opinions" id="totally" value="totally" />
  <label for="totally">Totally</label>


  <input type="radio" name="opinions" id="no-way" value="no-way" />
  <label for="no-way">You must be kidding</label>


  <input type="radio" name="opinions" id="whats-caddyshack"
  value="whats-caddyshack" />
  <label for="whats-caddyshack">What's Caddyshack?</label>


</fieldset>
```

Without any CSS, the radio button controls are clearly grouped with their question and completely usable. And if we add the radio buttons to the form we created earlier, the **fieldset**, legend, and **label** elements inherit the "safe" styles we created for the checkboxes.

Caddyshack is the greatest movie of all time, right?
◉ Totally   ◎ You must be kidding   ◎ What's Caddyshack?

Figure 15-11 Radio button foundation markup with safe styles applied

Enhanced markup and style

As with the checkboxes, the enhancement script will wrap each radio button **input** and **label** pair in a **div** with the class **custom-radio** so we can add the enhanced style and behavior:

```
<div class="custom-radio">
  <input type="radio" name="opinions" id="totally" value="totally" />
  <label for="totally">Totally</label>
</div>
```

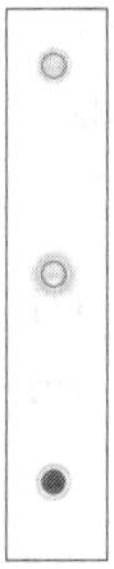

And we'll create a background image sprite for the radio buttons—again making sure that the sprite has an opaque background, that each state is large enough to obscure the native browser feedback, and that the image states are stacked vertically and spaced at our standard increment of 100px:

Figure 15-12 Custom radio button image sprite with unchecked, hover, and checked states

One difference you'll notice is that radio buttons don't have the checked hover state (for example, **.custom-checkbox label.checkedHover**) that we created for the checkboxes; radio buttons don't allow the user to toggle them off once they're checked, so this bit of visual feedback isn't necessary.

Since the custom radio button image is positioned over the native input exactly as it was with the checkboxes, we can simply add the radio button rules to the checkbox rules in the enhanced style sheet.

Without modifying the CSS rules, we'll add the **custom-radio** class selector to our rules for the wrapper, input, and label.

```css
.custom-checkbox, .custom-radio {
  position:relative;
}
.custom-checkbox input, .custom-radio input {
  position:absolute;
  left:2px;
  top:2px;
  margin:0;
}
.custom-checkbox label, .custom-radio label {
  display:block;
  position:relative;
  font-size:1.3em;
  padding-right:1em;
  line-height:1;
  padding:.5em 0 .5em 30px;
  margin:0 0 .3em;
  cursor:pointer;
}
```

And we'll set the image path for the **custom-radio** class background image sprite:

```css
.custom-radio label {
  background: url(../images/radio button.gif) no-repeat;
}
```

We were careful to space the radio button images out at exactly the same increment as with our checkbox sprite, so they can share the same image-positioning CSS rules for each state. We just need to add the selector for **custom-radio** label to each rule. Since the **checkedHover** state applies only to checkboxes, we'll leave that rule as is:

```css
.custom-checkbox label,
.custom-radio label {
  background-position:-10px -14px;
}
```

```
.custom-checkbox label.hover,
.custom-checkbox label.focus,
.custom-radio label.hover,
.custom-radio label.focus {
  background-position:-10px -114px;
}
.custom-checkbox label.checked,
.custom-radio label.checked {
  background-position:-10px -214px;
}
.custom-checkbox label.checkedHover, .custom-checkbox label.checkedFocus {
  background-position:-10px -314px;
}
```

At this point, the code is in place to give all three radio button states their desired style—unchecked, unchecked hover, and checked:

Figure 15-13 All three radio button states are created by changing the background position of the image sprite.

Radio button script

Our custom checkboxes and radio buttons share similar behavior as well as design, so it makes sense to incorporate the logic for radio button functionality into the script we've already created for the checkboxes.

First, we'll modify our starting selection to include radios as well, changing the variable name to **checksRadios** instead of **checkboxes**:

```
//find all checkboxes and radios on the page
var checksRadios = $('input[type=checkbox],input[type=radio]');
```

Then we'll need to modify the first loop to wrap our **input/label** pairs with a **div** of the appropriate class name:

```
//loop through each input
checksRadios.each(function(){
  //find associated label element
  var label = $('label[for='+ $(this).attr('id') +']');
  //bind a mouseover event to label
  label.mouseover(function(){
      //add hover class
      $(this).addClass('hover');
      //check if checkbox/radio has .checked class
      if( $(this).is('.checked') ){
          //add checkedHover class
          $(this).addClass('checkedHover');
      }
  });
  //bind mouseout event to label
  label.mouseout(function(){
      //remove all hover classes
      $(this).removeClass('hover checkedHover');
  });
  //get input type, for classname suffix
  var inType = input.attr('type');
  //wrap the input and label in div with appropriate class
  $(this).add(label).wrap('<div class="custom-'+ inType +'"></div>');
});
```

Our **updateState** event will need to reference our new **checksRadios** variable to accommodate the checkboxes and radios. The scripting contained in the **updateState** event won't need any modification:

```
//bind custom updateState event to all the checkboxes and radios
checksRadios.bind('updateState', function(){
```

```
   ...
});
```

Likewise, we'll trigger the **updateState** event on the **checksRadios** at page load:

```
//trigger updateState on all checkboxes and radios at page load
checksRadios.trigger('updateState');
```

Our **click** event will need a minor update to make sure that whenever a radio is clicked, the other radios in its set are updated to display their unchecked state. Since the radios will control each other's checked state natively, we'll simply need to trigger the **updateState** event on all inputs with the same **name** attribute as the one that was clicked (which, of course, will include the one that was clicked, as well):

```
//bind a click event to the checkboxes and radios
checksRadios.click(function(){
  //get this input's name attr
  var inName = $(this).attr('name');
  //trigger updateState on ALL inputs with same name
  $('input[name='+ inName +']').trigger('updateState');
});
```

Lastly, the **focus** and **blur** events won't need modification to support radios; we'll simply bind the event to our **checksRadios** variable to include them:

```
//bind a focus event to the checkboxes and radios
checksRadios.focus(function(){

  ...
});
//bind a blur event to the checkboxes and radios
checksRadios.blur(function(){

  ...
});
```

Now our script supports both checkbox and radio inputs, and provides a clean and reusable way to enhance the basic experience into a set of richly formatted custom controls for browsers that pass the capabilities test:

Which genres do you like?
Action / Adventure
Comedy
Epic / Historical
Science Fiction
Romance
Western
Caddyshack is the greatest movie of all time, right?
Totally
You must be kidding
What's Caddyshack?

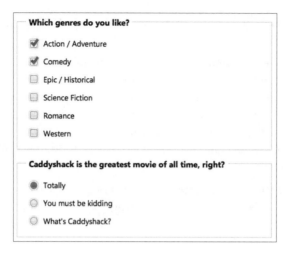

Figure 15-14 Enhanced custom checkboxes and radio buttons

This is a very robust approach that scales gracefully even when the user chooses to set their font size a few notches above the default size. (This is important to test when building any widget that uses advanced CSS styles.)

Best of all, this technique safely falls back to the fully visible and accessible native input if the visitor passes the capabilities test but for any reason doesn't see images displayed in their browser:

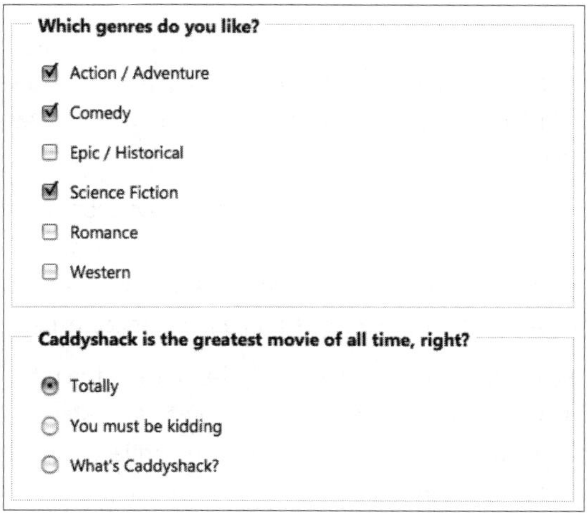

Which genres do you like?
Action / Adventure
Comedy
Epic / Historical
Science Fiction
Romance
Western
Caddyshack is the greatest movie of all time, right?
Totally
You must be kidding
What's Caddyshack?

Figure 15-15 Enhanced custom checkboxes and radio buttons with browser images disabled

Taking custom inputs further: a star rating widget

We've applied the technique for customizing checkboxes and radio buttons to create a rating widget. Rating widgets collect and display subjective user feedback based on a predefined scale. Star rating widgets are especially popular, and are generally structured with a five-star scale indicating how much the user likes a product or service (for example, 5 stars = very much to 1 star = very little, sometimes with an additional "ignore" option). Millions of people use star rating widgets when responding to online polls, evaluating products on Amazon, or rating movies on Netflix.

In keeping with the movie theme, we'll create a widget where users can rate movies they've seen on a scale of "unwatchable" to "Oscar-worthy."

Figure 15-16 Star rating widget design

Because users are limited to choosing only a single option in a continuum, a set of radio buttons is ideal for the foundation markup. But there are a few important exceptions to consider with the rating widget:

▶ Rating widgets are often treated as standalone components that submit data back to the server asynchronously with JavaScript when a rating value is chosen. To ensure that the rating functions without JavaScript, we'll need to add a submit input in the foundation markup, and then adjust the script to remove it in the enhanced experience.

▶ Unlike simpler standard radio buttons or checkboxes, the scale of the rating widget is additive—that is, when a user hovers the cursor on the fourth star, stars 1, 2, and 3 are also "on." We'll need to write a new script based on the customized checkboxes and radio buttons script that includes a mechanism to provide the appropriate feedback.

Foundation markup

The foundation markup and "safe" styles for the ratings widget radio button set should follow exactly the same process as outlined for the custom radio buttons. Be sure to:

▶ Assign a shared **name** attribute and value to all radio button inputs so they act as a single set.

▶ Assign a unique **id** to all inputs, and reference that id value in a **for** attribute assigned to each associated label.

The enhanced markup, styles, and script are also very similar to those for the standard custom radio button elements. We'll look at them in detail in our discussion of hover state treatment below.

To let users submit ratings when JavaScript isn't supported, include a submit **input** within each **fieldset** in the foundation code:

```
<fieldset>

  <legend>Star Wars</legend>

  <input type="radio" name="star-wars" id="star-wars-Unwatchable"
  value="Unwatchable" />

  <label for="star-wars-Unwatchable">Unwatchable</label>


  <input type="radio" name="star-wars" id=" star-wars-Bad" value="Bad" />

  <label for="star-wars-Bad">Bad</label>


  <input type="radio" name="star-wars" id="star-wars-OK" value="OK" />

  <label for="star-wars-OK">OK</label>


  <input type="radio" name="star-wars" id="star-wars-Good" value="Good" />

  <label for="star-wars-Good">Good</label>


  <input type="radio" name="star-wars" id="star-wars-Oscar-worthy"
  value="Oscar-worthy" />

  <label for="star-wars-Oscar-worthy">Oscar-worthy</label>


  <input type="submit" id="star-wars" value="Rate this" class=
  "rating-submit" />

</fieldset>
```

Once applied, the ratings foundation markup displays like this for browsers that support the basic experience:

Figure 15-17 Basic experience for the movie rating with "Rate this" buttons

Since a set of radio buttons and labels displays in a single line with default HTML rendering, the basic experience without CSS or JavaScript enabled still looks like a horizontal continuum of bad to good, so it is a solid approximation of the enhanced experience.

Enhanced markup and style

The enhanced version of the ratings widget will be served only to browsers that support JavaScript, in which case it's safe to use Ajax to submit the rating. With Ajax enabled, Submit buttons aren't necessary, so we hide them by setting the display property to **none** in the enhanced style sheet. We assigned a class of **rating-submit** to each **input**; we can use that class to hide them all at once by adding the following line to the enhanced styles:

```
.rating-submit { display: none; }
```

The rating widget radio button styles and behavior rules are slightly different than the standard radios—for example, the background image is a star graphic, and the text labels are hidden—so the wrapper **div** that groups the input and label pair needs a unique and descriptive class. For the rating widget, we'll use **rating-option**:

```
<div class="rating-option">
    <input type="radio" name="star-rating-opt" id="OK-1" value="OK" />
    <label for="OK-1">OK</label>
</div>
```

Enhanced styles applied to the **input** and **label** elements with the **rating-option** class share positioning and block properties with styles for the custom radio buttons, but with a few exceptions.

First, we need to adjust the top position value of the input from 2px to 3px to make sure it's totally obscured by the star icon:

```
.rating-option input {
  position: absolute;
  left: 2px;
  top: 3px;
  margin: 0;
}
```

We'll also adjust the widget label styles to reference the star background image sprite, hide the label text (we do this by applying a negative text-indent in combination with **overflow: hidden**, to keep the text "visible" to screen readers), and make a few small tweaks to the padding, margins, and dimensions to fit the star icons:

```
.rating-option label {
  background: url(../images/star.gif) no-repeat -14px -11px;
  display: block;
  position: relative;
  width: 25px;
  height: 25px;
  margin: 0;
  cursor: pointer;
  text-indent: -99999px;
  overflow: hidden;
}
```

The background image positions that set the checked and hover states should also be adjusted to work with the star background sprite:

```
.rating-option label.checked {
  background-position: -14px -211px;
}
.rating-option label.hover {
  background-position: -14px -111px;
}
```

Scripting the star rating widget

While based on the same markup as our custom radio inputs, the enhanced star rating widget has several behavioral changes that we'll need to account for in our scripting.

First, when the user hovers or clicks on a star label, all of the labels preceding it in its set should be styled too. Also, because the label text is hidden from view in the star rating widget, we'll need to add a tooltip to the label so users can hover to see the value each star represents. Lastly, when a star is chosen, we'll automatically send the rating information to the server using Ajax, removing the need for the user to click a Submit button.

To support these behavioral differences, we'll need to change our script in several ways. Rather than trying to write a single script with all the conditional logic we would need to keep the two cases clear, we'll duplicate the original custom checkbox and radio script and modify it for the star rating widget.

First, we'll modify our starting element selection to get only radio inputs, changing the variable name in the process to **starRadios** instead of **checksRadios**. Throughout the script, we'll refer to our inputs using the **starRadios** variable.

```
//find all radios on the page
var starRadios = $('input[type=radio]');
```

We'll need to modify our initial loop through the radios in a few ways:

▶ We'll pass an **index** argument to each function, which provides an incrementing number, increasing by **1** each time the loop runs.

▶ We'll store the **index** number on its **label** using a special jQuery property called **data**, which lets us set and get values on an HTML element.

▶ On hover, we'll toggle the hover class on both the label itself *and* all of the preceding star rating labels in the row:

```
//loop through each radio, pass index argument
starRadios.each(function(index){
  //find associated label element
  var label = $('label[for='+ $(this).attr('id') +']');
  //store the label's index number in memory for later
  label.data('index', index);
  //bind a mouseover event to label
  label.mouseover(function(){
      //loop through each of the radios
```

```
starRadios.each(function(){
    //find that radio's label, store it as var oLabel
    var oLabel = $('label[for='+$(this).attr('id')+']');
    //if oLabel comes before or IS the one being hovered
    if(oLabel.data('index') <= index) {
        //add hover class to it
        oLabel.addClass('hover');
    }
});
});
//bind mouseout event to label
label.mouseout(function(){
    //loop through each of the radios
    starRadios.each(function(){
        //find that radio's label, store it as var oLabel
        var oLabel = $('label[for='+$(this).attr('id')+']');
        //no need to check the index number,remove the class
        oLabel.removeClass('hover');
    });
});
//wrap the input and label in div with our rating-option class
$(this).add(label).wrap('<div class="rating-option"></div>');
});
```

Our **updateState** event will need to reference our new **starRadios** variable. The scripting contained in the **updateState** event will need similar modifications to the ones we made to the each loop, making each radio affect the appearance of the ones preceding it. This time, we'll remove any hover and checked classes from each label in the set, and add the checked class to all preceding star labels in the set:

```
//bind custom updateState event to all the radios
starRadios.bind('updateState', function(){
    //save reference to this label's index value
    var index = $('label[for='+$(this).attr('id')+']').data('index');
```

```
    //check if the clicked radio is checked
    if ( $(this).is(':checked') ){
        //loop through each of the radios
        radioSet.each(function(){
            //find that radio's label, store it as var oLabel
            var oLabel = $('label[for='+$(this).attr('id')+']');
            //remove both the hover and checked classes
            oLabel.removeClass('hover checked');
            //if oLabel comes before or IS the one being hovered
            if(oLabel.data('index') <= index) {
                //add the checked class
                oLabel.addClass('checked');
            }
        });
    }
});
```

We'll trigger the **updateState** event on the **checksRadios** at page load, so any existing star rating values will be visible to the user:

```
//trigger updateState on all radios at page load
starRadios.trigger('updateState');
```

Now that our **updateState** event toggles the states of all of a radio's siblings, our **click** event can simply trigger **updateState** on itself.

However, we do need to add some additional logic to the **click** event to submit the star rating data to the server. We can handle this simply by using jQuery's **ajax** function: we'll define the Ajax request parameters based on the markup, using the form's **method** attribute to specify whether it is sent as a **get** or **post** request (in this case, it should be a **post** request, since we are saving data to the server) and its **action** attribute for specifying the request URL; we'll use jQuery's **serialize** method to send the form's data into key value pairs:

```
//bind a click event to the radios
starRadios.click(function(){
    //trigger the updateState on this radio
    $(this).trigger('updateState');
```

```
//get the parent form element
var form = $(this).parents('form');
//send the form data with Ajax
$.ajax({
    type: form.attr('method'),
    url: form.attr('action'),
    data: form.serialize()
});
});
```

Now our radios will save their state to the server whenever they're clicked.

The **focus** and **blur** events won't need modification to support the star rating behavior. They'll simply toggle the focus class on the label:

```
//bind a focus event to the radios
starRadios.focus(function(){
  label.addClass('focus');
});
//bind a blur event to the radios
starRadios.blur(function(){
  label.addClass('focus');
});
```

Using the custom input and star rating scripts

The downloadable code that accompanies this book (available at www.filamentgroup.com/dwpe) includes two jQuery plugins that offer simple methods for creating custom checkboxes, radios, and star ratings: **jQuery.customInput.js** and **jQuery.starRating.js**.

To use the **jQuery.customInput.js** script, simply reference the necessary dependency files in the custom inputs demo page, and call the **customInput** method on any checkbox or radio button **input** you want to customize. If you apply this script to all **input**s, it's smart enough to enhance only checkboxes and radio buttons, not text or submit inputs:

```
$('input').customInput();
```

The **jQuery.starRating.js** script works the same way, except that it will only work on sets of radio inputs.

```
$('input').starRating();
```

Both plugins can accept any jQuery selector, allowing you to scope your selection of inputs to any specificity you'd like. For example, you might want to call the **starRating** method only on inputs within a div that has a class of **rating**:

```
$('.rating input').starRating();
```

And both plugins are designed to be as simple and lightweight as possible, so there aren't any configuration options or methods—just call these on your target inputs and they'll be enhanced into the customized version.

* * *

As we've discussed at length in this book, we strongly believe that whenever you need to extend a native element, you should exhaust the full potential of semantic HTML and CSS before you create a new element from scratch.

In this case, we applied creative CSS and a bit of scripting to the foundation HTML markup to create custom-styled checkbox and radio button form controls without having to reinvent the elements at all. Not only does this save a lot of work, it also retains the accessibility, keyboard shortcuts, and behavior of the native elements, so we can feel confident that this technique works reliably in a broad range of browsers.

As an added bonus, since we're really just styling the native element, the form-processing logic is identical for the basic and enhanced experiences.

chapter sixteen

slider

Slider controls are used to capture a single value, or data range, on a continuum. Many users find them to be immediately intuitive because they mimic the appearance and functionality of physical sliders in everyday objects like stereos, car dashboard controls, and appliances; the "track" constrains choices to the continuum of available options, and the "handle" position indicates clear feedback of the currently selected value.

Typically, sliders in web applications capture numeric values such as price and volume level, but they can be applied equally well to virtually any set of values in a continuum—like letter grades, financial bond ratings, or positive to negative sentiment. They can capture a single value or be extended with two or more slider handles to capture multiple values or a range.

Sliders are commonly used as:

▶ Filtering tools to set parameters like product size, weight, or capacity; minimum and maximum price range; the display size of photo thumbnails in an album; the length of abstracts to display in a RSS reader; or the zoom level in a map

▶ Playback controls for embedded audio or video, with the slider acting as the timeline for the media and the draggable handle auto-advancing to indicate the current playback position

There is no native HTML form control for a slider widget that currently works across browsers. Sites that employ them typically mark up a set of HTML elements (often **divs**) and use CSS and JavaScript to apply style and slider behavior. Accessibility-minded developers also build in essential keyboard support, and assign the ARIA attributes necessary to ensure that modern screen readers will understand how to communicate meaning and behavior to a non-sighted user.

But what happens when a user doesn't have JavaScript enabled, or can't render the CSS styles needed for the slider to work? Some popular sites that use sliders extensively—like the travel site Kayak, which offers sliders to filter flight times and prices—simply require script support. They offer no fallback option, and completely exclude users who don't have JavaScript enabled from accessing this functionality.

There's no reason to lock users out of key functionality; building with progressive enhancement, it's possible to start with a standard HTML form element like a text **input** or **select** element in the foundation markup to offer core functionality to all users in the basic experience, and then transform it into a slider widget in the enhanced experience. In this chapter, we'll explore how to create a slider that is universally accessible.

X-ray perspective

Online real-estate search sites frequently use sliders to simplify setting and adjusting target search criteria. In our sample design, we'll consider an apartment search form that features two groups of sliders: the first set collects numeric ranges for maximum price and minimum number of bedrooms and bathrooms; the second set collects qualitative values for the relative importance of amenities within a four-level continuum from "Not important" to "Must have," and displays feedback of the selected value to the right of the slider.

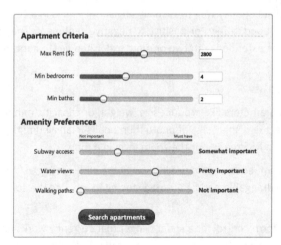

Figure 16-1 Target design for the enhanced experience

Looking at these sliders from an x-ray perspective, the text **input**, **select**, and radio button elements are all good candidates for the foundation markup. We can decide which element is optimal in the basic experience by analyzing the specific data-entry requirements for each form field, and considering how to balance the speed and flexibility of user input and the need to constrain data values to an acceptable range.

The first three sliders collect numeric values within specific minimum and maximum ranges. The maximum rent slider allows any dollar value between $0 and $5,000, while the bedroom and bathroom sliders accept a smaller range of numbers, from 0-10. If we used an HTML **select** element for the maximum price field, it would need to list up to 5,000 options in the markup for full flexibility, or even 50 values if we limit prices to $100 increments—these would be technically workable implementations, but probably not optimal from a user experience perspective. A text **input** is a far more flexible and friendly choice for the rent field's foundation markup—it's faster and easier to type a number into a field than to interact with a select menu either by mouse or keyboard. For consistency, we'll use a text **input** for the bedroom and bathroom fields, too.

The HTML5 specification offers an **input** attribute, **type=number**, which accepts attributes that define the minimum and maximum values to aid in validating the user's entry; these attributes let us more richly describe the rent, bedroom, and bathroom fields than the simpler **type=text**. And, since both the HTML 3 and 4 specifications stipulate that **input** elements default to **type=text** when no type (or an unknown type) is specified, we can safely use the HTML5 **number input** in our foundation markup and know that it will display as a still perfectly functional standard **text input** in browsers that don't understand the **number** type.

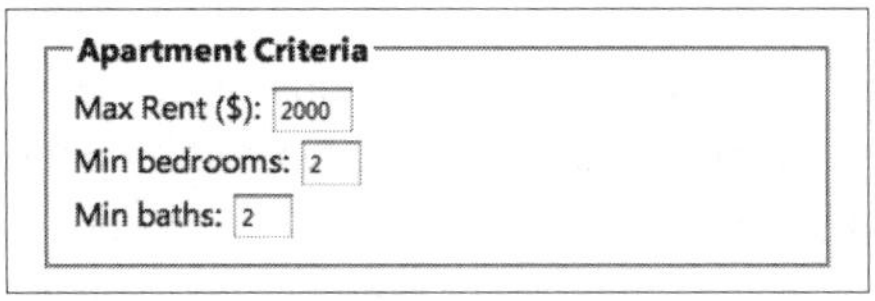

Figure 16-2 Text inputs in the basic experience for rent, bedroom, and bath values

One important consideration when using a **text** or **number input** is data validation. Unlike a **select**, an **input** doesn't provide constraints or real-time feedback to prevent users from entering invalid values like negative numbers, letters, symbols, or values outside the acceptable range. To ensure that the data entered is valid in the basic experience, each time the user submits the form to update results, the server should validate the entry, and provide an error message if it's not an acceptable value. In the enhanced experience, that same validation logic can be handled on the front-end with JavaScript for immediate feedback for users with capable browsers.

We should also consider data granularity when the user interacts with the slider control. The values a slider can capture are limited by the width of the slider track—in this design, roughly 300 pixels. Our minimum bedroom and bath entries accept only numbers between one and ten, so the sliders pose no problem: we simply divide our ten values evenly along the 300-pixel track.

But the rent field is another story: it has 5,000 acceptable values (0-$5,000 at $1 increments), but the slider handle offers only 300 possible pixel positions across the width of the track. This translates to $17 increments if we distribute the pixels evenly. While incrementing the handle by 17 might not cause any problems for users with a mouse—aside from being a seemingly arbitrary amount—it would be slow and inconvenient for someone to use with their keyboard arrow keys. To optimize the slider for quick selection of round numbers, we'll specify that the handle will move at $50 increments, either when a user drags the handle or uses the arrow keys to move it left or right.

By making both the slider and text **input** available in the interface, we can let users choose how they want to interact: moving the slider handle to specify a rent value (for quick, imprecise selections), or entering a number in a text **input** field (for precise entry of exact dollar amounts). Since both will actively collect data, we'll make sure they sync with each other: the slider handle position will update the **input** text value, and vice versa.

Figure 16-3 In the enhanced experience, both the slider and text **input** can be used.

The amenity preference sliders—the second set of three on our form—collect markedly different data from the rent, bedroom, and bathroom fields. Here, users can choose one of four preset values: Not important, Somewhat important, Pretty important, or Must have. To represent these choices in the foundation markup, we could use a radio button set, as it displays all possible options for easy scanning and constrains users to making a valid selection. However, given the space required for each radio and its label, a **select** element offers the same constraints but in a more compact and easier-to-read format in the basic experience—when a selection is made, the selected option will combine with the label to form an easily readable phrase (for example, Subway access: Somewhat important).

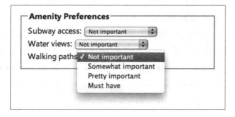

Figure 16-4 Select inputs in the basic experience for amenity preferences

There's no benefit to leaving the **select** visible on the page in the enhanced experience, since the slider is a complete replacement for the **select**'s functionality. In this case, we'll hide the original **select** and display text feedback for the currently selected value to the right of the slider. Since the slider itself will communicate its value to screen-reader users, we'll prevent duplication by using ARIA to hide the visual text feedback from those users.

Figure 16-5 In the enhanced experience, the `select` is hidden and replaced with text feedback.

A truly usable slider control must gracefully work with both mouse and keyboard, and requires refined logic to elegantly handle drag-and-drop functionality. Rather than create a slider from scratch, we recommend leveraging the robust slider included in the jQuery UI library (http://jqueryui.com/docs/slider) to save time and development effort; we'll use it here.

When called on an **input** or **select** element, our enhancement script will work as a sort of middle-man, parsing the foundation markup and culling the values needed to configure the jQuery UI slider. The jQuery UI slider plugin then injects the enhanced markup to generate the slider track and handle, apply drag and snap behavior, calculate value changes based on handle movement, and support keyboard actions.

Our plugin script will supplement the capabilities of the jQuery UI slider plugin by adding ARIA support, which the current version of jQuery UI does not include as of this writing (but will very soon). And finally, it proxies to ensure that any changes in data value are communicated between the enhanced slider and the native **input** or **select** element.

Now that we have a plan for how to handle the various sliders' functionality in the basic experience, we can dive into developing our custom sliders.

HTML5's input type=range element: a native slider for the future

The HTML5 specification adds a new **type=range** attribute for the **input** element that is intended to collect "imprecise" numeric values (the W3C's way to say "slider"). The latest versions of Opera and Webkit already render this **input** type as a slider, so browser support is slowly gaining ground for a native slider.

Technically, you could safely specify the **type=range input** in your foundation markup today; **input** elements will default to a type of **text** when no type, or an unknown type, is provided. Just keep in mind that, from a design perspective, Opera and Safari render the **range input** slider in dramatically different ways, both in terms of functionality and appearance. It feels a bit more like an experiment than an element we can safely use. We look forward to a time in the future when we can use these sliders in a consistent way.

Figure 16-6 Native sliders in the latest Safari (top) and Opera (middle) versions rendered from the **range** input. In Firefox (bottom), a standard text **input** is displayed, because the **range** type isn't supported.

Creating the slider

The first step in building the apartment search tool's sliders is to create the foundation markup that will capture their data values in the basic experience. Then, we'll create the enhanced markup for interactive sliders for capable browsers, as well as the scripts that apply their behavior and keep the data in sync between the sliders and **input** elements.

Foundation markup and style

For the first three fields, we'll use numeric **input** elements, and for the last three we'll use **select** elements, each coded with an associated **label** tag and wrapped in a **form** for submission.

As we discussed in the x-ray section, each numeric data field—for maximum rent price, number of bedrooms, and number of bathrooms—will be coded as an **input** with the HTML5 **type=number**, and with **min** and **max** value attributes. We'll prepopulate the **input** with an initial default value and specify a **size** attribute, which is a flexible way to tell the browser to display the **input** in a width that will hold a specific number of characters to match the acceptable data constraints.

```
<input type="number" name="price" id="price" value="2000" min="0"
max="5000" size="4" />
```

To add a bit of extra meaning that we can leverage to provide clearer feedback for screen readers in the enhanced experience, we'll create a custom attribute using the HTML5 **data-** prefix, called **data-units**, to specify the unit for the **input**'s value (in this case, dollars). When we set the **aria-valuenow** (current value) attribute on each slide movement, it will read aloud a more human-friendly "1,500 dollars" instead of just the value, "1,500." We'll also use this feedback text to populate the slider handle's **title** attribute, which will render in most browsers as a tooltip:

```
<input type="number" name="price" id="price" value="2000" min="0"
max="5000" size="4" data-units="dollars" />
```

We'll create a label for each **input** and properly associate it to its input with a **for** attribute that matches the **input**'s **id**:

```
<label for="price">Max Rent ($):</label>

<input type="number" name="price" id="price" value="2000" min="0"
max="5000" size="4" data-units="dollars" />
```

The markup for number of bedrooms and baths **input**s will be structured in the same way, with the properly associated label, and appropriate **min**, **max**, **size**, and **data-units** values.

The three amenities sliders will be coded as **select** elements in the foundation markup, also associating the **label**'s **for** attribute and **select**'s **id**, like this:

```
<label for="subway">Subway access:</label>

<select name="subway" id="subway">

  <option value="0">Not important</option>

  <option value="1">Somewhat important</option>

  <option value="2">Pretty important</option>

  <option value="3">Must have</option>

</select>
```

The **option** values in the **select**-based sliders are complete and readable as is and inherently constrained, so they don't require any additional attributes.

Now that the basic markup for each of the form fields is defined, we'll apply a single global font to the basic style sheet to make the basic experience look a bit nicer:

```
body, input { font-family: "Segoe UI", Arial, sans-serif; }
```

Enhanced markup and style

As we mentioned earlier, we'll use the jQuery UI slider plugin to take care of generating the enhanced markup and applying all the behavior for any element in the markup designated as a slider.

The jQuery UI slider generates an anchor link for the slider handle, wrapped in a **div** for the track. As the slider handle is dragged, the script dynamically sets an inline style on the anchor to set the CSS **left** property, reflecting the handle's current placement as a percentage of the track's maximum value:

```
<div class="ui-slider ui-slider-horizontal">

  <a href="#" class="ui-slider-handle" style="left:40%"></a>

</div>
```

■ Note
_____

For clarity, we've omitted a few classes from the jQuery UI slider markup that apply a jQuery UI theme.

Our enhancement script will need to add a number of ARIA attributes to make the slider accessible. These attributes are the same, regardless of whether the foundation markup is a numeric **input** or a **select**.

First, an ARIA **role** attribute with a value of **application** is added to the **body** element to make a screen reader recognize the slider control and respect any custom keyboard shortcuts we assign:

```
<body role="application">
```

Then, the script will assign a number of ARIA attributes to the anchor link that acts as the slider handle. (Since the handle delivers all interactive functionality on the slider, and the track is primarily visual feedback, all ARIA roles are addressed to the anchor.)

The **role** of **slider** on the anchor element tells the screen reader that it's playing the part of a slider control instead of a normal link, so it will read aloud a description of the control when the link gains focus:

```
<div class="ui-slider ui-slider-horizontal" role="application">
  <a href="#" class="ui-slider-handle" role="slider" style="left:40%"></a>
</div>
```

The **aria-labelledby** attribute allows us to associate the slider with an element on the page that describes it. The native foundation element that provides the slider's data and proxies with it when data is manipulated—in this case, the **input** element—already has an associated **label** on the page that accurately describes the slider as well. We can use the **input** element's **label** to serve as a label for the slider in the enhanced experience. The **aria-labelledby** attribute must reference another element by its **id**, so we'll use JavaScript to generate a unique **id** for the label by using the value of its **for** attribute, plus a suffix of **-label**:

```
<label for="price" id="price-label">Max Rent ($):</label>
```

Then we'll use the same ID to populate the **aria-labelledby** attribute on the slider's anchor, thereby associating it with the **label** element for screen reader users:

```
<div class="ui-slider ui-slider-horizontal" role="application">
  <a href="#" class="ui-slider-handle" role="slider" aria-labelledby=
"price-label" style="left:40%"></a>
</div>
```

The **aria-valuemin** and **aria-valuemax** attributes communicate the minimum and maximum values of the slider control—again, we'll borrow values from the foundation markup and use the **min** and **max** attributes for each **input**, or the first and last values of each **select**:

```
<div class="ui-slider ui-slider-horizontal" role="application"
style="left:40%"></a>

  <a href="#" class="ui-slider-handle" role="slider" aria-valuemin="0"
  aria-valuemax="5000" aria-labelledby="price-label" style="left:40%"></a>
</div>
```

Lastly, we'll use the script to dynamically update two additional ARIA attributes whenever the slider handle moves or its associated form field's value changes: **aria-valuenow** (the current number value of the slider) and **aria-valuetext** (the human-friendly value feedback text that's read aloud by screen readers). This process is slightly different for our two foundation elements. For the **select**-based sliders, we'll use the **option** text to populate the **data-units** attribute. To make the **aria-valuetext** more useful for the numeric **input**s, our script will take the current **input** value (2,000) and add in the string from the **data-units** attribute in the foundation markup ("dollars") to improve audible feedback ("2,000 dollars"):

```
<div class="ui-slider ui-slider-horizontal" role="application">

  <a href="#" class="ui-slider-handle" role="slider" aria-valuemin="0"
  aria-valuemax="5000" aria-valuenow="2000" aria-valuetext="2000 dollars"
  aria-labelledby="price-label" style="left:40%"></a>
</div>
```

We can leverage one ARIA attribute to improve the experience of non-screen-reader users. Our enhancement script will use feedback text from the **aria-valuetext** attribute to populate a **title** attribute on the handle link, which will render as a descriptive tooltip. (This isn't required, but is a "nice to have" feature, because the slider **input**s are still visible on the page.)

```
<div class="ui-slider ui-slider-horizontal" role="application">

  <a href="#" class="ui-slider-handle" role="slider" aria-valuemin="0"
  aria-valuemax="5000" aria-valuenow="2000" aria-valuetext="2000 dollars"
  aria-labelledby="price-label" title="2000 dollars" style="left:40%"></a>
</div>
```

The same markup structure will be used to create the sliders for the rest of the controls on the page. Now that the ARIA-enabled enhanced markup is roughed out, we'll write the enhanced styles to make the jQuery UI slider look like our target design.

CSS FOR ENHANCED EXPERIENCE

First, we'll style the slider container, which forms a track for the slider handle in our design. It has a fixed width and height, a background image to add some gradient texture to the track, rounded corners, and a border. It's also relatively positioned, to allow the slider handle and range elements to be absolutely positioned within it:

```
.ui-slider {
  position:relative;
  top:.8em;
  float: left;
  width:293px;
  height:1em;
  background:#ebebec url(../images/bg-slider.png) top repeat-x;
  border:1px solid #aaa;
  -moz-border-radius:.5em;
  -webkit-border-radius:.5em;
  border-radius:.5em;
}
```

Our slider track and its label now look like this:

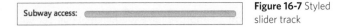

Figure 16-7 Styled slider track

The slider handle is absolutely positioned using negative **top** and **margin-left** properties to center it over the track. We'll style it using **width** and **height** properties to create a square, and then give it a solid border, a background image, and CSS3 **border-radius** properties to round the corners to look like a circle (which aren't supported everywhere, but degrade safely):

```
.ui-slider .ui-slider-handle {
  position:absolute;
  z-index:2;
  width:1.6em;
  height:1.6em;
  top:-.5em;
```

```
    margin-left:-.8em;

    cursor:pointer;

    border:2px solid #444;

    background:#fff url(../images/bg-slider-handle.png) 50% repeat-x;

    -moz-border-radius:.9em;

    -webkit-border-radius:.9em;

    border-radius:.9em;

}
```

With these styles added, our slider handle looks like this:

Figure 16-8 Styled slider handle and track

To create visual feedback on the slider handle when the user hovers with the mouse or focuses with the keyboard, we'll apply a different background image during **hover** and **focus** states. During an active state (click or keypress), the background image is removed, leaving a flat white appearance.

```
.ui-slider .ui-slider-handle:hover, .ui-slider .ui-slider-handle:focus {

    background-image:url(../images/bg-slider-handle-hover.png);

}

.ui-slider .ui-slider-handle:active {

    background-image:none;

}
```

For the numeric **input** sliders like maximum rent, we'll take advantage of the jQuery UI slider's **range-min** option, which uses a colored fill to highlight the range from the left edge of the slider track to the current handle position (like a thermometer) to visually indicate that users are selecting all rent prices or bedrooms *up to* the selected value, not just a single point in the continuum. When this option is enabled, the plugin adds an additional **div** element to the slider markup and dynamically sets an inline percentage **width** to match it to the handle's position:

```
<div class="ui-slider ui-slider-horizontal">

    <div class="ui-slider-range ui-slider-range-min" width="42%"></div>

    <a href="#" class="ui-slider-handle" style="left:42%"></a>

</div>
```

We'll style this range **div** with a dark background image to give the appearance that the slider track is filled up to the handle position:

```
.ui-slider .ui-slider-range {
  position:absolute;
  z-index:1;
  font-size:.7em;
  display:block;
  border:0;
  top:0;
  height:100%;
  background:#999 url(../images/bg-slider-range.png) 50% repeat-x;
  left:0;
}
```

Our numeric range sliders now have a range fill that makes it much clearer that the selected value is a maximum that includes every value below it.

We'll also style the numeric **input**s to look editable, since they can be used in addition to the slider. In the source order, the slider **div** appears before the **input**; setting both to **float:left** will display each slider to the left of its **input**. We'll set the **font-weight** to **bold**, specify the border color, and use the CSS3 **border-radius** property to round the corners of the **input**:

```
input#price, input#bedrooms, input#baths {
  float:left;
  font-size:1.3em;
  font-weight:bold;
  width:55px;
  border:1px solid #ccc;
  -moz-border-radius:3px;
  -webkit-border-radius:3px;
  border-radius:3px; padding:.2em;
}
```

Figure 16-9 Numeric slider with a colored range fill from the left of the track to the handle, and numeric **input** positioned to the right

For the three amenity sliders, we'll hide their **select** elements off-screen using CSS while keeping them on the page for form submission. Our enhancement script will assign the ARIA **aria-hidden=true** attribute to these elements to reinforce to ARIA-capable screen readers that the **select** elements are hidden.

```
select#subway, select#water, select#walking {
   display: none;
}
```

To provide visual feedback for each amenity slider's value, the script will append a feedback **div** with a class of **slider-status** after the slider and dynamically update it with the current value. We'll apply an **aria-hidden** attribute with a value of **true** to the **div** to hide it from screen readers, because the feedback text is redundant with the **aria-valuetext** attribute information in the slider itself.

```
<div class="slider-status" aria-hidden="true">Pretty important</div>
```

We'll style the feedback **div** elements alongside the sliders, similarly to how we styled the **input** elements with the first three sliders.

```
.slider-status {
   float:left;
   font-weight:bold;
   font-size:1.5em;
   color:#444;
}
```

Figure 16-10 Styled amenity slider with current selection feedback

Lastly, we'll add a legend above the amenity sliders to clarify the range of choices, from not important to must-have.

Figure 16-11 Amenity slider legend

We'll inject the legend markup via JavaScript. Its text content will be dynamically generated by the first and last text value of the first **select** menu (as it has the same options as all amenity sliders), and the color continuum is added with a background image:

```
<div class="sliders-labels">
  <span class="label-first">Not important</span>
  <span class="label-last">Must have</span>
</div>
```

The legend markup is for visual feedback only, so we'll apply an **aria-hidden** attribute with the value **true**, to convey that the **div** has no meaning to a screen reader.

```
<div class="sliders-labels" aria-hidden="true">
  <span class="label-first">Not important</span>
  <span class="label-last">Must have</span>
</div>
```

Finally, we'll style the legend to look like our target design:

```
.sliders-labels {
  height:2em;
  margin-left:145px;
  width:293px;
  background:url(../images/bg-continuum.png) bottom left no-repeat;
  padding-top:1em;
}
.sliders-labels span.label-first {
  float:left;
}
.sliders-labels span.label-last {
  float:right;
}
```

Slider script

We're using jQuery UI's slider plugin for the actual slider control, so our enhancement script will act as a bridge to parse the foundation markup into a format the slider can use, manage adding and updating of ARIA attributes, and ensure that the value of the slider and **input** or **select** are kept in sync at all times. The page will need to reference both the jQuery and jQuery UI libraries.

■ Note

The jQuery UI library and widget-specific plugins like slider can be downloaded at http://jqueryui.com/download.

Our script will deal with the numeric **input** sliders and the qualitative **select**-based sliders differently. We'll walk through the steps for each here.

GENERATING THE input-BASED SLIDERS

To generate sliders from our numeric **input** elements, the first thing our enhancement script needs to do is loop through each of the **input** elements on the page to collect the labels, values, and other information needed to generate the slider:

```
$('#price, #bedrooms, #baths').each(function(){
  //code per input goes here...
});
```

Within the **each** loop, the script starts by making a reference to the current **input** in the loop, and then applies a generated **id** to the **label** element, stores the unit name from the **data-units** attribute, and builds a variable that stores the human-friendly feedback text that will be used for ARIA and the slider handle's tooltip:

```
//save reference to input element
var input = $(this);

//find related label element
var thisLabel = $('label[for=' + input.attr('id') + ']');

//generate its unique ID using its for attribute + '-label'
thisLabel.attr('id', thisLabel.attr('for') + '-label');

//get units of input from custom data attr
var thisUnits = input.attr('data-units');
```

```
//get value of input and create a friendly version including units
var friendlyVal = input.val() + ' ' + thisUnits;
```

To ensure keyboard control to the slider for screen-reader users, we'll apply a **role** of **application** to the **body** element:

```
$('body').attr('role','application');
```

Next, the script adds a **div** for the jQuery UI plugin to insert the slider markup:

```
var slider = $('<div></div>');
```

This **div** is inserted into the page, just before the **input**. (Normally, we'd do this after creating the control, but the slider plugin requires that the markup be on the page before it can be configured.)

```
slider.insertBefore(input);
```

Then we can initialize each slider, passing options to the jQuery UI slider API in key/value pairs, separated by commas. We'll set the **min** and **max** options with the values of the **min** and **max** attributes from each **input**. The initial value of the slider is set with the **value** option, which we'll grab from the **input**'s **value** and parse into a number. The **range** option allows for a visual highlight either on a range between two slider handles, or from a handle to the end of the slider; we'll set the range to **min**, which tells the plugin to create a range element that stretches from the start of the slider to the handle. Lastly, the **step** option sets an increment by which the slider handle will move; we'll use a special conditional statement called the *ternary operator* to set the **step** option to **50** if the current **input** has an **id** of **price**, and **1** for all others:

```
slider.slider({
  min: input.attr('min'),
  max: input.attr('max'),
  value: parseInt(input.val(),10),
  range: 'min',
  step: input.is('#price') ? 50 : 1
});
```

With this information, the jQuery UI plugin creates the fully functional slider control, and inserts it into the **div** before the text **input**.

Now that the slider is functional, we'll make it more meaningful and usable for screen-reader users by adding ARIA attributes:

```
slider
  .find('a')
    .attr({
        'role': 'slider',
        'aria-valuemin': input.attr('min'),
        'aria-valuemax': input.attr('max'),
        'aria-valuenow': input.val(),
        'aria-valuetext': friendlyVal,
        'aria-labelledby': thisLabel.attr('id'),
        'title': friendlyVal
    });
```

Each slider should also sync with the original **input** element every time it updates. We'll take advantage of the slider plugin's custom **slide** event to update the **input** with the current slider value whenever it updates:

```
//bind a custom slide event to the slider (slide is a jQuery UI event)
slider.bind('slide', function(e, ui){
  //set the input's value to the slider's value
  input.val(ui.value);


  //get the friendly value
  friendlyVal = input.val() + ' ' + thisUnits;


  //update attribute values on slider handle
  slider.find('a').attr({
      'aria-valuenow': input.val(),
      'aria-valuetext': friendlyVal,
      'title': friendlyVal
  });
});
```

We also want the **input** to talk back to the slider control and update the slider handle position when users type a value into the **input** field. To do that, we'll use the plugin's **slider** method again. The first argument we'll provide is the slider option we'd like to update (**value**), and the second option is the **input**'s current value:

```
input.keyup(function(){
  slider.slider('value', parseInt($(this).val(),10));
});
```

We now have a slider built from a standard **input,** and the means to keep both synchronized. When the form is submitted, each **input**'s value will be sent with the form data the same way in both the basic and enhanced experiences.

GENERATING THE select-BASED SLIDERS

The basic steps to initialize the **select**-based slider widget by parsing the foundation HTML are quite similar to the input, but the methods and syntax are a bit different for a **select**.

The first step is to loop through each select that will have a slider:

```
$('#subway, #water, #walking').each(function(){
  //code for each select element
});
```

Inside the **each** loop, the script will create a variable reference to the current **select** element, apply **aria-hidden=true** on that **select**, apply a generated **id** to the **label** element, capture the text for the currently selected **option**, and then create a **div** that will hold the slider:

```
//reference current select element
var select = $(this);


//hide select element from ARIA-enabled screen readers
select.attr('aria-hidden','true');


//save reference to associated label
var thisLabel = $('label[for=' + select.attr('id') + ']');
```

```
//generate its unique ID using its for attribute + '-label'
thisLabel.attr('id', thisLabel.attr('for') + '-label');
```

```
//find user-friendly value
var friendlyVal = select.find('option')
        .eq( select[0].selectedIndex )
        .text();
```

```
//create div for building slider
var slider = $('<div></div>');
```

The slider **div** is inserted just before the **select** element:

```
slider.insertBefore(select);
```

The script then calls the jQuery UI **slider** method on the **div** and passes in the configuration options for the minimum, maximum, and current values to create a slider. The **min** and **max** options refer to the first and last index numbers of the options in the **select** (which start at **0**). The current value is found by checking the selected **option** in the original **select** element. We'll set the **step** option to 1, as it's critical that every **option** from the **select** will be available in the slider.

```
slider.slider({
  min: 0,
  max: select.find('option').length-1,
  value: select[0].selectedIndex,
  step: 1
});
```

We'll add the same ARIA attributes to the slider as we did with the **input**-based sliders to make it accessible to screen readers:

```
slider
  .find('a')
  .attr({
      'role': 'slider',
      'aria-valuemin': 0,
```

```
        'aria-valuemax': select.find('option').length-1,
        'aria-valuenow': select[0].selectedIndex,
        'aria-valuetext': friendlyVal,
        'title': friendlyVal,
        'aria-labelledby': thisLabel.attr('id')
    });
```

Next we'll insert a **div** with the current value to act as visual feedback, since the **select** is hidden. We'll also **bind** the plugin's **slide** event to watch for changes in the slider handle's position, and do two things when the slider value changes: update the selected value of the original **select,** and update the text in the feedback **div** with the user-friendly value. We'll also apply the **aria-hidden** attribute, to prevent duplication for screen-reader users who will get the value from the select's aria attribute.

```
//append status div after slider
slider.after('<div class="slider-status" aria-hidden="true">'+
        friendlyVal + '</div>');


//bind slide event
slider.bind('slide', function(e, ui){
        //set select menu value to match slider
        select[0].selectedIndex = ui.value;


        //figure out user friendly value
        friendlyVal = select.find('option')
                    .eq( select[0].selectedIndex ).text()


        //populate feedback div
        slider.next().text(friendlyVal);


        //apply attributes to slider handle
        slider.find('a').attr({
            'aria-valuenow': select[0].selectedIndex,
```

```
            'aria-valuetext': friendlyVal,]

            'title': friendlyVal

        });

});
```

Lastly, the script will insert the static markup needed to build the color-coded range legend's image and labels:

```
// generate legend markup

$('<div class="sliders-labels" aria-hidden="true"><span class="label-
first">'+

  $('#subway option:first').text() +

  '</span><span class="label-last">'+

  $('#subway option:last').text() +

  '</span></div>')

        // Inject before the first slider

        .insertBefore('label[for=subway]');
```

Using the slider script

The slider demo and code that accompanies this book (available at www.filamentgroup.com/dwpe/) includes the script, **jQuery.peSlider.js**, which packages the progressive enhancement slider features outlined in this chapter into a reusable plugin. The **peSlider** script is a "wrapper" for the jQuery UI slider plugin; it requires both jQuery and jQuery UI as dependencies.

To use this script in your page, download and reference the files listed in the slider demo page, and then call the **peSlider** method on a numeric **input, select** element, or any combination of the two. This plugin makes it possible to create all the sliders in our demo page with a single jQuery statement, such as the following:

```
$('#price, #bedrooms, #baths, #subway, #water, #walking').peSlider();
```

Calling the **peSlider** method will create a jQuery UI slider with all the data and proxy logic to sync the native element to the slider, an automatically calculated default increment, and all ARIA attributes for accessibility.

There are three custom options we described in the examples above that are not included by default in either the jQuery UI slider plugin or the **peSlider** plugin: the **range** option that adds a highlight color fill to the slider track to show the selected area; the modified **step** option for setting a custom increment; and the **div** that displays text feedback about the current selected value to the right of the **select**-based sliders. To support these specific examples, you'll need to either pass configuration options to the **peSlider** method, or generate some markup manually using jQuery. The examples that follow will walk through how each of these examples could be achieved using **peSlider**.

The first three **input**-based sliders use the range feedback element, which highlights the track from the slider's start to the handle. Our **peSlider** plugin wraps the native jQuery UI slider, so we can pass any native jQuery UI slider options, like the option to create range feedback, as key/value pairs. For example, we'll specify the **range min** option:

```
$('#price, #bedrooms, #baths').peSlider({range: 'min'});
```

You can pass any jQueryUI slider options in this way; keep in mind that the **min**, **max**, and **value** options are automatically populated from the **input** or **select** markup by our plugin and don't need to be passed in as arguments.

The **peSlider** plugin will also figure out a sensible default increment based on dividing the slider's maximum value by its width, and automatically set the slider's **step** option to that increment. This default can easily be overridden in favor of a custom increment by setting a specific **step** value:

```
$('#price').peSlider({step 50});
```

In our x-ray example, the **select**-based sliders update a read-only block of feedback text to the right of the slider. The **peSlider** plugin doesn't automate the process of generating and updating a feedback **div**, because this is a specific design element that may not be needed in every situation. However, this feature can be accomplished by using jQuery to key off the **slide** event of the slider to check the new value and update a feedback **div**.

The following code inserts a feedback **div** after each **select**-based slider and uses the slider's **slide** event to update the feedback **div** whenever the slider changes values. For the text in the feedback **div**, we'll simply grab the slider handle's **aria-valuetext** value, since it's already formatted as a user-friendly version of the slider's value:

```
$('select')
  //insert slider feedback divs
  .after('<div class="slider-status" aria-hidden="true"></div>')
```

```
//create sliders
.peSlider({
    //bind a callback function to the slider's slide event
    slide:function(){
        //find status div from slider element
        var statusDiv = $(this).next().next();


        //find slider handle
        var sliderHandle = $(this).find('a:eq(0)');


        //set statusDiv's text with aria-valuetext attribute
        statusDiv.text(sliderHandle.attr('aria-valuetext'));
    }
})
.each(function(){
    //find status div from select element
    var statusDiv = $(this).next();


    //find slider handle, from select element
    var sliderHandle = $(this).next().find('a:eq(0)');


    //set statusDiv's text with aria-valuetext attribute
    statusDiv.text(sliderHandle.attr('aria-valuetext'));
});
```

The **peSlider** plugin is very simple by design because the jQuery UI slider provides a wealth of features that can be easily accessed to extend it.

■ Note

To learn more about the wide variety of features available in the jQuery UI slider, including vertical orientation, additional callback events, and visual theming using ThemeRoller.com, read the documentation at http://jqueryui.com/demos/slider.

Taking the slider further

Two advanced features could be added to a slider to make it even more usable and interactive:

▶ Tooltips near the slider's handle—either during slide events or at all times—can provide feedback of the currently selected value.

▶ Tick marks and labels along the slider's axis provide additional visual context to help users understand the level of granularity on the continuum of options.

We explore how to extend the jQuery UI's slider to add both features in a lab article on our site (www.filamentgroup.com/lab/jquery_ui_selectmenu_an_aria_accessible_plugin_for_styling_a_html_select).

* * *

This chapter illustrates how we can build very interactive elements like a slider with progressive enhancement techniques in a way that will work on any device. Using scripting to parse data from foundation markup and generate enhanced JavaScript widgets is, we think, a very powerful way to take advantage of Web 2.0 features while still providing a semantic HTML equivalent that will work on any device.

We also demonstrate how to wrap an existing full-featured plugin to add progressive enhancement capabilities and ARIA accessibility support; we feel this is a good way to get a plugin with the features you want without having to reinvent the wheel and rewrite a plugin from scratch, and build in essential accessibility considerations.

chapter seventeen

select menu

Native **select** elements look pretty simple, but in fact are robust and sophisticated widgets: they include a host of interaction features such as keyboard mapping for navigating and selecting options, single-letter type-ahead, and scroll-wheel support, to name a few.

Often a design will call for a custom look and feel for a dropdown select menu. It would be ideal if you could simply use CSS to style a standard **select** element and preserve the native functionality that web users have come to expect. However, browsers offer very limited support for styling these elements—styles are defined per browser (including text style and size, box outline and arrow style, dropdown options menu format, and scrollbar), and are mostly non-configurable with CSS.

A lot of site designs (including many we've worked on) incorporate custom select menus for both visual and functional reasons. Common improvements include:

▶ Styling the **select** element's text content, box shape, or dropdown arrow presentation to match the distinct visual design of a site

▶ Adding icons next to each menu option to reinforce content choices, such as showing product colors for an ecommerce site or national flags on a country location or currency chooser

▶ Formatting the options menu into a hierarchical structure, or formatting **option** text into multiple lines with varying text styles (like mixed bold and normal font)

From both user experience and corporate brand perspectives, there are valid reasons to pursue these goals, and a custom select can achieve them—if it's implemented correctly.

In this chapter, we'll review how to transform a native HTML **select** element into a custom select widget that incorporates icons and advanced style formatting, and detail how to implement all the interaction features and accessibility you'd expect from a native

HTML **select**. Then we'll discuss how these principles can be extended to a range of other customizations—including complex option content formatting and single-letter type-ahead support—and show how to integrate a robust custom select widget into your projects.

X-ray perspective

Let's say we're building a retail application where shoppers can choose gift wrap for their purchase during the checkout process. We'd like to provide users with a select menu that offers good visual feedback about their options, so we'll add a thumbnail that shows the color and print for each style (see Figure 17-1). While we're at it, we also want to customize the select menu's typography and visual style to match our retail site design.

Here's our target design:

Figure 17-1 Target custom select design with icons next to each option

Taking an x-ray perspective, we see that the custom select has three elements: a label to identify the control, a clickable element that displays feedback of the currently selected option, and an options menu that opens below it to display the available choices.

The target design presents all the visual cues of a standard **select** element (button shape and outline, gradient texture, arrow indicator), so it's clear that we'll start with a native **select** element in the foundation markup. Our basic experience will simply display the **select** along with a **label** ("Gift wrap pattern:") and our options. We think it will help users make an informed decision to see an image, so we'll include a link after the **select** to a page that shows a preview of gift-wrap options:

Figure 17-2 The gift-wrap chooser in the basic experience is a standard **select** control.

When a browser passes the capabilities test, we'll use JavaScript to grab the **select** element's "data"—the label, classes and attributes, and option text—and use it to dynamically build a custom select widget that replaces the native control and communicates back to the native **select** element behind the scenes using a "proxy" pattern.

Markup for the clickable element must use an element that natively accepts keyboard focus; we could use a standard anchor link, an **input** with a **type** of **button**, or a **button** element. When we apply enhancements, we'll use JavaScript to override this element's primary function—to link to another page or resource or to submit form data—so the decision comes down to which element is easiest to style. We can rule out the **input** button, since it doesn't support background images (of which our design has several for its hover state and gift-wrap icon). This leaves the **button** or anchor elements, either of which could be used validly within our target design. In this example, we'll use an anchor.

The custom select's menu consists of a styled list of links. The closest semantic match for this structure is an unordered list (**ul**) with an anchor element inside a list item (**li**) for each menu option.

Our target design also specifies a unique icon image for each gift-wrap option. Many developers would build a background image reference for each option into the enhancement script. We recommend against this approach because it would limit our script to this single data set; if additional custom select widgets were required, we'd have to duplicate and customize this script for each—an inefficient use of JavaScript, difficult to maintain, especially if the data (in this case, gift-wrap designs) were to change.

Instead, we construct the foundation markup with attributes that "encode" the information we need for the enhanced experience. We add a **class** attribute to each **option** that specifies an icon style, and then use the enhancement script to transfer each class to its list item counterpart in the enhanced markup and use CSS to set a background image on each option. This adds extra attributes to the foundation markup, but doing so is harmless (**class** attributes won't effect how **option** elements are used or displayed), and it allows us to write the script in a generic way that can be applied to multiple select menus in our application.

The custom select will look much like a standard **select** element, so users will likely expect it to *act the same way* in reaction to mouse clicks and keyboard commands. Users should be able to tab into and away from the custom select, open the menu on mouse click or by tabbing to it and pressing the spacebar, move up and down the list of options with arrow keys, and click the mouse or press the spacebar or Enter key to select an option. To enable this behavior in the custom select, we'll need to write markup and script logic that changes the native behaviors of the anchor elements so they follow the patterns of a native **select** instead.

For screen readers, the custom select must be built in such a way that it's recognized as a custom select widget, rather than an anchor link and an unordered list. To do this, we'll add ARIA attributes that identify the roles played by the various components of the custom select, how they relate to each other, and their current states and values.

Finally, we need to ensure that the user's gift-wrap choice is submitted with the form. In the enhanced experience, we'll keep the native **select** element on the page, but hidden from users; whenever the custom select widget's value changes, we'll proxy its value to the native **select** element to keep it in sync for form submission.

Creating an accessible custom select

For our custom select, we'll create the foundation markup structure for the basic experience and encode it with attributes necessary for the enhancement script to build the custom widget. We'll then walk through how to mark up the custom select, assign the necessary ARIA attributes to provide feedback for screen-reader users, and style it to match our target design. Finally, we'll review how the enhancement script generates and inserts the custom select into the page, applies behavior (including keyboard support and type-ahead functionality), and creates a proxy to the hidden **select** element so that form data can be submitted the same way for both basic and enhanced experiences.

Foundation markup and styles

The foundation markup consists of a standard **select** element paired with a **label**. The **label** element's **for** attribute matches the select's **id**, which associates the elements for screen readers and allows users to click the **label** to focus the **select**:

```
<label for="giftwrap">Gift wrap pattern:</label>
<select name="giftwrap" id="giftwrap">
  <option value="pattern-bubbles">Purple bubbles</option>
  <option value="pattern-swirl">Yellow swirl</option>
  <option value="pattern-snow" selected="selected">Blue snow</option>
  <option value="pattern-sparks">Pink sparks</option>
  <option value="pattern-blobs">Green blobs</option>
</select>
<a href="giftwrap-patterns.html" id="giftwrap-patterns">view samples</a>
```

Next, we'll encode a unique **class** to each **option** value in the **select**, from which we'll use JavaScript to construct the custom select options and apply their icons in the enhanced experience.

```
<select name="giftwrap" id="giftwrap">

  <option class="purple-bubbles" value="pattern-bubbles">Purple bubbles
  </option>

  <option class="yellow-swirl" value="pattern-swirl">Yellow swirl</option>

  <option class="blue-snow" value="pattern-snow" selected="selected">
  Blue snow</option>

  <option class="pink-sparks" value="pattern-sparks">Pink sparks</option>

  <option class="green-blobs" value="pattern-blobs">Green blobs</option>

</select>
```

For the basic experience, we'll assign a **font-family** property to both the **body** and **select** elements (it's necessary to address the **select** element directly because some browsers don't allow form elements to inherit font styles):

```
body, select { font-family: "Segoe UI", Arial, sans-serif; }
```

With light CSS applied, the basic **select** looks like this:

Figure 17-3 Native HTML select with safe styles applied and a link to gift-wrap images

The basic experience is fully functional, and the link to the sample images page adds the missing bit of content that appears in the enhanced experience. Now we're ready to start assembling the custom select menu's markup and styles.

Enhanced markup and styles

Before we get to the widget markup, we need to first instruct screen readers to recognize application controls in our enhanced markup; doing so will allow us to take advantage of custom keyboard behavior. To do that, we'll add an ARIA **role** attribute with a value of **application** to the **body** element:

```
<body role="application">
```

Next, the JavaScript will generate two components for the custom select—a menu button and an options list—based on values from the foundation **select** element. The script will inject the menu button into the page markup after the foundation **select** element (which will be hidden once the full custom select is in place) and place the options list at the end of the page to ensure its menu will reliably layer over other elements in the page with absolute positioning.

The button is an anchor link, populated with the selected option's text, and the options menu is an unordered list of links populated with all options' text. Both are assigned a unique **id** based on the select element's **id**, **giftwrap**:

```
<a href="#" id="giftwrap-button">Blue snow</a>
<ul id="giftwrap-menu">
    <li><a href="#">Purple bubbles</a></li>
    <li><a href="#">Yellow swirl</a></li>
    <li><a href="#">Blue snow</a></li>
    <li><a href="#">Pink sparks</a></li>
    <li><a href="#">Green blobs</a></li>
</ul>
```

■ Note

Though the custom menu's behavior will be handled by JavaScript, it's worthwhile to take advantage of native behaviors built into HTML elements whenever possible. For that reason, we use an anchor link inside each list item, because anchors are natively focusable across browsers.

We'll assign classes to both components to style them later with CSS: the **custom-select** class will style the link like a clickable button, and **custom-select-menu** applied to the **ul** will make it look like a dropdown menu. The menu should be hidden when the page loads, so the list gets a second class, **custom-select-menu-hidden**:

```
<a href="#" class="custom-select" id="giftwrap-button">Blue snow</a>
<ul class="custom-select-menu custom-select-menu-hidden" id="giftwrap-menu">
    <li><a href="#">Purple bubbles</a></li>
    <li><a href="#">Yellow swirl</a></li>
    <li><a href="#">Blue snow</a></li>
    <li><a href="#">Pink sparks</a></li>
    <li><a href="#">Green blobs</a></li>
</ul>
```

When the script generates markup for these elements, it will comb through the original **select** element and note the selected option (or the first option, if none is marked as selected), and then grab the gift-wrap classes we assigned to the **option** elements and assign them to the enhanced markup to apply the correct icons to the menu link and list options:

```
<a href="#" class="custom-select blue-snow" id="giftwrap-button">Blue snow
</a>

<ul class="custom-select-menu custom-select-menu-hidden" id="giftwrap-menu">

  <li class="purple-bubbles"><a href="#">Purple bubbles</a></li>

  <li class="yellow-swirl"><a href="#">Yellow swirl</a></li>

  <li class="blue-snow selected"><a href="#">Blue snow</a></li>

  <li class="pink-sparks"><a href="#">Pink sparks</a></li>

  <li class="green-blobs"><a href="#">Green blobs</a></li>

</ul>
```

To make the anchor look like a menu button, the script will generate two **span** tags and insert them into the anchor link: the first, **custom-select-status**, styles the button text for the selected option, and the second, custom-select-button-icon, is for the end cap with an arrow icon:

```
<a href="#" class="custom-select blue-snow" id="giftwrap-button">

  <span class="custom-select-status">Blue snow</span>

  <span class="custom-select-button-icon"></span>

</a>
```

We should inform readers that this link is a select menu button, and not a simple hyper-link, so we'll add a few ARIA attributes: **role="button"** to inform screen readers that the link is acting as a button control, **haspopup="true"** to associate the button with popup content (in this case, a menu of options), and **aria-owns="giftwrap-menu"** to associate it specifically with the unordered list's ID:

```
<a href="#" class="custom-select blue-snow" id="giftwrap-button"
role="button" aria-haspopup="true" aria-owns="giftwrap-menu">

  <span class="custom-select-status">Blue snow</span>

  <span class="custom-select-button-icon"></span>

</a>
```

We'll also add a **span** to the button with the text " select"—note the space before the word—that we'll hide from sighted users. This text will serve as an additional role description for screen readers that don't fully support ARIA attributes. (For example, at the time of writing, Apple's VoiceOver screen reader supports the **button** role, but won't notify the user that an element has the **haspopup**=**"true"** attribute and is acting as a menu button. With this **span** in place, VoiceOver will speak aloud, "Blue snow select button," when the menu button gains focus.)

```
<a href="#" class="custom-select blue-snow" id="giftwrap-button"
role="button" aria-haspopup="true" aria-owns="giftwrap-menu">

  <span class="custom-select-status">Blue snow</span>

  <span class="custom-select-button-icon"></span>

  <span class="custom-select-roletext"> select</span>

</a>
```

Likewise, we'll add ARIA attributes to the options list so that screen readers understand that it's part of the custom select. We'll assign a **role** of **listbox** to the **ul** to identify it as a container with selectable items, and assign **aria-hidden**=**"true"** to tell screen readers that the options list is currently hidden. We'll associate the options list with the menu button specifically with an **aria-labelledby** attribute directed to the menu button's ID, **giftwrap-button**:

```
<ul class="custom-select-menu custom-select-menu-hidden" id="giftwrap-menu"
role="listbox" aria-hidden="true" aria-labelledby="giftwrap-button">

  ...

</ul>
```

To each option link we'll add the **role**=**"option"** attribute to indicate that it's selectable, and the **aria-selected** attribute to indicate the option's state:

```
<ul class="custom-select-menu custom-select-menu-hidden" id="giftwrap-menu"
role="listbox" aria-hidden="true" aria-labelledby="giftwrap-button">

  <li class="purple-bubbles">

      <a href="#" role="option" aria-selected="false">Purple bubbles</a>

  </li>

  ...

</ul>
```

■ Note

The script will update all `aria-hidden` and `aria-selected` attributes dynamically as the user interacts with the menu, and will also update the foundation `select` behind the scenes so that its selected option always matches the custom menu.

We'll also add a **tabindex** attribute to each option link. By default, all links on a page can receive focus when navigating with the Tab key. In this case, however, we want the menu to be treated as part of the custom select widget that gains access via a click of the menu button, not as a list of links on the page, so we'll remove each option link from the tab order by assigning a **tabindex** value of **-1**.

```
<ul class="custom-select-menu custom-select-menu-hidden" id="giftwrap-menu"
role="listbox" aria-hidden="true" aria-labelledby="giftwrap-button">

  <li class="purple-bubbles">

    <a href="#" tabindex="-1" role="option" aria-selected="false">Purple
    bubbles</a>

  </li>

  ...

</ul>
```

With the enhanced markup structure in place, we'll style it to match our target design.

The menu button looks like a dimensional, clickable object, so we'll float it left (which gives it block-level properties), specify a width value, and for browsers that support rounded corners and text shadow, add **border-radius** and **text-shadow** properties. We'll use a border and a gradient background image to add polish:

```
.custom-select {

  float:left;

  text-decoration:none;

  text-align:left;

  cursor:pointer;

  position:relative;

  background:#fff url(../images/button-silver.gif) left center repeat-x;

  border:1px solid #b3b3b3;

  font-size:1.3em;

  font-weight:bold;

  overflow:visible;

  -moz-border-radius:7px;

  -webkit-border-radius:7px;

  border-radius:7px;

  width:180px;
```

```
   text-shadow:1px 1px 0 #fff;
}
```

The two spans within the menu button—for the currently selected option's text and the menu's end cap with an arrow icon—are floated left. The end cap is assigned a background image and rounded corners:

```
.custom-select-status {
   float:left;
   line-height:2;
   color:#444;
   padding:.2em 8px;
}
.custom-select-button-icon {
   float:right;
   background:#fff url(../images/button-green.gif) left center repeat-x;
   height:2.5em;
   width:2em;
   -moz-border-radius-topright:7px;
   -webkit-border-top-right-radius:7px;
   border-top-right-radius:7px;
   -moz-border-radius-bottomright:7px;
   -webkit-border-bottom-right-radius:7px;
   border-bottom-right-radius:7px;
}
```

We'll also hide the View Samples link in the foundation markup, as it's no longer needed alongside the custom select:

```
#giftwrap-patterns { display: none; }
```

Figure 17-4 Custom select menu button with styles applied

Hover and focus states—assigned with the **:hover** and **:focus** pseudo-classes—will provide visual feedback when the user puts the mouse over the button or focuses by tabbing to it. We'll also create a **custom-select-open** class to apply these styles to the button via JavaScript to make it look pressed when the menu is open:

```
.custom-select:hover,

.custom-select:focus,

.custom-select-open {

  background-position:right center;

  border-color:#999;

}

.custom-select:hover .custom-select-button-icon,

.custom-select:focus .custom-select-button-icon,

.custom-select-open .custom-select-button-icon {

  background-position:-500px center;

}
```

Figure 17-5 Custom select menu button in the hover/focus state

We'll hide the **span** that contains audible role text ("select") from sighted users with absolute positioning so screen readers will still find it and read it aloud:

```
.custom-select-roletext {

  position: absolute;

  left: -99999px;

}
```

To the options list, we'll add a border, a background image, and a high **z-index** so the dropdown menu will appear above other elements on the page. We'll also apply **overflow** properties to conditionally show a vertical scrollbar, which we'll use in the enhancement script to programmatically limit the height of the menu:

```
.custom-select-menu {

  border: 1px solid #b3b3b3;

  background: #e9e9e9;

  z-index: 999999;

  position: absolute;
```

```css
  margin: 0;

  padding: 0;

  font-size: 1.3em;

  -moz-border-radius: 7px;

  -webkit-border-radius: 7px;

  border-radius: 7px;

  width: 180px;

  cursor: pointer;

  text-shadow: 1px 1px 0 #fafafa;

  overflow: auto;

  overflow-x: hidden;

}
```

We'll remove padding and margin from the list items, and instead apply those properties to the option links:

```css
.custom-select-menu li {

  padding: 0;

  margin: 0;

  list-style: none;

  clear: both;

}
```

Each list item's link is styled to look like a menu option, not like a standard link, so we'll give it block properties, padding, and a gray text color, and remove the link's default text underline:

```css
.custom-select-menu li a {

  text-decoration:none;

  color:#555;

  display:block;

  cursor:pointer;

  padding:.5em 5px;

  text-shadow:1px 1px 0 #f9f9f9;

}
```

We want to show the appropriate interaction feedback in the menu. First, we'll be sure not to override the browser's native focus state, which applies a dotted or glowing outline to the focus state by default when the user navigates to it with the keyboard. Additionally, the script will dynamically assign a class, **hover-focus**, to apply a slightly different background image when a user hovers or focuses on an option:

```
.custom-select-menu li.hover-focus {

  background:#e6e6e6 url(../images/button-silver.gif) right center
  repeat-x;

  color:#444;

}
```

When a user selects an option, the script will assign the **selected** class for visual feedback:

```
.custom-select-menu li.selected {

  background:#66b81e url(../images/menu-green.gif) left center repeat-x;

  color:#fff;

}

.custom-select-menu li.selected a {

  color:#fff;

  text-shadow:1px 1px 0 #2d7406;

}
```

We'll add the icons to the menu button and to each option link that identify the type of gift wrap. We'll assign a single background image sprite to the button text span (**custom-select-status**) and every option link, set padding so that text in these containers won't overlap the image, and adjust the background image's position for each class to show the relevant icon:

```
#giftwrap-button .custom-select-status,

#giftwrap-menu li a {

  background-image:url(../images/select-icons.gif);

  background-repeat:no-repeat;

  padding-left:40px;

}

.purple-bubbles .custom-select-status,

li.purple-bubbles a {
```

```
    background-position:5px 3px;
}
.yellow-swirl .custom-select-status,
li.yellow-swirl a {
    background-position:5px -47px;
}
.blue-snow .custom-select-status,
li.blue-snow a {
    background-position:5px -97px;
}
.pink-sparks .custom-select-status,
li.pink-sparks a {
    background-position:5px -147px;
}
.green-blobs .custom-select-status,
li.green-blobs a {
    background-position:5px -197px;
}
```

With styles applied, the custom select menu now looks like this:

Figure 17-6 Custom select menu with icons for each item

We're almost done with the enhanced markup and styles; to finish up, we need to address the native **select** element and its **label** in the foundation markup.

The custom select will replace the foundation **select**'s functionality outright, so it makes little sense to keep the original **select** visible on the page. We'll use JavaScript to add the class **select-hidden** to the **select** element, and an **aria-hidden="true"** attribute to hide the select from ARIA-enabled screen readers:

```
<select name="giftwrap" id="giftwrap" class="select-hidden" aria-hidden=
"true">

   ...

</select>
```

To hide the **select**, we'll apply the **display: none** property:

```
.select-hidden {

  display: none;

}
```

Finally, we'll associate the foundation label element ("Gift wrap pattern:") with the custom select's button, by updating its **for** attribute to point to the button's **id** (later, we'll reinforce the relationship between these elements by explicitly setting a **click** event on the label using JavaScript):

```
<label for="giftwrap-button">Gift wrap pattern:</label>
```

Planning for our enhanced markup and style is now complete. Next, we'll create the script to generate this markup and make it functional.

Enhanced custom select script

When a browser passes the capabilities test, we'll use JavaScript to transform the foundation markup's **select** element into the custom select widget, assign events to open and close the menu, add keyboard support, and apply ARIA attributes to make it all accessible. We'll also create a proxy connection between the native **select** and its custom counterpart so the form can be submitted consistently across both experiences.

GENERATING THE ENHANCED MARKUP

The script's first step is to generate the enhanced custom select markup and inject it into the page. To start, we'll create several variables to store references to the native **select** element and its option attributes (later in the script, we'll use them to construct the menu button and custom options list, and to set the currently selected option):

```
//reference to the native select element

var selectElement = $('#giftwrap');


//get select ID

var selectElementID = selectElement.attr('id');
```

```
//get initial selected index
var initialSelectedIndex = selectElement[0].selectedIndex;


//get the selected option's text value
var selectedOptionText = selectElement.find('option')
            .eq(initialSelectedIndex).text();


//get the selected option's class attribute value
var selectedOptionClass = selectElement.find('option')
            .eq(initialSelectedIndex).attr('class');


//get array of all select option classes, for quick removal
var allOptionClasses = selectElement.find('option')
    //convert option classes to array
    .map(function(){ return $(this).attr('class'); })
    //join array into string of classes separated by a space
    .get().join(' ');
```

Next, we'll create the custom select's button and menu IDs based on the native **select**'s ID, and construct the menu button markup and inject it into the page immediately after the native **select**:

```
//create IDs for button, menu
var buttonID = selectElementID + '-button';
var menuID = selectElementID + '-menu';


//create empty menu button
var button = $('<a class="custom-select" id="'+ buttonID
⇥+'" role="button" href="#" aria-haspopup="true" aria-owns="'
⇥+ menuId +'"></a>');


//create button text, icon, and roletext spans, and append to button
var selectmenuStatus = $('<span class="custom-select-status">'
⇥+ selectedOptionText +'</span>')
```

```
.appendTo(button);

var selectmenuIcon = $('<span class="custom-select-button-icon"></span>')
  .appendTo(button);

var roleText = $('<span class="custom-select-roletext"> select</span>')
  .appendTo(button);

//transfer tabindex attribute from select, if it's specified
if(selectElement.is('[tabindex]')){
  button.attr('tabindex', selectElement.attr('tabindex'));
}

//add selected option class defined earlier
button.addClass(selectedOptionClass);

//insert button after select
button.insertAfter(selectElement);
```

To complete the button markup, we'll associate the custom select button with the foundation markup's **label** element and apply a **click** event to the label so that it shifts focus to the button when the user clicks it:

```
//associate select's label to new button
$('label[for='+selectElementID+']')
  .attr('for', buttonID)
  .bind('click', function(){
      button.focus();
      return false;
});
```

Now we're ready to tackle the menu. We'll construct the options list by looping through all of the **option** elements in the native **select** and noting each **option**'s index number (its place in the list order) and **class** attribute. Then we'll append the complete options list to the **body**:

```
//create menu ul
var menu = $('<ul class="custom-select-menu" id="'+ menuID+'"
➥role="listbox" aria-hidden="true" aria-labelledby="'
➥+ buttonID+'"></ul>');


//find all option elements in selectElement
selectElement.find('option')
  //iterate through each option element, tracking the index
  .each(function(index){
      //create li with option's text and class attribute
      var li = $('<li class="'+ $(this).attr('class') +'">
      ➥<a href="#" tabindex="-1" role="option" aria-selected="false">'
      ➥$(this).text() +'</a></li>');
  //if option index matches selected index of select element
  if(index == initialSelectedIndex){
      //add selected class and aria
      li.addClass('selected').attr('aria-selected',true);
  }
  //append li to menu
  li.appendTo(menu);
});


//append menu to end of page and don't hide it yet
menu.appendTo('body');
```

As a failsafe feature, we'll check the menu's height and limit it to 300 pixels; we set **overflow** properties in the CSS so that if the maximum height is exceeded, the menu will scroll vertically:

```
//limit the menu's height
if(menu.outerHeight() > 300){
  menu.height(300);
}
```

After we check the menu's height, we'll hide it with the **custom-select-menu-hidden** class. As the user interacts with the menu button, we'll toggle this class on the menu to hide or show it:

```
//hide menu

menu.addClass('custom-select-menu-hidden');
```

To finish up the markup enhancements, we'll add the ARIA **role** of **application** to the **body** element to inform screen readers that the page now contains interactive widgets:

```
//add application role to body

$('body').attr('role','application');
```

APPLYING CUSTOM SELECT BEHAVIOR

We'll create jQuery custom events to define all the logic and behavior for opening and closing the options list, updating the menu button feedback when an option is chosen, and updating the native **select**'s value to keep it in sync. Each of these will be defined once in the script, and then triggered later based on user interaction with the mouse or keyboard.

Our custom **show** event will remove the menu's **custom-select-menu-hidden** class, set its **aria-hidden** attribute to **false**, and dynamically position it just beneath the button; it will also focus on the currently selected option in the menu, and add a class of **custom-select-open** to the button:

```
//custom show event

menu.bind('show', function(){
  $(this)
      //remove hidden class

      .removeClass('custom-select-menu-hidden')


      //remove aria hidden attribute

      .attr('aria-hidden', false)


      //position the menu under the button

      .css({
          top: button.offset().top + button.height(),
          left: button.offset().left
      })
```

```
    //send focus to the selected option
    .find('.selected a')[0].focus();


    //add open class from button
    button.addClass('custom-select-open');
});
```

The **hide** event reverses the **show** event's actions by removing the **custom-select-open** class from the button and adding the **custom-select-menu-hidden** class and **aria-hidden="true"** attributes back to the menu:

```
//custom hide event
menu.bind('hide', function(){
  //remove open class from button
  button.removeClass('custom-select-open');


  $(this)
      //remove hidden class
      .addClass('custom-select-menu-hidden')
      //remove aria hidden attribute
      .attr('aria-hidden', true);
});
```

The **toggle** event conditionally shows and hides the menu. If the menu is hidden, we'll trigger the **show** event; if the menu is already visible, we'll trigger the **hide** event:

```
//apply mousedown event to button
menu.bind('toggle', function(){
  //if the menu is hidden, first set its positioning
  if(menu.is(':hidden')){
      //show menu
      menu.trigger('show');
  }
  else{
      //hide menu
```

```
        menu.trigger('hide');
    }
});
```

The **select** event is bound to the anchor elements in the menu; it sets the currently selected option, updates the menu button text and icon, and proxies the selected option back to the native **select** so that the form can submit the data properly:

```
//event to update select menu with current selection (proxy to select)
menu.find('a').bind('select',function(){
    //deselect previous option in menu
    menu
        .find('li.selected')
        .removeClass('selected')
        .attr('aria-selected', false);


    //get new selected li's class attribute
    var newListItemClass = $(this).parent().attr('class');


    //update button icon class to match this li
    button.removeClass(allOptionClasses).addClass( newListItemClass );


    //update button text this anchor's content
    selectmenuStatus.html( $(this).html() );


    //update this list item's selected attributes
    $(this)
        .parent()
        .addClass('selected')
        .attr('aria-selected', true);


    //trigger the custom hide event to hide menu
    menu.trigger('hide');
```

```
  //update the native select with the new selection
  selectElement[0].selectedIndex = menu.find('a').index(this);
});
```

Next, we'll set up the logic to trigger our custom events based on user interaction. We'll trigger our **toggle** event on **mousedown** to show and hide the menu and **return false** to prevent the button from gaining focus:

```
//apply click to button
button.mousedown(function(){
  menu.trigger('toggle');
  return false;
});
```

■ Note

We use mousedown, rather than click, so that users can press the mouse button, drag over the menu, and release the mouse button to make a selection.

We'll disable the **click** event on the menu button by returning it **false**, because we don't want the browser to follow the anchor element's native **click** behavior:

```
//disable click event on button (use mousedown/up instead)
button.click(function(){
  return false;
});
```

We'll also hide the menu whenever the user clicks elsewhere on the page:

```
//bind click to document for hiding menu
$(document).click(function(){
  menu.trigger('hide');
});
```

Now that we've assigned the menu button behavior, we'll move on to the menu. First, we'll bind a **mouseup** event to each menu option link that triggers our **select** event, and **return false** to prevent the anchor from receiving focus:

```
//apply mouseup event to menu for selecting options
//this event allows the user to drag and release
menu.find('a').mouseup(function(event){
```

```
    //trigger select event on this anchor
    $(this).trigger('select');
    //prevent native event from following through
    return false;
});
```

To provide visual feedback, we'll bind **mouseover** and **focus** events to the menu option links that add the **hover-focus** class to their parent list items. We'll also bind events to remove that class when the user moves away from the option:

```
//hover and focus events
menu.find('a')
    .bind('mouseover focus',function(){
        //remove class from previous hover-focused option
        menu.find('.hover-focus').removeClass('hover-focus');


        //add class to this option
        $(this).parent().addClass('hover-focus');
    })
    .bind('mouseout blur',function(){
        //remove class from this option
        $(this).parent().removeClass('hover-focus');
    });
```

Next, we'll apply keyboard events to match the native **select** element's behavior, including the ability to:

▶ Open the menu with the spacebar or Enter key

▶ Navigate through the menu options using the Up, Down, Left, and Right Arrow keys

▶ Make a selection in the menu using the spacebar or Enter key

We'll bind a **keydown** event to the menu button that does a number of things. When triggered, the event stores a reference to the selected option, and then it uses a **switch** statement to apply logic based on the **keyCode** of the key that was pressed.

Pressing the spacebar or Enter key triggers the **toggle** event to show or hide the menu. Pressing the arrow keys changes the selected option to the previous or next option, and displays it in the button (without having to open the menu):

```
//if enter or space is pressed in menu, trigger mousedown
button.keydown(function(event){
  //find selected list item in menu
  var currentSelectedLi = menu.find('li')
        .eq( selectElement[0].selectedIndex );

  //handle different key events
  switch(event.keyCode){
      //if enter or space is pressed in menu, trigger toggle
      case 13:
      case 32:
          button.trigger('toggle');
          return false;
      break;


      //up or left arrow keys
      case 37:
      case 38:
          //if there's a previous option, select it
          if( currentSelectedLi.prev().length ){
              currentSelectedLi.prev().find('a')
                  .trigger('select');
          }
          //prevent native scroll
          return false;
      break;


      //down or right arrow keys
      case 39:
      case 40:
          //if there's a next option, select it
```

```
        if( currentSelectedLi.next().length ){
            currentSelectedLi.next().find('a')
                .trigger('select');
        }
        //prevent native scroll
        return false;
    break;
  }
});
```

We'll apply a **keydown** event to the menu with similar logic, except the arrow keys move focus without changing the selection. This allows a user to browse the options with their arrow keys and then tab away without making a selection. Pressing the spacebar or Enter key triggers the **select** event on the focused anchor, closes the menu, and directs focus back to the menu button. All of these keypresses return **false**.

When the Tab key is pressed, we hide the menu, and direct focus back to the menu button so that focus jumps to the next focusable element in the page, to ensure that tab focus follows the user's expected tab order:

```
//keydown events for menu
menu.keydown(function(event){
  //switch logic based on which key was pressed
  switch(event.keyCode){
      //if enter or space is pressed in menu, trigger mouseup
      case 13:
      case 32:
          // trigger select
          $(event.target).trigger('select');
          button[0].focus();
          return false;
      break;
      //up or left arrow keys
      case 37:
      case 38:
```

```
        //if there's a previous option, focus it
        if( $(event.target).parent().prev().length ){
            $(event.target).parent().prev().find('a')[0]
                .focus();
        }
        //prevent native scroll
        return false;
    break;
    //down or right arrow keys
    case 39:
    case 40:
        //if there's a next option, focus it
        if( $(event.target).parent().next().length ){
            $(event.target).parent().next().find('a')[0]
                .focus();
        }
        //prevent native scroll
        return false;
    break;
    //tab key returns focus to the menu button,
    //allowing the browser to automatically shift focus
    //to the next focusable element on the page
    case 9:
        menu.trigger('hide');
        button[0].focus();
    break;
    }
});
```

Lastly, because the native and custom selects perform the same function, we'll apply attributes to hide the native select:

```
selectElement.addClass('select-hidden').attr('aria-hidden', true);
```

Taking the custom select further: advanced option styling

The custom select example above addresses simple text formatting and images. A design may call also call for richer text formatting to apply visual hierarchy. Consider, for example, this custom select menu that asks the user to choose a photo album:

Figure 17-7 Custom select menu design with multi-line text formatting styles

We can't achieve this level of visual style in a native **select** element, given its limitations (its child **option** elements cannot contain HTML tags), and will have to create a custom select to accomplish it. The important question is: is there a way we can create this enhanced custom select with a native **select** element to keep it fully accessible, and use the data-mining approach we used in the example above to construct a generic script that transforms it?

While at first glance it may seem impossible to communicate this level of content hierarchy using content within a native select, it can be done. We simply need to format each native **option**'s text in a way that delineates the three separate lines—title, description, and date—to properly prepare for the styling in the custom select. Then we can use JavaScript to parse the text and format it with HTML in the custom select.

First, we'll think about how we can translate formatting in the enhanced version using HTML characters and punctuation without compromising the usability of the basic experience. For example, we can use hyphens and parentheses to delineate each line of text:

```
My Title -- This is a description (Created January 12, 2009)
```

So we'll include this text formatting in the **select** element's foundation markup:

```
<select name="album" id="album">

  <option value="albumA">Summer Party -- Fun at the lake house (Created
  August 12, 2009)</option>

  <option value="albumB">Kate's Birthday -- Cake and presents (Created May
  13, 2009)</option>
```

```
<option value="albumC">Dance Recital -- First one of the year (Created
February 6, 2009)</option>

</select>
```

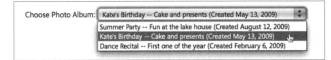

Choose Photo Album: Kate's Birthday -- Cake and presents (Created May 13, 2009)
Summer Party -- Fun at the lake house (Created August 12, 2009)
Kate's Birthday -- Cake and presents (Created May 13, 2009)
Dance Recital -- First one of the year (Created February 6, 2009)

Figure 17-8 Text formatted with simple punctuation in the basic experience.

Then, to transform the list item markup, we'll use a JavaScript regular expression to find and replace the punctuation we added with HTML. *Regular expressions* provide means to find strings of text using patterns of special characters, and JavaScript lets us take action on them. We'll write a regular expression to find the hyphens and parentheses and store it in a variable called **pattern**:

```
var pattern = /([\s\S]+)\-\- ([\s\S]+) (\([\s\S]+\))/;
```

This expression captures the three segments that we're trying to match—title, description, and date (highlighted in the code above).

Conveniently, JavaScript automatically assigns a variable name to each segment, so we can refer to each part of the regular expression with the variables **$1**, **$2**, and **$3**, respectively. We'll construct new enhanced markup for each line of text that references the three segments of our regular expression using these dollar-sign variables, and store it in a variable called **replacement**:

```
var replacement = '<span class="option-title">$1</span>'+
  '<span class="option-description">$2</span>'+
  '<span class="option-date">$3</span>';
```

After the enhancement script has generated the custom select menu, we'll run a short script that grabs each option's text from the enhanced markup and swaps it with a formatted equivalent by referencing our **pattern** and **replacement** variables inside a JavaScript **replace** method:

```
menu.find('li a').each(function(){

  //get the anchor's text

  var text = $(this).text();


  //replace anchor HTML with newly formatted markup
```

```
    $(this).html( text.replace(pattern,replacement) );

});
```

The resulting enhanced markup now contains **span** tags in place of the punctuation we used in the foundation markup:

```
<ul id="album-menu" class="custom-select">

  <li class="option-selected">

      <span class="option-title">Summer Party</span>

      <span class="option-description">Fun at the lake house</span>

      <span class="option-date">Created August 12, 2009</span>

  </li>

  ...

</ul>
```

Once that markup is injected into the page, we can use CSS to style the **span** elements to look like our target design:

```
#album-menu li a span.option-title {

  font-weight: bold;

  display:block;

}

#album-menu li a span.option-date {

  display:block;

  font-size: .9em;

  font-style: italic;

}
```

Using the custom select script

The demo and code that accompanies this book (available at www.filamentgroup.com/ dwpe) includes a script, **jQuery.selectmenu.js**, that automates the creation of custom selects using the principles outlined in this chapter, and includes full ARIA and keyboard navigation support. The script also mimics the search type-ahead behavior of a native **select**—when a letter key is pressed while the custom select is focused, it will select the first option that starts with that letter.

To use this script in your page, download and reference the files to match those shown in the select menu page, and call the **selectmenu** method on a **select** element in your page, as demonstrated in the following code:

```
$('select#foo').selectmenu();
```

The **maxHeight** option is used to set the maximum height of the options list menu in pixels. If the options list's height exceeds this value, a vertical scrollbar will appear:

```
$('select#foo').selectmenu({
  maxHeight: 300
});
```

To format the text of every menu option in the custom select, you can define a function that accepts a single argument, **text**, which represents the text of each list item. For example, this will wrap a **span** around each option in the custom select:

```
$('select').selectmenu({
  format: function(text){
        //wrap custom option text in a span
        return '<span class="error">'+text+'</span>';
    },
});
```

This format option can be used to create the multiple line-formatting example discussed in the "Taking it Further" section above.

★ ★ ★

When replacing any native form element, we always want to ensure that the enhanced component has at least the same set of capabilities as the native one before we extend the component with non-native features. This means that all features—like keyboard shortcuts and accessibility attributes—must work just as well as in the native control, to ensure that users who expect the custom select to act like a standard **select** control won't be frustrated or confused.

With our custom select menu widget, we find a way to mine all the goodness out of the native **select**, and layer on enhancements that enrich the user experience, while also applying generic logic to simplify the life of the developer.

chapter eighteen

list builder

As web applications start to more closely mirror the features of their desktop application cousins, we increasingly encounter situations where native HTML has no precedent for a UI element. One such example is the list builder widget.

In its simplest form, a list builder widget groups a number of words or phrases within an editable area. Each entry is typically "boxed" with a border or background color to make the list easy to scan, edit, and delete; and since each entry is treated like an independent unit, richer interactions like multi-select, drag-and-drop, action buttons, and context menus can be added.

List builder interactions can be found in a variety of common web applications, including:

▶ Sites with tagging systems where users enter words or phrases to characterize a photo, document, map point of interest, video, or bookmark

▶ Email applications that facilitate creating recipient lists in the To, Cc, and Bcc fields

▶ Grocery delivery or other list-based shopping websites, where list items can be quickly added, moved and deleted

Many complex list builders add auto-complete features to recommend values that already exist in the system, such as tags already applied to other objects, or email information stored in the user's address book.

Figure 18-1 A message-recipient list builder widget

In this chapter, we'll describe how to construct a simple list builder using standard, accessible HTML form controls and then transform it with JavaScript into an interactive widget that builds upon the basic version's functionality, while maintaining all accessible features of the native elements. Then, we'll discuss how to augment a standard list builder with more complex functionality like multiple selection, drag-and-drop sorting, auto-complete, and contextual menus.

X-ray perspective

To start, we'll consider a fairly simple list builder for adding descriptive tags to a photo:

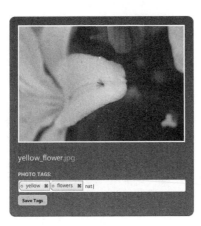

Figure 18-2 Target list builder design for tagging a photo

The target design shows a list of tags grouped inside an editable text box, each entry styled with a border and background image to look like an iconic tag. A small Remove button associated with each tag provides a one-click shortcut for deleting that tag, and users can add new tags by simply typing into the text box container.

The list builder design incorporates a number of advanced features—custom styling, Remove buttons for each entry, and a custom-styled Submit button (Save Tags). But when we look at this design from an x-ray perspective, we see that these features are not core to the tool: the list builder's essential function is to provide a way to enter and submit one or a series of words or phrases. Our foundation markup can accomplish all essential list builder functionality with a text-entry form element that accepts a space- or comma-delimited list, followed by a standard Submit button.

Two HTML elements—the text **input** and **textarea**—could satisfy these requirements. Each has unique features that could be useful:

▶ A text **input** has built-in constraints: it accepts a single line of text, and displays only as many characters as will fit within its fixed dimensions. (While technically, the **input** will accept more content than the element's size dimension, users need to use arrow keys to view characters that exceed the visible area.) It's ideal for cases where character limitations are encouraged.

▶ A **textarea** allows more flexibility: it can accept multi-line inputs, and automatically adds a scrollbar if the content exceeds the viewable area.

Savvy web users will often interpret the constraints of a system based on which type of element is displayed, and assume that field size suggests the length of an acceptable answer. In our photo-tagging example, we don't want to limit the number of tags a user can add to any one photo, so we'll use a **textarea** in our foundation markup to help them understand that.

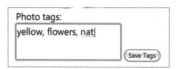

Figure 18-3 Basic experience for the list builder

The enhanced list builder widget incorporates more complex functionality than is supported natively by the **textarea**—for example, each photo tag is custom styled and has a built-in Remove button—so the enhanced widget should be constructed with new markup that's injected into the page via JavaScript. We'll style a standard unordered list (**ul**) to contain the tags; the last item in the list will always contain a blank text **input** to allow new inline entries.

To simplify form-processing on the server, we'll follow our standard proxy pattern: when the enhanced list builder widget is created on page load, the script will check the foundation markup's **textarea** and generate an unordered list item for each existing value; each time a tag is added or removed in the builder widget, the **textarea** will be updated so both are in sync at all times. On screen, we'll hide the foundation HTML element from users, but keep it in the page markup so that the form submits the same way for both the basic and enhanced versions of the page.

To maintain accessibility, the enhanced list builder must be constructed in a way that allows screen-reader users to understand what the component is and how to use it. We'll adequately describe the functionality using ARIA attributes in ways that assistive technology will understand.

Creating the list builder

We'll start by marking up the page with a standard **textarea** that can be populated with a simple list of comma-delimited values; we'll then transform those values into a group of styled, editable photo tags in the enhanced experience.

Foundation markup and style

The foundation markup for the list builder is simple: it consists of a **textarea** and an accompanying **label** to describe its purpose. The **label** element's **for** attribute matches the **textarea**'s **id** attribute to properly associate them for screen readers. Before the user has entered any tags, the **textarea** contains no value:

```
<label for="tags">Photo tags:</label>

<textarea id="tags" name="tags"></textarea>
```

If the user has previously entered tags for a photo, on page load the **textarea** element is prepopulated with a value of the existing, comma-separated photo tags. In this example, we'll assume that two tags were already assigned and saved to the photo ("yellow" and "flowers") and are present when the page loads:

```
<textarea id="tags" name="tags">yellow, flowers</textarea>
```

With the markup in place, we can apply a few very simple CSS rules to the list builder that are safe for pretty much any browser:

▶ A global **font-family** stack assigned to the **body** tag, and, specifically, to the **textarea** element, as text-entry form elements do not automatically inherit fonts in most browsers

▶ A block-level **display** property set for the **label**, to stack it above the **textarea** (otherwise it will sit to the left)

In the basic style sheet, our safe styles look like this:

```
body, textarea { font-family: "Segoe UI", Arial, sans-serif; }

label { display: block; }
```

And voilà! The list builder foundation markup is complete.

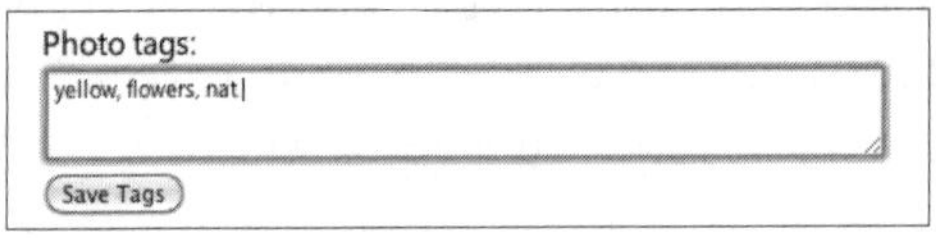

Photo tags:
yellow, flowers, nat|

Save Tags

Figure 18-4 Photo tag builder foundation markup with safe styles applied

We don't need to add any accessibility features to the basic experience, because all native HTML form elements are accessible. For example, the full complement of list builder features can be accessed and used with key commands: users can press the Tab key to focus on the **textarea**, type a comma-delimited list of values, and then tab to the Save Tags button to submit the form.

Enhanced markup and style

The enhanced markup for our list builder widget will be inserted into the page via JavaScript when the capabilities test passes, and communicate its content values back to the foundation **textarea** for form submission.

First, the **textarea**'s functionality will be replaced by the list builder widget, so we'll hide it from all users, including screen readers—we want everyone to manipulate the list builder widget and ignore the **textarea** entirely:

```
textarea#tags { display: none; }
```

■ Note

Keep in mind that the textarea is only hidden from users; when we build the list builder script, we'll set up the foundation textarea to serve as a proxy for submitting values entered into the list builder widget.

Now the decks are clear to structure the enhanced list builder. We'll use an unordered list with a **class** of **listbuilder** to group the tags together in a semantic way that can be styled to look like a box:

```
<ul class="listbuilder">

  ...

</ul>
```

Each list item (**li**) contained in the **ul** will represent a unique photo tag.

The unordered list should always contain a list item with a text **input** for entering a new tag; we'll identify it with a descriptive class, **listbuilder-entry-add**. A **title** attribute on the **input** provides a tooltip on hover and spoken instructions for screen readers:

```
<li class="listbuilder-entry-add">

  <input type="text" value="" title="To add an item to this list, type a
  name and press enter or comma." />

</li>
```

■ Note

We intentionally omitted the name attribute from this input because we're using it solely as a way to collect and temporarily hold a new tag entry; we don't need to submit its value along with the rest of the form data.

Our list builder script will generate a new tag for every entry it finds in the **textarea** when the page loads. The markup for each tag is a list item with a **span** wrapped around the photo tag's text:

```
<li class="listbuilder-entry">
  <span class="listbuilder-entry-text">yellow</span>
</li>
```

Whenever a user enters a word or phrase and either adds a comma or presses Enter, the script creates a new list item with the **input**'s value and inserts it at the end of the list of tags, just before the editable list item.

Each photo tag also has a Remove link with the class **listbuilder-entry-remove** and a text value of "Remove." We'll hide the link text with CSS and replace it with a compact "x" icon background image, and add a **title** attribute with a text explanation of the button's functionality, to be used by both a native tooltip and a screen reader's audible feedback, and an ARIA **role** of **button** that describe the link's purpose:

```
<li class="listbuilder-entry">
  <span class="listbuilder-entry-text">yellow</span>
  <a class="listbuilder-entry-remove" title="Remove yellow from the list."
  href="#" role="button">Remove</a>
</li>
```

To complete the list builder markup, we need to address the foundation **label** element. In the basic experience, the **label** describes only the **textarea**; in the enhanced experience, it needs to describe all of the new markup—the unordered list structure, new entry text input, text spans, and Remove buttons—in which case, a single **label** element is inadequate. To make it more meaningful in its enhanced role, we'll use JavaScript to transform it into an HTML heading:

```
<h2>Photo tags:</h2>
```

At this stage, we've established the enhanced markup for the list builder—it's a simple unordered list of tags with Remove links and an editable text input at the end.

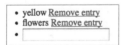

Figure 18-5 Unstyled enhanced markup for two tags and the text input

Next, we'll add CSS to style the list builder for the enhanced experience, applying a larger font size and adding weight to the list builder heading that replaces the **label** element:

```
h2 {
  font-size:1.3em;
  margin:.5em 0;
```

```
  font-weight:bold;

  text-transform:uppercase;

}
```

We'll apply a few styles to the list builder's container (**ul**), like **border** and **overflow** properties, to approximate the look and scrolling behavior of a standard **textarea**. The list builder has a medium-gray background color to let the individual tags stand out, and uses the CSS3 **border-radius** property to round the corners in browsers that support it:

```
ul.listbuilder {

  padding: 0;

  margin: 0;

  background:#88898a;

  list-style:none;

  border:1px solid #4D4D4D;

  overflow:auto;

  cursor:text;

  -moz-border-radius:5px;

  -webkit-border-radius:5px;

  border-radius:5px;

}
```

When the cursor is focused in the list builder, the background color will change to white to make it look more like an active, editable text field. This color change will occur when the **listbuilder-focus** class is appended to the list based on the **input**'s focus state:

```
ul.listbuilder-focus { background: #fff; }
```

Figure 18-6 Default (top) and focused (bottom) states for the list builder widget

We'll float all list items and the editable input to the left so they sit side by side, and add a little margin to space them apart:

```
ul.listbuilder li {

  float:left;
```

```
    font-size:1.3em;

    margin: 2px 0 2px 2px;

    color: #333;

}
```

The editable text input should be seamless within the list builder container, so we'll remove the border, padding, margin, and outline, and set the font size to **1em** so that it inherits the list's font size:

```
ul.listbuilder input {

    font-size:1em;

    margin:0;

    padding:0;

    background:transparent;

    border:0;

    outline:0;

    line-height:1.7;

    color: #fff;

    width: 3em;

}
```

To make each tag appear tag-like, we'll apply two background images: one for the top that we'll assign to the **li,** and one for the bottom that we'll assign to the **span**. Using two "sliding door" background images in this way will ensure that the background accommodates flexible text sizes when the user adjusts text size using browser controls. We'll set the **span** to **display: block** to make it fill the available space, and add an extra 25 pixels of padding the right to leave room for the Remove link:

```
ul.listbuilder li.listbuilder-entry {

    position:relative;

    cursor:default;

    border-right:1px solid #7d7d7d;

    background:#eee url(../images/bg-tag-top.png) top left no-repeat;

}
ul.listbuilder span.listbuilder-entry-text {

    display:block;
```

```
padding:.2em 25px .4em 18px;
background:url(../images/bg-tag-bottom.png) bottom left no-repeat;
}
```

Finally, we'll hide the Remove link's text using a large negative **text-indent** value, and replace it with an icon background image; we'll also absolutely position the link so that it always sits to the right of the tag text:

```
ul.listbuilder li.listbuilder-entry a.listbuilder-entry-remove {
    position:absolute;
    right:.3em;
    top:50%;
    margin-top:-5px;
    width:11px;
    height:11px;
    text-indent:-99999px;
    overflow:hidden;
    background:url(../images/icon_remove.png) 0 0 no-repeat;
}
```

List builder script

When the capabilities test runs, it inserts the enhanced CSS and scripts that create the list builder widget for passing browsers. The list builder enhancement script does a number of things:

1 Generates the enhanced list builder markup and populates the list with any initial values found in the **textarea**.

2 Adds new tags as they're entered by watching for keyboard events in the text input.

3 Creates a proxy function to continually update the original **textarea** with the set of tags in the list builder, so they always stay in sync for form submission.

4 Applies mouse-click behavior to the list for removing tags, showing visual feedback, and focusing the cursor into the editable text input.

5 Transforms the **label** element in the foundation markup into a more semantically correct heading for the enhanced control.

■ Note

The scripting principles described in this chapter could work with either a textarea or input,
since the enhanced experience is the same for both.

GENERATING THE ENHANCED MARKUP

The list builder script generates the widget based on the characteristics of a specific
textarea in the foundation markup. First, we'll identify which **textarea** will become a
list builder, and then gather information about it, including its width and current value
(in case it's pre-filled with a set of tags). As with other script examples, we'll use jQuery
notation for these variables:

```
var textarea = $('textarea#tags');

var textareaWidth = textarea.width();

var textareaValue = textarea.val();
```

We'll use these variables to create an empty **ul** for the list builder container and set its
width to match the original **textarea**:

```
var listbuilder = $('<ul class="listbuilder"></ul>')
        .width( textareaWidth );
```

The first step in populating the contents of the list builder widget is to create a tag
for any existing value in the **textarea**. We'll use the **textarea**'s value, stored in the
textareaValue variable, and generate a new **li** for each word or phrase, separated
by a comma or a line break, and append it to the list builder as a tag.

To do that, we'll separate the **textarea**'s value into an array of values with JavaScript's
native **split** method, specifying the characters that delimit each entry. For example,
to split the value at every comma, we'd pass a comma string as an argument to the
split method:

```
textareaValue.split(',');
```

The **split** method can also accept regular expressions to match more complicated patterns. To split the value string in the appropriate places for our list builder, we'll use the
regular expression **/[,\n]/**, which looks for any occurrence of a comma (**,**) or line break
(**\n**). (The slashes denote the beginning and end of the expression, and the square brackets describe one or more characters that constitute a match.) We'll create a new variable, **textareaValueArray**, to capture the resulting array of split values:

```
var textareaValueArray = textareaValue.split(/[,\n]/);
```

Using jQuery's **each** method, we'll iterate through the array and generate a list item for each tag value, and then append them all at once to the **ul** to optimize performance. If the array has no values, the **each** method will simply iterate zero times and cause no errors:

```
$.each( textareaValueArray, function(){

  /* create a reference to the value of the current item */

  var val = this;


  /* append a new list item to the list builder */

  listbuilder.append('<li class="listbuilder-entry">
  ➥<span class="listbuilder-entry-text">'+val+'</span>
  ➥<a href="#" class="listbuilder-entry-remove"
  ➥title="Remove '+val+' from the list." role="button">
  ➥Remove</a></li>');

};
```

Next, we'll append the editable list item that lets users add new tags to the list. If there are no pre-existing tags, the input will be the only item in the list builder container; when other items are present, it will always be the last item in the list.

```
listbuilder.append('<li class="listbuilder-editable">
➥<input type="text" value=""
➥title="Type a name and press enter or comma
➥to add it to the list." /></li>');
```

Finally, we'll insert the list builder into the page:

```
listbuilder.insertAfter( textarea );
```

KEEPING THE ORIGINAL TEXTAREA IN SYNC

Though the original foundation **textarea** is hidden from view, it's still necessary behind the scenes for capturing tag values to submit to the server when the user clicks the Save Tags button. By using the hidden **textarea** this way, we can use a single method to process the form in both the basic and enhanced experiences.

To do this, we'll use a "proxy" pattern: when the user interacts with the enhanced list builder, our script will update the original, hidden **textarea** with the current set of values. The script will loop through all the entries in the list, store their values in a comma-delimited string, and use that string to set the **textarea**'s value. We'll write this logic into its own function, **updateValue**, which we can call whenever the user updates the list by adding, editing, or deleting tags:

```
function updateValue(){
  /* create array to hold new values */
  newTextareaValue = [];

  /* loop through each list item's text and add it to the array */
  listbuilder.find('span.listbuilder-entry-text').each(function(){
      newTextareaValue.push( $(this).text() );
  });

  /* add the value of the input element in the last list item */
  newTextareaValue.push( listbuilder.find('input').val() );

  /* populate the textarea with the list items, joined with commas */
  textarea.val( newTextareaValue.join(',') );
};
```

APPLYING CLICK BEHAVIOR TO THE LIST

The script for removing entries from the list is very simple: when a Remove icon is clicked, its list item is removed from the page, and the **textarea**'s value is updated with the new list by calling our **updateValue** function. We'll assign this click event once to the list builder container and use event delegation to ensure that all Remove links—those already in the list *and* any that might be added to the list later—will receive this behavior.

```
listbuilder.click(function(ev){
  //create reference to the element that was clicked
  var clickedElement = $(ev.target);

  //check if the clicked element as a remove link
  if(clickedElement.is('a.listbuilder-entry-remove') ){

      //remove the parent list item
      clickedElement.parent().remove();
  }
```

```
//return the click event false
return false;
});
```

We need to add one more scenario to the click event on our list builder: when the user clicks on the list builder container but is not removing a tag, we want to direct the cursor's focus to the editable input field. With this, the list builder will feel like a native **textarea**:

```
listbuilder.click(function(ev){
    var clickedElement = $(ev.target);
    if(clickedElement.is('a.listbuilder-entry-remove') ){
        clickedElement.parent().remove();
    }
    else {
        //direct focus to the last item's input element
        listbuilder.find('input').focus();
    }
    return false;
});
```

We also want to provide visual feedback when focus is on the list builder. To do this, we'll use the input's **focus** and **blur** events to add or remove the **listbuilder-focus** class we created earlier:

```
listbuilder.find('input')
    .focus(function(){
        listbuilder.addClass('listbuilder-focus');
    })
    .blur(function(){
        listbuilder.removeClass('listbuilder-focus');
    });
```

ADDING NEW TAGS

When the user presses a key while focused in the text **input**, we transfer that key's value back to the foundation **textarea** to keep the controls in sync. If the user happens to press one of the two keys we've identified for adding tags—the comma or Enter key—we'll generate a tag in the enhanced list builder control that contains the **input**'s value. We'll bind all of this logic to the list builder container using the **keydown** event, which fires when a key is first pressed but before the character specified (Enter or comma) is added to the input's value:

```
listbuilder.find('input')
  //add keydown event
  .keydown(function(ev){

      //save reference to the input
      var input = $(this);

      //check if key was either comma (188) or enter (13),
      //and the value isn't blank or just a single comma
      if( (ev.keyCode == 188 || ev.keyCode == 13)
          && input.val() != '' ){

          //save reference to the value before the comma
          var val = input.val().split(',')[0];

          //inject a new list item before this one,
          //including the new text
          input.parent().before( '<li class="listbuilder-entry">
          <span class="listbuilder-entry-text">'+val+'</span>
          <a href="#" class="listbuilder-entry-remove"
          title="Remove '+val+' from the list." role="button">
          Remove</a></li>');

          //reset the input's value
          input.val('');
      }

      //regardless of conditions above,
      //if key pressed was comma or enter,
```

```
//prevent it from finishing keypress
if(ev.keyCode == 188 || ev.keyCode == 13){
    ev.preventDefault();
}
});
```

When the **keyup** event fires, the script will run the **updateValue** function to make sure the **textarea** is always up to date with all entries in the list builder, including any incomplete entries currently being typed:

```
listbuilder.find('input')
//assign keyup event
.keyup(function(){
  //update the textarea
  updateValue();
});
```

As a final touch, we'll replace the foundation **label** element with a heading for the entire list builder control:

```
//find label by its for attribute
var label = $('label[for='+ textarea.attr('id') +']');


//use jQuery's replaceWith method to change the label to an h2
label.replaceWith('<h2>'+label.text()+'</h2>');
```

Our script now transforms an ordinary **textarea** into a richly interactive list builder that can be styled to fit any application.

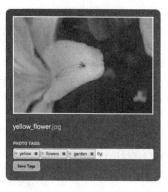

Figure 18-7 Final enhanced list builder widget

Taking the list builder further: multi-select, sorting, auto-complete, and contextual menus

So far we've reviewed the basic mechanics for creating a list builder from a **textarea**. Once created, there are a range of additional features that could be layered on to further improve the list builder's usefulness and usability.

Multiple selection

The ability to select and take action on multiple items simultaneously—by pressing the Control or Shift key while clicking individual items in the list builder—could make it feel more like an advanced desktop-style component, and dramatically boost user efficiency by eliminating the need for repetitive actions. This can be accomplished by adding logic that watches for specific keyboard events each time the user clicks on an item.

For example, a user may want to edit a long list of email addresses in the To field. With multiple selection enabled, they could hold down the Shift key and click (or use arrow keys) to select a number of consecutive email addresses, or hold down the Control key to select addresses at different points in the list.

Note that the list builder plugin script that accompanies this book (available at www.filamentgroup.com/dwpe) incorporates this functionality automatically.

Drag-and-drop sorting

In situations where the sequence of items in the list builder is important, consider incorporating click-and-drag functionality to support reordering items in the list. This behavior could be added with jQuery UI's sortable plugin, available at jQueryUI.com. By including jQuery UI's core and sortable plugins, and then calling the **sortable** method on the list builder container, the list items will gain the ability to be reordered with drag and drop.

Auto-complete

Many list builder implementations include auto-complete functionality that suggests a list of values as the user types a new entry. This could easily be added using jQuery UI's auto-complete widget, which can be found at jQueryUI.com. The configuration for auto-complete varies depending on the source and structure of the data; to learn more about jQuery UI auto-complete's features and download the plugin, visit jQueryUI.com.

When implementing auto-complete, it's worth considering whether the choices offered in an auto-complete list should also be offered in the basic experience—which can be supported with a link that navigates to a separate HTML page with suggested values in radio buttons or checkboxes. For example, an email recipient list builder could have an Address Book link next to the **textarea** that navigates users to a separate page with a checklist of contacts; the user could select a number of contact addresses to populate the recipient list when they click an Add Recipients button. In the enhanced experience, the list of contacts could be retrieved with Ajax as HTML, JSON, or XML, and fed into the auto-complete menu for a faster and more interactive experience.

Contextual menus

Another powerful way to extend the list builder is to add context menus to each list item so the user has quick access to related actions. For example, in Apple Mail, the list items in the To, Cc, and Bcc fields include a context menu with links to easily copy or save the email address, remove the address from the list, or start a new chat or email with that person.

This feature isn't included in our plugin, but there are a host of jQuery and other plugins available that offer ways to attach a menu's event behavior to each list item.

Using the list builder script

The list builder demo and code that accompanies this book (www.filamentgroup.com/dwpe) includes a script, **jQuery.listbuilder.js**, that has all the basic features described in this chapter, along with additional keyboard behavior for multiple selection and removing items with the Backspace key. Here's how you use this script:

1　Download and reference the jQuery library (version 1.3.1 or later), the script included on the book website (**jQuery.listbuilder.js**), and the CSS files and images included in the online demo.

2　Point the plugin to a specific **textarea** or text **input**, and call the **listbuilder** method:

```
$('textarea').listbuilder();
```

3　Set options as desired. The plugin can be configured with the following options:

- **delimChar** — the character(s) used to split **textarea** content into separate entries, like a comma or line break

- **width** — the width of the list builder container, which defaults to the width of the **textarea** it replaces.

- **completeChars** — an array of key codes used to create a new item. For example, when the user types in a word or phrase, they can press the comma or Enter key to add a tag. A complete list of key codes is listed at the Mozilla Developer Center (https://developer.mozilla.org/en/DOM/Event/UIEvent/KeyEvent).

- **userDirections** — instruction text applied as a **title** attribute on the new input. The default direction text is "Type a name and press enter or comma to add it to the list."

- **labelReplacement** — a new tag, or set of nested tags, in the form of an HTML string to replace the **label** element originally associated with the **textarea**, for example, **<h2 class="list-builder-heading"></h2>**. The script will grab the **label**'s content and inject it into the innermost tag of the specified string. For a good example of this option, view the list builder JavaScript in the code accompanies this book.

4 Override the default values for any option by passing an object into the **listbuilder** method, with a key/value pair:

```
//split the text area value by dashes instead of comma/line breaks
$('textarea').listbuilder( {delimChar: '-'} );
```

The elements and classes generated by the list builder plugin match those explained in this chapter; you can grab the CSS file included with the code samples posted on the book website to use the design presented in this chapter as a starting point for your project.

★ ★ ★

The list builder provides a rich example of how the x-ray approach allows us to map a complex, interactive widget back to very simple HTML elements to ensure compatibility with all devices. It also illustrates the fact that not every enhanced feature (such as auto-complete and contextual menus) needs to be implemented in the basic experience to still provide a perfectly usable interaction.

chapter nineteen
file input

As websites expand their content-sharing and collaboration features, users are electing to upload files—photos, videos, documents, even secure data—and store them via web applications in "cloud"-based systems instead of locally on their own computers. Common applications that rely on file uploading from a web browser include photo or video sharing sites like Flickr or YouTube, social networking sites like Facebook, and web-based productivity suites like Google Docs.

Conveniently, HTML provides a native form control to access local files: a standard **input** element with the **type** set to **file**. The file **input** renders with a text field for feedback and a button that launches a standard operating-system dialog box to allow users to browse the contents of their local hard drive. When a file is selected, the text feedback field is populated with the selected file's path.

But the standard file **input** is less than optimal from both a style and usability standpoint. It's not possible to style the native file **input** with CSS, and the appearance and dimensions of both the text field and button can vary widely—even button wording may differ—across browsers and operating systems. Most importantly, the fixed-size text field rendered by most browsers is often too small to display the full file path, so the user must scroll within the text field to view the most essential piece of user feedback—the filename (Safari on the Mac is the notable exception; it shows the filename, but does not display the rest of the path):

Figure 19-1 Examples of a native file input in popular browsers and platforms—IE 8 Windows (top), Firefox 3 Windows (middle), Safari 4 Mac (bottom)

There are a number of situations where a custom-designed file input would work better than the native control in a website or application:

▶ Sites where the file input's look and feel must match the rest of the user interface design, or its dimensions must be controlled to fit into a specific layout

▶ Cases when the Browse (or Choose File) button has an icon, or requires different wording to more accurately fit the context (such as Choose Image or Upload Profile Picture) or to support variations in language

▶ Situations in which feedback for the selected file, including the filename, must be visible or accompanied by a custom icon

▶ Cases when users can upload multiple files, and where it would be helpful to display thumbnail images and file sizes, or a progress bar that shows real-time feedback on the upload process

It's common to see a plugin-based solution like Flash for creating a custom file input, but as we've discussed, the proprietary nature of plugins makes them less than fully available on all platforms and devices. For that reason, we prefer to enhance the standard HTML file **input** using a little CSS and JavaScript, which are more broadly accessible.

In this chapter, we'll walk through the process of building a custom file input that leverages the native **input**, with a creative twist. We'll discuss more complex scenarios, like multiple file inputs that run in parallel, at the end of this chapter.

X-ray perspective

Our design for a social networking site has a form that lets users upload a profile photo. The photo upload form has a custom-designed file input to match the look and feel of our site:

Figure 19-2 Custom file input design

As with a native file input, a standard operating-system dialog box appears when the user clicks the Browse button:

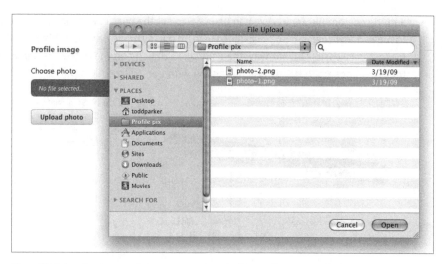

Figure 19-3 A native browse dialog appears when the Browse button is clicked.

In our target design, the custom input will display the name of the file along with an icon to identify the file type. As an enhanced touch, we'll swap the label on the button from Browse to Change to reflect the fact that a file has already been selected:

Figure 19-4 Filename and icon feedback for a selected file

Looking at this design from the x-ray perspective, our foundation markup choice for this element is clear: a standard file **input** is the only way to upload files in HTML.

However, the native file **input** can't be styled to match our target design. To work around this problem, we'll hide the native file **input** visually, and generate additional markup in its place that looks like our custom widget. Whenever that custom widget is clicked, we'll need to transfer that **click** event to the native **input**, which will open the operating system's Browse dialog. This allows us to essentially "piggyback" on the native control to open the Browse dialog.

Ordinarily, we would use JavaScript to trigger that **click** event on the native file **input** whenever the custom widget is clicked. However, because the file **input** interacts directly with a user's file system, browser developers have built in protections to prevent hackers from exploiting JavaScript-triggered **click** events, sometimes referred to as *hijacking clicks*, or *click-jacking*, so we'll need a clever workaround.

Since we can't programmatically trigger the **click** on the native file **input**, we'll dynamically position the input itself to make sure it receives the *actual* click. To do this, we'll make the native file **input** transparent, and position it directly between the user's cursor and the custom file **input**. We can use CSS to set the **opacity** of the native **input** to zero to make it invisible, but still clickable (using **display:none** or **visibility:hidden** would make it inaccessible). That way, the user clicks directly on the native file **input**, even though it appears that they are interacting with the custom file input:

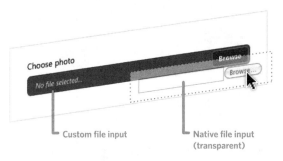

Figure 19-5 The native file input is positioned under the user's cursor to open the browse dialog.

Custom file input

Native file input
(transparent)

The best part of this approach is that we're able to use the native file **input** control for both the basic and enhanced experiences, so we can leverage all the functionality and accessibility that it provides—the custom file input is really just a visual feedback mechanism. Though the native **input** is invisible, it's still keyboard-accessible, so there's no need to add any accessibility features or ARIA attributes to it. We will, however, add one ARIA attribute to the custom widget to hide it from screen readers, since it's relevant only to sighted users.

And the basic experience is perfectly usable with the native file **input**:

Figure 19-6 Basic experience of the image uploader

A tip of the hat

This solution was inspired by the work of Michael McGrady and Shaun Inman, who developed this tricky bit of CSS and JavaScript to position the native file **input** under the user's cursor to create custom file inputs.

www.shauninman.com/archive/2007/09/10/styling_file_inputs_with_css_and_the_dom

www.quirksmode.org/dom/inputfile.html

Creating the custom file input

Now that we have an overall approach in hand, we'll dig into the foundation markup for the basic experience, and then add markup, style, and script enhancements.

Foundation markup and style

The basic markup consists of a standard **input** tag with the **type** attribute set to **file**:

```
<input type="file" name="file" />
```

We'll add a unique ID to the **input** to associate it with its **label** and provide a hook (an easy way to locate it) for our enhancement script:

```
<label for="file">Choose photo</label>
<input type="file" name="file" id="file" />
```

To complete the foundation markup, we'll wrap this markup in a **form** tag and add a standard **input** with a type of **submit** for the Upload Photo button. In order to properly submit file-input data, the opening **form** tag must include the **method="post"** and **enctype="multi-part/form"** attributes and values, which let the form submit binary file data in addition to standard text values:

```
<form action="profilePhoto.php" method="post" enctype="multipart/form-data">
```

Figure 19-7 Basic experience before safe styles are applied

Next, we'll add a few safe styles to the basic style sheet that will be served to all users. We'll include a simple font stack to set the default font for the page, and add a rule to set the **label** to **display: block** to stack it above the file **input**:

```
body { font-family: "Segoe UI", Arial, sans-serif; }
label { display:block; }
```

Figure 19-8 Basic experience with safe styles applied

Enhanced markup and style

Now that we have the foundation markup established, we'll move on to the enhanced markup and styles for the custom file input.

First we'll create a container **div** for the custom file input markup, and give it a class of **customfile**, and an **aria-hidden** attribute with a value of **true** (later we'll style this as the outer container around the feedback box and button):

```
<div class="customfile" aria-hidden="true"></div>
```

Within this container, we'll add two **span** elements: the first will be used to display the icon and text feedback of the selected file; the second will serve as the Browse button. By default, the native file **input** will be blank, so the initial feedback message is "No file selected..." and the button label is Browse:

```
<div class="customfile" aria-hidden="true">
  <span class="customfile-button">Browse</span>
  <span class="customfile-feedback">No file selected...</span>
</div>
```

We'll style the outer container with a dark gray background color, border, and padding, and apply rounded corners with the CSS3 **border-radius** property. We'll also set the **cursor:pointer** property, so users will see the hand icon to indicate that the file input is clickable:

```
.customfile {
  width: 400px;
  background: #666;
  cursor: pointer;
  overflow: auto;
  padding: 2px;
  border: 1px solid #444;
  -moz-border-radius:7px;
  -webkit-border-radius:7px;
  border-radius:7px;
}
```

We'll float the Browse button to the right of the feedback box, and style it with a gradient background image and rounded corners:

```
.customfile-button {
  border: 1px solid #999;
  background: #333 url(../images/bg-submit.gif) bottom repeat-x;
  color: #fff;
  font-weight: bold;
  float: right;
  width: 50px;
  padding: .3em .6em;
  text-align: center;
  text-decoration: none;
  font-size: 1.2em;
  -moz-border-radius:5px;
  -webkit-border-radius:5px;
  border-radius:5px;
}
```

The feedback text is styled with italicized type for the initial, empty state (before the user has selected a file):

```
.customfile-feedback {
  display: block;
  margin: 1px 1px 1px 5px;
  font-size: 1.2em;
  color: #fff;
  font-style: italic;
  padding: .3em .6em;
}
```

Figure 19-9 Enhanced experience with no file selected

To provide visual feedback when a user hovers over the button with the mouse or focuses on the **input** with the keyboard, we'll create a common rule to style the hover and focus states, and then add a dotted outline for keyboard focus feedback:

```
.customfile-hover .customfile-button,

.customfile-focus .customfile-button {

  color:#111;

  background: #aaa url(../images/bg-btn.png) bottom repeat-x;

  border-color:#aaa;

  padding: .3em .6em;

}

.customfile-focus .customfile-button {

  outline: 1px dotted #ccc;

}
```

Figure 19-10 Example of keyboard focus feedback—the button is styled like the hover state with the addition of a dotted outline

When a file is chosen, the script will add another class to the feedback box, **customfile-feedback-populated**, with a few style overrides that make the feedback text bold and add a file-icon background image:

```
.customfile-feedback-populated {

  color: #fff;

  font-style: normal;

  font-weight: bold;

  padding-left: 20px;

  background: url(../images/icon-generic.gif) left 4px no-repeat;

}
```

Figure 19-11 File feedback with generic file icon

By default, a generic file-icon background is set, which will be overridden if the script recognizes a more specific file-type icon that matches one of those referenced in the style sheet. To update the icon image, the script will parse the filename of the selected file to find its extension, and then dynamically add a class to the feedback box for that extension. For example, a file called photo.png will be assigned **class="png"**. In the enhanced style sheet, style rules for these classes will point to unique background images.

When multiple file types share an icon, several class selectors (PNG, JPG, etc.) can be chained and directed to the same style rule. Here, we'll set four common image extensions to use the same image icon. Since our interface is focused on choosing a photo, these are the primary extensions that we'll accept:

```
.jpg, .gif, .png, .jpeg, .bmp {
    background-image: url(../images/icon-image.gif);
}
```

Figure 19-12 Image icon feedback

We'll set the **opacity** of the original file **input** to **0** to make it invisible in most modern browsers (later, we'll script the opacity for Internet Explorer 6). When the user hovers the mouse over the custom input, the script will append the native file **input** to the end of the **body** before showing it, to ensure that it's positioned at the proper mouse coordinates relative to the window. We'll set the **z-index** of the **input** to **99999** to ensure that it's positioned in front of the custom input, regardless of the other **z-index** properties applied to elements on the page:

```
.customfile-nativeinput {
    position: absolute;
    cursor: pointer;
    opacity: 0;
    z-index: 99999;
}
```

Finally, we'll style the original **label** from the foundation markup to match our target design, because it will remain visible on the page in the enhanced experience:

```
label {
    font-size: 1.4em;
    display: block;
    margin: .5em 10px .5em 0;
}
```

Custom file input script

The first thing the enhancement script does when called is to add a **customfile-nativeinput** class to the native file **input** so we can apply styles. We'll also use jQuery's **css** method to make the element invisible for Internet Explorer (Internet Explorer **6** doesn't support CSS **opacity**, so jQuery automatically applies a proprietary **filter** as a workaround):

```
var fileInput = $('#file')

  // add class for CSS

  .addClass('customfile-nativeinput')


  // visually hide element with jQuery's opacity method

  .css('opacity',0);
```

Next, we'll generate the container **div** with two **span** elements for the enhanced markup, and append it to the page after the native **input**. The custom file input is empty (contains no value) by default, so it will contain the "No file selected..." feedback text:

```
// create custom control container

var upload = $('<div class="customfile" aria-hidden="true"></div>');


// create custom control button

var uploadButton = $('<span class="customfile-button">Browse</span>').
appendTo(upload);


// create custom control feedback

var uploadFeedback = $('<span class="customfile-feedback">No file
selected...</span>').appendTo(upload);


// insert enhanced markup after the native file input

upload.insertAfter(fileInput);
```

To position the native file **input** under the user's cursor, the script binds the **mousemove** event to detect when the mouse is located over the custom file input. The script then dynamically repositions the left and top screen coordinates for the native **input**, and places it between the user's cursor and the custom input. When a user clicks the custom input's button, they're actually clicking the invisible native file **input**'s button, which opens the Browse dialog:

```
// on mousemove, keep file native input under the cursor to capture click
upload.mousemove(function(e){
  fileInput.css({

    // position 3px above cursor Y
    top: e.pageY - 3,

    // position right side 20px right of cursor X
    left: e.pageX - fileInput.outerWidth() + 20
  });
});
```

To ensure that this x and y repositioning works reliably in all browsers and layouts, it's essential that the native **input** always be positioned relative to the document body. The script accomplishes this by placing the native **input** at the end of the HTML document in the source order when the cursor hovers over it. When the user moves the mouse over the custom file input and prompts a **mouseenter** event, we'll append (using the **appendTo** method) the native **input**'s markup to the end of the **body** tag. When the user moves the mouse away from the custom input, we'll fire the **mouseleave** event and return the native file **input** to its original position in the HTML source, right before the custom file input code, using the **insertBefore** method:

```
upload
  // move native file input to the end of the body on mouseover
  .mouseover(function(){
     fileInput.appendTo('body');
  })
  // move native file input back to original location on mouseout
  .mouseout(function(){
     fileInput.insertBefore(upload);
  });
```

Now when the user clicks the button, the native **input** will open the operating system's Browse dialog box as it normally would—the script doesn't need to do anything else to make this happen.

To replicate the native **input**'s hover and focus states, we'll amend the script to detect when the user focuses on or hovers over the native **input**, and then programmatically add a **hover** class to the custom file input, which we can use to style its hover state. When the user moves the mouse away from the native **input** and triggers a **blur** event, we'll remove the **hover** class and return the custom input's button to its default appearance. Similarly, as a user tabs through the page using keyboard commands, we'll detect when the native **input** has focus, and toggle a **customfile-focus** class to make it appear as if the user has focused on the custom widget (though technically focus remains on the native input):

```
fileInput
    // add hover mouse class on mouseover
    .mouseover(function(){
        upload.addClass('customfile-hover');
    })
    // remove mouse hover class on mouseout
    .mouseout(function(){
        upload.removeClass('customfile-hover');
    })
    // add keyboard focus class on focus
    .focus(function(){
        upload.addClass('customfile-focus');
    })
    // remove keyboard focus class on blur
    .blur(function(){
        upload.removeClass('customfile-focus');
    })
```

We also need to populate the feedback box in the custom file input with the filename and icon. When a user selects a file from the Browse dialog, we'll look for the **change** event fired by the native **input** and parse the **input**'s new value. Using regular expressions, we can extract the filename from the full path to update the feedback text, generate the proper icon **class** based on the file extension, add the **customfile-feedback-populated** class to swap the style of the feedback area, and update the custom file input's button to say "Change:"

```
fileInput
    .change(function(){
        // find text after the last backslash in path for filename
        var fileName = $(this).val().split(/\\/).pop();
```

```
        // find text after the last period in path for extension
        var fileExt = 'customfile-ext-' +
        fileName.split('.').pop().toLowerCase();


        // update the feedback
        uploadFeedback

            // add class to containter to show populated state
            .addClass('customfile-feedback-populated');


            // set feedback text to filename
            .text(fileName)


            // add file extension class
            .addClass(fileExt)


        // change text of button
        uploadButton.text('Change');
    });
```

Finally, the custom file input should replicate all native file **input** functionality, including the ability to programmatically disable it. When it makes sense to prevent user interaction with the custom file input, we append the **disabled="disabled"** attribute to the native **input** and provide a visual style to make the custom version look disabled and not accept user interaction. (We provide a detailed walkthrough of how to handle disabling custom controls in Chapter 17, "Select menu.")

Using the custom file input script

The custom file input demo and code that accompany this book (available on the book's website, www.filamentgroup.com/dwpe) references a script, **jQuery.fileinput.js**, that automates the creation of custom file inputs using the principles described in this chapter.

To use this script in your page, download and reference the files listed on the demo page, and call **customFileInput()** on a native file **input** in your page you want to transform into a custom file input:

```
//convert an input with an ID of "file" into a custom file input
$('input#file').customFileInput();
```

Or, to customize all file inputs on a page, change the selector to find them all:

```
//convert all inputs with a type attribute of "file"
$('input[type=file]').customFileInput();
```

* * *

In the case of the custom file input, we have no choice but to use the native file **input** because of security limitations. This chapter is a good illustration of how we can creatively reuse a native element from the foundation markup in the enhanced experience instead of re-implementing its features from scratch with JavaScript. This not only simplifies coding, but also allows us to take advantage of the accessibility features of the native element.

Richer uploading on deck with HTML5

The HTML5 working group has written a number of specifications that will add more native features and capabilities for file inputs and uploading once they gain browser support. These specifications include a new File API that offers a standards-based approach to many features that are currently available only through proprietary plugins like Adobe Flash or Sun Java. Some notable HTML5 file uploading features include:

► *Drag-and-drop file selection*: As web applications become more seamless with desktop environments, users expect that it will be possible to upload files by dragging them from an OS window to a browser. This functionality is frequently offered on photo-printing sites, for example, where users must upload photos to order prints. The HTML 5 **dataTransfer** and **dragEvent** interfaces provide specifications for native implementations of this behavior.

► *Tracking upload progress*: Web applications that accept file uploads sometimes provide progress indicators to update the user on the upload status. This functionality is typically handled using Flash, since most browsers don't provide information on upload progress. The HTML5 specification has drafted a recommendation for events to track upload progress—including **onloadstart** and **loadprogress**—that will make feedback possible without proprietary plugins.

► *Uploading multiple files with a single input*: The HTML5 specification describes the new **multiple** attribute for the native file input element, which will allow a user to select more than one file at a time within a single native operating system Browse dialog.

A number of these features will soon be natively available in browsers, with Firefox 3.5 already providing significant support for much of the HTML5 file API at the time of this writing.

summary

looking ahead

Universal access is not only a worthy goal, but also an attainable one, when approached with test-driven progressive enhancement.

We believe that progressive enhancement will quickly become the new baseline for all web development. As more complex functionality moves to the Internet—and users continue to embrace new web-enabled devices and expect all functionality to work seamlessly on those devices—considering accessibility, mobile device support, and broad browser compatibility isn't something that can be pushed off as a nice-to-have feature.

Progressive enhancement—and specifically, test-driven progressive enhancement that factors in accessibility—is the only practical way to cope with the complex range of user needs and Internet devices we now need to support. The fact that it's also a future-friendly approach that will inherently work for any new browsers and devices that adopt web standards is another strong argument in its favor.

We're thrilled that many popular JavaScript libraries are beginning to embrace progressive enhancement and accessibility. As adoption increases, their developer communities will create more prebuilt plugins to make development easier. For example, the jQuery UI team is implementing many of the progressive enhancement techniques described in this book in forthcoming plugins and is committed to having full ARIA support in the near future.

We also look forward to a future when more HTML5 and CSS3 features are broadly supported—this will allow us to create even more powerful experiences with less JavaScript and cleaner semantics. Happily, when this happens, the customizable nature of the EnhanceJS test suite will be there, letting us test for and deliver these new features to browsers that can handle them, and still accommodate the full complement of legacy browsers with a basic experience that works everywhere.

But for today's projects, the core set of tools and techniques covered in this book should empower you to confidently tackle your next project with progressive enhancement. By following the x-ray perspective, coding best practices, capabilities test script, and prebuilt widget plugins provided with this book, you have the tools to ensure that your project will work for everyone.

Index